Lecture Notes in Computer Science 15231

The series Lecture Notes in Computer Science (LNCS), including its subseries Lecture Notes in Artificial Intelligence (LNAI) and Lecture Notes in Bioinformatics (LNBI), has established itself as a medium for the publication of new developments in computer science and information technology research, teaching, and education.

LNCS enjoys close cooperation with the computer science R & D community, the series counts many renowned academics among its volume editors and paper authors, and collaborates with prestigious societies. Its mission is to serve this international community by providing an invaluable service, mainly focused on the publication of conference and workshop proceedings and postproceedings. LNCS commenced publication in 1973.

Gianluca Demartini · Katja Hose ·
Maribel Acosta · Matteo Palmonari ·
Gong Cheng · Hala Skaf-Molli · Nicolas Ferranti ·
Daniel Hernández · Aidan Hogan
Editors

The Semantic Web – ISWC 2024

23rd International Semantic Web Conference
Baltimore, MD, USA, November 11–15, 2024
Proceedings, Part I

Springer

Editors
Gianluca Demartini
University of Queensland
St. Lucia, QLD, Australia

Maribel Acosta
Technical University of Munich
Heilbronn, Baden-Württemberg, Germany

Gong Cheng
Nanjing University
Nanjing, China

Nicolas Ferranti
Vienna University of Economics
and Business
Vienna, Austria

Aidan Hogan
University of Chile
Santiago, Chile

Katja Hose
Technical University of Vienna
Vienna, Austria

Matteo Palmonari
University of Milano-Bicocca
Milan, Italy

Hala Skaf-Molli
University of Nantes
Nantes, France

Daniel Hernández
University Stuttgart
Stuttgart, Baden-Württemberg, Germany

ISSN 0302-9743 ISSN 1611-3349 (electronic)
Lecture Notes in Computer Science
ISBN 978-3-031-77843-8 ISBN 978-3-031-77844-5 (eBook)
https://doi.org/10.1007/978-3-031-77844-5

This Springer imprint is published by the registered company Springer Nature Switzerland AG
The registered company address is: Gewerbestrasse 11, 6330 Cham, Switzerland

Preface

The 2024 edition of the International Semantic Web Conference (ISWC) took place in Baltimore, Maryland, USA. It was my honour to be the General Chair of ISWC 2024, and to collaborate with the Organising Committee whose talent and dedication were essential for the success of the conference. Particular thanks are due to Karuna Joshi, the Local Chair, and the rest of the Local Organisers from the University of Maryland, Baltimore County (UMBC), namely Tim Finin, Manas Gaur, Anupam Joshi, and Roberto Yus for their important contributions to ISWC 2024. I would also like to express my thanks to the Semantic Web Science Association (SWSA), and in particular SWSA President Elena Simperl, for their guidance and assistance in organising ISWC 2024. I also warmly thank all those involved as Senior Programme Committee members, Programme Committee Members, Workshop and Tutorial Organisers, and Challenge Organisers, for their important contributions to ISWC 2024.

The conference ran for five days and returned to the USA for the first time after the COVID-19 pandemic, and the first time since ISWC 2018 in California. The first two days of ISWC 2024 were dedicated to Workshops, Tutorials, a Doctoral Consortium, and an NSF Open Knowledge Network Symposium. The last three days of ISWC 2024 were dedicated to presentations of Research, Resources, In-Use and Industry Track papers, Challenges & Special Session papers, Poster & Demo papers, keynotes, a panel, and more besides. The following proceedings present 44 accepted papers from the Research, Resources, and In-Use Tracks.

The Research Track of ISWC 2024, which forms the heart of the ISWC programme, was chaired by Gianluca Demartini and Katja Hose. The track received 159 abstract submissions, and 111 full submissions. Of the full submissions, 12 were desk rejected, and 99 sent for review. In the end, 26 papers were accepted, and are included in these proceedings, giving an acceptance rate of 23.4%. Instrumental to the peer review process were the 171 Programme Committee Members and 22 Subreviewers who conducted reviews, and 28 Senior Programme Committee Members who oversaw the review process and provided meta-reviews and recommendations.

The Resources Track of ISWC 2024 focused on describing published artefacts that are relevant to research on the Semantic Web, including benchmarks, knowledge graphs, tools, and vocabularies. The track was chaired by Maribel Acosta and Matteo Palmonari, and received 41 abstract submissions and 34 full submissions of which all 34 full submissions were sent for review. Of these submissions, 10 were accepted, and appear in these proceedings, equating to an acceptance rate of 29.4%. Key to making this selection were the 60 Programme Committee Members and 11 Subreviewers who provided detailed reviews for these papers, and 11 Senior Program Committee Members who provided meta-reviews for the papers.

The In-Use Track of ISWC 2024 solicited papers describing applications of Semantic Web and Knowledge Graph technologies in concrete, practical use cases, in contexts ranging from industry to government and society. The track was chaired by Gong Cheng and Hala Skaf-Molli, and received 23 abstract submissions, which translated into 22 full submissions, which were all sent for review. Of these submissions, 8 were accepted, and appear in these proceedings, giving an acceptance rate of 36.4%. Key to deciding which papers to accept were the 23 Programme Committee Members and 5 Subreviewers who provided expert reviews for the submissions.

We were delighted to have three esteemed keynote speakers at ISWC 2024, namely Chaitan Baru from the National Science Foundation (NSF), Ioana Manolescu from Inria & L'École polytechnique, and Ora Lassila from Amazon Neptune. These keynotes covered seminal topics relating to the use of Semantic Web technologies for improving the work of data journalists, the ongoing seminal initiatives in the USA relating to the Open Knowledge Network, and the ongoing development of the Amazon Neptune graph database. We were thrilled, in particular, to have keynotes representing academia, industry, and the public sector.

The Workshop and Tutorial Chairs, Irene Celino and Raghava Mutharaju, were instrumental in organising the programme for the first two days of the conference. For the first time, this year the chairs opted to separate the timelines for workshop and tutorial proposals, having workshop submissions early in the year (as traditional) but postponing tutorial proposals until after the deadlines for the main track, which resulted in a significant uptick in terms of tutorial proposals. Specifically, of 14 workshop proposals, 8 were accepted (6 of which were established workshops appearing in previous years, with 2 new workshop series). Of 14 tutorial proposals, 10 were accepted (an increase from 2 accepted for ISWC 2023). These workshops and tutorials covered a wide range of topics of interest to the ISWC audience, with a notable increase in events relating to Deep Learning, Knowledge Graphs, and Language Models.

The Industry Track Chairs, Vanessa Lopez and Francesco Osborne, provided an essential forum for participants from industry to showcase their latest results and applications relating to Semantic Web technologies (primarily) in the private sector. The track received 14 abstract submissions, of which 13 led to full submissions. These 13 papers were reviewed by 23 Programme Committee Members and 1 Subreviewer. Of these papers, 11 were accepted, representing a wide range of topics and industries all centring around Semantic Web and Knowledge Graph technologies.

This year's Doctoral Consortium Chairs, Kerry Taylor and Antoine Zimmermann, were involved in organising a key opportunity at ISWC 2024 for PhD students in the community to present their doctoral topics at the conference, to receive feedback from a diverse panel of experienced researchers, and also to establish relations with peers at a similar stage of their academic career. Of the 16 submissions to the track, a total of 12 submissions were accepted, covering a diverse set of emerging topics at the frontier of Semantic Web research. Key to making decisions on which papers to accept were the 24 Programme Committee Members who provided constructive feedback and recommendations for the 16 submissions. We hope to see all authors become integral members of the Semantic Web community in future years.

Another integral part of the conference programme was expertly overseen by Lorena Etcheverry and Romana Pernisch as the Poster & Demo Track Chairs. The Poster & Demo Session has long formed a highlight of the ISWC conference series, offering an interactive session in which attendees and presenters can converse in a more reciprocal manner. The track received 18 demo submissions and 34 poster submissions, of which 13 demo papers and 28 poster papers were accepted. These decisions were made based on the expert reviews of 91 Programme Committee Members and 6 Subreviewers.

Carrying on the ISWC tradition of bolstering empirical methods for advancing science, the Semantic Web Challenge Chairs this year were Agnieszka Ławrynowicz and Giuseppe Pirrò. This track solicited proposals of initiatives that provide benchmarks and other resources in order to empirically compare competing approaches that address a particular challenge relevant to the community. A total of six challenges were proposed and accepted, covering tasks relating to knowledge graph construction, question answering, extraction from tabular data, using language models for ontology learning, anomaly detection, and knowledge graph predictions.

Another jewel of the ISWC programme is the Panel Session, in which invited members of the community debate timely topics of core interest to the community. Chairing the Panel Session this year were Sabrina Kirrane and Juan Sequeda, who, keen to revamp the format, proposed an innovative debate format to discuss the relation between Knowledge Graphs and Large Language Models. The four panellists, Oscar Corcho, Anna Lisa Gentile, Paul Groth, and Irene Celino debated what the future holds for these key technologies, and in particular, the importance of Knowledge Graphs in the current age of Large Language Models.

In an effort to expand and create a more inclusive Semantic Web Research community, the Student Grants Chairs, namely Diego Torres, Roberto Yus, and Veruska Zamborlini, were successful in acquiring over US$50,000 to support the travel of students who otherwise would not be able to attend ISWC. With these funds, we were successful in supporting the travel of 35 students from 25 countries, 42% of whom were women. In this context, we warmly thank the Semantic Web Science Association (SWSA) and the National Science Foundation (NSF) for their generous contributions towards supporting the participation of the next generation of Semantic Web researchers.

With such a multifaceted and rich programme, communicating calls, dates and new initiatives to the community was an essential (and occasionally Herculean) task for ensuring the success of ISWC 2024. In this sense, a well-deserved thanks is due to the Web Presence & Publicity Chairs of ISWC 2024, namely Sebastián Ferrada, Manas Gaur, and Varish Mulwad, who publicised key information relating to ISWC 2024 on social media, and kept the conference website up to date with the latest developments.

Another essential task in the organisation of any conference is to secure sponsorship to financially support the event. Here the contributions of the ISWC 2024 Sponsor Chairs, namely Evgeny Kharlamov, Nandana Mihindukulasooriya, and Haofen Wang, were essential to acquire funding from the private sector. Among all of the sponsors of ISWC 2024, we acknowledge in particular our Gold Sponsors, which included eBay and IBM Research, as well as the generous contributions from UMBC.

New to ISWC this year was the organisation of Special Sessions, which were intended to offer a more interactive format for discussing topics of key strategic importance to the community during the conference. The Special Sessions this year focused on Large Language Models, and included three slots relating to benchmarking, knowledge enhancement, and applications in the intersection of Generative A.I. and the Semantic Web. These sessions were proposed and organised by the Special Session Chairs, namely Reham

Alharbi, Jacopo de Berardinis, Paul Groth, Albert Meroño-Peñuela, Elena Simperl, and Valentina Tamma.

Taking advantage of the geographic context of ISWC 2024 in the USA, we are also immensely grateful to the Chairs of the National Science Foundation (NSF) Open Knowledge Network (OKN) Symposium, namely Chaitan Baru, Jemin George, Pascal Hitzler, and Cogan Shimizu. This symposium, proposed by the chairs, provides a unique forum for members of such initiatives in the USA to present and discuss collaboration opportunities with international attendees relating to the research and deployment of large-scale knowledge graphs in the USA under the OKN umbrella.

Finally, much gratitude is due to the Proceedings Chairs, Nicolas Ferranti and Daniel Hernández, without whom the proceedings you are currently reading would not be possible. There are many details involved in putting together such proceedings, including collating camera-ready sources, copyright agreements, and indeed sending multiple gentle reminders to the General Chair to prepare the preface.

Having been a participant, author, reviewer, and co-organiser of ISWC conferences spanning close to two decades, it was my distinguished honour to be General Chair of ISWC 2024. The conference series has evolved in many ways in these past years, and I hope (and believe) that ISWC 2024 provides another positive step in the evolution of the series looking to the future.

Aidan Hogan, ISWC 2024 General Chair, on behalf of all the editors.

September 2024

Gianluca Demartini
Katja Hose
Maribel Acosta
Matteo Palmonari
Gong Cheng
Hala Skaf-Molli
Nicolas Ferranti
Daniel Hernández
Aidan Hogan

Organisation

General Chair

Aidan Hogan	University of Chile, Chile

Local Chair

Karuna Joshi	University of Maryland, Baltimore County, USA

Local Co-chairs

Tim Finin	University of Maryland, Baltimore County, USA
Manas Gaur	University of Maryland, Baltimore County, USA
Anupam Joshi	University of Maryland, Baltimore County, USA
Roberto Yus	University of Maryland, Baltimore County, USA

Research Track Chairs

Gianluca Demartini	University of Queensland, Australia
Katja Hose	TU Wien, Austria

Resources Track Chairs

Maribel Acosta	Technical University of Munich, Germany
Matteo Palmonari	University of Milan-Bicocca, Italy

In-Use Track Chairs

Gong Cheng	Nanjing University, China
Hala Skaf-Molli	Nantes University, France

Workshops and Tutorials Chairs

Irene Celino	Cefriel, Italy
Raghava Mutharaju	IIIT Delhi, India

Industry Track Chairs

Vanessa Lopez	IBM Research Europe, Ireland
Francesco Osborne	KMi, The Open University, UK

Doctoral Consortium Chairs

Kerry Taylor	Australian National University, Australia
Antoine Zimmermann	École des Mines de Saint-Étienne, France

Posters, Demos, and Lightning Talks Chairs

Lorena Etcheverry	Universidad de la República, Uruguay
Romana Pernisch	Vrije Universiteit Amsterdam, Netherlands

Semantic Web Challenge Chairs

Agnieszka Ławrynowicz	Poznań University of Technology, Poland
Giuseppe Pirrò	University of Calabria, Italy

Panel Chairs

Sabrina Kirrane	Vienna University of Economics and Business, Austria
Juan Sequeda	Data.world, USA

Sponsor Chairs

Evgeny Kharlamov	Bosch Center for Artificial Intelligence, Germany and University of Oslo, Norway
Nandana Mihindukulasooriya	IBM, USA
Haofen Wang	Tongji University, China

Proceedings and Metadata Chairs

Nicolas Ferranti	Vienna University of Economics and Business, Austria
Daniel Hernández	University of Stuttgart, Germany

Student Grants Chairs

Diego Torres	Universidad Nacional de La Plata, Argentina
Roberto Yus	University of Maryland, Baltimore County, USA
Veruska Zamborlini	Universidade Federal do Espírito Santo, Brazil

Web Presence and Publicity Chairs

Sebastián Ferrada	Universidad de Chile, Chile
Manas Gaur	University of Maryland, Baltimore County, USA
Varish Mulwad	GE Aerospace Research, India

Special Session Chairs

Reham Alharbi	University of Liverpool, UK
Jacopo de Berardinis	University of Liverpool, UK
Elena Simperl	King's College London, UK
Paul Groth	University of Amsterdam, Netherlands
Valentina Tamma	University of Liverpool, UK
Albert Meroño-Peñuela	King's College London, UK

NSF OKN Symposium Chairs

Chaitan Baru	NSF, USA
Jemin George	NSF, USA
Pascal Hitzler	Kansas State University, USA
Cogan Shimizu	Wright State University, USA

Research Track Senior Program Committee

Maribel Acosta	Technical University of Munich, Germany
Carlos Buil Aranda	Universidad Técnica Federico Santa María, Chile
Gong Cheng	Nanjing University, China
Michael Cochez	Vrije Universiteit Amsterdam, Netherlands
Oscar Corcho	Universidad Politécnica de Madrid, Spain
Julien Corman	Free University of Bozen-Bolzano, Italy
Anastasia Dimou	KU Leuven, Belgium
Mauro Dragoni	Fondazione Bruno Kessler, Italy
Aldo Gangemi	Università di Bologna & CNR-ISTC, Italy
Peter Haase	metaphacts, Germany
Olaf Hartig	Linköping University, Sweden
Laura Hollink	Centrum Wiskunde & Informatica, Netherlands
Ernesto Jimenez-Ruiz	City St George's, University of London, UK
Sabrina Kirrane	Vienna University of Economics and Business - WU Wien, Austria
Markus Luczak-Roesch	Victoria University of Wellington, New Zealand
Boris Motik	University of Oxford, UK
Terry Payne	University of Liverpool, UK
Catia Pesquita	Universidade de Lisboa, Portugal
Axel Polleres	Vienna University of Economics and Business - WU Wien, Austria
María Poveda-Villalón	Universidad Politécnica de Madrid, Spain
Anisa Rula	University of Brescia, Italy
Uli Sattler	University of Manchester, UK
Hala Skaf-Molli	University of Nantes - LS2N, France
Kavitha Srinivas	IBM, USA
Kostas Stefanidis	Tampere University, Finland
Valentina Tamma	University of Liverpool, UK
Maria-Esther Vidal	Leibniz University Hannover, TIB- Leibniz Information Center for Science and Technology, L3S Research Center, Germany
Domagoj Vrgoc	Pontificia Universidad Católica de Chile, Chile

Research Track Program Committee

Shqiponja Ahmetaj	Vienna University of Technology, Austria
Ines Akaichi	WU Vienna, Austria
João Paulo Almeida	Federal University of Espírito Santo, Brazil
Julián Arenas-Guerrero	Universidad Politécnica de Madrid, Spain
Luigi Asprino	University of Bologna, Italy
Carlos Badenes-Olmedo	Universidad Politécnica de Madrid, Spain
Pierpaolo Basile	University of Bari, Italy
Christian Bizer	University of Mannheim, Germany
Peter Bloem Vrije	Universiteit Amsterdam, Netherlands
Carlos Bobed	University of Zaragoza, Spain
Pieter Bonte	KU Leuven, Belgium
Paolo Bouquet	University of Trento, Italy
Alessandro Bozzon	Delft University of Technology, Netherlands
Janez Brank	Jožef Stefan Institute, Slovenia
Davide Buscaldi	LIPN, Université Paris 13, Université Sorbonne Paris Nord, France
Jean-Paul Calbimonte	University of Applied Sciences and Arts Western Switzerland HES-SO, Switzerland
Pablo Calleja	Universidad Politécnica de Madrid, Spain
Antonella Carbonaro	University of Bologna, Italy
Remzi Çelebi	Maastricht University, Netherlands
Pierre-Antoine Champin	LIRIS, Université Claude Bernard Lyon 1, France
Nathalie Charbel	Neo4j, France
Victor Charpenay	Mines Saint-Étienne, France
Vinay Chaudhri	none, USA
David Chaves-Fraga	Universidade de Santiago de Compostela, Spain
Jiaoyan Chen	University of Oxford, UK
Sijin Cheng	Linköping University, Sweden
Philipp Cimiano	Bielefeld University, Germany
Andrei Ciortea	University of St. Gallen, Switzerland
Pieter Colpaert	Ghent University – imec, Belgium
Philippe Cudre-Mauroux	University of Fribourg, Switzerland
Claudia d'Amato	University of Bari, Italy
Victor de Boer	Vrije Universiteit Amsterdam, Netherlands
Christophe Debruyne	Université de Liège, Belgium
Stefan Dietze	Heinrich-Heine-University Düsseldorf & GESIS, Germany
Shusaku Egami	National Institute of Advanced Industrial Science and Technology, Japan
Paola Espinoza-Arias	BASF Digital Solutions, Spain

Lorena Etcheverry	Universidad de la República, Uruguay
David Eyers	University of Otago, New Zealand
Alessandro Faraotti	IBM, Italy
Daniel Faria	INESC-ID, Instituto Superior Técnico, Universidade de Lisboa, Portugal
Catherine Faron	Université Côte d'Azur, France
Anna Fensel	Wageningen University & Research, Netherlands
Javier D. Fernández	F. Hoffmann-La Roche AG, Switzerland
Alba Fernandez-Izquierdo	BASF Digital Solutions, Spain
Sebastián Ferrada	Universidad de Chile, Chile
Erwin Filtz	Siemens AG Österreich, Austria
Giorgos Flouris	ICS-FORTH, Greece
Kathleen Fontaine	Rensselaer Polytechnic Institute, USA
Carolina Fortuna	Jožef Stefan Institute, Slovenia
Naoki Fukuta	Shizuoka University, Japan
Mohamed H. Gad-Elrab	Bosch Center for Artificial Intelligence, Germany
Luis Galárraga	Inria, France
Fabien Gandon	Inria, France
Daniel Garijo	Universidad Politécnica de Madrid, Spain
Pouya Ghiasnezhad Omran	Australian National University, Australia
Shrestha Ghosh	Max Planck Institute for Informatics, Germany
Martin Giese	University of Oslo, Norway
Rafael Gonçalves	Harvard Medical School, USA
Jorge Gracia	University of Zaragoza, Spain
Paul Groth	University of Amsterdam, Netherlands
Tudor Groza	Rare Care Centre, Perth Children's Hospital, Australia
Claudio Gutierrez	Universidad de Chile, Chile
Andreas Harth	Friedrich-Alexander-Universität Erlangen-Nürnberg and Fraunhofer IIS, Germany
Mounira Harzallah	LS2N, University of Nantes, France
Oktie Hassanzadeh	IBM Research, USA
Daniel Hernandez	University of Stuttgart, Germany
Sven Hertling	University of Mannheim, Germany
Ryohei Hisano	University of Tokyo, Japan
Rinke Hoekstra	Elsevier, Netherlands
Andreas Hotho	University of Würzburg, Germany
Andreea Iana	University of Mannheim, Germany
Luis Ibanez-Gonzalez	University of Southampton, UK
Ana Iglesias-Molina	Universidad Politécnica de Madrid, Spain
Oana Inel	University of Zurich, Switzerland

Valentina Ivanova	RISE Research Institutes of Sweden, Sweden
Prateek Jain	The Trade Desk, Inc., USA
Krzysztof Janowicz	University of California, Santa Barbara, USA
Tobias Käfer	Karlsruhe Institute of Technology, Germany
Jan-Christoph Kalo	University of Amsterdam, Netherlands
Zoi Kaoudi	IT University of Copenhagen, Denmark
Takahiro Kawamura	National Agriculture and Food Research Organization, Japan
Mayank Kejriwal	University of Southern California, USA
Ilkcan Keles	Booking.com, Netherlands
Neha Keshan	Rensselaer Polytechnic Institute, USA
Elmar Kiesling	Vienna University of Economics and Business, Austria
Haridimos Kondylakis	University of Crete & FORTH-ICS, Greece
George Konstantinidis	University of Southampton, UK
Roman Kontchakov	Birkbeck, University of London, UK
Manolis Koubarakis	National and Kapodistrian University of Athens, Greece
Markus Krötzsch	TU Dresden, Germany
Jose Emilio Labra Gayo	Universidad de Oviedo, Spain
Davide Lanti	Free University of Bozen-Bolzano, Italy
Agnieszka Lawrynowicz	Poznań University of Technology, Poland
Danh Le Phuoc	TU Berlin, Germany
Maxime Lefrançois	Mines Saint-Etienne, France
Huanyu Li	Linköping University, Sweden
Maria Maleshkova	Helmut Schmidt University Hamburg, Germany
Jose L. Martinez-Rodriguez	Autonomous University of Tamaulipas, Mexico
Albert Meroño-Peñuela	King's College London, UK
Thomas Meyer	University of Cape Town and CAIR, South Africa
Pascal Molli	University of Nantes - LS2N, France
Deshendran Moodley	University of Cape Town, South Africa
Varish Mulwad	GE Aerospace Research, India
Summaya Mumtaz	University of Oslo, Norway
Raghava Mutharaju	IIIT-Delhi, India
Hubert Naacke	Sorbonne Université, LIP6, France
María Navas-Loro	Universidad Politécnica de Madrid, Spain
Sebastian Neumaier	St. Pölten University of Applied Sciences, Austria
Tuan-Phong Nguyen	Max Planck Institute for Informatics, Germany
Vinh Nguyen	National Library of Medicine, NIH, USA
Andriy Nikolov	AstraZeneca, UK
Werner Nutt	Free University of Bozen-Bolzano, Italy
Andrea Giovanni Nuzzolese	University of Bologna, Italy

Femke Ongenae	Ghent University - imec, Belgium
Julian Padget	University of Bath, UK
Peter Patel-Schneider	USA
Evan Patton	Massachusetts Institute of Technology, USA
Rafael Peñaloza	University of Milano-Bicocca, Italy
Bernardo Pereira Nunes	Australian National University, Australia
Alina Petrova	University of Oxford, UK
Francesco Piccialli	University of Naples Federico II, Italy
Dimitris Plexousakis	Institute of Computer Science, FORTH, Greece
Cédric Pruski	Luxembourg Institute of Science and Technology, Luxembourg
David Ratcliffe	Microsoft, Australia
Juan L. Reutter	Pontificia Universidad Católica, Chile
Martin Rezk	Google, USA
Mariano Rico	Universidad Politécnica de Madrid, Spain
Philipp D. Rohde	TIB Leibniz Information Centre for Science and Technology, Germany
Edelweis Rohrer	Universidad de la República, Uruguay
Oscar Romero	Universitat Politècnica de Catalunya, Spain
Miguel Romero Orth	Pontificia Universidad Católica de Chile, Chile
Marco Rospocher	Università degli Studi di Verona, Italy
Jože Rožanec	Jožef Stefan Institute, Slovenia
Sebastian Rudolph	TU Dresden, Germany
Harald Sack	FIZ Karlsruhe, Leibniz Institute for Information Infrastructure & KIT Karlsruhe, Germany
Tomer Sagi	Aalborg Universitet, Denmark
Angelo Salatino	Open University, UK
Muhammad Saleem	University of Leipzig, Germany
Emanuel Sallinger	TU Wien, Austria
Marco Luca Sbodio	IBM Research, Ireland
Francois Scharffe	Knowledge Graph Conference, USA
Konstantin Schekotihin	Alpen-Adria Universität Klagenfurt, Austria
Ralf Schenkel	Trier University, Germany
Juan F. Sequeda	data.world, USA
Cogan Shimizu	Wright State University, USA
Kuldeep Singh	Cerence GmbH and Zerotha Research, Germany
Martin G. Skjæveland	University of Oslo, Norway
Sebastian Skritek	TU Wien, Austria
Nadine Steinmetz	University of Applied Sciences Erfurt, Germany
Armando Stellato	University of Rome Tor Vergata, Italy
Fabian M. Suchanek	Institut Polytechnique de Paris, France
Chang Sun	Maastricht University, Netherlands

Vojtěch Svátek	Prague University of Economics and Business, Czechia
Ruben Taelman	Ghent University – imec, Belgium
Hideaki Takeda	National Institute of Informatics, Japan
David Tena Cucala	University of Oxford, UK
Krishnaprasad Thirunarayan	Wright State University, USA
Steffen Thoma	FZI Research Center for Information Technology, Germany
Ilaria Tiddi	Vrije Universiteit Amsterdam, Netherlands
Dominik Tomaszuk	University of Bialystok, Poland
Riccardo Tommasini	INSA Lyon - LIRIS, France
Cassia Trojahn	Université Grenoble Alpes, France
Antonis Troumpoukis	NCSR Demokritos, Greece
Takanori Ugai	Fujitsu Limited, Japan
Ricardo Usbeck	Leuphana University Lüneburg, Germany
Guillermo Vega-Gorgojo	Universidad de Valladolid, Spain
Ruijie Wang	University of Zurich, Switzerland
Simon Werner	Trier University, Germany
Xander Wilcke	Vrije Universiteit Amsterdam, Netherlands
Fouad Zablith	American University of Beirut, Lebanon
Antoine Zimmermann	École des Mines de Saint-Étienne, France

Research Track Additional Reviewers

Tilahun Abedissa	Leuphana University of Lüneburg, Germany
Mark Adamik	Vrije Universiteit Amsterdam, Netherlands
Debayan Banerjee	Leuphana University of Lüneburg, Germany
Roberto Barile	University of Bari Aldo Moro, Italy
Miguel Ceriani	Universitá di Bari Aldo Moro, Italy
Antrea Christou	Wright State University, USA
Nikos Fanourakis	Institute of Computer Science, FORTH; University of Crete, Greece
Genet Asefa Gesese	FIZ Karlsruhe, Leibniz Institute for Information Infrastructure, Germany
Junbo Huang	University of Hamburg, Germany
Mayank Kharbanda	Indraprastha Institute of Information Technology Delhi, India
Antonis Klironomos	Bosch Center for Artificial Intelligence, University of Mannheim, Germany
Anna Sofia Lippolis	Università di Bologna, Italy
Dehai Min	Southeast University and Monash University Joint Graduate School, China

Cedric Möller	University of Hamburg, Germany
Elio Musacchio	University of Bari Aldo Moro, Italy
Sergi Nadal	Universitat Politècnica de Catalunya, Spain
Janna Omeliyanenko	Julius-Maximilians University of Würzburg, Germany
Panagiotis Papadakos	Institute of Computer Science, FORTH; University of Crete, Greece
Fina Polat	University of Amsterdam, Netherlands
Simone Sandri	Okkam s.r.l, Italy
Sarah Binta Alam Shoilee	Vrije Universiteit Amsterdam, Netherlands
Sebastian Wankerl	University of Würzburg, Germany

Resources Track Senior Program Committee

Enrico Daga	Open University, UK
Anastasia Dimou	KU Leuven, Belgium
Michel Dumontier	Maastricht University, Netherlands
Milan Markovic	University of Aberdeen, UK
Lionel Medini	LIRIS, University of Lyon, France
Heiko Paulheim	University of Mannheim, Germany
Valentina Presutti	University of Bologna, Italy
Tong Ruan	ECUST, China
Ruben Taelman	Ghent University – imec, Belgium
Maria-Esther Vidal	Leibniz University Hannover; TIB-Leibniz Information Center of Science and Technology; L3S Research Center, Germany
Xiaowang Zhang	Tianjin University, China

Resources Track Program Committee

Vladimir Alexiev	Ontotext Corp, Bulgaria
Elvira Amador-Domínguez	Universidad Politécnica de Madrid, Spain
Vito Walter Anelli	Politecnico di Bari, Italy
Ghislain Atemezing	European Union Agency for Railways (ERA), France
Debanjali Biswas	GESIS Leibniz Institute for the Social Sciences, Germany
Germán Alejandro Braun	Universidad Nacional del Comahue, Argentina
David Chaves-Fraga	Universidade de Santiago de Compostela, Spain
Philipp Cimiano	Bielefeld University, Germany

Andrea Cimmino Arriaga	Universidad Politécnica de Madrid, Spain
Oscar Corcho	Universidad Politécnica de Madrid, Spain
Francesco Corcoglioniti	Free University of Bozen-Bolzano, Italy
Jennifer Daniel Onwuchekwa	University of Siegen, Germany
Jérôme David	Inria, France
Dimitar Dimitrov	GESIS, Germany
Pablo Fillottrani	Universidad Nacional del Sur, Argentina
Peter Haase	metaphacts, Germany
Fatma-Zohra Hannou	EDF Research & Development, France
Lars Heling	Stardog Union, Germany
Fabian Hoppe	VU Amsterdam, Netherlands
Ana Iglesias-Molina	Universidad Politécnica de Madrid, Spain
Antoine Isaac	Europeana & VU University Amsterdam, Netherlands
Clement Jonquet	MISTEA (INRAE) and LIRMM (U. Montpellier), France
Yavuz Selim Kartal	GESIS Leibniz Institute for Social Sciences, Germany
Christian Kindermann	Stanford University, USA
Tomas Kliegr	Prague University of Economics and Business, Czech Republic
Jakub Klímek	Charles University, Czech Republic
Agnieszka Lawrynowicz	Poznań University of Technology, Poland
Maxime Lefrançois	MINES Saint-Etienne, France
Xiaoze Liu	Purdue University, USA
Zola Mahlaza	University of Cape Town, South Africa
Patricia Martín-Chozas	Universidad Politécnica de Madrid, Spain
Hande McGinty	Kansas State University, USA
Albert Meroño-Peñuela	King's College London, UK
Nandana Mihindukulasooriya	IBM Research AI, USA
Pascal Molli	University of Nantes - LS2N, France
Alessandro Mosca	Institute for Cognitive Sciences and Technologies (ISTC-CNR), Italy
Andrea Giovanni Nuzzolese	University of Bologna, Italy
Mariano Rodríguez Muro	Google, USA
María del Mar Roldán-García	Universidad de Málaga, Spain
Marta Sabou	Vienna University of Economics and Business, Austria
Sebastian Schellhammer	GESIS Leibniz Institute for the Social Sciences, Germany
Stefan Schlobach	Vrije Universiteit Amsterdam, Netherlands
Umutcan Serles	University of Innsbruck, Austria
Patricia Serrano Alvarado	University of Nantes - LS2N, France

Cogan Shimizu	Wright State University, USA
Blerina Spahiu	University of Milan-Bicocca, Italy
Vojtěch Svátek	Prague University of Economics and Business, Czech Republic
Mary Ann Tan	FIZ Karlsruhe, Germany
Walter Terkaj	CNR-STIIMA, Italy
Tabea Tietz	FIZ Karlsruhe, Germany
Mahsa Vafaie	FIZ Karlsruhe, KIT, Germany
Joerg Waitelonis	FIZ Karlsruhe, Germany
Meng Wang	Tongji University, China
Zhichun Wang	Beijing Normal University, China
Tianxing Wu	Southeast University, China
Guohui Xiao	University of Bergen, Norway
Ondřej Zamazal	Prague University of Economics and Business, Czech Republic
Ningyu Zhang	Zhejiang University, China
Ziqi Zhang	Accessible Intelligence, UK

Resources Track Additional Reviewers

Cristobal Barba-Gonzalez	Universidad de Málaga, Spain
Antonio Benítez Hidalgo	Universidad de Málaga, Spain
Debanjali Biswas	GESIS, Germany
Susmita Gangopadhyay	GESIS, Germany
Sergio Alejandro Gomez	Universidad Nacional del Sur, Argentina
Stephan Linzbach	GESIS, Germany
Sarah Rebecca Ondraszek	FIZ Karlsruhe, Germany
Ritten Roothaert	Vrije Universiteit Amsterdam, Netherlands
Sebastian Schellhammer	GESIS, Germany
Ilaria Tiddi	Vrije Universiteit Amsterdam, Netherlands
Sharmila Upadhyaya	GESIS, Germany

In-Use Track Program Committee

Nathalie Aussenac-Gilles	CNRS, Institut de Recherche en Informatique de Toulouse, France
Martin Bauer	NEC Laboratories Europe, Germany
Sonia Bergamaschi	Università degli Studi di Modena e Reggio Emilia, Italy
Carlos Buil Aranda	Universidad Técnica Federico Santa María, Chile

Shumin Deng	National University of Singapore, Singapore
Alban Gaignard	CNRS, France
Daniel Garijo	Universidad Politécnica de Madrid, Spain
Damien Graux	Huawei Technologies R&D (UK) Ltd., UK
Peter Haase	metaphacts GmbH, Germany
Nicolas Heist	metaphacts GmbH, Germany
Tomi Kauppinen	Aalto University, Finland
Mayank Kejriwal	University of Southern California, USA
Evgeny Kharlamov	Bosch, Germany
Pavel Klinov	Stardog Union, USA
Craig Knoblock	University of Southern California, USA
Michael Luggen	University of Fribourg, Switzerland
Ioanna Lytra	Semantic Web Company, Austria
Beatrice Markhoff	Université de Tours, France
Pascal Molli	University of Nantes - LS2N, France
Andriy Nikolov	AstraZeneca, UK
Declan O'Sullivan	Trinity College Dublin, Ireland
Josiane Xavier Parreira	Siemens AG Österreich, Austria
Zequn Sun	Nanjing University, China

In-Use Track Additional Reviewers

Domenico Beneventano	Università degli Studi di Modena e Reggio Emilia, Italy
Fandel Lin	University of Southern California, USA
Giovanni Sullutrone	Università degli Studi di Modena e Reggio Emilia, Italy
Lisa Trigiante	Università degli Studi di Modena e Reggio Emilia, Italy
Binh Vu	University of Southern California, USA

Sponsors

Below we list the sponsors confirmed before the preparation of the proceedings, i.e., September 29th, 2024. The full up-to-date list of sponsors is available at the ISWC 2024 Website: https://iswc2024.semanticweb.org/.

Diamond Sponsors

UMBC

University of Maryland, Baltimore County

Gold Sponsors

ebay

IBM Research

Silver Sponsors

AllegroGraph
Franz Inc.

metaphacts

Other Sponsors

Keynotes and Panel

Knowledge as Infrastructure – and a National Research Resource

Chaitan Baru

Directorate for Technology, Innovation, and Partnership, National Science Foundation, Alexandria, VA, USA

We are amid three revolutions in AI: deep learning, knowledge graphs, and automated reasoning, as articulated by Prof. Kenneth Forbus during the AI Session at the National Science Board Meeting on May 1, 2024. Technology in each of these areas has progressed to the extent that it is used daily and is delivering significant value. While deep learning, which has unleashed powerful tools like ChatGPT, is a large focus of today's AI, knowledge graphs and reasoning are complements to deep learning. Knowledge graphs already power key web and e-commerce services provided by large corporations. Automated reasoning techniques are in wide use in many areas—for example, in the auto industry to find flaws in electrical systems and verify behavior with respect to design specifications. In this talk, we will discuss techniques, technologies, and strategies for building out the knowledge infrastructure that will be essential and necessary to support the next generation of AI. The National Science Foundation's Open Knowledge Network (OKN), envisioned as part of NSF's Harnessing the Data Revolution Big Idea, provides an important start. The Prototype-OKN (https://www.proto-okn.net/) is a coordinated effort among 18 projects funded under the NSF Proto-OKN project, in collaboration with NASA, NIH, NIJ, NOAA, USGS, and other agencies, to create an open knowledge network structure linking disparate, heterogenous information from diverse sources. Of these, 15 projects are "Theme 1" efforts focused on providing solutions for specific problems working in conjunction with federal, state, or other government agencies. Two projects—FRINK and SPIDER—are working towards providing a common Proto-OKN "fabric", or technical infrastructure, to deploy Theme 1 solutions, and one project—EduGate—focuses on the education, training, and outreach for this effort.

Knowledge representation and reasoning are not new topics in Computer Science. However, to make translational impact in real-world applications we need to make a shift towards treating the development and operation of computer science-based knowledge structures as infrastructure—in addition to just bespoke solutions to specific problems. This would begin with the hosting of repositories of knowledge in computational form based on open-source government, science, and other open data. The term "translational" implies focus on use-inspired, solution-oriented R&D efforts with the potential to directly impact people's everyday lives. An important focus is on education and training and teaching of knowledge representation at every level from high school to computer science undergraduates, and above. A key consideration is to pay attention to issues from governance to ethics to help build trust in the system.

Retrieve (and Leverage) the Inner Graph Behind the Data

Ioana Manolescu

Inria, IP Paris, France

Many challenging data integration problems, in particular in data journalism, feature heterogeneity at the level of the schema and the data model. To overcome the heterogeneity, we have shown how data of many (semi)structured models can be converted into fine-granularity graphs, enriched and densified with the help of information extraction. Such fine-grained graphs, however, are hard to grasp for non-technical users. To help them get acquainted with a dataset, we devised an abstraction method, which identifies, in fine-granularity data graphs, structured objects endowed with an internal structure, and relationships between them. Given a semistructured dataset, we automatically produce an Entity-Relationship style diagram; in contrast with traditional E-R models, our entities may feature deep nesting, reflecting the nested and possibly recursive structure present in some data models. We thus obtain an automated way of "rescuing" the conceptual model, which we argue is best viewed as a graph, behind any application dataset. We then describe automatic techniques for finding the most interesting paths connecting entities in a dataset.

The keynote describes joint work with Nelly Barret, Madhulika Mohanty, Prajna Upadhyay and many other colleagues. Further information can be found at the following web sites: https://connectionstudio.inria.fr/, https://team.inria.fr/cedar/projects/abstra/.

Semantic Web and AI: Can We Finally Realize the Original Vision?

Ora Lassila

Amazon Neptune, Amazon Web Services, Seattle, WA, USA

The original idea of the Semantic Web was not just to bring knowledge representation and reasoning to the Web, but to make these technologies pervasive in our use of information technology. The idea has matured into modern enterprise knowledge graphs, and – according to Gartner – has become a major mainstream trend. Organizations are using knowledge graphs without feeling the need to advertise this fact. Getting here took a long time, however: the original Semantic Web vision was introduced at the tail end of the so-called "AI winter", and the close relationship with AI greatly slowed its adoption. Now, given the popularity of generative AI, we should re-examine the vision and understand what is the role of AI in the Semantic Web, and what is the role of the Semantic Web in AI.

In this talk I will reflect on the more than a quarter century of work on building the technologies for the Semantic Web and how this work still continues. I will discuss the "wins", the "losses", the lessons learned, and describe how I see the future. I believe we are now ready for the next step: to finally realize the original Semantic Web vision, that of agents, planning, and reasoning.

Knowledge Graphs in the Era of Large Language Models: A Debate

Sabrina Kirrane[1] and Juan Sequeda[2]

[1] Vienna University of Economics and Business, Austria
[2] data.world

The rapid development of Large Language Models (LLMs) has sparked debate about the role and future of Knowledge Graphs (KGs). LLMs offer impressive capabilities in natural language understanding and generation. Many argue that they already have the ability to understand and reason and that this ability will only be further enhanced. Today, LLMs face limitations in delivering structured, precise, and explainable knowledge. Knowledge Graphs, by contrast, provide a robust framework for representing and linking data and knowledge in a structured manner, facilitating interoperability and reasoning.

This debate explores the complementarity and potential conflicts between LLMs and KGs, examining their respective roles in driving advancements in artificial intelligence and knowledge representation. To what degrees are KGs and LLMs complementary? Will LLMs subsume KG capabilities? Or will KGs be essential to provide context and refine the results of LLMs? What are the implications for our research community?

To explore this topic, we are excited to organize a debate where we will have two sides: Team KG and Team LLM. Our debaters will be Paul Groth, Irene Celino, Oscar Corcho, and Anna Lisa Gentile. Who will take which side? What will their arguments be? You will have to come to the debate!

Contents – Part I

Research Track

Contents – Part II

Research Track

Contents – Part III

Resource Track

In-Use Track

Research Track

SnapE – Training Snapshot Ensembles of Link Prediction Models

Ali Shaban[1,2] and Heiko Paulheim[1(✉)]

[1] University of Mannheim, Data and Web Science Group, Mannheim, Germany
heiko.paulheim@uni-mannheim.de
[2] Amazon Web Services, Seattle, USA
shaban-a@live.com

Abstract. Snapshot ensembles have been widely used in various fields of prediction. They allow for training an ensemble of prediction models at the cost of training a single one. They are known to yield more robust predictions by creating a set of diverse base models. In this paper, we introduce an approach to transfer the idea of snapshot ensembles to link prediction models in knowledge graphs. Moreover, since link prediction in knowledge graphs is a setup without explicit negative examples, we propose a novel training loop that iteratively creates negative examples using previous snapshot models. An evaluation with four base models across four datasets shows that this approach constantly outperforms the single model approach, while keeping the training time constant.

Keywords: Link Prediction · Knowledge Graphs · Snapshot Ensembles

1 Introduction

Knowledge Graphs (KGs) are a crucial instrument for structuring complex, inteld dan a way that is interpretable both by humans and machines [14,15]. They are used in many applications ranging from search engines to recommendation systems and from natural language processing to computer vision.

KGs often exhibit sparseness and incompleteness [7,22]. This link sparseness can significantly hinder the KGs' potential use in applications like semantic search. As a result, filling the missing links has gained traction in the AI community. This task is called *Link Prediction*, and it is one of the primary applications of machine learning and embedding methods on Knowledge Graphs [4]. Various research efforts have validated the efficacy of link prediction in addressing the sparsity issue in KGs and reinforcing their potential [21].

Link prediction with knowledge graph embeddings (KGEs) faces many challenges that have been the subject of research [2], including the sparsity of graphs [27], noisy or erroneous data [42], and scalability [8], among others. In

A. Shaban—This work is not related to the position at Amazon.

G. Demartini et al. (Eds.): ISWC 2024, LNCS 15231, pp. 3–22, 2025.
https://doi.org/10.1007/978-3-031-77844-5_1

machine learning, many of those challenges are addressed by ensemble methods. Ensembles can improve generalization by reducing the overfitting often seen in individual predictors [43], and better handle incomplete or noisy data by leveraging the robustness resulting from the combination of multiple models that make errors on different instances [24]. Finally, ensemble methods can be used to address the scalability challenges of link predictions by training different models on different sub-graphs and combining them [8] or by training smaller models on the whole graphs and combining them into an ensemble [40]. The approach followed in this paper falls into the latter category.

Snapshot Ensembles are an effective way of training ensembles without increasing the training time or computation cost [16]. By storing snapshots of a single model at distinct points in its training process and combining them into an ensemble, they require the same training time as a single model [16]. These snapshots, stored at the end of each cycle during training with cyclic learning rate schedules, have diverse model behaviors, ensuring less correlation among base models and avoiding the model being stuck in local minima. In many fields, snapshot ensembles have been shown to outperform single base models.

In this paper, we show how to apply the idea of snapshot ensembles to link prediction in KGs. We train an ensemble of base models in the same time as we would classically train a single model, and show that the ensemble outperforms the single base model in many cases. Moreover, we propose a new technique of negative sampling, where the previous snapshots are used to generate adversarial samples for the next training cycle. The contributions of this paper are as follows:

- We propose SnapE, a new *training method* which can be applied to existing link prediction models.[1]
- We show that using the same resources for training (measured by training time or memory), we can improve the performance of existing link prediction models.
- We propose a new negative sampling method which can be used with SnapE.

The rest of this paper is structured as follows. We provide a brief overview of ensemble methods for link prediction in knowledge graphs in Sect. 2. We sketch our approach in Sect. 3, followed by an evaluation and an ablation study in Sect. 4. We conclude with a summary and an outlook on future work.

2 Related Work

Link prediction in knowledge graphs is an extensively researched area. Approaches can be roughly categorized as geometric, matrix factorization, and neural network based approaches [30,38].

One of the earliest approaches to use ensembles for link prediction has been proposed by Krompass et al. [18]. They train three different heterogeneous models (i.e., a TransE, a RESCAL, and an mwNN model), and make a prediction

[1] Note: we do *not* propose a new link prediction model, but a new training method for existing models.

by averaging the probabilities for each predicted triple. Similar approaches are pursued by Rivas-Barragan et al. [29] and Gregucci et al. [12]. They can improve the prediction quality, but also signficantly increase the training efforts.

Prabhakara et al. [26] divide a knowledge graph into separate subgraphs, and train an embedding model on each subgraph. The predictions of each single embedding model are aggregated using the min, max, or mean of the individual scores. The results are mixed, and no evidence of an actual performance improvement is given, i.e., there is no evidence that training m models on a smaller subgraph is computationally cheaper than training one model on the full graph. Wan et al. [37] also consider the training on subgraphs, but instead of combining predictions, they combine the embedding vectors of entities and relations. While they can show that the resulting model is more robust to noise in the knowledge graph, their paper also lacks a discussion of training cost.

The approach closest to ours is Xu et al. [40], which proposes an approach of training different models of the same base class at a lower dimensionality independently, initialized with different random seeds, and combining their scores. They show that training the ensemble of different models with the same memory footprint exposes a better prediction quality than a single large model. Unlike our approach, they train the set of different models in multiple parallel runs, rather than a single training run (i.e., Xu et al. train m models in N epochs *each*, which requires a total of $N \times m$ epochs, whereas we train m models in N epochs *in total*). Since this approach is the closest to SnapE, we compare our work to theirs, also empirically.

While most of the approaches above can show an improvement in the link prediction quality, they usually require a larger training effort, e.g., by training more than one full model. In contrast, SnapE, as proposed in this paper, is the **first approach to train an ensemble of link prediction models at the same training cost of one single full model**.

3 Approach

KGE models are trained by iteratively adapting their weights in order to maximize a target function. In each iteration, the model's weights are adapted so that the error function is lowered. The amount by which each weight can be changed in each iteration is called the *learning rate*. A high learning rate leads to a fast convergence of the model, but may not yield the best possible solution. A low learning rate, on the other hand, requires more time for convergence, but may yield better results. Therefore, many models are trained with a decaying learning rate, as shown in Fig. 1a. There are different decay functions for learning rates, such as step decay [11] or cosine annealing [19].

The idea of Snapshot Ensembles, introduced by Huang et al. in 2017 [16], uses a cyclic learning rate, as shown in Fig. 1b. Each time the learning rate schedule reaches a local minimum, a snapshot of the model is stored. At prediction time, each stored model is used to predict, and the predictions are combined. The original snapshot ensemble paper uses cyclic cosine annealing, as shown in

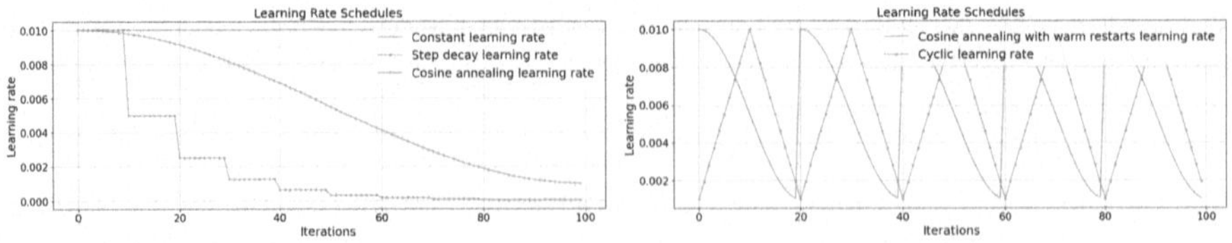

(a) Non-cyclic (b) Cyclic

Fig. 1. Non-cyclic vs. cyclic learning rate schedules

Fig. 1b, and averages the predictions. In this paper, we use the same mechanism for training an ensemble of link prediction models. We experiment with different learning rate schedulers, score aggregation functions, and negative samplers.

3.1 Learning Rate Schedulers

As discussed above, the original snapshot ensemble uses the cosine cyclic annealing schema (CCA), defined as [19]:

$$\alpha(t) = \frac{\alpha_0}{2}\left(\cos\left(\left(\frac{\pi mod(t-1, \lceil T/M \rceil)}{\lceil T/M \rceil}\right) + 1\right)\right) \tag{1}$$

where α_0 is the initial maximum learning rate, t is the iteration number, T is the total number of training iterations, and M is the number of cycles. A later paper used a variation called max-min cyclic cosine learning rate (MMCCLR), defined as [39]:

$$\eta_t = \eta_{\min} + \frac{1}{2}\left(\eta_{\max} - \eta_{\min}\right)\left(1 + \cos\left(\frac{mod(\lceil t/b \rceil, \lceil T/Mb \rceil)}{\lceil T/Mb \rceil}\pi\right)\right) \tag{2}$$

where η_t is the learning rate at step t, η_{min} and η_{max} are the minimum and maximum learning rates, respectively, and b is the batch size. The difference to cyclic cosine annealing is that the learning rate does not get as close to 0, which may lead to local minima being exploited a little better in the case of CCA.

In addition to those two schedulers, we explore two further variants, called *deferred* cyclic annealing. Assuming that a link prediction model requires some initial training in order to learn the principal structure of a knowledge graph, we defer the cyclic annealing by using a constant learning rate for the first k epochs before starting the cyclic annealing. The first model is then stored when the learning rate hits the first minimum. The result is a smaller number of models in a fixed set of epochs, but, on the other hand, those models may be a better fit due to the longer warmup time of the snapshot model.

Figure 2 illustrates the learning rate schedulers used in this paper.

3.2 Combining Predictions

In order to come up with a final prediction from the individual base models, their scores need to be aggregated. We follow different strategies:

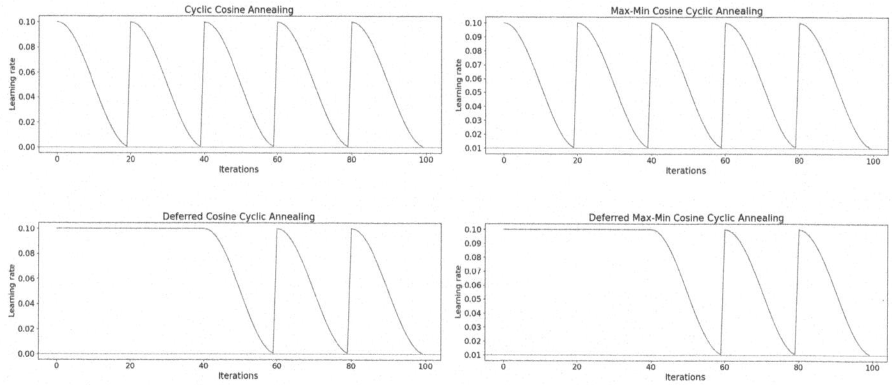

Fig. 2. Learning rate schedules used in this paper. Snapshots are always stored at the minima of the learning rate schedules.

Simple average: For each prediction made with the base models, we normalize the scores of each model with a min-max scaler (so that each model's scores fall into a $[0, 1]$ range), and average those normalized scores.

Weighted average: Instead of using a simple average, we weigh each model by (a) a weight derived from the model's last training loss[2], or (b) with descending weights from the last stored base model, assigning the highest weight to the last model, assuming that this is the best fit.

Borda rank aggregation: The rankings are unified using the Borda rank algorithm [9] (without considering the scores).

3.3 Negative Samplers

Unlike many other machine learning problems, link prediction in knowledge graphs only comes with positive examples. Therefore, link prediction requires the creation of negative examples, which is usually done via randomly corrupting positive examples, i.e., for a given triple $< s, p, o >$, either s or o is replaced with a random other entity to form a corrupted triple $< s', p, o >$ or $< s, p, o' >$, respectively.

In addition to this standard sampling, we propose an extended negative sampler, which uses the last snapshot to create negative examples for the next cycle. The idea is similar to boosting [10], where an ensemble of models is trained in a sequence, with each model focusing on the mistakes made by the previous ones.

After storing a snapshot model, the model is used to predict o' or s' for a triple $< s, p, o >$ in the training set. The highest scoring negative $< s, p, o' >$ or $< s', p, o >$ is then added as a negative example. With that approach, we guide the optimization to learn more diverse models, where subsequent models correct mistakes made by models stored in previous iterations.

[2] $max + min - loss$, where max and min are the maximum and minimum loss of the models in the ensemble.

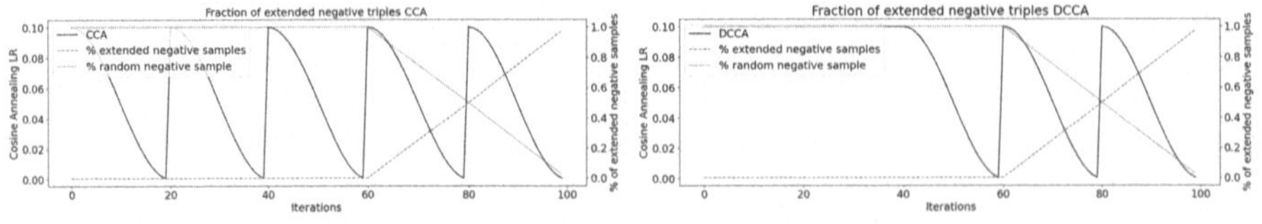

Fig. 3. Usage of the extended negative sampler in the cosine annealing (left) and deferred cosine annealing (right) setting.

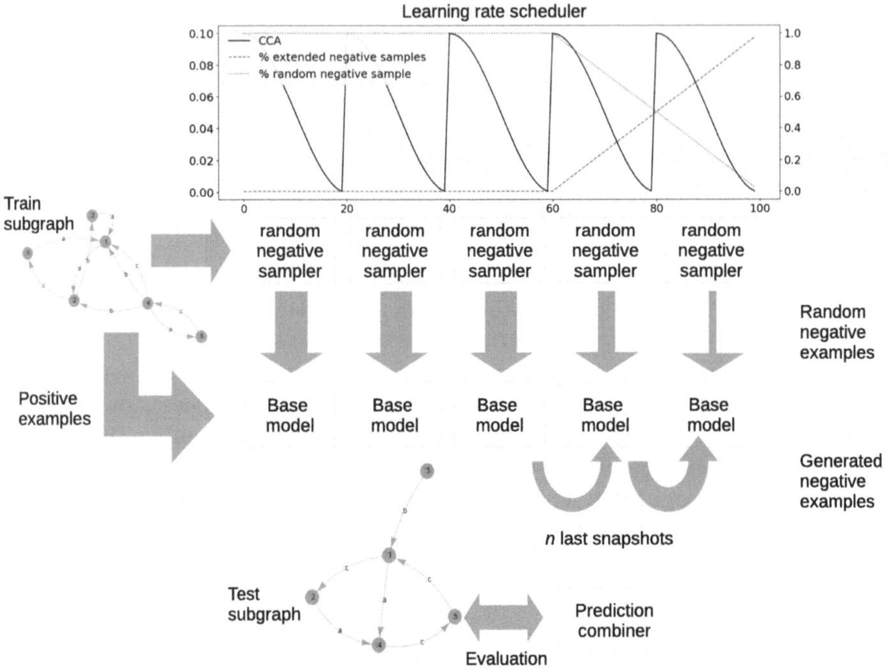

Fig. 4. Illustration of the overall approach

Like for the deferred cyclic annealing variants, we want to make sure that the models first learn the basic information in the graph before focusing on the edge cases. Therefore, we use random negative samples in the first iterations and successively use the extended sampling mechanism in the later stages. Figure 3 illustrates this idea.

Figure 4 illustrates the big picture. Following a learning rate schedule, the approach trains a base model and stores several snapshots. The last n snapshots are used for forming the final ensemble and computing a combined prediction. It is possible to use all snapshots, but since the later ones are expected to have a higher quality, we foresee the possibility to also only combine the latest ones. The negative samples in the first rounds are generated randomly; in later iterations, they can be successively replaced by the extended sampler, which uses the (wrong) predictions of the previous snapshots as non-trivial negative examples.

Table 1. Datasets used for the Evaluation

	Entities	Relations	Triples
DBpedia50	24,624	351	34,421
FB15k237	14,505	237	310,079
WN18RR	40,559	11	92,584
AristoV4	42,016	1,593	279,425

4 Evaluation

We run experiments with our approach and four different base models and compare them to the results achieved with the respective baseline models. In our evaluation, we consider two different setups:

1. **Equal training time budget.** We train a model with d dimensions and m snapshots, and compare it to a single base model with d dimensions.
2. **Equal memory budget.** We train a model with $\frac{d}{m}$ dimensions and m snapshots, and compare it to a single base model with d dimensions.

The code for reproducing the results is available online.[3]

We compare our approach to the one proposed by Xu et al. [40], who also train an ensemble of lower dimensional models, coined as M*base*, i.e., MTransE, MDistMult, MComplEx, and MRotatE. In order to ensure comparability to our approach, we use the same number of epochs for those models, train a total of 10 models (which is the maximum number of models for SnapE in our experiments, see Sect. 4.3), and stick to the parameters in the original paper otherwise (i.e., a learning rate of 0.0003, Adam optimizer, and random negative sampling).[4] All experiments were run on a server with 24 NVIDIA A100 GPUs with 32 GB of RAM each.

4.1 Datasets

We evaluate our approach on four different datasets, i.e., DBpedia50 [33], FB15k-237 [35], WN18RR [6], and AristoV4 [5]. The characteristics of the four datasets are depicted in Table 1.[5]

[3] https://github.com/Alishaba/pykeen-snapshot-ensembles.

[4] Note that the setup is pretty similar to SnapE. The only differences are that each model is initialized randomly, that the sampling is always random, i.e., never uses a previous model to generate negative samples, and that the combination uses uniform weights. Therefore, and due to the implementation of Xu et al. [40] not being available, we use the SnapE implementation to emulate MTransE etc. This also allows for a fair comparison of training and prediction times.

[5] We use the training, test, and validation split as provided in PyKEEN [1].

Table 2. Results of SnapE compared to baselines and to the M*base* ensemble approach. Ensemble approaches outperforming their representative baselines are marked in bold. The best overall results are underlined. The last column shows the average change in HITS@10 over the respective base model across all four datasets. Moreover, we show the average change of each metric for each dataset across all models.

Model	DBpedia50			FB15k237			WN18RR			AristoV4			avg.
	H@1	H@10	MRR	H@1	H@10	MRR	H@1	H@10	MRR	H@1	H@10	MRR	ΔHITS@10
Baselines													
$TransE_d = 64$	0.068	0.276	0.150	0.116	0.418	0.216	0.005	0.319	0.123	0.067	0.221	0.120	–
$TransE_d = 128$	0.056	0.245	0.125	0.097	0.427	0.206	0.002	0.301	0.112	0.037	0.224	0.102	–
$DistMult_d = 64$	0.262	0.378	0.309	0.090	0.318	0.167	0.292	0.309	0.299	0.047	0.151	0.084	–
$DistMult_d = 128$	0.299	0.418	0.345	0.105	0.343	0.185	0.293	0.328	0.308	0.060	0.170	0.098	–
$ComplEx_d = 64$	0.191	0.319	0.239	0.091	0.416	0.197	0.271	0.381	0.313	0.038	0.130	0.067	–
$ComplEx_d = 128$	0.002	0.008	0.005	0.094	0.402	0.195	0.282	0.360	0.311	0.064	0.176	0.105	–
$RotatE_d = 64$	0.223	0.269	0.242	0.167	0.455	0.265	0.315	0.348	0.328	0.089	0.220	0.135	–
$RotatE_d = 128$	0.227	0.288	0.250	0.178	0.483	0.281	0.328	0.379	0.346	0.038	0.130	0.069	–
SnapE - Same Memory Budget													
$TransE_d = 64$	0.062	0.250	0.131	0.108	0.395	0.202	0.003	0.289	0.106	0.055	0.184	0.100	−10.23%
$TransE_d = 128$	**0.058**	0.243	0.124	**0.128**	**0.445**	**0.231**	**0.004**	0.289	0.110	**0.067**	**0.226**	**0.120**	+0.05%
$DistMult_d = 64$	0.256	0.351	0.292	**0.097**	0.299	0.165	0.276	0.305	0.288	0.045	0.145	0.080	−4.52%
$DistMult_d = 128$	0.263	0.394	0.313	**0.138**	**0.355**	**0.211**	0.291	0.319	0.303	**0.060**	**0.175**	**0.101**	−0.49%
$ComplEx_d = 64$	**0.266**	**0.349**	**0.296**	**0.150**	**0.479**	**0.258**	**0.321**	**0.391**	**0.347**	**0.056**	**0.174**	**0.097**	+15.29%
$ComplEx_d = 128$	**0.006**	**0.029**	**0.014**	**0.171**	**0.512**	**0.283**	**0.318**	**0.389**	**0.344**	0.060	0.172	0.098	+75.44%
$RotatE_d = 64$	0.208	0.261	0.227	0.148	0.431	0.243	0.310	0.337	0.319	0.064	0.190	0.107	−6.25%
$RotatE_d = 128$	**0.227**	**0.289**	0.250	0.174	0.470	0.274	0.318	0.357	0.332	**0.086**	**0.204**	**0.127**	+12.21%
avg. Δ	+28.02%	+31.57%	+22.25%	+24.63%	+3.85%	+10.53%	+8.93%	−1.94%	−0.78%	+24.64%	+7.27%	+12.57%	
SnapE - Same Training Time Budget													
$TransE_d = 64$	**0.141**	**0.348**	**0.223**	**0.135**	**0.427**	**0.231**	0.005	0.313	0.122	**0.076**	**0.244**	**0.133**	+9.26%
$TransE_d = 128$	**0.086**	**0.284**	**0.161**	**0.140**	**0.457**	**0.246**	**0.004**	0.299	0.111	**0.082**	**0.258**	**0.142**	+9.38%
$DistMult_d = 64$	**0.288**	**0.395**	**0.327**	**0.141**	**0.354**	**0.214**	**0.303**	**0.338**	**0.317**	**0.059**	**0.179**	**0.102**	+10.94%
$DistMult_d = 128$	**0.326**	**0.433**	**0.367**	**0.146**	**0.366**	**0.221**	**0.299**	**0.346**	**0.316**	**0.064**	0.170	**0.102**	+3.86%
$ComplEx_d = 64$	**0.250**	**0.334**	**0.280**	**0.221**	**0.543**	**0.329**	**0.323**	**0.403**	**0.352**	**0.095**	**0.232**	**0.143**	+29.90%
$ComplEx_d = 128$	**0.030**	**0.068**	**0.044**	**0.198**	**0.518**	**0.305**	**0.312**	**0.367**	**0.332**	**0.072**	**0.181**	**0.110**	+194.82%
$RotatE_d = 64$	**0.256**	**0.321**	**0.280**	**0.167**	0.453	0.262	**0.323**	**0.364**	**0.339**	**0.084**	**0.224**	0.132	+6.31%
$RotatE_d = 128$	**0.264**	**0.336**	**0.290**	**0.180**	0.481	**0.282**	**0.335**	**0.388**	**0.353**	**0.100**	**0.246**	**0.149**	+26.94%
avg. Δ	+207.64%	+104.56%	+115.13%	+51.50%	+10.72%	+24.46%	+14.64%	+3.36%	+3.97%	+61.12%	+27.07%	+38.49%	
M*base*													
$MTransE_d = 64$	0.016	**0.487**	**0.214**	**0.184**	**0.558**	**0.314**	0.000	**0.368**	**0.154**	**0.078**	**0.340**	**0.169**	+44.74%
$MTransE_d = 128$	0.013	**0.479**	**0.210**	**0.113**	**0.582**	**0.283**	**0.003**	**0.349**	**0.164**	0.014	**0.360**	**0.142**	+52.13%
$MDistMult_d = 64$	**0.301**	**0.381**	**0.332**	**0.095**	0.259	0.149	0.028	0.028	0.028	0.041	0.116	0.068	−33.04%
$MDistMult_d = 128$	**0.326**	0.326	0.293	0.090	0.304	0.165	0.241	0.279	0.265	**0.072**	**0.224**	**0.124**	−4.09%
$MComplEx_d = 64$	0.005	0.028	0.013	**0.243**	**0.592**	**0.361**	0.009	0.035	0.018	**0.051**	**0.153**	**0.088**	−30.55%
$MComplEx_d = 128$	0.000	0.001	0.001	**0.197**	**0.522**	**0.310**	0.266	0.268	0.267	0.043	0.115	0.043	−29.53%
$MRotatE_d = 64$	0.195	0.255	0.219	**0.234**	**0.594**	**0.357**	**0.325**	**0.384**	**0.344**	**0.133**	**0.311**	**0.193**	+19.27%
$MRotatE_d = 128$	**0.228**	**0.344**	**0.268**	**0.236**	**0.615**	**0.366**	**0.437**	0.354	**0.382**	**0.122**	**0.277**	**0.174**	+38.28%
avg. Δ	−42.35%	−1.72%	−9.23%	+51.96%	+21.24%	+33.54%	−28.01%	−23.35%	−15.76%	+29.14%	+32.48%	+32.00%	

4.2 Base Models

As base models, we chose TransE [4], DistMult [41], ComplEx [36], and RotatE [34]. For each base model, we train two baseline models, one with 64 and one with 128 dimensions, and a batch size of 128 each. We determine the optimal number of epochs by applying early stopping, using $relative\_delta = 0.000001$ and $patience = 2$, and $Hits@10$ as a target metric. Furthermore, we pick the best learning rate $lr \in \{10, 1, 0.1, 0.01\}$ and the best optimizer out of stochastic gradient descent (SGD), Adam, and AdaGrad by applying grid search. The number of epochs that worked best for each base model is then also used for the snapshot ensemble (while the learning rate is controlled by the respective decay scheme).[6] The parameters used for each model are listed in the appendix.

Note that the goal is not to achieve the best possible baseline results [31]. We are more interested in analyzing the performance gains that can be obtained by using snapshot ensembles, compared to the standard training loop.

4.3 Parameters

For the parameters of the snapshot ensemble, we use the number of episodes that worked best on for the baseline model on the respective dataset (see Table 5 in the appendix). Moreover, we use scores weighted by last training loss as an aggregation method, min-max-scaling to normalize the scores before, and deferred CCA as a scheduler. We pick the no. of cycles C out of $\{5, 10\}$ and the number of models M to be used out of $[2, C]$ ((cf. Fig. 2)[7], as well as the best performing optimizer. The parameters used for each model are listed in the appendix.

4.4 Results

Table 2 shows a comparison of SnapE against the baselines. We show the results both for the setup with the same memory budget as well as for the setup with the same time budget.

We can observe that training with SnapE outperforms the standard training mechanism in about a third of the cases when considering the same memory budget case, and in almost all cases when considering the same training time budget case (in that case at the price of a larger overall model). Moreover, in all cases, the best overall result is achieved by an ensemble model.

It can also be observed that not all models benefit equally from the SnapE training. The gains for RotatE are moderate, while the other models, especially DistMult and ComplEx, benefit much more strongly. In particular, ComplEx (and, to a lesser extent, DistMult) strongly benefit on FB15k237 and WN18RR, whereas the improvements for TransE and RotatE are not that strong on those two datasets. As stated in the original RotatE paper, composition patterns are very important in those two datasets, and ComplEx and DistMult are not capable of learning those patterns. So one possible explanation is that the ensembling compensates for the inability of those models to learn composition patterns.

Comparing to the M*base* models proposed by [40], we can observe that while they sometimes achieve the best overall performance, their average gains are less (and often even negative) than those of SnapE. Hence, we conclude that while SnapE is occasionally outperformed by M*base*, it is more stable overall. Given the observations about the runtime below, we observe that SnapE provides a better trade-off of computational efforts and prediction quality than M*base*.

[6] For all other parameters, we use the default values from PyKEEN, including negative sampling rate (1 negative sample per positive example) and loss function (MarginRankingLoss for TransE, DistMult, and Rotate, SoftplusLoss for ComplEx).

[7] Note that when $M = C$, then there is actually no warmup phase, i.e., the schedule is equal to a non-deferred one.

4.5 Runtime Behavior

Table 3 shows the runtime behavior of the baselines as well as the SnapE configurations for the same memory and the same training time budget.[8]

In both cases, we can observe that the training time is similar to or even smaller than the one for the baseline method.

On the other hand, the prediction time is significantly larger for the same training time budget setup. The reason is that instead of making one model predict, *each* of the snapshot models has to make a prediction, which leads to the higher prediction time. The combination of the individual predictions also contributes to the prediction time, but to a lesser extent. For the same memory setup, this effect is not observed, since a prediction with a number of smaller models is not more time-consuming than a prediction with one large model.

For the M*base* approach, we observe significantly larger training times[9], as already discussed in Sect. 2, since SnapE trains all its models in the same number of epochs that M*base* uses per model. The fact that the prediction time of M*base* is also higher is due to the fact that M*base* always uses all base models trained, while in SnapE, this is a hyperparameter, and often a smaller number of models is used (see appendix).

4.6 Model Variety

One essential prerequisite for using ensemble methods successfully is that the base models expose some variety. Generally, the more diverse the single models in an ensemble are, the better the ensemble.

To measure the model variety, we look at the triple scores produced by the individual models, and compute their correlation for each pair of models. Table 4 shows the average of those correlations for all models in the ensemble, together with the HITS@10 of the best single base model and the ensemble.

We can see that the approach is indeed effective, since in most cases, the ensembles do not only outperform the baseline, but also the single best model.[10] Exceptions are only observed for the same memory setup for WN18RR, where in half of the cases, the best individual model is slightly better than the ensemble. Moreover, the gains over the best single model are often more considerable in cases of less correlated models, i.e., when SnapE learns more diverse base models.

What is also important is that the best performing model is only rarely the last one – otherwise, the overhead of storing all intermediate models would be even more questionable. Moreover, also in the cases where the best single model

[8] While it might seem surprising that the larger baseline models with d = 128 often train faster than the smaller ones with d = 64, despite having a larger number of parameters, this is due to the early stopping criterion, which allowed the larger models to be trained in a smaller number of episodes (see appendix), leading to overall lower training times.

[9] However, the training in M*base* can be parallelized, which is not possible for SnapE.

[10] Otherwise, one could have assumed that SnapE performs better simply due to a smaller model size and hence, e.g., a lesser tendency to overfit.

Table 3. Training and prediction time (s) of the baselines, the SnapE-trained approaches, and the M*base* ensembles

Model	DBpedia50		FB15k237		WN18RR		AristoV4	
	train	predict	train	predict	train	predict	train	predict
Baselines								
$\text{TransE}_{d=64}$	58.427	0.190	358.516	1.466	303.580	0.656	645.440	1.994
$\text{TransE}_{d=128}$	48.723	0.316	1,687.463	2.134	128.592	0.517	599.860	2.831
$\text{DistMult}_{d=64}$	84.571	0.340	196.292	1.490	49.885	0.411	186.774	2.417
$\text{DistMult}_{d=128}$	22.309	0.234	185.398	1.626	77.129	0.517	1,690.012	2.768
$\text{ComplEx}_{d=64}$	256.092	0.333	2,643.319	1.706	370.614	0.401	1,463.573	1.956
$\text{ComplEx}_{d=128}$	29.171	0.372	1,319.236	1.805	344.264	0.566	11,334.286	5.792
$\text{RotatE}_{d=64}$	62.807	0.241	1,130.800	1.620	1,109.552	0.532	1,962.201	2.764
$\text{RotatE}_{d=128}$	92.876	0.393	1,687.463	2.135	169.264	0.743	1,677.724	4.825
SnapE – Same Memory Budget								
$\text{TransE}_{d=64}$	54.006	0.203	296.375	1.314	275.402	0.649	578.863	1.878
$\text{TransE}_{d=128}$	38.658	0.236	443.577	1.503	103.982	0.755	619.845	2.258
$\text{DistMult}_{d=64}$	55.419	0.203	126.954	1.638	31.698	0.648	182.741	1.781
$\text{DistMult}_{d=128}$	13.182	0.239	258.389	1.599	49.283	0.783	198.814	2.474
$\text{ComplEx}_{d=64}$	180.451	0.185	2,470.871	1.252	322.798	0.544	1,050.948	1.569
$\text{ComplEx}_{d=128}$	23.597	0.282	836.381	1.518	300.829	0.738	2,243.378	2.129
$\text{RotatE}_{d=64}$	56.665	0.219	1,119.917	1.452	99.450	0.784	1,336.407	2.317
$\text{RotatE}_{d=128}$	66.058	0.362	1,594.601	1.689	128.422	1.143	1,482.312	3.306
avg. Δ	−23.86%	−17.77%	−17.07%	−13.18%	−30.21%	+40.17%	−31.16%	−24.21%
SnapE – Same Training Time Budget								
$\text{TransE}_{d=64}$	91.298	0.637	397.608	2.374	291.219	0.782	930.551	5.007
$\text{TransE}_{d=128}$	68.966	0.871	653.377	3.213	118.345	1.106	1,202.238	10.263
$\text{DistMult}_{d=64}$	14.589	0.293	153.939	3.491	57.423	2.426	256.140	7.571
$\text{DistMult}_{d=128}$	18.579	0.672	294.357	4.472	60.385	1.506	1,784.194	3.241
$\text{ComplEx}_{d=64}$	200.428	0.269	842.800	2.881	329.754	0.734	1,652.348	6.809
$\text{ComplEx}_{d=128}$	34.277	1.069	925.995	3.910	306.544	1.094	2,410.949	3.123
$\text{RotatE}_{d=64}$	80.620	1.034	149.655	4.392	223.709	4.574	1,733.061	5.713
$\text{RotatE}_{d=128}$	120.118	1.825	1,752.696	2.535	613.024	7.561	1,772.830	5.028
avg. Δ	+6.47%	+180.78%	−24.25%	+99.65%	+17.71%	+333.58%	+14.43%	+119.61%
M*base*								
$\text{MTransE}_d = 64$	547.341	1.070	2,856.178	3.301	2,773.676	3.598	5,496.94	8.27
$\text{MTransE}_d = 128$	424.415	1.615	4,343.727	5.108	1,061.422	4.234	5,078.27	12.73
$\text{MDistMult}_d = 64$	547.341	1.070	903.491	3.290	195.154	2.558	836.39	7.31
$\text{MDistMult}_d = 128$	167.593	0.981	965.005	5.410	516.893	4.229	15,772.17	13.29
$\text{MComplEx}_d = 64$	1,925.209	1.217	23,684.887	3.681	962.539	2.319	12,888.71	7.55
$\text{MComplEx}_d = 128$	147.732	1.058	11,655.125	5.773	2,895.896	5.013	10,317.45	12.48
$\text{MRotatE}_d = 64$	589.339	1.674	11,047.856	5.361	1,029.588	4.473	18,374.42	13.92
$\text{MRotatE}_d = 128$	713.364	2.362	16,925.643	9.354	1,287.857	7.531	6,434.62	22.24
avg. Δ	+671.36%	+369.21%	+624.30%	+190.34%	+494.37%	+665.77%	+571.36%	+301.59%

Table 4. Analysis of the variance of models in the SnapE ensembles. The table contrasts the HITS@10 scores achieved by SnapE and by the best single model in the ensemble (the better of the two marked in bold). The column N-# shows which is the best performing single model (0 means the last, 1 means the second to last, etc.). Moreover, we depict the average pairwise correlation of the models in the ensemble. For M*base*, we do not report the number of the best performing model, since all models are independent.

Model	DBpedia50				FB15k237				WN18RR				AristoV4			
	Ensemble	Best Single		avg.	Ensemble	Best Single		avg.	Ensemble	Best Single		avg.	Ensemble	Best Single		avg.
	H@10	H@10	N-#	corr.	H@10	H@10	N-#	corr.	H@10	H@10	N-#	corr.	H@10	H@10	N-#	corr.
SnapE - Same Memory Budget																
$TransE_d = 64$	0.250	**0.252**	0	0.324	**0.395**	0.390	1	0.484	**0.289**	0.289	1	−0.235	**0.184**	0.179	1	0.628
$TransE_d = 128$	**0.243**	0.243	1	0.632	**0.445**	0.440	5	0.408	0.289	**0.290**	1	−0.211	**0.226**	0.217	1	0.512
$DistMult_d = 64$	**0.351**	0.336	1	0.962	**0.299**	0.119	4	0.222	0.305	**0.306**	1	0.996	**0.145**	0.066	3	0.274
$DistMult_d = 128$	**0.394**	0.389	1	0.652	**0.355**	0.260	7	0.105	0.319	**0.322**	1	0.991	**0.175**	0.112	3	0.178
$ComplEx_d = 64$	**0.349**	0.337	1	0.005	**0.479**	0.462	2	-0.007	**0.391**	0.386	1	−0.308	**0.174**	0.137	1	0.349
$ComplEx_d = 128$	**0.029**	0.005	0	0.393	**0.512**	0.419	2	0.439	**0.389**	0.384	1	−0.224	**0.172**	0.162	1	−0.079
$RotatE_d = 64$	**0.261**	0.226	0	0.133	**0.431**	0.428	1	0.189	0.337	**0.337**	1	0.228	**0.190**	0.180	1	−0.245
$RotatE_d = 128$	**0.289**	0.259	1	0.037	**0.470**	0.467	6	0.158	0.357	0.357	1	0.079	**0.204**	0.203	1	−0.204
SnapE - Same Training Time Budget																
$TransE_d = 64$	**0.348**	0.345	1	0.416	**0.427**	0.381	5	0.719	0.313	**0.313**	1	−0.110	**0.244**	0.206	7	0.620
$TransE_d = 128$	**0.284**	0.231	0	0.837	**0.457**	0.401	5	0.837	**0.299**	0.299	1	0.085	**0.258**	0.175	3	0.504
$DistMult_d = 64$	**0.395**	0.365	1	0.489	**0.354**	0.288	8	0.153	**0.338**	0.281	7	0.219	**0.179**	0.116	9	0.323
$DistMult_d = 128$	**0.433**	0.401	4	0.375	**0.366**	0.338	8	0.101	**0.346**	0.333	2	0.967	**0.170**	0.167	1	0.743
$ComplEx_d = 64$	**0.334**	0.291	2	0.397	**0.543**	0.383	7	0.638	**0.403**	0.398	1	−0.236	**0.232**	0.088	1	0.325
$ComplEx_d = 128$	**0.068**	0.008	0	0.264	**0.518**	0.400	6	0.654	**0.367**	0.358	1	0.033	**0.181**	0.176	1	−0.100
$RotatE_d = 64$	**0.321**	0.263	1	0.085	**0.453**	0.344	8	0.102	**0.364**	0.277	0	0.006	**0.224**	0.205	3	0.000
$RotatE_d = 128$	**0.336**	0.264	2	0.089	**0.481**	0.476	1	0.224	**0.388**	0.314	9	0.003	**0.246**	0.245	1	−0.260
M*base*																
$MTransE_d = 64$	**0.487**	0.129	–	0.571	**0.558**	0.393	–	0.871	**0.368**	0.274	–	0.716	**0.340**	0.195	–	0.880
$MTransE_d = 128$	**0.479**	0.140	–	0.494	**0.582**	0.422	–	0.840	**0.349**	0.184	–	0.686	**0.360**	0.211	–	0.716
$MDistMult_d = 64$	**0.381**	0.306	–	0.936	**0.259**	0.212	–	0.954	**0.028**	0.021	–	0.979	**0.116**	0.075	–	0.969
$MDistMult_d = 128$	**0.326**	0.258	–	0.981	**0.304**	0.292	–	0.931	**0.279**	0.183	–	0.962	**0.224**	0.204	–	0.879
$MComplEx_d = 64$	**0.028**	0.002	–	0.551	**0.592**	0.404	–	0.658	**0.035**	0.001	–	0.474	**0.153**	0.070	–	0.827
$MComplEx_d = 128$	0.001	0.001	–	0.007	**0.522**	0.260	–	0.586	**0.268**	0.003	–	0.561	**0.115**	0.052	–	0.705
$MRotatE_d = 64$	**0.255**	0.228	–	0.540	**0.594**	0.518	–	0.755	**0.384**	0.349	–	0.417	**0.311**	0.240	–	0.797
$MRotatE_d = 128$	**0.344**	0.286	–	0.286	**0.615**	0.529	–	0.738	**0.437**	0.373	–	0.303	**0.277**	0.205	–	0.827

is found early on in the training process (indicated by a high value in the N-# column in Table 4), there are often considerable performance gains compared to the best single model, meaning that the subsequent models are not better individually, but are able to capture information and cases not solved correctly by the best single model. Interestingly, negative correlations are also observed (i.e., SnapE learns *contradicting* models). In many of those cases, we can see that the ensemble still performs well.

In comparison to M*base*, we observe that SnapE most often produces less correlated (i.e., more diverse) models, and, at the same, also better single models, which are then often learned late in the training process.

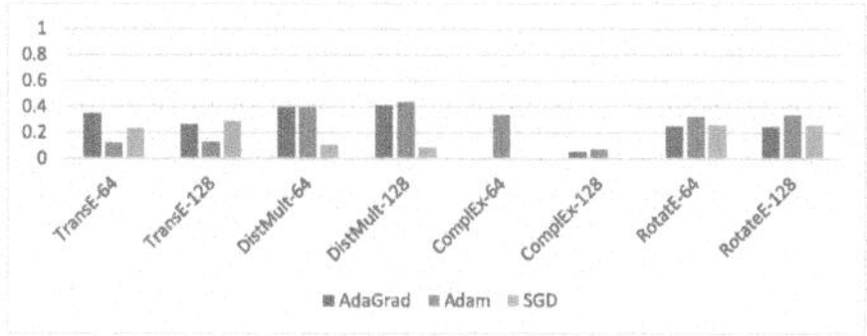

(a) DBpedia50

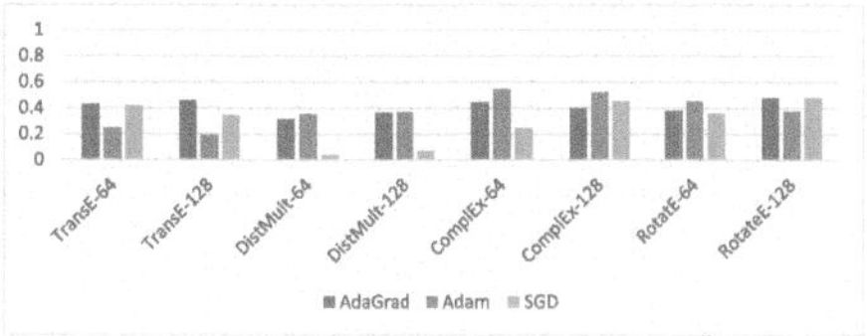

(b) FB15k-237

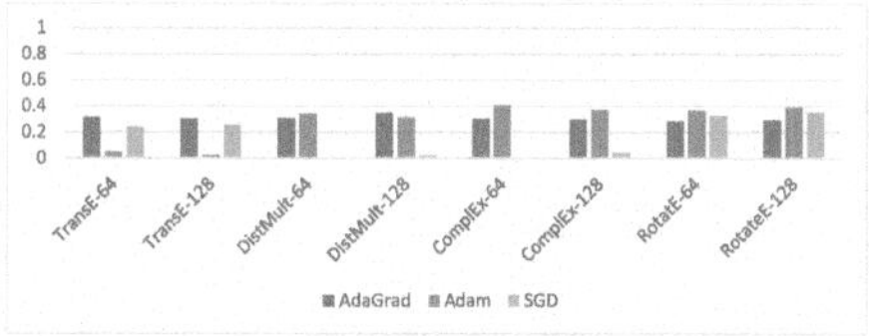

(c) WN18RR

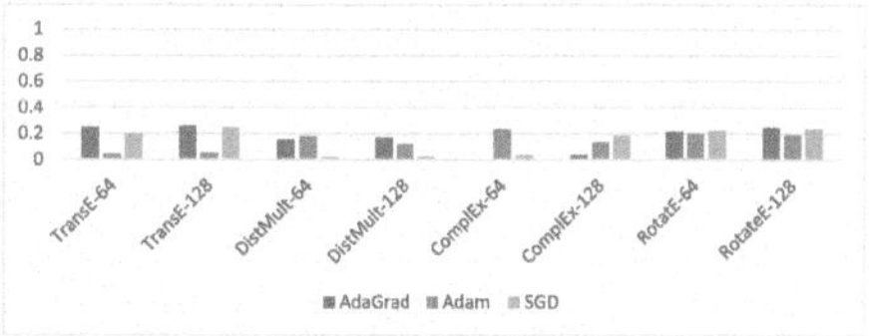

(d) AristoV4

Fig. 5. Ablation study on using different optimizers

4.7 Ablation Study

We analyze the impact of (1) different optimizers, (2) different learning rate schedulers (see Fig. 2), (3) different negative samplers, (4) different strategies for combining the predictions of the snapshots. In all the ablation studies, we use the best performing parameter sets, and vary only the respective parameter of study. For the sake of space, we show only the impact on Hits@10, and we only consider the setting with the same training time budget.

Figure 5 shows results obtained with varying the optimizer. There is quite a bit of variation between using different optimizers. It can be observed that, in most cases, the Adam optimizer works best with SnapE. Only when using SnapE for TransE (and ocassionally RotatE), AdaGrad and SGD are preferred.

Figure 6 shows the results for using different scheduling mechanisms. It can be observed that in general, the influence of the scheduler is rather minimal. In cases where the results differ, the deferred variants have an advantage over the non-deferred variants (i.e., those scheduling variants may help, but rather do not hurt). There is only a small difference between standard CCA and MMC-CLR. More detailed experiments have shown that CCA occasionally outperforms MMCCLR, but not vice versa.

Figure 7 shows the results obtained with standard negative sampling and the proposed extended negative sampler, which uses snapshots from previous iterations for negative sampling. It can be observed that the proposed extended negative sampler yields better results in most cases. There is a clear outlier, which is the result for DistMult with d = 128 on WN18RR. As shown in the analysis above, in that case, the variety of the models is very low when using the extended sampler (yielding a correlation of 0.967). This means that the individual models do not learn any different patterns (and, hence, the extended sampler cannot produce any interesting negatives for the subsequent iterations).

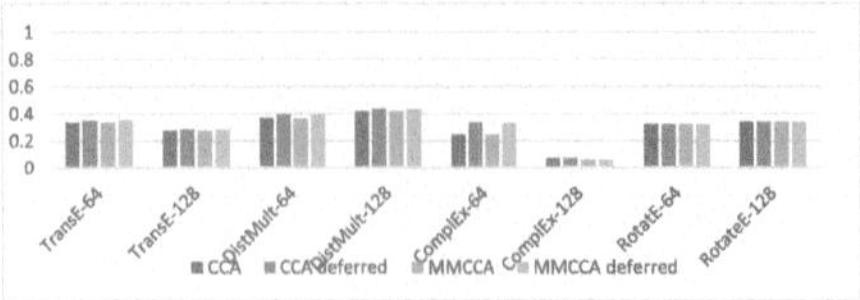

(a) DBpedia50

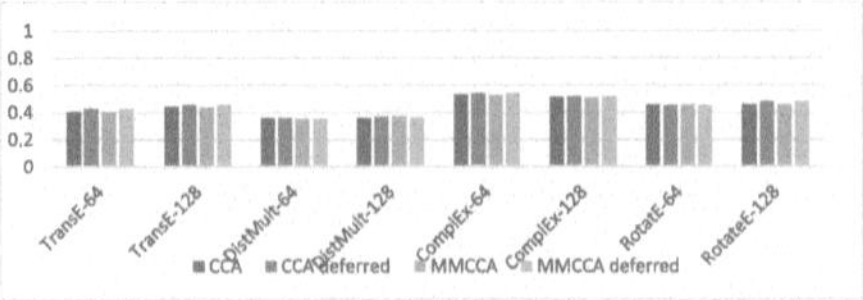

(b) FB15k-237

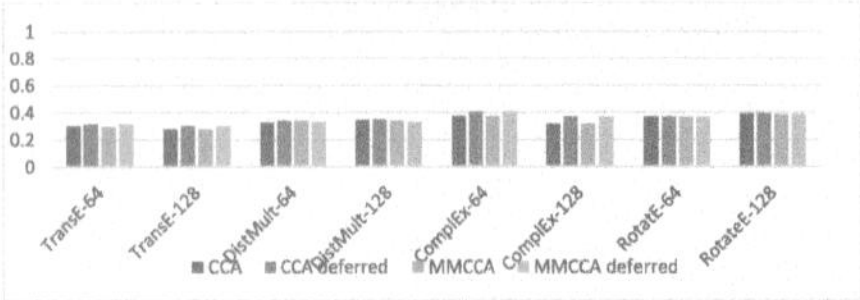

(c) WN18RR

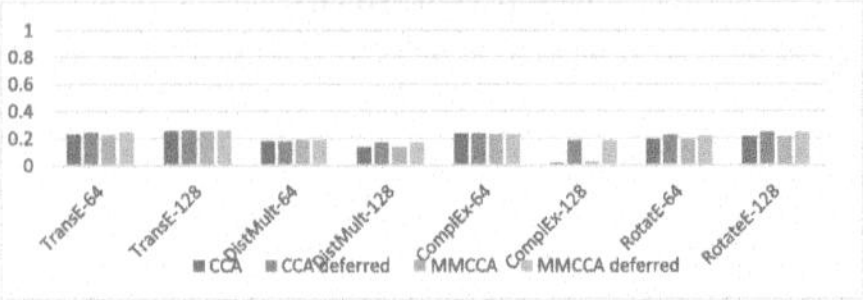

(d) AristoV4

Fig. 6. Ablation study on using different schedulers

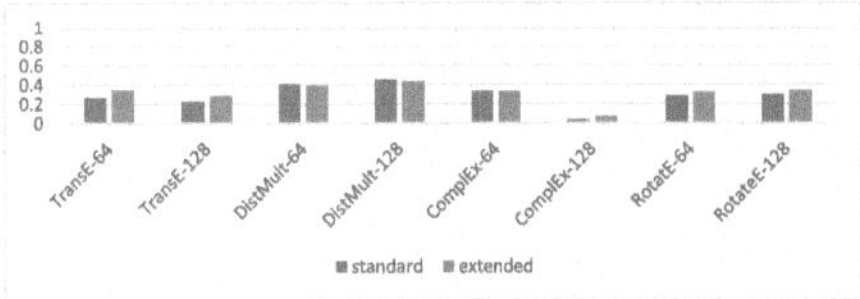

(a) DBpedia50

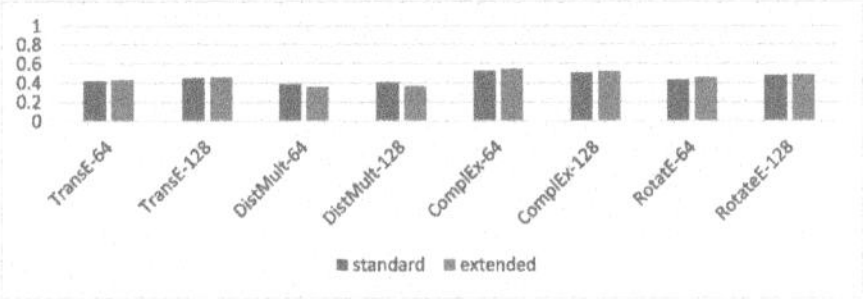

(b) FB15k-237

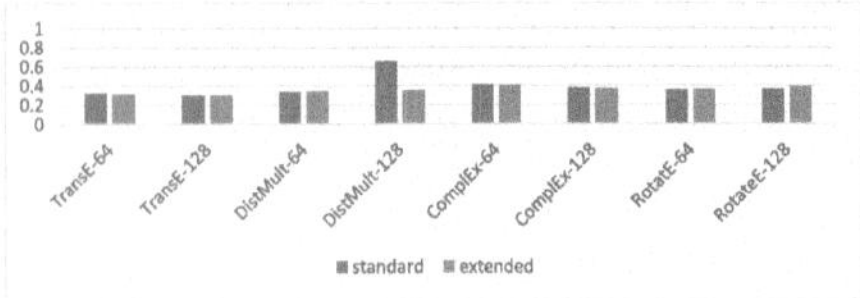

(c) WN18RR

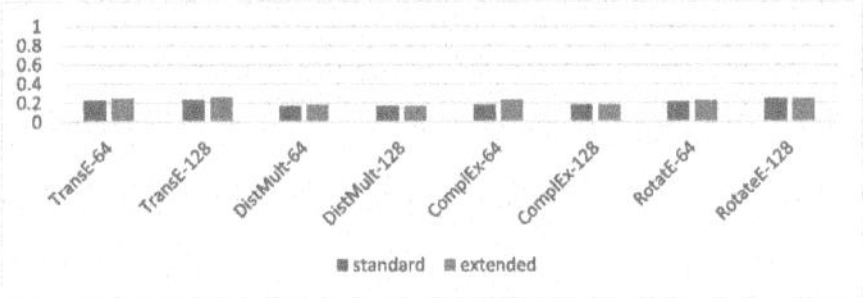

(d) AristoV4

Fig. 7. Ablation study on using the standard vs. the extended sampler

Lastly, Fig. 8 shows a study of the impact of using different techniques for combining the results. We can observe that in general, the worst results are achieved with Borda rank aggregation, while the other methods are en par in many cases (with the exception of some cases with TransE, which work significantly better with equal weights).

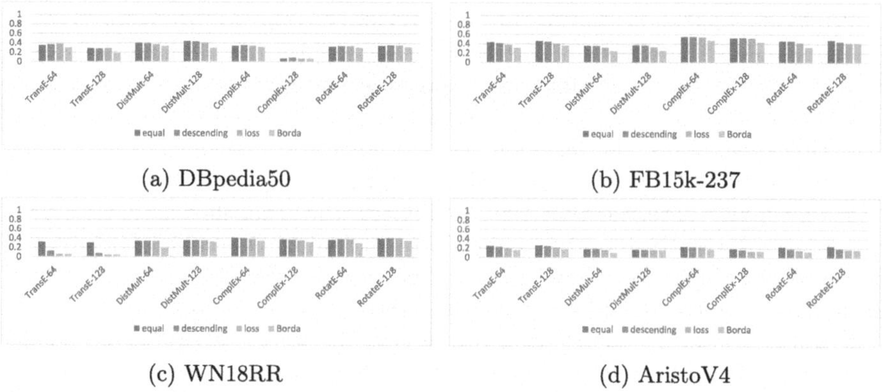

(a) DBpedia50

(b) FB15k-237

(c) WN18RR

(d) AristoV4

Fig. 8. Ablation study on different strategies for combining predictions

5 Conclusion and Outlook

In this paper, we have introduced SnapE, which is a training mechanism for knowledge graph embedding models based on snapshot ensembles. Instead of training one single model in N epochs, SnapE trains a sequence of C models with shorter training cycles of length N/C each, using a decaying learning rate in each cycle. We have conducted experiments on four datasets, each time training SnapE with TransE, DistMult, ComplEx, and RotatE as base models. The resulting ensemble method has been shown to often deliver superior results to an individual model, without increasing the training cost.

The SnapE framework allows for further experimentation. We have observed that learning rate schedulers and combination approaches have an impact on the overall results, thus, we can assume that more experimentation with different variants here might yield even better results. As far as the learning rate schedulers go, early stopping could also be applied in each of the learning cycles, allowing for further optimization of the training time. The deferred training schedules could also allow to train the first iteration on a condensed version of the graph, as proposed in [17]. For combining the predictions of snapshot models, techniques like mixture of experts [20] could be a promising candidate for creating even more powerful snapshot ensembles.

While we could show that SnapE models can be trained at the same training cost as standard baseline models, we have observed a drastic increase in prediction time. At the same time, we could observe that it is often sufficient or even beneficial to only use a subset of the snapshots, which in turn lowers the prediction time. Thus, the selection strategy for the subset of snapshots seems a crucial property for further optimizing SnapE.

We have also observed that the possibilities that snapshot ensembles yield with respect to creating negative samples are intriguing. One could think of more elaborate techniques for exploiting negative samples from previous snapshots, e.g., mixing negative samples created by several previous snapshots.

Finally, it would be interesting to see how the idea of snapshot ensembles can be carried over to different kinds of embedding and graph learning methods, like R-GCNs [32] or walk-based methods like RDF2vec [28] and its variants [25], and other downstream tasks, such as node classification [3,23]. Moreover, they might be an interesting approach to embedding versioned knowledge graphs [13] by forming an evolving ensemble of snapshots trained on different versions.

Appendix: Configurations Used

In this appendix, we show the configurations used for the baselines (Table 5) as well as the SnapE models (Table 6) in Sect. 4.

Table 5. Learning rate (lr), epochs (ep), and optimizer (Ad = Adam, AG = Adagrad) chosen for each base model as the best performing approach, based on HITS@10.

Model	DBpedia50			FB15k237			WN18RR			AristoV4		
	LR	ep	O	LR	ep	O	LR	ep	O	LR	ep	O
TransE$_{d=64}$	1.0	110	AG	0.1	80	AG	0.1	220	AG	0.1	170	AG
TransE$_{d=128}$	1.0	80	SGD	0.1	120	AG	0.1	80	AG	0.1	150	AG
DistMult$_{d=64}$	0.1	90	AG	0.1	20	AG	0.1	10	AG	0.1	20	AG
DistMult$_{d=128}$	0.1	20	AG	0.1	20	AG	0.1	30	AG	0.01	400	AG
ComplEx$_{d=64}$	0.01	210	Ad	1.0	350	AG	0.01	40	Ad	10	210	SGD
ComplEx$_{d=128}$	0.1	10	Ad	10	170	SGD	0.01	120	Ad	10	160	SGD
RotatE$_{d=64}$	10	100	SGD	1.0	270	SGD	10	70	SGD	0.1	490	AG
RotatE$_{d=128}$	10	110	SGD	1.0	400	SGD	10	80	SGD	0.1	150	AG

Table 6. Number of cycles (C), of models (M), and optimizer (O) for the best performing SnapE models, based on HITS@10.

Model	DBpedia50			FB15k237			WN18RR			AristoV4		
	C	M	O	C	M	O	C	M	O	C	M	O
SnapE – Same Memory Budget												
$\text{TransE}_{d=64}$	10	2	Adagrad	10	2	Adagrad	10	2	Adagrad	10	2	Adagrad
$\text{TransE}_{d=128}$	10	2	SGD	10	2	Adagrad	10	2	Adagrad	5	2	Adagrad
$\text{DistMult}_{d=64}$	5	2	Adagrad	10	9	Adam	10	2	Adagrad	5	5	Adam
$\text{DistMult}_{d=128}$	10	2	Adam	5	5	Adam	10	2	Adagrad	5	5	Adam
$\text{ComplEx}_{d=64}$	10	2	Adam	10	2	Adagrad	10	2	Adam	5	2	Adam
$\text{ComplEx}_{d=128}$	10	10	Adam	5	3	Adam	10	2	Adam	10	2	SGD
$\text{RotatE}_{d=64}$	5	5	Adam	10	2	SGD	10	2	SGD	5	2	SGD
$\text{RotatE}_{d=128}$	5	4	Adam	10	2	SGD	10	2	SGD	10	2	Adagrad
SnapE – Same Training Time Budget												
$\text{TransE}_{d=64}$	10	9	Adagrad	10	6	Adagrad	10	2	Adagrad	10	6	Adagrad
$\text{TransE}_{d=128}$	10	8	SGD	10	6	Adagrad	10	2	Adagrad	10	8	Adagrad
$\text{DistMult}_{d=64}$	10	3	Adam	10	10	Adam	10	9	Adam	10	10	Adam
$\text{DistMult}_{d=128}$	10	6	Adam	10	9	Adam	10	3	Adagrad	10	2	Adagrad
$\text{ComplEx}_{d=64}$	10	3	Adam	10	9	Adam	10	2	Adam	10	10	Adam
$\text{ComplEx}_{d=128}$	10	10	Adam	10	7	Adam	10	2	Adam	10	2	SGD
$\text{RotatE}_{d=64}$	10	10	Adam	10	9	Adam	10	10	Adam	10	4	SGD
$\text{RotatE}_{d=128}$	10	10	Adam	10	2	SGD	10	10	Adam	10	2	Adagrad

Acknowledgements. The authors acknowledge support by the state of Baden-Wrttemberg through bwHPC.

References

1. Ali, M., et al.: Pykeen 1.0: a python library for training and evaluating knowledge graph embeddings. J. Mach. Learn. Res. (2021)
2. Biswas, R., et al.: Knowledge graph embeddings: open challenges and opportunities. Trans. Graph Data Knowl. **1**(1), 1–4 (2023)
3. Bloem, P., Wilcke, X., van Berkel, L., de Boer, V.: kgbench: a collection of knowledge graph datasets for evaluating relational and multimodal machine learning. In: Verborgh, R., et al. (eds.) ESWC 2021. LNCS, vol. 12731, pp. 614–630. Springer, Cham (2021). https://doi.org/10.1007/978-3-030-77385-4_37
4. Bordes, A., Usunier, N., Garcia-Duran, A., Weston, J., Yakhnenko, O.: Translating embeddings for modeling multi-relational data. In: Burges, C., Bottou, L., Welling, M., Ghahramani, Z., Weinberger, K. (eds.) Advances in Neural Information Processing Systems. vol. 26. Curran Associates, Inc. (2013). https://proceedings.neurips.cc/paper_files/paper/2013/file/1cecc7a77928ca8133fa24680a88d2f9-Paper.pdf

5. Chen, Y., Minervini, P., Riedel, S., Stenetorp, P.: Relation prediction as an auxiliary training objective for improving multi-relational graph representations. In: 3rd Conference on Automated Knowledge Base Construction (2021). https://openreview.net/forum?id=Qa3uS3H7-Le
6. Dettmers, T., Minervini, P., Stenetorp, P., Riedel, S.: Convolutional 2D knowledge graph embeddings. CoRR abs/1707.01476 (2017). http://arxiv.org/abs/1707.01476
7. Dong, X.L., Gabrilovich, E., Heitz, G., Horn, W., Lao, N., Murphy, K., Strohmann, T., Sun, S., Zhang, W.: Knowledge vault: a web-scale approach to probabilistic knowledge fusion. In: The 20th ACM SIGKDD International Conference on Knowledge Discovery and Data Mining, KDD '14, New York, NY, USA - August 24 - 27, 2014, pp. 601–610 (2014). http://www.cs.cmu.edu/~nlao/publication/2014.kdd.pdf, evgeniy Gabrilovich Wilko Horn Ni Lao Kevin Murphy Thomas Strohmann Shaohua Sun Wei Zhang Geremy Heitz
8. Duan, L., Aggarwal, C., Ma, S., Hu, R., Huai, J.: Scaling up link prediction with ensembles. In: Proceedings of the Ninth ACM International Conference on Web Search and Data Mining, pp. 367–376. Association for Computing Machinery (2016)
9. Dwork, C., Kumar, R., Naor, M., Sivakumar, D.: Rank aggregation methods for the web. In: Proceedings of the 10th International Conference on World Wide Web, pp. 613–622 (2001)
10. Freund, Y., Schapire, R.E.: A decision-theoretic generalization of on-line learning and an application to boosting. J. Comput. Syst. Sci. **55**(1), 119–139 (1997)
11. Ge, R., Kakade, S.M., Kidambi, R., Netrapalli, P.: The step decay schedule: a near optimal, geometrically decaying learning rate procedure. CoRR abs/1904.12838 (2019). http://arxiv.org/abs/1904.12838
12. Gregucci, C., Nayyeri, M., Hernández, D., Staab, S.: Link prediction with attention applied on multiple knowledge graph embedding models. In: WWW '23: Proceedings of the ACM Web Conference, pp. 2600–2610 (2023)
13. Hahn, S.H., Paulheim, H.: Rdf2vec embeddings for updateable knowledge graphs–reuse, don't retrain! In: ESWC Posters and Demos (2024)
14. Heist, N., Hertling, S., Ringler, D., Paulheim, H.: Knowledge graphs on the web–an overview. In: Knowledge Graphs for eXplainable Artificial Intelligence: Foundations, Applications and Challenges, pp. 3–22 (2020)
15. Hogan, A., et al.: Knowledge graphs. ACM Comput. Surv. (CSUR) **54**(4), 1–37 (2021)
16. Huang, G., Li, Y., Pleiss, G., Liu, Z., Hopcroft, J.E., Weinberger, K.Q.: Snapshot ensembles: train 1, get m for free. In: International Conference on Learning Representations (2017)
17. Hubert, N., Paulheim, H., Monnin, P., Brun, A., Monticolo, D.: Schema first! learn versatile knowledge graph embeddings by capturing semantics with maschine. In: Proceedings of the 12th Knowledge Capture Conference 2023, pp. 188–196 (2023)
18. Krompass, D., Tresp, V.: Ensemble solutions for link-prediction in knowledge graphs (2015)
19. Loshchilov, I., Hutter, F.: SGDR: stochastic gradient descent with warm restarts. In: International Conference on Learning Representations (2017). https://openreview.net/forum?id=Skq89Scxx
20. Masoudnia, S., Ebrahimpour, R.: Mixture of experts: a literature survey. Artif. Intell. Rev. **42**, 275–293 (2014)
21. Nickel, M., Murphy, K., Tresp, V., Gabrilovich, E.: A review of relational machine learning for knowledge graphs. In: Proceedings of the IEEE (2015)

22. Paulheim, H.: Knowledge graph refinement: a survey of approaches and evaluation methods. Semantic Web **8**(3), 489–508 (2017)
23. Pellegrino, M.A., Altabba, A., Garofalo, M., Ristoski, P., Cochez, M.: GEval: a modular and extensible evaluation framework for graph embedding techniques. In: Harth, A., et al. (eds.) ESWC 2020. LNCS, vol. 12123, pp. 565–582. Springer, Cham (2020). https://doi.org/10.1007/978-3-030-49461-2_33
24. Polikar, R.: Ensemble based systems in decision making. IEEE Circuits Syst. Mag. **6**(3), 21–45 (2006). https://doi.org/10.1109/MCAS.2006.1688199
25. Portisch, J., Paulheim, H.: The rdf2vec family of knowledge graph embedding methods. Semantic Web (Preprint), 1–32
26. Prabhakar, V., Vu, C., Crawford, J., Waite, J., Liu, K.: An ensemble learning approach to perform link prediction on large scale biomedical knowledge graphs for drug repurposing and discovery. bioRxiv (2023)
27. Rahman, M., Saha, T., Hasan, M., Xu, K., Reddy, C.: Dylink2vec: effective feature representation for link prediction in dynamic networks (2018)
28. Ristoski, P., Paulheim, H.: RDF2Vec: RDF graph embeddings for data mining. In: Groth, P., et al. (eds.) ISWC 2016. LNCS, vol. 9981, pp. 498–514. Springer, Cham (2016). https://doi.org/10.1007/978-3-319-46523-4_30
29. Rivas-Barragan, D., Domingo-Fernández, D., Gadiya, Y., Healey, D.: Ensembles of knowledge graph embedding models improve predictions for drug discovery. Brief. Bioinforma. **23**(6), bbac481 (2022)
30. Rossi, A., Barbosa, D., Firmani, D., Matinata, A., Merialdo, P.: Knowledge graph embedding for link prediction: a comparative analysis. ACM Trans. Knowl. Discov. Data (TKDD) **15**(2), 1–49 (2021)
31. Ruffinelli, D., Broscheit, S., Gemulla, R.: You can teach an old dog new tricks! on training knowledge graph embeddings. In: International Conference on Learning Representations (2019)
32. Schlichtkrull, M., Kipf, T.N., Bloem, P., van den Berg, R., Titov, I., Welling, M.: Modeling relational data with graph convolutional networks. In: Gangemi, A., et al. (eds.) ESWC 2018. LNCS, vol. 10843, pp. 593–607. Springer, Cham (2018). https://doi.org/10.1007/978-3-319-93417-4_38
33. Shi, B., Weninger, T.: Open-world knowledge graph completion. CoRR abs/1711.03438 (2017). http://arxiv.org/abs/1711.03438
34. Sun, Z., Deng, Z.H., Nie, J.Y., Tang, J.: Rotate: knowledge graph embedding by relational rotation in complex space. CoRR abs/1902.10197 (2019). http://arxiv.org/abs/1902.10197
35. Toutanova, K., Chen, D.: Observed versus latent features for knowledge base and text inference (2015). https://doi.org/10.18653/v1/W15-4007
36. Trouillon, T., Welbl, J., Riedel, S., Gaussier, E., Bouchard, G.: Complex embeddings for simple link prediction. In: Proceedings of the 33rd International Conference on International Conference on Machine Learning - Volume 48, pp. 2071–2080 (2016)
37. Wan, G., Du, B., Pan, S., Wu, J.: Adaptive knowledge subgraph ensemble for robust and trustworthy knowledge graph completion. World Wide Web **23**(1), 471–490 (2020)
38. Wang, M., Qiu, L., Wang, X.: A survey on knowledge graph embeddings for link prediction. Symmetry **13**(3), 485 (2021)
39. Wen, L., Gao, L., Li, X.: A new snapshot ensemble convolutional neural network for fault diagnosis. IEEE Access **7**, 32037–32047 (2019)
40. Xu, C., Nayyeri, M., Vahdati, S., Lehmann, J.: Multiple run ensemble learning with low-dimensional knowledge graph embeddings, pp. 1–8 (2021)

41. Yang, B., tau Yih, W., He, X., Gao, J., Deng, L.: Embedding entities and relations for learning and inference in knowledge bases. In: Proceedings of the International Conference on Learning Representations (ICLR) (2015)
42. Zhang, P., Wang, X., Wang, F., Zeng, A., Xiao, J.: Measuring the robustness of link prediction algorithms under noisy environment. Sci. Rep. **6** (2016)
43. Zhou, Z.H.: Ensemble Methods: Foundations and Algorithms, 1st edn. Chapman and Hall/CRC (2012). https://doi.org/10.1201/b12207

Numerical Literals in Link Prediction: A Critical Examination of Models and Datasets

Moritz Blum[1(✉)], Basil Ell[1,2(✉)], Hannes Ill[1(✉)], and Philipp Cimiano[1(✉)]

[1] Bielefeld University, CITEC, Inspiration 1, 33619 Bielefeld, Germany
{mblum,bell,cimiano}@techfak.uni-bielefeld.de, hannes.ill@tum.de
[2] University of Oslo, Problemveien 11, 0313 Oslo, Norway
basile@ifi.uio.no

Abstract. Link Prediction (LP) is an essential task over Knowledge Graphs (KGs), traditionally focussed on using and predicting the relations between entities. Textual entity descriptions have already been shown to be valuable, but models that incorporate numerical literals have shown minor improvements on existing benchmark datasets. It is unclear whether a model is actually better in using numerical literals, or better capable of utilizing the graph structure. This raises doubts about the effectiveness of these methods and about the suitability of the existing benchmark datasets.

We propose a methodology to evaluate LP models that incorporate numerical literals. We propose i) a new synthetic dataset to better understand how well these models use numerical literals and ii) dataset ablations strategies to investigate potential difficulties with the existing datasets. We identify a prevalent trend: many models underutilize literal information and potentially rely on additional parameters for performance gains. Our investigation highlights the need for more extensive evaluations when releasing new models and datasets.

Keywords: Link Prediction · Numerical Literals · Evaluation

1 Introduction

Knowledge Graphs (KGs) store information in a graph-structured form as sets of relational triples (i.e., triples with a relation that connects two entities) and attributive triples (i.e., triples with a relation that annotates an entity with literal information). Prominent KGs are *Freebase* [5] and *Wikidata* [28]. A small example KG is shown in Fig. 1. KGs have emerged as a method to represent and store knowledge in various domains and applications, and will, as the authors believe, play an important role in generative AI as they complement LLMs for Retrieval Augmented Generation [16]. Nevertheless, KGs are inherently incomplete for various reasons [7]. In the past, efforts have been made to develop Link

G. Demartini et al. (Eds.): ISWC 2024, LNCS 15231, pp. 23–46, 2025.
https://doi.org/10.1007/978-3-031-77844-5_2

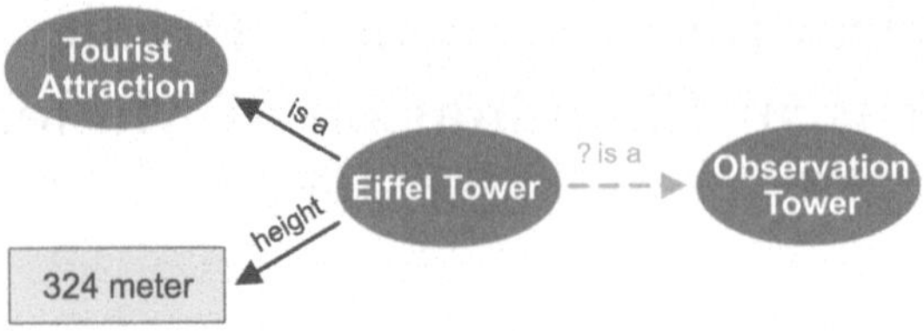

Fig. 1. Example KG about the *Eiffel Tower*. The KG contains the entities *Eiffel Tower*, *Tourist Attraction*, and *Observation Tower*; and the literal value *324 m*: the height of the *Eiffel Tower*.

Prediction (LP) methods to predict missing triples based on the triples already available.

Most LP approaches focus on relational triples, i. e., only use relational triples to predict missing relational triples. Neither do these models make use of attributive triples when predicting relational triples, nor do these models predict attributive triples – these models ignore information encoded in literals that might be valuable. In the example shown in Fig. 1, a model should predict the *is a* relation between *Eiffel Tower* and *Observation Tower*. Ideally, a model has learned from the data that a *Tourist Attraction* that has a certain height (e.g., above some threshold) is an *Observation Tower*. Here, a model needs to incorporate information expressed by the relational triple (*Eiffel Tower*, *is a*, *Tourist Attraction*) and information expressed by the attributive triple (*Eiffel Tower*, *height*, *324 m*) to predict the missing triple.

To incorporate literals, specialized models [30,34] or extensions of models were proposed [3,8,13,24,31]. Most models only operate on one and only some on multiple types of literals. Even though some models are technically able to predict literal values (e. g., [17,31,32]), we focus on the more prominent task of incorporating literals into the prediction of relational triples. Language Models (LMs) that operate on textual entity descriptions recently set state-of-the-art performance for LP [20]. The inclusion of numerical literals has shown only small improvements in models that do not use literals on common benchmark datasets [13,31]. However, we assume that numerical literals are highly valuable, especially for scientific KGs about physical experiments [4] or manufacturing processes [23], which store a large amount of information as numerical data. We focus on numerical literals as there is a lack of research on how well LP models that were designed to be able to use numerical literals can and do make use of numerical literals.

Typically, when new models or model extensions that can incorporate literals are published, then they are compared to state-of-the-art models that can incorporate numerical literals and to the base model they extend by standard metrics like Mean Reciprocal Rank (MRR) on benchmark datasets. As the improvements through incorporating literals is minor, we can not be sure whether the models are using the attributive triples, or whether the attributive triples in the existing datasets are valuable.

The benchmark datasets that contain literals are often created by enriching standard LP datasets, e. g., FB15k-237 or YAGO3-10, with literal information from their larger source KGs. These datasets might not be perfectly suited for the evaluation of LP models that incorporate literals, as, e. g., a certain amount of attributive triples in FB15k-237 connect entities to identifiers (IDs) for other databases that are not exploitable by a model.[1] Here, we only point to the ID relations, but other attributive triples might also not be valuable. Something similar might be the case for most of these datasets. To the best of our knowledge, no published evaluation has proven that the numerical literals in these datasets provide information relevant for LP. Therefore, we can not investigate whether the literals are used by the models, making them not suitable for benchmarking.

Overall, research on LP with numerical literals lacks a detailed evaluation of and comparison with the existing models and lacks insights on the used benchmark datasets. Therefore, we present the following contributions: i) We propose a method to extend a dataset with relational and attributive triples, where the prediction of relational triples of that kind can only then be carried out successfully if a model makes use of the attributive triples. ii) We propose ablation strategies for the existing evaluation datasets to investigate whether the numerical literals provide any additional knowledge, or whether the numerical literals only add information already contained in the relational triples. iii) We evaluate existing LP models which state to incorporate numerical literals on our semi-synthetic benchmark dataset and on datasets that we obtained by applying our ablation strategies to existing benchmark datasets, to gain insights into the models capabilities to incorporate literals and to gain insights into the suitability and difficulty of the existing datasets.

2 Preliminaries

With G we denote a directed labeled multi-graph with numerical literals. G is a set of triples $(s, p, o) \in \mathcal{U} \times \mathcal{U} \times (\mathcal{U} \cup \mathbb{R})$, where $\mathcal{U}$, and $\mathbb{R}$ are disjoint sets of URIs and numerical values.[2] The set of triples can be categorized into relational triples G_E and attributive triples G_A:

$$G_E = \{(s, p, o) \mid \exists (s, p, o) \in G \ \text{ s.t. } \ o \in \mathcal{U}\} \tag{1}$$

$$G_A = \{(s, p, v) \mid \exists (s, p, v) \in G \ \text{ s.t. } \ v \in \mathbb{R}\} \tag{2}$$

[1] Table 3 in Appendix A shows that for FB15k-237, 3/10 of the triples related to the most frequent attributive relations hold such IDs, overall 6.9% of all attributive triples in the dataset.

[2] Although typically KGs contain various types of literals, such as string literals or date literals, here we focus only on numerical literals and we do not distinguish between different types of numerical literals such as integer and float.

The set of entities $\mathcal{E} \subseteq \mathcal{U}$, the set of entity relations $\mathcal{R}_E \subseteq \mathcal{U}$, and the set of attributive relations $\mathcal{R}_A \subseteq \mathcal{U}$ are defined as follows:

$$\mathcal{E} = \{x \mid \exists(s,p,o) \in G \text{ s.t. } x{=}s \vee (x{=}o \wedge o \in \mathcal{U})\} \tag{3}$$

$$\mathcal{R}_E = \{p \mid \exists(s,p,o) \in G_E\} \tag{4}$$

$$\mathcal{R}_A = \{p \mid \exists(s,p,v) \in G_A\} \tag{5}$$

2.1 Link Prediction Models

LP models are trained to predict missing triples using triples already available.

Traditional Link Prediction Models. Traditional LP models can be considered as a function f that assigns a score $f(\vec{s},\vec{p},\vec{o}) \in \mathbb{R}$ to each triple (s,p,o) where $s,p,o \in \mathcal{U}$ and $\vec{e}$ denotes the embedding of the entity e. These models are trained to score true triples (i. e., triples in $\mathcal{G}_E$) higher than false triples (i. e., triples not in $\mathcal{G}_E$). Notably, the conventional LP models do not incorporate literals. Popular models are TransE [6], DistMult [33], ComplEx [27], and TuckER [2].

Link Prediction Approaches Incorporating Numerical Literals. Some LP models that are able to incorporate numerical literals are extensions of traditional LP models. These models use a feature vector $\vec{x}_e$ for each entity $e \in \mathcal{E}$. Each dimension of the feature vector $\vec{x}_e$ corresponds to a relation $r \in \mathcal{R}_A$. The value for a dimension is randomly selected from $\{v \mid \exists(e,r,v) \in G_A\}$ or is set to *"0"*, when the entity e has no value for the relation r in G_A.[3] These models can be categorized into two types.

Fusion via a Modification of the Scoring Function. Such models use the numerical features $\vec{x}_e$ as (additional) input features, i. e., they modify the scoring function explicitly. We investigate two established approaches: i) *LiteralE* [13], by Kristiadi et al., extends traditional LP models by adding a learnable parametric gate function $g(\vec{e},\vec{x}_e)$ to obtain a literal-enriched entity embedding that replaces the initial embedding in the scoring function. This makes LiteralE universally combinable with most existing embedding methods. In this paper, we evaluate LiteralE$_{DistMult}$ and LiteralE$_{ComplEx}$. ii) *KBLN* [8] is a reduced variant of KBLRN by García-Durán et al. KBLRN is a product of experts model that combines relational (vectors that describe in which graph patterns an entity occurs), latent (entity and relation embeddings), and numerical literal features. KBLN leaves out the expert for relational information.

[3] Replacing non-existing features with *"0"* can be considered critical as *"0"* might also be a valid literal value. Established methods like, e. g., LiteralE, make this abstraction. To ensure no negative effect, we computed the proportion of *"0"* literal values in the used datasets which is marginally small: FB15k-237 0.006%, YAGO3-10 0%, LitWD48K 1.67%.

Fusion via a Modification of the Objective Function. Such models learn to predict numerical features jointly with the LP objective.[4] Thereby, the entity embeddings incorporate information from both the graph structure and numerical literals. In this paper, we investigate two established approaches: i) *MTKGNN* [25], by Tay et al., introduces a neural network for numerical value regression in addition to a neural network for triple scoring. ii) *TransEA* [31], by Wu et al., is an extension of TransE [6] that learns a set of functions $g = \{g_p \mid p \in \mathcal{R}_A\}$ for numerical value regression.

A different line of research investigates methods applied to the datasets instead of the models.

Fusion via Literal Transformations. Models that transform attributive triples into relational triples allow traditional LP models to incorporate literal information without modifying the scoring function or objective function. In this paper, we investigate the following approach considered state-of-the-art in LP with numerical literals: *KGA* [29], by Wang et al., transforms numerical attributive triples into relational triples by discretizing numerical values into bins, and chaining these bins, modeling multiple levels of granularity.

For a broader overview of literal-aware LP models, we refer to [10].

2.2 Datasets

Widely used LP datasets that contain numerical literals are: FB15k-237 [26], YAGO3-10 [15], and LitWD48K [9]. An extensive overview about existing datasets and their types of literals can be found in [9].

We briefly describe the datasets used in this paper. These datasets are publicly accessible under *CC-BY* licenses. i) *FB15k-237* is a subset of FB15k which is a subset of Freebase. Toutanova et al. created FB15k-237 by removing inverse relations from FB15k that allowed even simple models to achieve high scores by simply inverting triples [26]. We use the version of FB15k-237 that was extended with numerical literal as provided by Kristiadi et al. [13].[5] ii) *YAGO3-10* is a subset of *YAGO3* [14] that only contains triples associated with entities that occur in at least ten relations leading mostly to triples related to people. YAGO3-10 does not contain literals, but they can be derived from *YAGO3*. Again, we use the numerical literals provided by Kristiadi et al. iii) *LiterallyWikidata* [9] comprises three datasets designed to evaluate LP models utilizing literal data, sourced from *Wikidata* and *Wikipedia*. These datasets vary in size and structure; we use the largest, LitWD48K.

Table 2 in Appendix A shows the general characteristics of the datasets used in this paper.

[4] The literal information is implicitly encoded into the embeddings and not explicitly provided during inference.

[5] See https://github.com/SmartDataAnalytics/LiteralE/tree/master/data.

2.3 Evaluation Metrics

The models are compared via the filtered mean rank (MR) metric, the mean reciprocal rank (MRR) metric, and Hits@k for $k \in \{1, 3, 10\}$, as proposed by [6]. For each triple in the test set, the subject and the object entities are corrupted by replacing them by any $e \in \mathcal{E}$. The score for each triple is used to rank the test triple among all of those triples by sorting in ascending order. Triples already contained in the graph are removed before ranking to not cause true triples to increase the rank of the test triples.

The MR is the mean rank, the MRR is the mean of the multiplicative inverse of the ranks, and Hits@k is the proportion of ranks $\leq k$.

3 Related Work

To the best of our knowledge, no existing work focuses on a methodology for evaluating LP models with numerical literals or other types of literals.

LP models are evaluated according to standard metrics such as *MR* and *MRR*, following the evaluation protocol proposed by Bordes [6], where models are treated as black-boxes. Safavi et al. raise concerns about the reliability of these ranking-based metrics [19]. They point out that while a ranking metric may suggest good performance because the correct triple is ranked high, it could still receive a significantly lower score than an incorrectly top-ranked triple.

In-depth evaluations, e. g., analyzing particular relations or distinguishing between head and tail predictions (as done by Bordes et al. [6]), are uncommon. Such an analysis can be useful to investigate how specific KG characteristics can be learned by a model, e. g., if symmetric relations can be properly represented by the model.

Explainability methods could provide insights into the behavior of LP models. Whereas rule-based approaches [12] and explainers over graph neural network-based approaches [35,36] can offer explanations for model predictions, particularly shallow models like TransE or DistMult are difficult to explain. Ismaeil et al. generate interpretable vectors for entity embeddings [11]. They employ embedded feature selection techniques to extract propositional features from the KG that are important for a given KG embedding model.

Another way to gain insights into the specific behavior and capabilities of LP models is to build datasets in a way such that obtaining good LP results requires the models to have specific capabilities, thus these datasets enable to test to what extent a model has these capabilities. E. g., recent work stated a lack of evaluation datasets covering certain KG properties like a given entity type system, pairs of mutually inverse relations, or mediator objects to represent n-ary relationships. Shirvani-Mahdavi et al. evaluate these properties on a newly proposed version of the Freebase KG [22].

The outlined open challenge of evaluating and explaining traditional LP models without considering literals results in a scarcity of research on the evaluation and explainability of LP with literals.

Although the original releases of existing LP datasets such as FB15k-237 and YAGO3-10 lack attributive triples, they have been extended with textual and numerical attributes sourced from their respective KGs. However, these enriched datasets contain numerous entities without numerical attributes,[6] and the provided numerical attributes are not proven to be helpful for LP. Consequently, Gesese et al. introduced a series of LP datasets called LiterallyWikidata, constructed from Wikidata and Wikipedia, specifically for LP involving numerical and textual literals [9]. The graph structure of LiterallyWikidata was designed for benchmarking LP models, avoiding issues such as that inverse relations could leak information or the existence of any shortcut features.

Despite the existence of datasets tailored for LP tasks involving (numerical) literals, these datasets are derived from real KGs, making it challenging to accurately assess the true advantages of integrating (numerical) literal information.

The most related work is García-Durán et al.'s input feature ablation study, which investigated which graph structure features improved their model's performance [8].

4 Methodology

We i) propose a method to enrich an existing dataset with synthetic information that enables us to find out if numerical literal-aware models are capable of using numerical literals to make predictions about relational triples. Furthermore, ii) we develop a set of ablation methods to gain further insights into the existing literal-aware datasets, whether in some datasets attributive triples might not be used for LP, or whether information is represented redundantly as attributive and relational triples.

When elucidating the derivable conclusions from the following ablation experiments, we denote a model trained on the dataset D as $m(D)$ and define $\sigma(m(D))$ as the result of evaluating $m(D)$ according to some measure of performance σ (such that a higher value indicates better performance).

4.1 Semi-synthetic LP Dataset with Literals

To ensure attributive triples to be relevant, we propose a dataset extension methodology with the intention to introduce a new learning goal given by a function h into the dataset.

For simplicity, we restrict h to be a function that predicts a relation r_{syn-r} from an existing entity e to one of two entities representing classes, added to the dataset, namely c_{high} and c_{low}, based on the attributive triple (e, r_{syn-a}, v). More precisely, our function h is defined as:

$$h(e) = \begin{cases} (e, r_{\text{syn-}r}, c_{\text{high}}) & \text{if } \exists (e, r_{\text{syn-}a}, v) \in G' \quad \text{with } v > 0.5 \\ (e, r_{\text{syn-}r}, c_{\text{low}}) & \text{if } \exists (e, r_{\text{syn-}a}, v) \in G' \quad \text{with } v \leq 0.5 \end{cases}$$

[6] See Table 2 in Appendix A.

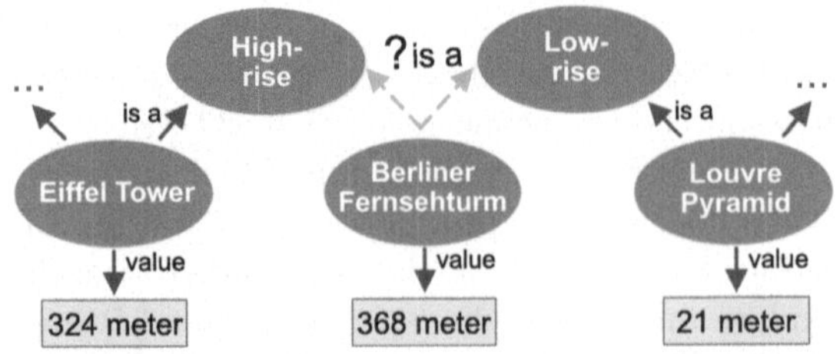

Fig. 2. Example of the synthetic dataset enrichment. The entitites *High-rise* and *Low-rise* represent c_{high} and c_{low} and *is a* is used as the r_{syn-a} relation. Ideally, an LP model predicts the tail entity *High-rise* for the given head *Berliner Fernsehturm* and the *is a* relation.

To remove any noise and biases from the original G_A, we replace it by G'_A defined as $\{(e, r_{syn-a}, v) \mid e \in \mathcal{E}'\}$ where $v \sim \text{Uniform}(0, 1)$ and $\mathcal{E}' \subseteq \mathcal{E}$. We then apply h to every $e \in \mathcal{E}'$ to obtain relational triples that are added to G_E to create G'_E. The new dataset is defined as $G' = G'_E \cup \mathcal{G}'_A$. An example is shown in Fig. 2.

Note that the function h could be more complex, taking into account multiple relational and attributive triples, make use of more than the one target relation r_{syn-r} and the two target entities c_{high} and c_{low}, and realize something more complex than comparing a value against a threshold value.

Let $\mathcal{E}_{high}$ and $\mathcal{E}_{low}$ be defined as follows: $\mathcal{E}_{high} := \{e \in \mathcal{E}' \mid \exists (e, r_{syn-a}, v) \in G'_A \wedge v > 0.5\}$ and $\mathcal{E}_{low} := \{e \in \mathcal{E}' \mid \exists (e, r_{syn-a}, v) \in G'_A \wedge v \leq 0.5\}$. (Note that $\mathcal{E} = \mathcal{E}_{high} \cup \mathcal{E}_{low}$ and $\mathcal{E}_{high} \cap \mathcal{E}_{low} = \varnothing$.)

Our goal is to measure the models' ability to score the synthetic relational triples according to h. As this is a binary classification task, we define the accuracy, denoted by *Acc*, as follows:

$$Acc := \frac{true_{high} + true_{low}}{|\mathcal{E}_{high}| + |\mathcal{E}_{low}|} \tag{6}$$

where $true_{high}$ is the number of $e \in \mathcal{E}_{heigh}$ for which $r(e, r_{syn-a}, c_{high}) \geq r(e, r_{syn-a}, c_{low})$. $true_{low}$ is defined analogously.

We consider the following situations where we can derive conclusions:

i) if $\sigma(m(G_E \cup G'_A)) < \sigma(m(G_E \cup G_A))$, i. e., the model that has no access to the original attributive triples performs worse, then the attributive triples are used for the prediction;
ii) if $\sigma(m(G_E \cup G'_A)) \geq \sigma(m(G_E \cup G_A))$, i. e., both models perform equally well, or the model that used the random features performs better, then the model is not capable of making use of literals.

4.2 Literal Features Ablation

If a model has proven to incorporate literals from a synthetic dataset into the prediction, this model should be evaluated on the established benchmark datasets.

To gain insights into the performance increase by using literals, one has to compare models that use literals against the same model without access to literals.

For some models, e.g., MTKGNN, we cannot remove the attributive triples from the dataset, as these models directly operate on the numerical features only, and do not learn a separate entity embedding. For other models, e. g., LiteralE, removing the attributive triples from the dataset reduces the number of model parameters.

Therefore, we propose an ablation method where each entity is related with each attributive relation to a certain value. Given $G = G_E \cup G_A$, we create $G' = G_E \cup G'_A$ where G'_A is created as follows: for each entity $e \in \mathcal{E}$ and each relation $p \in \mathcal{R}_A$, we add the triple (e, p, v) to G'_A where v is a certain literal value we assign.

As some models only operate on numerical features, assigning the same value to all attributive triples would lead to identical features for all entities. Consequently, such models would lose the ability to distinguish the entities. Therefore, we propose to sample v randomly from Uniform$(0, 1)$.

We consider the following situations where we can derive conclusions about a model and a dataset, under the assumption that the model can make use of literals according to the experiments of the model on the semi-synthetic dataset:

i) if $\sigma(m(G_E \cup G'_A)) < \sigma(m(G_E \cup G_A))$, i. e., the model that has no access to the original attributive triples performs worse, then the attributive triples are relevant for the prediction task;
ii) if $\sigma(m(G_E \cup G'_A)) \geq \sigma(m(G_E \cup G_A))$, i. e., both models perform equally well, or the model that used the random features performs better, then, either the information represented via attributive triples is redundantly represented via relational triples, the literal information is difficult to use by the models, or no information relevant for LP is represented via attributive triples.

4.3 Relational Features Ablation

The previous experiments may leave open whether attributive triples are not relevant for the prediction task, challenging to leverage, or whether information is represented redundantly as relational and attributive triples. To gain insights into the redundancy of relational and attributive triples for a given dataset, we propose an ablation method that targets relational triples, thus modifies G_E. We reduce G_E to $G_{E_{-\alpha}}$ s. t.

1) $|G_{E_{-\alpha}}| = (1 - \alpha)|G_E|$ where $\alpha \in [0, 1]$ is a user-defined real value.
2) $\forall e \in \mathcal{E} : (\exists p, o : (e, p, o) \in G_{E_{-\alpha}}) \vee (\exists s, p : (s, p, o) \in G_{E_{-\alpha}})$
3) $\forall p \in \mathcal{R}_{\mathcal{E}} : (\exists s, o : (s, p, o) \in G_{E_{-\alpha}})$

This means, we remove relational triples from G until $|G_{E_{-\alpha}}| = (1 - \alpha)|G_E|$. We ensure that there remains at least one triple per entity $e \in \mathcal{E}$ and relation $p \in \mathcal{R}_{\mathcal{E}}$ such that embeddings are learned. Note that for some G_E and $\alpha \in \mathbb{R}^+$ it can be the case that there is no $G_{E_{-\alpha}}$ that satisfies both constraints. Thus, there is a limit to how much G_E can be reduced.

We consider the following situations where we can derive conclusions:

i) if with the reduced set of relational triples the random feature ablation has an effect on model performance (i.e., $\sigma(m(G_{E_{-\alpha}} \cup G_A)) \gg \sigma(m(G_{E_{-\alpha}} \cup G'_A))$), then that means that information is represented redundantly as attributive and relational triples and that attributive triples are relevant for the prediction task;
ii) if with the reduced set of relational triples the random feature ablation has still no effect on the model performance (i.e., $\sigma(m(G_{E_{-\alpha}} \cup G_A)) \approx \sigma(m(G_{E_{-\alpha}} \cup G'_A))$), then attributive triples are either difficult to incorporate or not relevant for the prediction task.

5 Experimental Setup

We apply our methodology to all numerical literal-aware models mentioned in [10] and the state-of-the-art model KGA [29].

Implementation. We run our experiments with LiteralE$_{DistMult}$, Literal E$_{ComplEx}$, KBLN, and MTKGNN with the code of Kristiadi et al. [13].[7]

We implemented TransEA in PyTorch Geometric[8] due to the absence of a public implementation.

We decided to use the model variants that achieve the overall best performance and the model that shows the largest performance gains through incorporating literals, which are KGA$_{TuckER}$ and KGA$_{DistMult}$ according to [29].[9]

All hyperparameters are reported in Appendix B. We ran all experiments three times and computed mean and standard deviation for each metric.

Semi-Synthetic FB15k-237. We apply our dataset enrichment method to the FB15k-237 dataset. We decided that $\mathcal{E}$ is the set of entities of type person. FB15k-237 contains 4,505 entities of type person, i. e. ≈30% of the entities.[10]

For evaluation, we create a training, validation, and test split as follows: we add 70% of the new synthetic relational triples to the original train set, 15% to the original validation set, and 15% to the original test set. The new synthetic literal values replace the original literal values. The models are trained for LP as usual.

---

7 See https://github.com/SmartDataAnalytics/LiteralE.

8 See https://pytorch-geometric.readthedocs.io. We extended the existing TransE implementation to TransEA.

9 The KGA transformations approximately create as many additional relational triples as attributive triples. As our proposed attributive features ablation creates a large number of literals with random values, the number of relational triples increases significantly. Consequently, we had to limit the number of attributive relations. Instead of relating each entity with each attributive relation, we only replace the numerical values of attributive triples in the original dataset by a random value. Thereby, the model is provided with some literal information, i. e., the existence of the attributive relation.

10 By assigning numerical literals only to certain entities, we enable further analysis, such as determining if the model learns that only certain entities have a specific literal.

Computing Resources. Our evaluation required numerous experiments, due to the combinations of investigated models and datasets. We used 10 A100 GPUs for two weeks. The evaluated models have similar sizes, e. g., $\text{Literale}_{DistMult}$ trained on FB15k-237 has ≈3M parameters.

6 Results

6.1 Synthetic LP Dataset with Literals

We created a semi-synthetic FB15-237 dataset and used it to investigate the models' ability to utilize the necessary numerical literal information for predicting relational triples. The results are shown in Table 1. The accuracy for all models is shown in the column Acc_{org}. A score slightly above 0.5 suggests that the models' performance is only marginally better than random guess, and a score close to 1 suggests that the model is capable of making correct predictions by using the numerical literals.

As a baseline, we train the models with random features following the introduced literal features ablation method, which we applied after the creation of the semi-synthetic dataset. Acc_{rand} is the score of the models when the literals provide no information, forcing the models to guess randomly.

The variance across runs is small; hence, these values indicate a measure of reliable performance.

The KGA models are capable of using the provided numerical literals for their prediction as they achieve Acc_{org}'s of 0.999, both. The Acc_{rand} scores range from 0.482 to 0.510, proving the models' random guessing. Note that due to the randomness of the features, the models cannot make a justified prediction. The Acc_{org} scores achieved by the other models are much lower and in the same range as the Acc_{rand} scores', showing that these models do not or do only to a small extent use the information provided via literals.

6.2 Literal Features Ablation

The results for our experiments for the random literal features ablation method are visualized for three models in Fig. 3 as box plots, showing the mean and variance of the MRR scores across three runs. For each combination of model and dataset, the plot shows two boxes. The first box shows the score achieved by the model trained with the original literal features and the second box shows the score achieved by the model trained on the random features.[11]

In general, as shown in Fig. 3, replacing original features by random features has no significant negative impact on most of the models as the box for the original features and the box for the random features overlaps in many cases and the differences are very small. The details reported in Appendix C show that in 9 of the 21 cases we see the models with random literals outperform

[11] The box-plots for all experiments and the scores of all computed metrics for these experiments are in Appendix C.

the models that use real literals regarding the MRR score, and only in 10 of the 15 cases models showed a benefit regarding the MRR score in using the real attributive triples provided by the datasets. The Hits@k scores follow this trend. When looking at the MR scores, this trend exists, too. The KGA models show the best usage of literals as the predictions with the original features are better, but only marginally, than with the random features for all combinations of KGA models and datasets investigated, except for $KGA_{DistMult}$ on the YAGO3-10 dataset.

Table 1. Scores achieved on the synthetic dataset. Acc_{org} denotes the Acc score achieved on the synthetic dataset when we provide the meaningful synthetic literal values, whereas Acc_{rand} denotes the Acc score on the synthetic dataset if we apply the random feature ablation after the dataset creation.

Model	$\mathbf{Acc}_{org}$	$\mathbf{Acc}_{rand}$
$LiteralE_{DistMult}$	0.512±0.003	0.482±0.001
$LiteralE_{ComplEx}$	0.493±0.005	0.498±0.020
KBLN	0.482±0.009	0.493±0.005
MTKGNN	0.472±0.006	0.495±0.009
TransEA	0.489±0.022	0.496±0.020
KGA_{TuckER}	0.999±0.000	0.510±0.007
$KGA_{DistMult}$	0.999±0.000	0.487±0.011

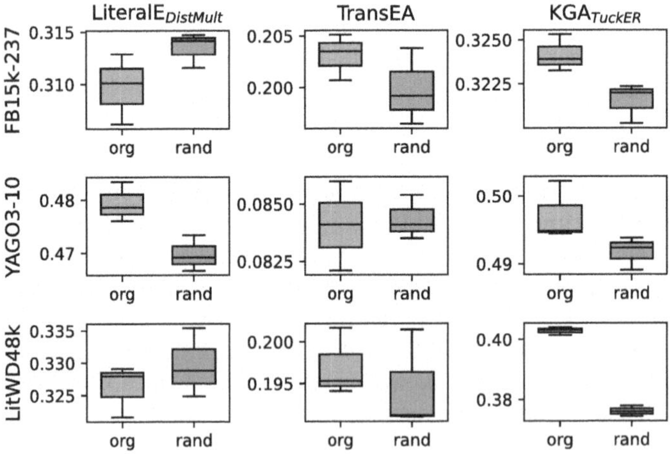

Fig. 3. MRR scores over three runs for models and datasets that either include the original literal features or that include random literal features.

6.3 Relational Features Ablation

The ablation effect of relational triples from FB15k-237 on KGA_{TuckER} is shown in Fig. 4.[12] We plot the mean and standard deviation of the MRR score while reducing the amount of relational triples from 100% (representing the original dataset) to 10% (equivalent to removing 90% of the relational triples) in steps of 10%. As expected, the MRR score decreases significantly when reducing the available relational triples, showing that important information is eliminated.

We compared these models against the ones we applied the random literal feature ablation strategy on. The curves of the models operating on random features are very close to the curves of the models operating on the original features, not showing any advantages of the original features when reducing the relational triples.

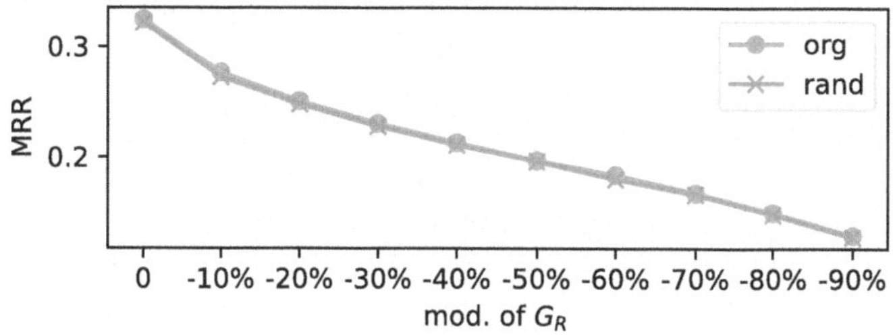

Fig. 4. KGA_{TuckER}'s MRR scores (mean and variance over three runs) after removing x% relational triples from FB15k-237. The model is provided either with the original or with random numerical features. The variance is marginally small and not visually recognizable in the figure.

7 Discussion

The synthetic dataset creates a scenario where numerical literals are necessary for predictions. KGA converts these continuous literals into discrete entities, allowing models to bypass the need to incorporate the concrete literal values. Thereby, KGA translates the task created by our semi-synthetic dataset into a more simple graph-structure learning task,[13] but might struggle with more complex synthetic datasets. The other models behaved similar to random guessing, as the scores are close to 0.5. We assume that these model's objective function does not enforce the models to integrate numerical information valuable for LP into the entity embeddings. Even though TransEA forces the embeddings to contain information to reconstruct the numerical literals, this information is not necessarily valuable for LP.

[12] Plots for further models are contained in Appendix C.

[13] Entities with similar literals obtain similar embeddings as entities with similar literals are connected to the same bins.

Even though we proposed our synthetic dataset to overcome a certain issue with the existing real-world benchmark datasets, we, nevertheless, believe that real-world datasets are relevant. Therefore, we also evaluated all models on these datasets and compared the scores to the scores of their random feature variant to confirm the previous results.

One would expect significant performance drops after applying the random feature ablation methods. We do not observe any significant performance drop, and in some cases even an improvement. Interestingly, the KGA models do only show small benefits of using numerical literals even though they showed good performances on our synthetic dataset. This brings us to the conclusion that either the literals are not relevant for the prediction task, or the information contained in attributive triples is difficult to use, or the information represented via the attributive triples is redundantly represented via relational triples.

We are not sure about the reason for the increase in performance after introducing random literals. Possibly, in some cases unintentionally good features are created which can be used by the models. A similar increase in performance through random node initialization has been observed by Abboud et al. for GNNs, which gain additional expressivity in the neighborhood encoding from random node initialization [1]. However, all models we investigated are shallow models that do not perform any neighborhood encoding.

We have to note that our scores of the LiteralE models slightly differ from the ones reported by Kristiadi et al. [13], even though we used their implementation and hyperparameters. Interestingly, the base ComplEx model achieves higher MRR and Hits@k scores than the LiteralE$_{ComplEx}$ model on FB15k-237 in our experiments. However, the similarity of the results from three runs confirm our results' reliability.

Lastly, we investigated if relational and attributive triples redundantly represent information, which leads to the LP performance to remain similar even though numerical literals are incorporated. If the attributive triples were redundant, one would expect the model with the real literal features to obtain less worse results when ablating the relational triples than the one with the random features, i. e., at some point the literal features should become important. As Fig. 4 does not show any benefit of incorporating numerical literals when reducing the amount of available relational triples, we conclude that either the attributive triples are not relevant for the prediction task, or the information contained in attributive triples is difficult to use by the models.

8 Conclusion and Future Work

In this work, we investigated the capability of LP models that incorporate numerical literal information and the suitability of the corresponding benchmark datasets. We propose a methodology to create semi-synthetic datasets and a dataset ablation methodology.

With a semi-synthetic dataset we showed that many models underutilize literal information, even in a setting where the numerical data is crucial for the prediction. We showed that under the established evaluation schema, the performance gains of many models can be attributed to the additional model parameters rather than the models's capabilities to exploit literals.

Future work could investigate real-world KGs regarding their suitability for evaluating numerical LP more deeply. Additionally, developing more challenging synthetic dataset extensions requiring the combination of literal information and graph structure for predicting missing links could offer valuable insights into the potentially more advanced LP models proposed in the future.

9 Limitations

We see three limitations of our work:

i) Our synthetic dataset implements one simple learning goal that requires the model to learn a threshold value to make correct predictions. This learning goal is simple and does not provide any information about the models' capabilities in understanding more complex scenarios. More complex learning goals could go beyond numerical literals and could also require to combine information from numerical literals and relational triples. However, we did not investigate complex learning goals, as we believe that if models fail in simple scenarios, they will also fail in more complex ones.
ii) We did not find a model that consistently shows benefits from the numerical literals provided by the existing benchmark datasets, not even in the relational triples ablation scenario. Therefore, we can not make any conclusions about the value of the literals provided for these datasets. The numerical literals are either not relevant for the prediction task, or the information contained is difficult to use by the existing models.
iii) We exclude the evaluation of Graph Neural Network models, such as R-GCN [21], which have the ability to process numerical literals as node features. This decision is based on the absence of published research specifically advocating for these models' application in LP with numerical literal data.

Supplemental Material Statement

You can find all our source code, datasets, training result logs, and visualization Jupyter Notebooks on GitHub.[14]

Acknowledgements. This work was supported by: the Ministry of Culture and Science of the State of North Rhine-Westphalia (Germany) through SAIL, Grant No. NW21-059A; the Deutsche Forschungsgemeinschaft (DFG) through the priority program RATIO (SPP-1999), Grant No. 376059226; the Research Council of Norway through its Centres of Excellence scheme, Integreat – Norwegian Centre for knowledge-driven machine learning, project number 332645.

[14] See https://github.com/moritzblum/LiteralEvaluation.

Ethical Statement. We address concerns related to the experimental design and the significance of results of existing methods. Our objective is not to criticize the creators of the models and datasets, but rather to assist the community by providing practical guidance for future research.

In this work, efforts are made to interpret and understand how well-established models respond to changes in literal data. However, it is important to note that explainability methods still encounter challenges in interpreting such models.

All datasets utilized in this research adhere to ethical standards and are obtained from publicly available sources.

A Dataset Statistics

Table 2 shows the statistics of the evaluated LP datasets FB15k-237, YAGO3-10k, LitWD48K, and of our Synthetic dataset.

Table 2. Dataset statistics.

Dataset	**FB15k-237**	**YAGO3-10**	**LitWD48K**	**Synthetic**
# entities ($\|\mathcal{E}\|$)	14,541	123,182	47,998	14,541
# relations ($\|\mathcal{R}_E\|$)	237	37	257	237
# attributes ($\|\mathcal{R}_A\|$)	121	5	246	1
# relational triples ($\|\mathcal{G}_E\|$)	310,116	1,089,040	336,745	310,116
# attributive triples ($\|\mathcal{G}_A\|$)	70,257	111,406	148,707	14,541
# entities w/o num.	4600	31,030	8,198	0
# train	272,115	1,079,040	303,117	272,115
# test	17,535	5,000	16,838	17,535
# valid	20,466	5,000	16,838	20,466

In FB15k-237, 3/10 of the triples related to the most frequent attributive relations hold IDs for other databases, overall devoting to 6.9% of the attributive triples in the dataset. Table 3 shows the 10 most frequent attributive relations in FB15k-237.

Table 3. Ten most frequent attributive relations in FB15k-237. The original relation URIs are `http://rdf.freebase.com/ns/ + relation name`.

Relation	# triples
topic_server.population_number	52764
people.person.height_meters	2871
location.location.area	2166
film.film.netflix_id	1883
organization.organization.date_founded	844
user.robert.default_domain.rated_film.ew_rating	739
location.location.gnis_feature_id	645
sports.sports_team.founded	643
location.hud_county_place.countyplace_id	568
tv.tv_program.episode_running_time	493

B Hyperparameters

We either used the hyperparameters reported as best in the original publications, or performed a hyperparameter optimization in case we re-implemented a model.

We refrained from performing a new hyperparameter optimization for the models trained on our ablated datasets, as it is common practice to use the same hyperparameters across multiple datasets [13,29]. Further, Ruffinelli et al. show that the relative performance difference between various LP model architectures often shrunk through hyperparameter optimization and re-implementation when compared to prior results [18].

We use the following hyperparameters:

LiteralE$_{DistMult}$*, LiteralE*$_{ComplEx}$*, KBLN, and MTKGNN* We use the best hyperparameters reported in the original publication to ensure a fair comparison: embedding dim. 200, epochs 100, learning rate 0.001, batch size 128, embedding dropout prob. 0.2, and label smoothing 0.1. The same hyperparameters are used across all models and datasets.

TransEA. We carried out a grid-search hyperparameter optimization: embedding dim. {50, **100**}, learning rate {0.01, **0.001**}, and α {**0.1**, 0.2, ..., 0.9}.[15] The best hyperparameters are highlighted. Further, we set: epochs 500, and batch size 128.

KGA. We used the Quantile Hierarchy augmentation method, which showed the best results across all models on FB15K-237 according to [29]. For KGA$_{TuckER}$ we use the hyperparameters: embedding dim. 200, epochs 500, learning rate 0.003, batch size 128, embedding dropout prob. 0.2, and hidden dropout 0.3. For KGA$_{DistMult}$ we use additional label smoothing 0.1.

[15] We did not apply dropout or label smoothing, thereby following [31].

All models are trained for LP as usual. We applied early stopping by monitoring the MRR score on the validation set every three epochs.

C Detailed Results

We report the MR, MRR, and Hits@10 scores (their mean and variance) obtained over three runs for models and datasets either including original features or including random features in Table 4.

Furthermore, the effect of the relational triples ablation from FB15k-237 on MTKGNN and LiteralE$_{DistMult}$ is shown in Fig. 5.

Table 4. Comparison of scores of models trained on the datasets provided with the original literal feature versus those trained on datasets provided with random features.

Model	Original features			Random features		
	MR	MRR	Hits@1	MR	MRR	Hits@1
			FB15k-237			
LiteralE$_{DistMult}$	285±001	.310±.003	.224±.003	286±008	.313±.001	.229±.002
LiteralE$_{ComplEx}$	429±002	.272±.000	.193±.001	414±022	.278±.001	.198±.001
KBLN	486±004	.295±.000	.213±.001	618±007	.285±.002	.207±.003
MTKGNN	563±006	.282±.001	.202±.001	575±004	.282±.001	.202±.001
TransEA	303±002	.203±.002	.132±.002	305±001	.200±.003	.128±.002
KGA$_{TuckER}$	200±004	.324±.001	.234±.000	200±001	.322±.001	.231±.001
KGA$_{DistMult}$	372±007	.307±.001	.221±.002	389±004	.304±.001	.220±.002
			YAGO3-10			
LiteralE$_{DistMult}$	1860±018	.479±.003	.400±.004	1925±058	.470±.003	.388±.004
LiteralE$_{ComplEx}$	2086±034	.475±.002	.400±.002	2303±116	.480±.004	.408±.004
KBLN	2850±129	.485±.023	.405±.024	4243±057	.483±.001	.401±.001
MTKGNN	3287±048	.449±.017	.362±.016	3235±094	.467±.001	.379±.002
TransEA	2226±041	.084±.002	.048±.001	2325±055	.084±.001	.049±.001
KGA$_{TuckER}$	1046±003	.497±.004	.412±.005	1094±020	.492±.002	.407±.002
KGA$_{DistMult}$	1554±005	.495±.003	.407±.004	1696±071	.496±.002	.410±.004
			LitWD48k			
LiteralE$_{DistMult}$	886±060	.326±.003	.250±.003	875±041	.330±.004	.250±.001
LiteralE$_{ComplEx}$	1489±109	.268±.005	.200±.007	1358±067	.305±.005	.238±.003
KBLN	1741±042	.329±.004	.246±.004	1836±044	.334±.002	.262±.002
MTKGNN	3085±208	.289±.002	.227±.003	2743±137	.297±.001	.235±.001
TransEA	947±019	.197±.003	.131±.003	952±032	.195±.005	.129±.004
KGA$_{TuckER}$	353±010	.403±.001	.315±.001	395±007	.376±.001	.293±.001
KGA$_{DistMult}$	504±005	.335±.001	.250±.001	1422±094	.227±.004	.169±.003

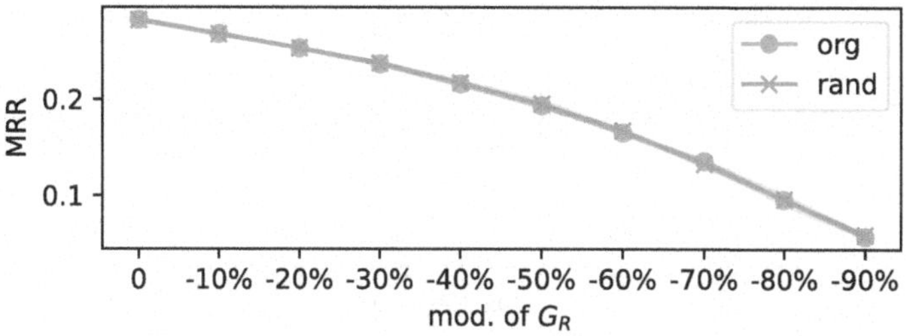

(a) MTKGNN

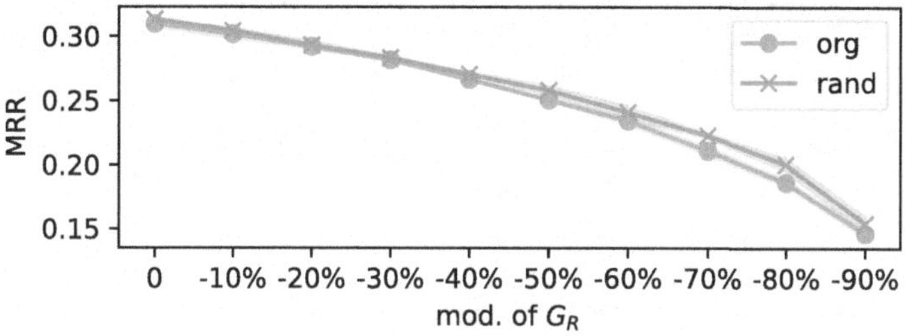

(b) LiteralE$_{DistMult}$

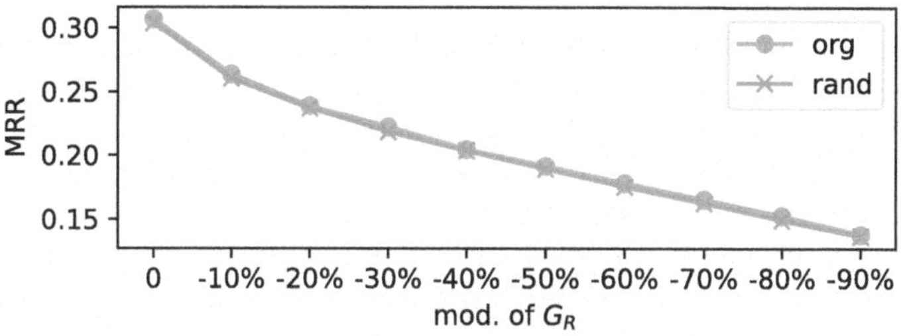

(c) KGA$_{DistMult}$

Fig. 5. MRR score after removing some percentage of relational triples from FB15k-237. The models are provided either with the original numerical features or with random features. Mean score and variance are shown across three runs.

D Further Ablation Experiments: Attributive Value Ablation

In order to provide further insights into the literal features of existing datasets, we apply an additional literal ablation method that allows to investigate whether the concrete literal value is important, or whether only the existence of such an attribute is important, or whether only the existence of an attribute can be taken into account by a model.

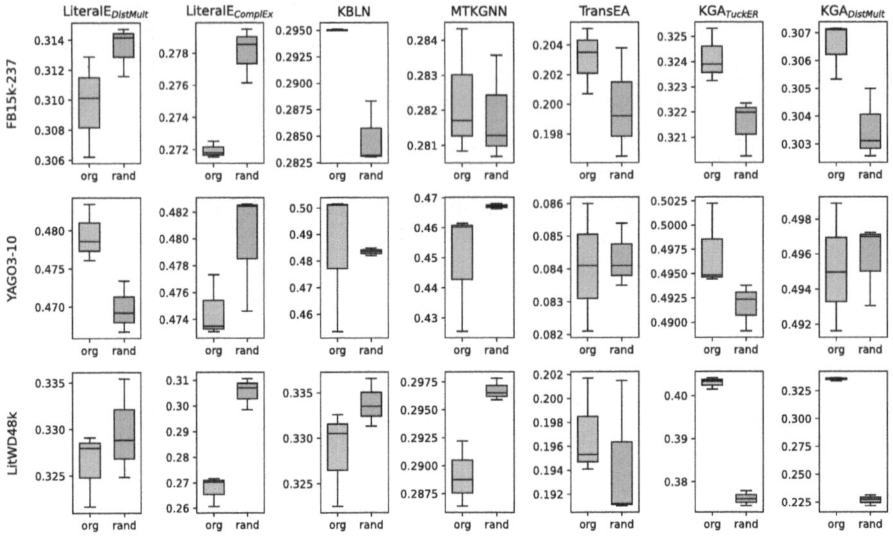

Fig. 6. MRR scores obtained over three runs for models and datasets either including original features or including random features. The variance is marginally small and not visually recognizable in the figure.

Therefore, we propose an ablation method that removes the concrete literal values but adds literal values that indicate whether the attribute exists. Given $G = G_E \cup G_A$, we create $G' = G_E \cup G'_A$ where G'_A is created as follows: if there exists a value v such that $(e, p, v) \in G_A$, then we add the triple $(e, p, 1)$ to G'_A.

We evaluate the two models, KGA$_{TuckER}$ and KGA$_{DistMult}$, which exhibit the highest benefits when provided with literals. Table 5 displays the scores of these models on three datasets. The MRR scores show no consistent trend, but the MR scores are consistently worse for the models that are provided only with the existence of attributes of entities compared to those provided with original or random features. We hypothesize that the lower performance resulting from abstracting the concrete literal values is due to the transformations that transform attributive triples into relational triples, which create a disadvantageous graph structure where most entities are connected to the two entities representing the literal values "0" and "1".

Table 5. Comparison of models trained and evaluated on datasets, each subjected to all proposed literal ablations. The model that uses the literals provided with the dataset is named *original*. The models that use only the relation type and not the concrete literal value are are named *relation type*.

	features	MR	MRR	Hits@1	Hits@3	Hits@10
FB15k-237				$\mathbf{KGA}_{TuckER}$		
	original	200±.004	.324±.001	.234±.000	.355±.002	.508±.001
	random	200±.001	.322±.001	.231±.001	.354±.000	.505±.001
	relation type	217±.002	.319±.001	.229±.001	.351±.001	.502±.001
				$\mathbf{KGA}_{DistMult}$		
	original	372±.007	.307±.001	.221±.002	.336±.001	.478±.001
	random	389±.004	.304±.001	.220±.002	.333±.001	.472±.001
	relation type	401±.011	.303±.002	.218±.002	.333±.001	.474±.005
YAGO3-10				$\mathbf{KGA}_{TuckER}$		
	original	1046±.003	.497±.004	.412±.005	.546±.005	.651±.001
	random	1094±.020	.492±.002	.407±.002	.539±.002	.646±.002
	relation type	1320±.064	.521±.005	.439±.005	.570±.003	.671±.005
				$\mathbf{KGA}_{DistMult}$		
	original	1554±.005	.495±.003	.407±.004	.543±.002	.661±.001
	random	1696±.071	.496±.002	.410±.004	.543±.002	.655±.002
	relation type	1755±.061	.509±.002	.423±.002	.559±.004	.668±.002
LitWD48k				$\mathbf{KGA}_{TuckER}$		
	original	353±.010	.403±.001	.315±.001	.435±.002	.584±.000
	random	395±.007	.376±.001	.293±.001	.403±.002	.545±.002
	relation type	672±.013	.386±.001	.303±.001	.418±.000	.556±.001
				$\mathbf{KGA}_{DistMult}$		
	original	504±.005	.335±.001	.250±.001	.360±.002	.513±.003
	random	1422±.094	.227±.004	.169±.003	.243±.005	.339±.006
	relation type	786±.015	.359±.001	.268±.001	.388±.002	.557±.003

References

1. Abboud, R., Ceylan, İ.İ., Grohe, M., Lukasiewicz, T.: The surprising power of graph neural networks with random node initialization. In: Proceedings of the 13th International Joint Conference on Artificial Intelligence (2021)
2. Balazevic, I., Allen, C., Hospedales, T.: TuckER: tensor factorization for knowledge graph completion. In: Inui, K., Jiang, J., Ng, V., Wan, X. (eds.) Proceedings of the 2019 Conference on Empirical Methods in Natural Language Processing and the 9th International Joint Conference on Natural Language Processing (EMNLP-IJCNLP), pp. 5185–5194. Association for Computational Linguistics, Hong Kong, China (2019)
3. Blum, M., Ell, B., Cimiano, P.: Exploring the impact of literal transformations within Knowledge Graphs for Link Prediction. In: Proceedings of the 11th International Joint Conference on Knowledge Graphs, pp. 48–54. Association for Computing Machinery (2023)

4. Blum, M., Ell, B., Cimiano, P.: Insights from an OTTR-centric ontology engineering methodology. In: Proceedings of the 14th Workshop on Ontology Design and Patterns (2023)
5. Bollacker, K., Evans, C., Paritosh, P., Sturge, T., Taylor, J.: Freebase: a collaboratively created graph database for structuring human knowledge. In: Proceedings of the ACM SIGMOD International Conference on Management of Data, pp. 1247–1250 (2008)
6. Bordes, A., Usunier, N., Garcia-Duran, A., Weston, J., Yakhnenko, O.: Translating embeddings for modeling multi-relational data. In: Advances in Neural Information Processing Systems, vol. 26 (2013)
7. Dong, X., et al.: Knowledge vault: a web-scale approach to probabilistic knowledge fusion. In: Proceedings of the 20th ACM SIGKDD International Conference on Knowledge Discovery and Data Mining, pp. 601–610. Association for Computing Machinery (2014)
8. García-Durán, A., Niepert, M.: KBlrn: end-to-End Learning of Knowledge Base Representations with Latent, Relational, and Numerical Features. In: Proceedings of the Thirty-Fourth Conference on Uncertainty in Artificial Intelligence, pp. 372–381. AUAI Press (2018)
9. Gesese, G.A., Alam, M., Sack, H.: LiterallyWikidata - a benchmark for knowledge graph completion using literals. In: Hotho, A., et al. (eds.) ISWC 2021. LNCS, vol. 12922, pp. 511–527. Springer, Cham (2021). https://doi.org/10.1007/978-3-030-88361-4_30
10. Gesese, G.A., Biswas, R., Alam, M., Sack, H.: A survey on knowledge graph embeddings with literals: which model links better literal-ly? Semantic Web **12**, 617–647 (2021)
11. Ismaeil, Y., Stepanova, D., Tran, T.K., Blockeel, H.: FeaBI: a Feature Selection-Based Framework for Interpreting KG Embeddings. In: Payne, T.R., et al. (eds.) ISWC 2023. LNCS, vol. 14265, pp. 599–617. Springer, Cham (2023). https://doi.org/10.1007/978-3-031-47240-4_32
12. Khajeh Nassiri, A., Pernelle, N., Saïs, F.: REGNUM: generating logical rules with numerical predicates in knowledge graphs. In: Pesquita, C., et al. (eds.) ESWC 2023. LNCS, vol. 13870, pp. 139–155. Springer, Cham (2023). https://doi.org/10.1007/978-3-031-33455-9_9
13. Kristiadi, A., Khan, M.A., Lukovnikov, D., Lehmann, J., Fischer, A.: Incorporating literals into knowledge graph embeddings. In: Ghidini, C., et al. (eds.) ISWC 2019. LNCS, vol. 11778, pp. 347–363. Springer, Cham (2019). https://doi.org/10.1007/978-3-030-30793-6_20
14. Mahdisoltani, F., Biega, J., Suchanek, F.: YAGO3: a knowledge base from multilingual Wikipedias. In: 7th Biennial Conference on Innovative Data Systems Research. CIDR Conference (2014)
15. Nickel, M., Tresp, V., Kriegel, H.P.: Factorizing YAGO: scalable machine learning for linked data. In: Proceedings of the 21st International Conference on World Wide Web, pp. 271–280 (2012)
16. Pan, J.Z., Razniewski, S., Kalo, J.C., et al.: Large Language Models and Knowledge Graphs: opportunities and Challenges. Trans. Graph Data Knowl. **1**, 2:1-2:38 (2023)
17. Pezeshkpour, P., Chen, L., Singh, S.: Embedding multimodal relational data for knowledge base completion. In: Proceedings of the Conference on Empirical Methods in Natural Language Processing, pp. 3208–3218. Association for Computational Linguistics (2018)

18. Ruffinelli, D., Broscheit, S., Gemulla, R.: You can teach an old dog new tricks! on training knowledge graph embeddings. In: International Conference on Learning Representations (2020)
19. Safavi, T., Koutra, D., Meij, E.: Evaluating the calibration of knowledge graph embeddings for trustworthy link prediction. In: Proceedings of the 2020 Conference on Empirical Methods in Natural Language Processing, pp. 8308–8321. Association for Computational Linguistics (2020)
20. Saxena, A., Kochsiek, A., Gemulla, R.: Sequence-to-sequence knowledge graph completion and question answering. In: Proceedings of the 60th Annual Meeting of the Association for Computational Linguistics (2022)
21. Schlichtkrull, M., Kipf, T.N., Bloem, P., van den Berg, R., Titov, I., Welling, M.: Modeling relational data with graph convolutional networks. In: Gangemi, A., et al. (eds.) ESWC 2018. LNCS, vol. 10843, pp. 593–607. Springer, Cham (2018). https://doi.org/10.1007/978-3-319-93417-4_38
22. Shirvani-Mahdavi, N., Akrami, F., Saeef, M.S., Shi, X., Li, C.: Comprehensive analysis of freebase and dataset creation for robust evaluation of knowledge graph link prediction models. In: Payne, T.R., et al. (eds.) ISWC 2023. LNCS, vol. 14266, pp. 113–133. Springer, Cham (2023). https://doi.org/10.1007/978-3-031-47243-5_7
23. Strötgen, J., et al.: Towards the Bosch materials science knowledge base. In: Proceedings of the ISWC Satellite Tracks co-located with 18th International Semantic Web Conference, pp. 323–324. Springer (2019)
24. Tay, Y., Tuan, L.A., Phan, M.C., Hui, S.C.: Multi-task neural network for non-discrete attribute prediction in knowledge graphs. In: Proceedings of the 2017 ACM on Conference on Information and Knowledge Management, pp. 1029–1038. Association for Computing Machinery (2017)
25. Tay, Y., Tuan, L.A., Phan, M.C., Hui, S.C.: Multi-task neural network for non-discrete attribute prediction in knowledge graphs. In: Proceedings of the 2017 ACM on Conference on Information and Knowledge Management, pp. 1029-1038. Association for Computing Machinery (2017)
26. Toutanova, K., Chen, D.: Observed versus latent features for knowledge base and text inference. In: Proceedings of the 3rd Workshop on Continuous Vector Space Models and their Compositionality, pp. 57–66. Association for Computational Linguistics (2015)
27. Trouillon, T., Welbl, J., Riedel, S., Gaussier, É., Bouchard, G.: Complex embeddings for simple link prediction. In: International Conference on Machine Learning, pp. 2071–2080 (2016)
28. Vrandečić, D., Krötzsch, M.: Wikidata: a free collaborative knowledgebase. Commun. ACM **57**, 78–85 (2014)
29. Wang, J., Ilievski, F., Szekely, P., Yao, K.T.: Augmenting knowledge graphs for better link prediction. In: Raedt, L.D. (ed.) Proceedings of the Thirty-First International Joint Conference on Artificial Intelligence, IJCAI-22, pp. 2277–2283. International Joint Conferences on Artificial Intelligence Organization (2022). main Track
30. Wang, L., Zhao, W., Wei, Z., Liu, J.: SimKGC: simple contrastive knowledge graph completion with pre-trained language models. In: Proceedings of the 60th Annual Meeting of the Association for Computational Linguistics, pp. 4281–4294. Association for Computational Linguistics (2022)
31. Wu, Y., Wang, Z.: Knowledge graph embedding with numeric attributes of entities. In: Proceedings of the Third Workshop on Representation Learning for NLP, pp. 132–136. Association for Computational Linguistics (2018)

32. Xue, B., Li, Y., Zou, L.: Introducing semantic information for numerical attribute prediction over knowledge graphs. In: Sattler, U., et al. (eds.) ISWC 2022. LNCS, vol. 13489, pp. 3–21. Springer, Cham (2022). https://doi.org/10.1007/978-3-031-19433-7_1
33. Yang, B., Yih, S.W.T., He, X., Gao, J., Deng, L.: Embedding entities and relations for learning and inference in knowledge bases. In: Proceedings of the International Conference on Learning Representations (2015)
34. Yao, L., Mao, C., Luo, Y.: KG-BERT: BERT for knowledge graph completion. arXiv preprint arXiv:1909.03193 (2019)
35. Ying, Z., Bourgeois, D., You, J., Zitnik, M., Leskovec, J.: GNNExplainer: generating explanations for graph neural networks. In: Advances in Neural Information Processing Systems, vol. 32 (2019)
36. Zhang, S., et al.: PaGE-link: path-based graph neural network explanation for heterogeneous link prediction. In: Proceedings of the ACM Web Conference, pp. 3784–3793 (2023)

Relationships Are Complicated! An Analysis of Relationships Between Datasets on the Web

Kate Lin(✉), Tarfah Alrashed(✉), and Natasha Noy(✉)

Google Research, Google, San Francisco, USA
{kateslin,tarfah,noy}@google.com

Abstract. The Web today has millions of datasets, and the number of datasets continues to grow at a rapid pace. These datasets are not standalone entities; rather, they are intricately connected through complex relationships. Semantic relationships between datasets provide critical insights for research and decision-making processes. In this paper, we study dataset relationships from the perspective of users who discover, use, and share datasets on the Web: what relationships are important for different tasks? What contextual information might users want to know? We first present a comprehensive taxonomy of relationships between datasets on the Web and map these relationships to user tasks performed during dataset discovery. We develop a series of methods to identify these relationships and compare their performance on a large corpus of datasets generated from Web pages with `schema.org` markup. We demonstrate that machine-learning based methods that use dataset metadata achieve multi-class classification accuracy of 90%. Finally, we highlight gaps in available semantic markup for datasets and discuss how incorporating comprehensive semantics can facilitate the identification of dataset relationships. By providing a comprehensive overview of dataset relationships at scale, this paper sets a benchmark for future research.

Keywords: Web datasets · dataset relationships · semantic markup

1 Introduction

As the world becomes increasingly data-driven, researchers rely on open data to answer scientific questions and to understand complex phenomena [45]. This reliance on data has led to dataset publication becoming the norm in many scientific disciplines [39]. Unlike scientific publications, however, datasets are not static and standalone entities: dataset providers publish new versions of datasets as the data evolves, researchers produce new datasets by combining existing datasets, and meaningful subsets of large datasets may gain a life of their own. When a user chooses a dataset for her work, these distinctions become critical. For instance, when reproducing results from a publication, we must identify which specific dataset snapshot the authors used. When evaluating the

G. Demartini et al. (Eds.): ISWC 2024, LNCS 15231, pp. 47–66, 2025.
https://doi.org/10.1007/978-3-031-77844-5_3

trustworthiness of a dataset available on multiple platforms, users may want to choose the repository that they trust the most. If a scientist wants to compare slices of a large dataset, she wants to ascertain that these slices come from the same snapshot of the larger dataset. Therefore, understanding the semantics of relationships between datasets can be just as important as understanding other metadata about them.

How can we identify relationships between datasets? The most straightforward method is to look at information provided by dataset publishers. The industry standard for describing semantic metadata for any Web content (including datasets) is through structured markup in `schema.org` [16]. Standards like `schema.org` and W3C DCAT [2] provide means to identify pages containing datasets as well as the semantics of relationships between them. In addition to these Web standards, approaches such as datasheets [14] provide mechanisms to describe dataset origins, biases, and recommended usage. These methods of providing additional context for datasets enable publishers to link versions of the same dataset to one another, link a dataset in one repository to the original dataset in another repository, or to declare that one dataset is based on another. However, semantic markup is often unreliable and incomplete, [4,19,27] and only a small fraction of dataset metadata on the Web contains values for properties that link them to other datasets [8]. Furthermore, dataset authors often update or restructure datasets without providing notice or documentation [20,41,43]. Finally, current markup frameworks do not fully capture the variety and nuance of dataset relationships.

To illustrate the richness of dataset relationships, consider the collection of datasets provided by the United States Census Bureau. This collection captures a wide variety of measures (e.g., income data) over many decades at various levels of granularity, such as national, statewide, county-wide, and so on. On the Web, one can find various slices of this large dataset that may be relevant in a specific context: for example, there may be a dataset containing income data for California in 2008 or a dataset containing income data for the entire US in the same year. Each of these datasets is a subset of the larger 2008 Census dataset, but researchers may publish them in different Web sites and contexts. Figure 1 presents another example—a collection of datasets published by the US National Oceanic and Atmospheric Administration (NOAA). We have found more than 140 forms of this dataset on the Web, including annual, monthly, and daily sets. Many variations have multiple versions, and some of these datasets are subsets of larger ones. Additionally, many of the datasets in this collection are replicated across various Web sites. Critically, the information that helps us understand these relationships often must come from *metadata*: the data itself may not have enough context for us to understand the provenance or coverage of the datasets.

In this paper, we explore the relationships between datasets from the perspective of users who want to discover and analyze datasets. Rather than define these relationships in an abstract way, we take a user-centric view and ground the relationships in user tasks performed during dataset discovery. We analyze a large dataset corpus, generated from dataset pages on the Web with `schema.org/Dataset` markup, to identify these relationships between datasets. Our evaluation focuses specifically on provenance-based relationships, which we can infer from metadata. There is a large body of work (Sect. 2) that infers relationships from data. Our focus on metadata and specifically on provenance-based relationships complements related work.

Specifically, we make the following contributions in this paper:

- We define a taxonomy of relationships between datasets on the Web and ground it in essential user tasks that rely on understanding these relationships (Sects. 3 and 4). To our knowledge, this taxonomy is the most comprehensive in the literature to date.
- We propose and compare several methods for identifying dataset relationships (Sects. 5). We show that machine-learning methods that use dataset metadata achieve a multi-class classification accuracy of 90%, outperforming `schema.org` and heuristics-based methods (Sect. 6).
- We analyze the prevalence of provenance-based relationships in a corpus of 2.7 million datasets on the Web. We found that 20% of datasets have at least one relationship with another dataset (Sect. 6).
- We present recommendations for enhancing dataset metadata, facilitating the discovery of more relationships between datasets (Sect. 7).
- We publish a collection of 2.7 million dataset pages with their basic metadata, along with the connections and interrelationships among these datasets.[1]

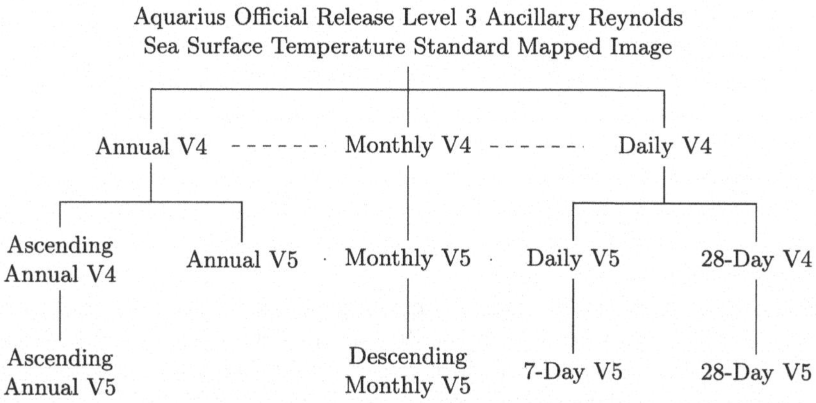

Fig. 1. The *"Aquarius Official Release Level 3 Ancillary Reynolds Sea Surface Temperature Standard Mapped Image"* dataset has annual, monthly, and daily variants with multiple versions. Variants are derived from each other and can have different replicas (e.g., *"Annual V4"* on three sites) and reconfigurations (ascending, descending). (See, for example, dozens of versions of this dataset in Google Dataset Search: https://bit.ly/3IrdEb2)

[1] https://figshare.com/articles/dataset/Metadata_for_Datasets_and_Relationships/22790810.

2 Related Work

Our research focuses on relationships between datasets on the Web. In this section, we examine approaches to tackling this topic, including exploring dataset provenance, understanding dataset evolution, identifying conceptually similar or joinable datasets, and linking datasets to scientific publications.

Research reproducibility benefits from understanding dataset provenance and relationships between datasets. Herschel et al. [18] proposed user-focused methods for capturing and analyzing provenance, emphasizing relationship presentation. Klump et al. [22] introduced a contextual framework and versioning principles surpassing simple revisions. Rauber et al. [33] identified subsets of large datasets supporting research findings, while Silvello [37] detailed citing linked open data subsets. Rauber et al. [32] stressed the importance of exact version citation for research reproducibility.

Semantic vocabularies like `schema.org` [16], DCAT [2], and VoID [3] enable dataset providers to specify relationships between datasets (e.g., `schema.org/isBasedOn` for derivations, `schema.org/sameAs` and `void:Linkset` for replicas, DCAT's `dct:isVersionOf` for versioning). However, these standards lack a comprehensive vocabulary for diverse dataset relationships. The PROV Data Model [6] offers a standardized framework for describing provenance information between entities, including `wasDerivedFrom` for dataset derivation. Indeed the PROV notion of derivation can form the basis for some of the relationships that we discuss later. However, because datasets and their relationships are not the focus of PROV, it does not capture many of the dataset-specific relationships, such as subsets, slices, or datasets that can be integrated.

Research in data evolution addresses challenges of detecting, tracking, and explaining dataset changes over time. Roussakis et al. [35] introduced a flexible framework for dynamic dataset analysis, offering various granularity levels and rich visualizations. Umbrich et al. [41] quantified change frequency in linked open data (LOD) for improved understanding of dataset dynamics. Shraga and Miller [36] proposed a semantic data versioning method using explanations to aid users in comprehending dataset changes.

Other LOD research focuses on recommending interconnected datasets. Lopes et al. [30] proposed collaborative filtering and content-based methods using dataset metadata, both validated through real-world evaluation. Leme et al. [25] suggested using core datasets for interlinking recommendations, demonstrating effectiveness on a large-scale dataset. Ellefi et al. [7] introduced an intensional approach based on conceptual similarity. The LOD research focuses on linking entities within datasets [1,9,13,42], complementary to our focus on complete datasets rather than individual datapoints.

In addition to finding conceptually similar datasets, researchers emphasize identifying joinable datasets to enrich information without foreign keys [12]. Zhu et al. introduced Josie to find joinable tables using overlap set similarity search [44]. Dong et al. developed a clustering-based method for grouping joinable tables [10]. Recent work includes DeepJoin, a deep learning model for efficient joinable table discovery [11]. These efforts streamline dataset discovery for data analysts.

Efforts to link datasets with scientific publications are significant. The Research Graph dataset [5] consolidates publication, dataset, and software details into a unified knowledge graph, simplifying research output discovery. Ayush et al. [38] applied natural language processing to extract data-related information from publications and match it to online datasets. Google Dataset Search [28] connects datasets with scholarly articles referencing them, enhancing scientific discovery by simplifying dataset finding for researchers.

The highlighted research emphasizes the importance of dataset relationships in scientific research. Our aim is to offer a broader framework for future research by identifying more relationships, evaluating their impact, and thus advancing the development of better dataset management tools and techniques.

3 Grounding Dataset Relationships in User Tasks

The data ecosystem relies on a continuous cycle of discovery, analysis, and sharing, necessitating a nuanced understanding of dataset relationships. To ground our taxonomy of dataset relationship, we begin by defining the tasks users undertake during data discovery and sharing.

Finding Datasets: The proliferation of data on the Web has complicated dataset discovery through traditional search engines [23]. Users face challenges in sorting through vast amounts of data and navigating diverse search criteria, especially when their intent varies. For instance, reproducing an experiment from a paper demands sorting through dataset versions, formats, and sources [22], while augmenting a dataset requires finding compatible data in structure, schema, and topic. Understanding dataset relationships facilitates efficient and accurate dataset selection, aiding in reliable data-driven decision-making.

Evaluating Dataset Trustworthiness: Evaluating whether to use a dataset involves an assessment of dataset trustworthiness [15,18]. Unlike research publications, datasets published on the Web rarely undergo peer review. As a result, users must rely on dataset attributes and metadata as proxies for dataset trustworthiness. User-experience studies reveal users weigh data provider, format, prior usage, and update frequency [15]. Hence, comprehending dataset provenance, identifying citations, and locating reliable sources aid in evaluation.

Citing and Referencing Datasets: Noy et al. [29] note that well-described datasets drive new research. Citing datasets like papers encourages better data collection and curation [18]. Proper citation requires persistent identifiers, metadata, and accurate provenance descriptions, including version number, source, and whether it is a subset of another dataset [22]. Proper dataset identification promotes transparency and collaboration, enhancing research quality.

Curating Datasets: Dataset curation involves collecting, organizing, and maintaining datasets from diverse sources to ensure availability for users. The goal is to create high-quality datasets beneficial for researchers, developers, and users. Curators must understand a dataset's relationships with others, including versions, replicas, and usage in research or projects [14].

While the list of user tasks in this section is by no means exhaustive, it demonstrates the need for improving our understanding of the relationships between datasets, capturing these relationships explicitly, and using these relationships to improve researchers' experiences with data.

4 Defining Dataset Relationships

We base our categorization of dataset relationships on the analysis of user tasks in dataset discovery (Sect. 3), prior research (Sect. 2), and observations from analyzing a large corpus of datasets on the Web. Specifically, we collected a corpus of datasets by relying on `schema.org/Dataset` markup (Sect. 6.1).

We broadly group dataset relationships on the Web into provenance-based and non-provenance-based relationships. *Provenance-based relationships* are relationships between the datasets that share a common original dataset, such as being derived or modified versions of the same original dataset. *Non-provenance-based relationships* involve connections between datasets based on content, topic, or task rather than their origin. For each relationship, we highlight which of the tasks from Sect. 3 it is particularly useful for.

4.1 Provenance-Based Relationships

We define a dataset on the web $D = (P, O, S, W)$ as consisting of a set of data points P, origin of dataset O (i.e., primary data-collection process), schema S, and a web site that hosts the dataset W. Note that in the context of dataset discovery, we may not have complete information about a given dataset and, in particular, may not know origin or schema.

We define schema S for the most common dataset types in our corpus. Relational (tabular) datasets are characterized by a header row with column names, data types, and constraints such as primary keys. Document datasets, such as PDFs, are defined by collections of key-value pairs, arrays, or nested documents. Structured datasets, like JSON, are defined by the structure and properties of elements, including data types, relationships, and constraints. RDF data is defined by RDF Schema.

Replica: Datasets $D_1 = (P_1, O_1, S_1, W_1)$ and $D_2 = (P_2, O_2, S_2, W_2)$ are *replicas* of each other iff their underlying data and origin are identical, but they are hosted on different sites: $P_1 = P_2$, $O_1 = O_2$, $S_1 = S_2$, and $W_1 \neq W_2$.

In today's Web data ecosystem, a common pattern is one repository aggregating datasets from multiple other repositories. For instance, the European data portal (europa.eu) offers access to datasets from member state data portals. In the United States, an open data site for a state government might include datasets from county data repositories, which in turn may include datasets from individual towns. Therefore, datasets from local governments (e.g., county) are *replicated* in the state repository. Identifying and grouping replicas of datasets in a dataset-discovery context helps users easily locate datasets and provides choices of sources. It also enables users to obtain data from their most trusted source when available from multiple sources. For example, a user may trust their local government site more and opt to retrieve the dataset from there.

Version and Revision: Datasets $D_1 = (P_1, O_1, S_1, W_1)$ and $D_2 = (P_2, O_2, S_2, W_2)$ are *versions* of each other iff $P_1 \approx P_2$, $O_1 = O_2$, $S_1 \approx S_2$. W_1 may or may not be the same as W_2. This relationship captures evolution of a dataset over time, where changes between subsequent versions are usually relatively small to the size of the dataset.

Published datasets resemble software more than research publications, as they continue evolving after release. Evolution can range from error corrections and data adjustments to continuous updates with new observations. The Research Data Alliance Data Versioning Working Group stipulates that any alteration to a dataset forms a new version that authors must identify, encompassing minor changes such as data additions/removals [32]. However, authors often label only significant checkpoints as new versions, thus, we refer to stable, labeled releases as versions. Minor, unlabeled changes are revisions. For instance, if a dataset covers sales data from January to November and is updated with December data and give it a new label, they create a new version of a dataset. Converting Fahrenheit to Celsius in a weather dataset is typically a revision, not a new version. Identifying all dataset versions is crucial for research reproducibility, data quality assessment, and maintaining transparency and proper attribution when citing the data source.

Subset: A dataset $D' = (P', O', S', W')$ is a *subset (or slice)* of $D = (P, O, S, W)$ iff $P' \subset P$, $O' = O$, $S' \subset S$. W' may or may not be the same as W. There is usually an extraction function $F(x)$ that determines which data points from P are in P': $P' = \{x \in P | F(x) = true\}$

A dataset subset is a smaller, more focused set of data extracted from a larger dataset, published independently. The subset typically contains data selected based on specific criteria, like time period, geographical region, or variables. For example, a dataset containing weather information for a country may have subsets for specific regions or time periods. Researchers using a subset of a dataset in their work benefit from transparency, accuracy, and appropriate attribution.

Note that there is a complementary **superset** relationship. For simplicity, we refer only to the subset relationship in the paper.

Derivation: A dataset $D' = (P', O', S', W')$ is a *derivation* from a collection of datasets $\Delta = \{D_1, \ldots, D_n\}$ iff there exists a derivation function $M(x_1, \ldots, x_m)$ that transforms, combines, or otherwise manipulates data points for datasets in Δ. Thus, O' is different from $O_1, ..., O_n$. Schemas and web sites may or may not be the same.

A healthy data ecosystem enables users to build new datasets from published ones. A dataset can be derived from one or more datasets as a result of transforming, aggregating, or otherwise manipulating existing datasets. Examples of derived datasets include summaries, aggregations of multiple datasets, and variables created by combining or transforming existing variables. Understanding which datasets served as input for a given dataset can help users evaluate trustworthiness of datasets and understand whether a given dataset has properties they are looking for. For dataset curation in particular, it is usually not sufficient to specify a dataset is derived from another dataset; rather, dataset authors must provide details on changes and modifications to ensure users understand implications and could reproduce the dataset[2].

Variant: Datasets $D_1 = (P_1, O_1, S_1, W_1)$ and $D_2 = (P_2, O_2, S_2, W_2)$ are *variants* of each other iff $P_1 \cap P2 \approx \emptyset$, $O_1 = O_2$, $S_1 = S_2$. W_1 may or may not be the same as W_2.

Consider two weather datasets covering different regions of the country and different years; the two datasets use the same schema and were collected in the same way. Teams in these regions may have collected these datasets independently or may have generated them by creating subsets of a larger dataset. The variant relationship captures the link between these two "sibling" datasets. Formally, two datasets are variants of each other if they share the schema, origin, and collection methods but differ in coverage along some dimension. This dimension is often temporal or spatial: the same statistics may be collected and published annually over multiple years, for example. These annual datasets would be variants of each other. Identifying dataset variants allows users to compare and analyze datasets to identify patterns and trends that may be obscured if we look only at one dataset in isolation. By comparing variants of datasets, users gain a more comprehensive understanding of the phenomena that the data represents and make more informed decisions.

4.2 Non-provenance-Based Relationships

With the wealth of datasets on the Web, users can gain useful insights from serendipitous relationships between datasets. These post-hoc relationships can be based on metadata, dataset usage, or similarity in content. Many of these relationships are context-dependent: a specific dimension makes sense in the context of a specific user task. We define several such relationships in this section. This list is not exhaustive as we cannot predict all possible uses of datasets.

Topically Similar: Datasets D_1 and D_2 are *topically similar* iff their topical similarity score exceeds a defined threshold θ: $Sim(D_1, D_2) \geq \theta$, where Sim represents a similarity function that yields a value within the range of 0 (indicating no similarity) to 1 (reflecting perfect similarity). The choice of threshold θ and

[2] Technically, we can consider a subset to be a derived dataset. We distinguish between the two relationships in our taxonomy; for derived datasets, their authors applied some processing or analysis to the data, while for subsets they simply selected the data from an existing dataset.

similarity function Sim relies on the context and desired similarity level. The function $Sim(D_1, D_2)$ can be implemented using methods like cosine similarity, Jaccard index, or others, depending on the nature of the datasets at hand.

Topically similar datasets cover the same subject or capture similar topics along the dimensions relevant to the user context. For instance, datasets covering ocean temperature and salinity can be topically similar when understanding the effects of climate on the oceans. In a different context, a dataset of stock prices might be compared to a benchmark index to assess performance; thus these two datasets would be topically similar.

Task-Similar: Datasets D_1 and D_2 are *task-similar* if $Sim(T(D_1), T(D_2)) \geq \theta$, where $T(D_1)$ and $T(D_2)$ are the tasks for which the two datasets have been designed, and Sim is a similarity function that yields values between 0 (indicating no similarity) and 1 (reflecting perfect similarity). The selection of the threshold θ and similarity function Sim depends on the specific context and the degree of similarity one aims to capture.

Dataset metadata may include not only intrinsic properties of a dataset but also a collection of tasks that a dataset may be best suited for or that dataset creators had in mind. Task-similar datasets share similarities in the tasks or problems they are used for. Datasets created for similar tasks allow for comparison and benchmarking of different algorithms or models, aiding in the evaluation and selection of the best model for a given task. For example, Human3.6M and KITTI datasets are each used for video prediction, yet their subjects vary drastically: humans versus cars.

Integratable: Datasets D_1 and D_2 are *integratable* if they share schema or content enabling the integration. Integratable datasets, D_1 and D_2, are *joinable* when their attribute sets have a non-empty intersection, serving as common attributes or foreign keys: $A(D_1) \cap A(D_2) \neq \emptyset$, where A represents the attribute set (data fields or columns) in the dataset. Integratable datasets, D_1 and D_2, are *unionable* when their attribute sets have a non-empty intersection $A(D_1) \cap A(D_2) \neq \emptyset$, and they share similar schemas $S_1 \approx S_2$, and the overlap between their data points is insignificant: $P_1 \cap P_2 \approx \emptyset$.

Integratable datasets share schema or content, allowing their combination. Datasets are *joinable* if they share common attributes or foreign keys, like traffic patterns and accident reports linked by location and time. Datasets are *unionable* if they capture similar data about complementary concepts, such as weather patterns in different cities. Unionable datasets differ from variants as they do not have the same schema or collection methodology.

4.3 Discussion

A dataset can have *multiple relationships* with other datasets. For instance, a national dataset of education statistics with state-level information can be a source for multiple state-specific datasets. The state-specific datasets are *variants* of each other, but all the state-specific datasets are the *subsets* of the national dataset. Two datasets can have multiple relationships with each other. For example, a Monthly dataset and a Daily dataset in Fig. 1 are *variants* of each other. However, if the Monthly dataset was created by aggregating the Daily datasets, it is also *derived from* the Daily datasets.

Certain relationships are *bidirectional*, while others are *directional*. For instance, if datasets D_1 and D_2 are replicas, then D_1 is a replica of D_2 and D_2 is also a replica of D_1 (bidirectional $D_1 \leftrightarrow D_2$). However, if D_1 is a subset of or derived from D_2, it implies that $D_1 \rightarrow D_2$ is true, but not $D_2 \rightarrow D_1$.

Dataset providers can explicitly capture some relationships that we identify in this section. Specifically, `schema.org` supports two of these relationships: *replica* (`schema.org/sameAs`) and *derivation* (`schema.org/isBasedOn`). For other provenance-based relationships, we can rely on analyzing metadata (e.g., *versions, variants*) or the data itself (e.g., *integratable* datasets). *Topical and task similarity* relationships depend on the user context. Because `schema.org` metadata is not always reliable [4,19,27], combining it with metadata analysis helps identify relationships.

In our empirical analysis, we prioritize metadata, deferring relationships reliant on data or user context for future exploration. Moreover, extensive research exists on deriving dataset relationships directly from the data itself [10,21,44].

5 Empirical Analysis Methods

Earlier research has shown that `schema.org` metadata is not always reliable [4,19,27]. Furthermore, the markup for dataset relationships is extremely incomplete [28]. Thus, in addition to extracting relationships from `schema.org` markup, we propose a series of automatic approaches to infer dataset relationships. We focus specifically on evaluating the value of metadata (not data); thus, we concentrate on provenance-based relationships.

We evaluate four methods: First, we extract relationships directly using `schema.org`. Second, we develop a set of heuristics tailored to each relationship type. Heuristics-based approaches are usually efficient to implement. Finally, we propose two machine-learning-based approaches: a classical ML approach consisting of a gradient boosted decision trees classifier and a generative AI approach using a LLM-based classifier. Each of these models represents a larger class of methods that can be used to tackle this problem setting. Section 6 compares the accuracy of these approaches on a large ground-truth set.

5.1 Semantic Markup Analysis

We use the `schema.org` relationships that metadata explicitly captures: *replica* (`schema.org/sameAs`) and *derivation* (`schema.org/isBasedOn`). We consider datasets A and B to be replicas if one contains the DOI or URL of the other in its `sameAs` field. Dataset A is considered derived from dataset B if dataset A contains the DOI or URL of dataset B in its `isBasedOn` field.

5.2 Heuristics-Based Methods

We define a set of heuristics based on regularities observed by analyzing a large corpus of metadata for datasets on the Web. All comparisons in this section use normalized names and descriptions; specific rules are tailored to each relationship type. Two datasets are **replicas** if their normalized names and descriptions are exact matches or one is a non-trivial prefix of the other. Two datasets are **versions** if their normalized names are the same except for the version number, which we extract using a regular expression. Two datasets are **variants** if their normalized names are the same except for months or dates, which we extract using a regular expression. Two datasets are also variants if their prefixes before a common delimiter are the same, but suffixes are different. Here we consider two dimensions for variants: temporal and spatial.

Directional relationships require complex rules to identify. We identify **subsets** by splitting dataset names into prefixes and suffixes based on a common delimiter. Dataset A is a subset of Dataset B if the name prefix of A and B are exact matches and only Dataset A has a suffix. Additionally, Dataset A is a subset of Dataset B if the two dataset names are the same after extracting a year or month from Dataset A but not from Dataset B. To identify the **derived** relationship, we use observed text patterns in the corpus, such as "analysis of." Dataset A is derived from Dataset B if the processed names are the same after removing these patterns from Dataset A but not B. Table 1 shows an example of one of the heuristics used to identify the subset relationship.

Table 1. An example of a heuristic to discover subsets in our corpus. We consider D_a to be a subset of D_b

ID	Dataset Name	Prefix	Suffix
D_a	"Survey of Earned Doctorates - 2019"	"Survey of Earned Doctorates"	"2019"
D_b	"Survey of Earned Doctorates"	"Survey of Earned Doctorates"	""

5.3 Gradient Boosted Decision Trees Based Classification

We used the ydf-implementation of GradientBoostedTreesLearner in TensorFlow2 [17] to train a GBDT-based multi-class classifier using manually annotated examples described in Sect. 6.1. We trained the model with a batch size of 128, a local growth method to optimize a cross entropy loss function, a random sampling method, a maximum depth of 4, a sparse oblique splitting method [40] and a shrinkage of 0.0887 as set by a hyperparameter sweep.

5.4 LLM-Based Classification

We fine-tuned the t5x [34] implementation of the T5.1.1 large-language model [31] to perform a multi-class classification task using the same manually annotated training examples described in Sect. 5.3. We used a batch size of 64 with 1,050,000 training steps and a learning rate of $1e-3$ set by a hyperparameter sweep.

6 Evaluation and Results

To understand which approach works best in practice, we compared the performance of the four methods from the previous section on manually annotated ground truth data. We then apply the best-performing method to a large corpus of datasets on the Web in order to understand the prevalence of different provenance relationships between datasets.

6.1 Training and Evaluation Data

Dataset Corpus. We generated a corpus of dataset metadata by crawling the Web to find pages with `schema.org` metadata indicating that the page contains a dataset. We then selected a subset of citable datasets: we categorize a dataset as *citable* if it has a persistent de-referencible identifier, like a digital object identifier (DOI). This corpus includes 2.7 million dataset-metadata entries.

Ground Truth. To generate ground truth for training and evaluation, the paper authors manually labeled 2,178 dataset pairs. The labelers had access to all metadata fields for these datasets, not just their names and descriptions.

We observed that some relationships (e.g., replica) are much more common than others (e.g., subset). Thus, our goal when generating a set of pairs for manual labeling was to ensure that this set likely had examples of all the relationships. We used the following procedure: We randomly sampled 125 *seed datasets* from the corpus. Each seed dataset must have between 1 and 10 replicas, as identified by a heuristic-based method (Sect. 5). Note that we required that a dataset *has* a replica but not that the replica is included in the sample. We observed that datasets with replicas are also likely to have other related datasets. Seed datasets also had to come from hosts with more than 30 datasets. We limited seed datasets to a maximum of 2 datasets per host to ensure diversity of the set. We projected the metadata of the datasets in our sample and our corpus into the NewsEmbed [26] embedding space (an embedding space that we found worked particularly well for datasets). Given a seed dataset S and its 20 nearest neighbors $\mathcal{D} = \{D_1, ..., D_{20}\}$, we label manually each relationship $\{\langle S, D_1\rangle, \ldots, \langle S, D_{20}\rangle\}$ and a random sample of 20 relationships between $\langle D_x, D_y\rangle$ where $D_x \in \mathcal{D}$ and $D_y \in \mathcal{D}$.

The number of subset and derived relationships in a random sample was still very low. Typical data interpolation techniques were not possible because subset and derived relationships are non-reflexive. To address the sparse label space, we added government datasets used in Show US the Data Kaggle Competition [24]. We observed that these datasets were more likely to have subsets or derivations.

For machine-learning based methods, we used 70:15:15 split for training, validation, and evaluation data. For other methods, we used the same evaluation data as for the ML-based methods (the 15% of the labeled pairs).

6.2 Results

Table 2 presents the comparison of evaluating the four methods from Sect. 5. Our experiments find that `schema.org` metadata alone is insufficient for identifying relationships between datasets, even for the two types for which `schema.org` exist (replica and derived): Indeed, *no* pairs of datasets in our random sample had an explicit relationship defined between them.

Table 2. Precision (P), recall (R), and F1 scores for each method and relationship type. The scores for the method with the top F1 score for each relationship is bolded.

Relationship	Schema.org			Heuristics			GBDT			T5		
	P	R	F1	P	R	F1	P	R	F1	P	R	F1
Replica	0.00	0.00	0.00	1.00	0.35	0.51	**0.97**	**0.95**	**0.96**	0.92	0.92	0.92
Version	N/A	N/A	N/A	0.96	0.53	0.68	0.92	0.80	0.86	**0.87**	**0.87**	**0.87**
Subset	N/A	N/A	N/A	0.49	1.00	0.65	**1.00**	**0.80**	**0.89**	0.82	0.90	0.86
Derived	0.00	0.00	0.00	0.00	0.00	0.00	0.67	0.33	0.44	**0.80**	**0.67**	**0.73**
Variant	N/A	N/A	N/A	1.00	0.50	0.67	**0.90**	**0.85**	**0.87**	**0.81**	**0.93**	**0.87**
None	0.33	1.00	0.49	**1.00**	**0.80**	**0.89**	**0.85**	**0.93**	**0.89**	**0.94**	**0.85**	**0.89**

Heuristics-based methods perform reasonably well for certain relationship types, such as *none* (i.e., there is no relationship between two datasets) and *version*. These methods often have low recall because they are brittle: small perturbations in names or descriptions of datasets significantly affect their performance. The GBDT Classifier and T5-Based Classifier both perform quite well and have similar F1 scores for all relationships except *derived*. For the *derived* relationship, which is more semantically complex, the T5-Based classifier outperforms the GBDT Classifier.

Figure 2 compares the overall accuracy of the methods. We opt to calculate accuracy as opposed to macro-average precision and recall because there exists a large imbalance between the prevalence of each relationship on the Web.

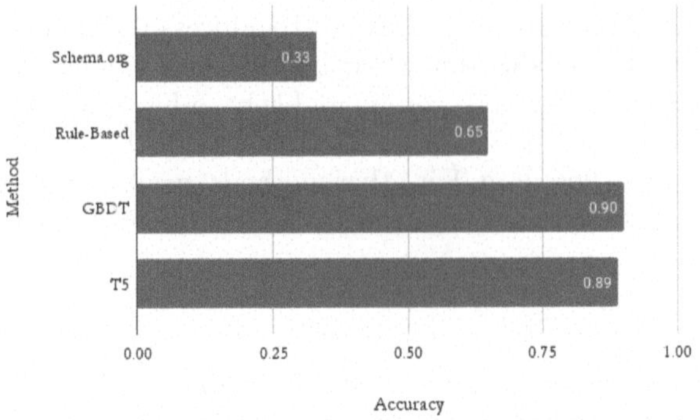

Fig. 2. The overall accuracy for each method type.

6.3 Corpus-Level Analysis

We analyzed the corpus of 2.7 million citable datasets (Sect. 6.1) using the GBDT classifier because it had the highest overall accuracy. Because classifying all of the $O(N^2)$ pairs of datasets is extremely expensive computationally, we clustered datasets first and then classified pairs within each cluster. Specifically, we used the NewsEmbed embedding space and classified a relationship between each dataset and its 20 nearest neighbors. This process gave us 42.4 million unique dataset pairs for the GBDT classifier to classify.

Out of 2.7M datasets in the corpus, 20.1% had at least one relationship with another dataset, and 22% had multiple relationships. Table 3 shows the distribution of the identified relationships, with the *replica* relation being the most prevalent. Only a handful of datasets had *derived* or *version* relation.

Table 3. The distribution of relationship in the corpus.

Relationship Type	Percentage
Replica	77.8%
Subset	14.2%
Variant	5.2%
Derived	1.8%
Version	1.0%

Datasets in each replica pair come from different sites by definition. In order to understand the publishing ecosystem better, we looked at whether or not pairs of datasets in other relationships come from the same repository or tend to be distributed. Out of 61,485 dataset subsets, 59% are from the same site as the parent dataset; the rest are from different sites. Conversely, the majority of variants, derived datasets, and versions exist on the same site: 79% of variants, 83% of derived datasets, and 97% of versions.

7 Discussion and Future Work

Our categorization of dataset relationships and corpus analysis highlighted both the complexity of and the need for identifying these relationships.

7.1 Relationships Are, Indeed, Complicated

Several previous works categorized dataset relationships (see Sect. 2). Our categorization in Sect. 4 complements this effort. Critically, the user-centric approach gave us a unique view. Consider, for example, the *subset* and the *integrated* relationships. In both cases, datasets share some of the content: with the subset relationship, they share some or parts of records. For datasets to be joinable, they must share a subset of foreign keys. However, if we approach the distinction from a user point of view, these two relationships are quite different. Usually we seek *subset* relationships for a manageable dataset slice, whereas for joinable datasets, we aim to expand existing data for new insights.

The user-centric view also helps us decide whether to include specific relationships in our taxonomy. For instance, we have not found the *replica* relationship in other categorizations. However, in the context of Web-based dataset discovery, users need to understand the relationships between original sources of datasets and repositories that aggregate datasets from multiple sources. Users then can choose a site that they find reliable and trustworthy to download the dataset.

Having the grounding in user tasks did not eliminate the need for difficult decisions. For example, determining topic similarity between datasets raises questions. While two datasets covering different weather aspects in the same region for the same timespan are clearly related, the situation differs with education outcome datasets. If one covers high schools and the other elementary schools, they may be considered topically similar only if the user's interest spans all school education. Topic similarity varies based on user task granularity.

In Google Dataset Search, we use several of the relationships from Sect. 4 directly in the tool. In dataset results, we group together *replicas* of a dataset giving the user an option to get the dataset from their preferred site. We also group versions and variants in order to simplify navigation and show the larger diversity of search results.

7.2 Semantic Markup for Dataset Relationships

Our analysis found that over 20% of datasets have at least one relationship with another dataset. These relationships are not captured by `schema.org` metadata. While some researchers noted the low quality of semantic markup (e.g., [4]), we found it to be extremely incomplete. If `schema.org/sameAs` relationships were accurate and complete, our replica-identification mechanism would not be needed. The metadata connecting datasets is often incomplete or inaccurate for several reasons. First, the community can improve and expand `schema.org/Dataset` properties, as some definitions are vague. For example, `isBasedOn` can capture subset, revision, or version relationships. `Schema.org` also lacks relationships like linking to a previous version. Second, our analysis, supported by [18,22,45], highlights the need for data sharing best practices, including publishing datasets with digital object identifiers, linking datasets to papers, and capturing provenance information in metadata. Additionally, the lack of tools utilizing metadata may deter authors from providing accurate metadata; developing such tools could incentivize authors to improve metadata accuracy.

7.3 Limitations in Future Work

We analyzed millions of datasets, optimizing the process to find pairs of datasets to label. The ground truth datasets were limited to pairs that are neighbors in an embedding space, focusing on datasets with similar names and descriptions. Our methods may miss relationships when dataset names change significantly, although minor changes like adding acronyms should not be affected.

We used a few metadata fields to infer relationships, with future analysis planned to explore the impact of fields like authors, providers, and explicit temporal or spatial coverage values.

We derived our relationships using the corpus of datasets on the Web. These relationships likely paint a different picture for datasets in specific dataset repositories (e.g., Figshare, Zenodo), and also among the datasets that constitute the linked open data (LOD) cloud. Understanding how these relationships apply to the datasets in LOD will enable us to highlight similarities and differences between linked data and more traditional data.

Identifying provenance-based relationships lays the groundwork to studying data quality and trustworthiness of data changes on the Web, aiding users in finding reliable data sources and identifying information gaps.

Finally, understanding non-provenance relationships is the first step in helping users find the right data for their tasks. Users often seek data to complete specific tasks (e.g., training an ML model for weather prediction). Understanding dataset relationships helps us better assist users in finding the necessary data.

8 Conclusion

Understanding relationships between datasets is crucial for extracting valuable insights that can drive innovation and positively impact various domains. Using even simple analysis methods, we can see that datasets on the Web are connected in many different ways. However, while this analysis can help in identifying some of the relationships, research communities must develop best practices that encourage dataset authors to specify metadata. Overall, our paper sets a benchmark for future research and highlights the importance of understanding dataset relationships for scientific research and decision-making processes.

Supplemental Material Statement: We publish metadata and dataset relationships for the collection of 2.7 million dataset pages analyzed in Sect. 6 *on Figshare (see Footnote 1). While the source code for the methods outlined in Sect.* 5 *references proprietary libraries and therefore cannot be released, we have reproduced the overall code logic in pseudocode, also available at the aforementioned link. The base t5x implementation described in Section* 5.3 *can be found on GitHub.*[3] *The GBDT training algorithm described in Sect.* 5.4 *can be found on GitHub.*[4]

References

1. Achichi, M., Bellahsene, Z., Ellefi, M.B., Todorov, K.: Linking and disambiguating entities across heterogeneous RDF graphs. Web Semant. **55**(C), 108–121 (2019). https://doi.org/10.1016/j.websem.2018.12.003
2. Albertoni, R., Browning, D., Cox, S.J.D., González-Beltrán, A.N., Perego, A., Winstanley, P.: Data catalog vocabulary (DCAT) - Version 2, W3C recommendation (2020). https://www.w3.org/TR/2020/REC-vocab-dcat-2-20200204/
3. Alexander, K., Cyganiak, R., Hausenblas, M., Zhao, J.: Describing linked datasets. In: LDOW (2009)
4. Alrashed, T., Paparas, D., Benjelloun, O., Sheng, Y., Noy, N.: Dataset or not? a study on the veracity of semantic markup for dataset pages. In: Hotho, A., et al. (eds.) ISWC 2021. LNCS, vol. 12922, pp. 338–356. Springer, Cham (2021). https://doi.org/10.1007/978-3-030-88361-4_20
5. Aryani, A., et al.: A research graph dataset for connecting research data repositories using RD-Switchboard. Sci. Data **5**(1), 1–9 (2018). https://doi.org/10.1038/sdata.2018.99
6. Belhajjame, K., et al.: PROV-DM: the Prov data model. W3C Recommend. **14**, 15–16 (2013)
7. Ben Ellefi, M., Bellahsene, Z., Dietze, S., Todorov, K.: Dataset recommendation for data linking: an intensional approach. In: Sack, H., Blomqvist, E., d'Aquin, M., Ghidini, C., Ponzetto, S.P., Lange, C. (eds.) ESWC 2016. LNCS, vol. 9678, pp. 36–51. Springer, Cham (2016). https://doi.org/10.1007/978-3-319-34129-3_3
8. Benjelloun, O., Chen, S., Noy, N.: Google dataset search by the numbers. In: Pan, J.Z., et al. (eds.) ISWC 2020. LNCS, vol. 12507, pp. 667–682. Springer, Cham (2020). https://doi.org/10.1007/978-3-030-62466-8_41
9. Bizer, C., Heath, T., Berners-Lee, T.: Linked Data - The Story So Far, 1 edn., pp. 115–143. Association for Computing Machinery, New York (2023). https://doi.org/10.1145/3591366.3591378
10. Dong, Y., Takeoka, K., Xiao, C., Oyamada, M.: Efficient joinable table discovery in data lakes: A high-dimensional similarity-based approach. In: 2021 IEEE 37th International Conference on Data Engineering (ICDE), pp. 456–467. IEEE (2021). https://doi.org/10.48550/arXiv.2010.13273
11. Dong, Y., Xiao, C., Nozawa, T., Enomoto, M., Oyamada, M.: Deepjoin: joinable table discovery with pre-trained language models (2023), https://arxiv.org/abs/2212.07588

[3] https://github.com/google-research/t5x.

[4] https://github.com/google/yggdrasil-decision-forests.

12. Fan, G., Wang, J., Li, Y., Miller, R.J.: Table discovery in data lakes: state-of-the-art and future directions. In: Companion of the 2023 International Conference on Management of Data. SIGMOD '23, New York, NY, USA, pp. 69–75. Association for Computing Machinery (2023). https://doi.org/10.1145/3555041.3589409
13. Färber, M., Lamprecht, D.: The data set knowledge graph: creating a linked open data source for data sets. Quantitative Science Studies **2**(4), 1324–1355 (2022). https://doi.org/10.1162/qss_a_00161
14. Gebru, T., et al.: Datasheets for datasets. Commun. ACM **64**(12), 86–92 (2021). https://doi.org/10.48550/arXiv.1803.09010
15. Gregory, K., Groth, P., Scharnhorst, A., Wyatt, S.: Lost or found? discovering data needed for research. Harvard Data Sci. Rev. (2020). https://doi.org/10.1162/99608f92.e38165eb
16. Guha, R.V., Brickley, D., Macbeth, S.: Schema.org: evolution of structured data on the web. Commun. ACM **59**(2), 44–51 (2016). https://doi.org/10.1145/2844544
17. Guillame-Bert, M., Bruch, S., Stotz, R., Pfeifer, J.: Yggdrasil decision forests: a fast and extensible decision forests library. In: Proceedings of the 29th ACM SIGKDD Conference on Knowledge Discovery and Data Mining. KDD '23, New York, NY, USA, pp. 4068–4077. Association for Computing Machinery (2023). https://doi.org/10.1145/3580305.3599933
18. Herschel, M., Diestelkämper, R., Ben Lahmar, H.: A survey on provenance: what for? what form? what from? VLDB J. **26**, 881–906 (2017). https://doi.org/10.1007/s00778-017-0486-1
19. Hogan, A., Harth, A., Passant, A., Decker, S., Polleres, A.: Weaving the pedantic web. LDOW **628**, 26 (2010)
20. Kery, M.B., John, B.E., O'Flaherty, P., Horvath, A., Myers, B.A.: Towards effective foraging by data scientists to find past analysis choices. In: Proceedings of the 2019 CHI Conference on Human Factors in Computing Systems. CHI '19, New York, NY, USA, pp. 1–13. ACM (2019). https://doi.org/10.1145/3290605.3300322
21. Khatiwada, A., Shraga, R., Gatterbauer, W., Miller, R.J.: Integrating data lake tables. Proc. VLDB Endowment **16**(4), 932–945 (2022). https://doi.org/10.14778/3574245.3574274
22. Klump, J., Wyborn, L., Wu, M., Martin, J., Downs, R.R., Asmi, A.: Versioning data is about more than revisions: a conceptual framework and proposed principles. Data Sci. J. (2021). https://doi.org/10.5334/dsj-2021-012
23. Koesten, L.M., Kacprzak, E., Tennison, J.F.A., Simperl, E.: The trials and tribulations of working with structured data: a study on information seeking behaviour. In: Proceedings of the 2017 CHI Conference on Human Factors in Computing Systems. CHI '17, New York, NY, USA, pp. 1277–1289. ACM (2017). https://doi.org/10.1145/3025453.3025838
24. Lane, J., Gimeno, E., Levitskaya, E., Zhang, Z., Zigoni, A.: Data inventories for the modern age? Using data science to open government data. Harvard Data Sci. Rev. **4**(2) (2022). https://hdsr.mitpress.mit.edu/pub/g6e8noiy
25. Leme, L.A.P.P., Lopes, G.R., Nunes, B.P., Casanova, M.A., Dietze, S.: Identifying candidate datasets for data interlinking. In: Daniel, F., Dolog, P., Li, Q. (eds.) ICWE 2013. LNCS, vol. 7977, pp. 354–366. Springer, Heidelberg (2013). https://doi.org/10.1007/978-3-642-39200-9_29
26. Liu, J., Liu, T., Yu, C.: NewsEmbed: modeling news through pre-trained document representations. In: Proceedings of the 27th ACM SIGKDD Conference on Knowledge Discovery & Data Mining. KDD 2021, New York, NY, USA, pp. 1076–1086. ACM (2021). https://doi.org/10.1145/3447548.3467392

27. Meusel, R., Paulheim, H.: Heuristics for fixing common errors in deployed schema.org microdata. In: Gandon, F., Sabou, M., Sack, H., d'Amato, C., Cudré-Mauroux, P., Zimmermann, A. (eds.) The Semantic Web. Latest Advances and New Domains. pp. 152–168. Springer (2015). https://doi.org/10.1007/978-3-319-18818-8_10
28. Noy, N., Burgess, M., Brickley, D.: Google dataset search: building a search engine for datasets in an open web ecosystem. In: The World Wide Web Conference, pp. 1365–1375 (2019). https://doi.org/10.1145/3308558.3313685
29. Noy, N., Goble, C.: Are we cobblers without shoes? making computer science data fair. Commun. ACM **66**(1), 36–38 (2022). https://doi.org/10.1145/3528574
30. Rabello Lopes, G., Paes Leme, L.A.P., Pereira Nunes, B., Casanova, M.A., Dietze, S.: Two approaches to the dataset interlinking recommendation problem. In: Benatallah, B., Bestavros, A., Manolopoulos, Y., Vakali, A., Zhang, Y. (eds.) WISE 2014. LNCS, vol. 8786, pp. 324–339. Springer, Cham (2014). https://doi.org/10.1007/978-3-319-11749-2_25
31. Raffel, C., Shazeer, N., Roberts, A., Lee, K., Narang, S., Matena, M., Zhou, Y., Li, W., Liu, P.J.: Exploring the limits of transfer learning with a unified text-to-text transformer. J. Mach. Learn. Res. **21**(1) (2020)
32. Rauber, A., Asmi, A., van Uytvanck, D., Proell, S.: Data Citation of Evolving Data: Recommendations of the Working Group on Data Citation (WGDC) (2015). https://doi.org/10.15497/RDA00016
33. Rauber, A., Asmi, A., van Uytvanck, D., Pröll, S.: Identification of reproducible subsets for data citation, sharing and re-use. Bull. IEEE Technical Committee Dig. Lib. **12**(1) (2016). https://doi.org/10.5281/zenodo.4048304
34. Roberts, A., et al.: Scaling up models and data with t5x and seqio. J. Mach. Learn. Res. **24**(377), 1–8 (2023). http://jmlr.org/papers/v24/23-0795.html
35. Roussakis, Y., Chrysakis, I., Stefanidis, K., Flouris, G., Stavrakas, Y.: A flexible framework for understanding the dynamics of evolving RDF datasets. In: Arenas, M., et al. (eds.) ISWC 2015. LNCS, vol. 9366, pp. 495–512. Springer, Cham (2015). https://doi.org/10.1007/978-3-319-25007-6_29
36. Shraga, R., Miller, R.J.: Explaining dataset changes for semantic data versioning with Explain-Da-V (technical report) (2023). https://doi.org/10.48550/arXiv.2301.13095
37. Silvello, G.: A methodology for citing linked open data subsets. D-Lib Magazine **21**(1/2), 1505–1524 (2015). https://doi.org/10.1045/january2015-silvello
38. Singhal, A., Srivastava, J.: Research dataset discovery from research publications using web context. In: Web Intelligence, vol. 15, pp. 81–99. IOS Press (2017). https://doi.org/10.3233/WEB-170354
39. Tedersoo, L., et al.: Data sharing practices and data availability upon request differ across scientific disciplines. Sci. Data **8**(1), 192 (2021). https://doi.org/10.1038/s41597-021-00981-0
40. Tomita, T.M., et al.: Sparse projection oblique randomer forests. J. Mach. Learn. Res. **21**(104), 1–39 (2020). https://doi.org/10.48550/arXiv.1506.03410, http://jmlr.org/papers/v21/18-664.html
41. Umbrich, J., Hausenblas, M., Hogan, A., Polleres, A., Decker, S.: Towards dataset dynamics: change frequency of linked open data sources. In: Proceedings of the WWW2010 Workshop on Linked Data on the Web (LDOW2010) (2010)
42. Volz, J., Bizer, C., Gaedke, M., Kobilarov, G.: Discovering and maintaining links on the web of data. In: Bernstein, A., et al. (eds.) ISWC 2009. LNCS, vol. 5823, pp. 650–665. Springer, Heidelberg (2009). https://doi.org/10.1007/978-3-642-04930-9_41

43. Zhang, A.X., Muller, M., Wang, D.: How do data science workers collaborate? roles, workflows, and tools. Proc. ACM Hum.-Comput. Interact. **4**(CSCW1) (2020). https://doi.org/10.1145/3392826
44. Zhu, E., Deng, D., Nargesian, F., Miller, R.J.: JOSIE: overlap set similarity search for finding joinable tables in data lakes. In: Proceedings of the 2019 International Conference on Management of Data. SIGMOD '19, pp. 847–864, New York, NY, USA. ACM (2019). https://doi.org/10.1145/3299869.3300065
45. Zuiderwijk, A., Shinde, R., Jeng, W.: What drives and inhibits researchers to share and use open research data? A systematic literature review to analyze factors influencing open research data adoption. PLoS ONE **15**(9), e0239283 (2020). https://doi.org/10.1371/journal.pone.0239283

Multi-view Transformer-Based Network for Prerequisite Learning in Concept Graphs

Zhichun Wang[1,2](✉), Yifeng Shao[1], Boci Peng[3], Bangqi Li[4], Yun Li[5], Qianren Wang[5], and Nijun Li[5]

[1] School of Artificial Intelligence, Beijing Normal University, Beijing, China
zcwang@bnu.edu.cn
[2] Engineering Research Center of Intelligent Technology and Educational Application, Ministry of Education, Beijing, China
[3] School of Intelligence Science and Technology, Peking University, Beijing, China
[4] School of Computer Science and Engineering, Beihang University, Beijing, China
[5] Advanced Cognitive AI Lab, Shanghai Huawei Technologies, Shanghai, China

Abstract. Prerequisite learning is the task of identifying prerequisite relations among concepts, which is important for many AI-based educational applications. Previous approaches explore different kinds of learning resources to obtain useful features for predicting prerequisites. Early approaches use handcrafted features while recent approaches use neural networks to encode information of concepts. To further improve the results of prerequisite learning, we build concept graphs to include comprehensive information about concepts from open data and learning resources, and propose a **M**ulti-view **T**ransformer-based **N**etwork (MTN) to encode multi-view features of concepts in the graph. Multi-view features are fused to make accurate predictions of concept prerequisites. We evaluate our approach on four public datasets and compare it with recently published approaches. The results show that our approach can achieve state-of-the-art results in the task of prerequisite learning. The source code and data are available at https://github.com/kg-bnu/MTN.

Keywords: prerequisite learning · concept embedding · concept graph

1 Introduction

Prerequisite relations identify the underlying dependencies among concepts, which provide a reasonable learning order of concepts. If a concept A is a prerequisite of B, it means that it is difficult to learn B without the knowledge of A. For example, in Calculus, the concept *Limit* is a prerequisite of concept *Derivative*. To understand *Derivative*, one is required to learn the knowledge of *Limit* first. Concept prerequisites are very important for many educational applications, including intelligent tutoring [5], curriculum planning [1], learning materials generation [7], and recommendation [4]. Prerequisites among courses are usually given in university curricula or by Massive Open Online Courses (MOOCs) platforms, but concept prerequisites are often not provided.

The original version of the chapter has been revised. The authors name has been modified as "Bangqi Li". A correction to this chapter can be found at
https://doi.org/10.1007/978-3-031-77844-5_14

G. Demartini et al. (Eds.): ISWC 2024, LNCS 15231, pp. 67–86, 2025.
https://doi.org/10.1007/978-3-031-77844-5_4

Prerequisite learning is the task of automatically discovering concept prerequisites from different kinds of data, and many approaches have been proposed in recent years. Typically, prerequisite learning is solved as a binary classification of concept pairs. Features of concept pairs can be obtained from Wikipedia [16,17], MOOCs [2,23], university course curriculums [18], textbooks [34], scientific corpora [8], or lecture files [13,15]. Early approaches extracted manually defined features from learning resources for prerequisite learning. For example, the work in [17] designed 15 graph-based features and 17 text-based features from Wikipedia, [23] defined 7 features for finding prerequisites in MOOCs. For these approaches, the results of prerequisite learning highly depend on the used features. The pre-defined features cannot be easily adapted to new types of resources. Recently, several neural-based approaches for prerequisite learning have been proposed, including PREREQ [25], VGAE [14], CPRL [10], ConLearn [29], and MHAVGAE [39], etc. These approaches first obtain initial concept features by using topic models or language models, and then utilize neural networks to predict prerequisites. Deep models can effectively model useful information of concepts, which achieve promising results without hand-crafted features.

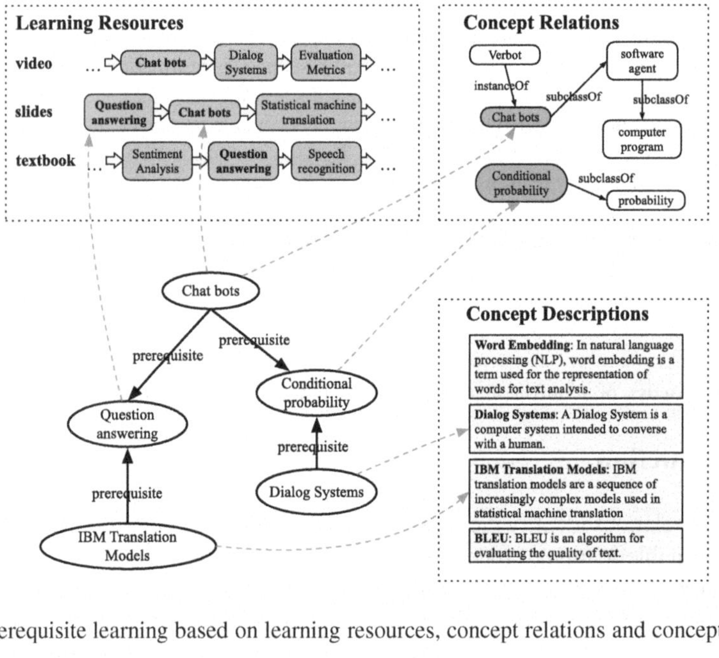

Fig. 1. Prerequisite learning based on learning resources, concept relations and concept descriptions.

Although continuous progress has been made by previous studies, we find that there are still challenging problems when using neural models for prerequisite learning. First, there lacks a unified framework for representing useful features of different types of learning resources. Previous approaches extracted texts from lecture slides [13] or MOOC transcripts [25], but the lengths and styles of sentences from these resources are quite different, which were handled with different techniques. For example, GAE [14] employs Doc2Vec model [11] to obtain concept representations from documents, while

PREREQ [25] uses the pairwise-link LDA [22] model for concept representation. Second, background knowledge of concepts is not fully utilized in the existing approaches. There are open knowledge bases containing descriptions and rich relations of concepts, such as ConceptNet [28], Wikidata [33], and Wikipedia[1]. Both structural and textual knowledge of concepts can be obtained from these open resources, but such knowledge is not well utilized in previous neural models. Previous approaches [14, 25] only treated known prerequisites as the background knowledge of concepts, without considering concept relations like *subclassOf*, *partOf*, etc. It is important to study whether such background knowledge is useful and how to incorporate the knowledge into prerequisite learning models.

To solve the above challenges, we propose a **M**ulti-view **T**ransformer-based **N**etwork (MTN) for prerequisite learning. We first gather different kinds of information to build a multi-relational concept graph (as shown in Fig. 1), which contains learning resources, concept relations, and concept descriptions. MTN encodes multi-view features of concepts in the concept graph to predict prerequisite relations among them. Specifically, the main contributions of this paper include:

- We propose a method to build a multi-relational concept graph from learning resources and open knowledge bases. Concept prerequisites are predicted based on the multi-view features of the concept graph, including *resource-view*, *relation-view*, and *text-view*.
- We propose a multi-view transformer-based network (MTN) for prerequisite learning. MTN uses three transformer encoders to obtain concept features from different views, and fuses these features with an attention-based aggregation method to accurately predict concept prerequisites.
- We evaluate our approach on four public datasets, our approach overall outperforms the compared approaches and achieves the state-of-the-art results.

The rest of this paper is organized as follows: Sect. 2 formalizes the problem of prerequisite learning, Sect. 3 describes the proposed multi-view transformer-based network (MTN), Sect. 4 introduces the multi-view features aggregation method, Sect. 5 presents the evaluation results, Sect. 6 discusses some related work, Sect. 7 is the conclusion, and discusses limitations of this work.

2 Problem Formulation

In this work, we formalize the prerequisite learning as the task of link prediction in a multi-relational concept graph, which aims to identify missing prerequisites among entities already in the concept graph. We include rich relations and concept descriptions in the concept graph, which provides comprehensive information about concepts. The concept graph in our approach is built using three kinds of inputs:

- **Learning Resources**. Learning resources are those materials used in teaching and learning activities, including MOOCs, textbooks, scientific papers, etc. Concepts are

[1] https://www.wikipedia.org.

usually defined or introduced in learning resources, which contain important clues for prerequisite learning. Learning resources may be in different types and forms, we consider the order of appearance of concepts in them as the most important information, which contains clues of concept relatedness and dependencies. In this work, we identify concepts appearing in learning resources, and record the occurrence order of concepts in each learning resource. Concepts and learning resources are represented as nodes in the concept graph, there will be a $hasConcept$ link from a learning resource to a concept if the concept appears in the learning resource. The order of concepts appearing in a learning resource is recorded as a node attribute of the learning resource.

- **Concept Relations**. To predict prerequisite relationships among concepts, we believe that having knowledge of other types of concept relationships is helpful, such as $subClassOf$, $partOf$, and $instanceOf$. The previous prerequisite learning approaches built concept graphs containing only known prerequisite relations, while in this work we include more relation types in the graph by integrating concept knowledge from the open knowledge base Wikidata. Let $C_{core} = \{c_i\}_{i=1}^{K}$ denote a set of core concepts among which prerequisite relations are to be predicted, where K is the number of concepts and c_i is the i-th concept in C_{core}. We locate them in Wikidata and extract their one-hop neighbors with the associated relations to populate the concept graph in our approach. A set of new extended concepts C_{ext} will be introduced in the population process. To control the size of the concept graph and exclude irrelevant concepts, we only keep new concepts linked with at least two concepts in C_{core}. In this way, the concept graph will include rich links among concepts while retaining a modest size.
- **Concept Descriptions**. Concept descriptions can usually be found in textbooks or online wikis, which formally define concepts with important information. In this work, we take Wikipedia as the source of concept descriptions, because it covers a huge number of concepts and provides generally high-qualified descriptions of concepts. Given the set of core concepts $C_{core} = \{c_i\}_{i=1}^{K}$, we locate each concept in Wikipedia and extract the first sentence in its wiki page as the concept description.

To learn concept prerequisites in a certain domain, we first build a multi-relational concept graph $\mathcal{G} = \{C, E, R, T, D\}$ by using the above inputs, where $C = C_{core} \cup C_{ext}$ consists of core concepts with partially annotated prerequisites and extended concepts from Wikidata, E is a set of learning resources, R is a set of relations, T is a set of triples representing relations among concepts and learning resources, D is the set of descriptions of concepts in C. Given the concept graph $\mathcal{G}$ and a set of known prerequisites among concepts in C_{core}, the problem of prerequisite learning is to predict missing prerequisite relations between concepts, i.e. mapping any concept pair (c, c'), $c, c' \in C_{core}$, to a binary class indicating whether c is a prerequisite of c'.

3 Multi-view Transformer-Based Network

To accurately predict prerequisites in a multi-relational concept graph, we propose a **M**ulti-view **T**ransformer-based **N**etwork (MTN). Figure 2 shows the framework of

MTN. Given inputs from the resources-view, relation-view, and text-view of the concept graph, MTN first uses three Transformer models to get important features of concept pairs; it then aggregates features from different views and determines whether they have prerequisite relations or not.

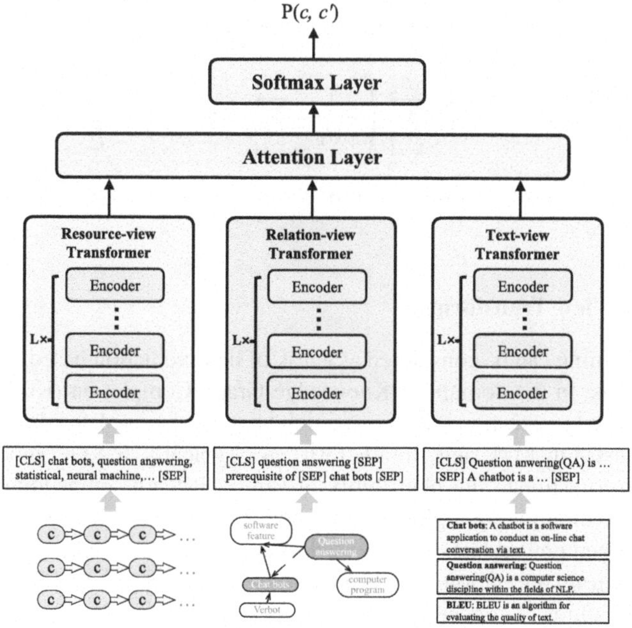

Fig. 2. Framework of MTN.

3.1 Resource-View Transformer

Resource-view Transformer aims to encode concept features based on the relationships between concepts and learning resources in a concept graph. The underlying assumption is that concepts linked to the same learning resources are related, and the order in which concepts appear may indicate their prerequisite relations. To capture the relatedness and dependencies among concepts, we train a Resource-view Transformer following the scheme of Masked Language Modeling in BERT [6].

Let $\mathcal{G}res = \{C, E, T\}$ denote the resource-view of the original concept graph $\mathcal{G}$. We first obtain a set of concept sequences $\{(c_{i1}, c_{i2}, ..., c_{il})\}_{i=1}^{|E|}$ from $\mathcal{G}$, where $c_{ij} \in C$, $(e_i, hasConcept, c_{ij}) \in T$, the subscript j is the index of concepts appearing in learning resource $e_i \in E$. Concept names in each sequence are separated by tabs. During training, a certain percentage of the input concept tokens are randomly masked. These masked tokens are then predicted based on the context provided by the surrounding sequence. Specifically, for each masked token, a masking probability is applied to determine whether it should be replaced with a special [MASK] token, a wrong concept token, or remain unchanged. The objective is to maximize the likelihood of predicting the original concept names given the contextual information.

Let $\mathcal{D} = \{(x_k, M_k)\}_{k=1}^{|E|}$ represent the set of masked sequences and the set of masked tokens in them (i.e. x_k denotes the masked input sequence, and M_k is the set of masked tokens), $|E|$ is the number of concept sequences. The Resource-view Transformer is trained by optimizing the following loss:

$$\mathcal{L}_{\text{res}} = -\frac{1}{|E|}\sum_{k=1}^{|E|}\left(\frac{1}{|M_k|}\sum_{y\in M_k}\log P(y|x_k)\right), \tag{1}$$

where $P(y|x_k)$ is predicted probability of the true token y given the context of the masked input x_k.

3.2 Relation-View Transformer

Prerequisite learning can be considered as a task of link prediction based on the existing concept relations. In the domain of Knowledge Graph Completion (KGC) [27], there are many knowledge graph embedding models that can be used for this task, such as TransE [3], DistMult [37], and RotatE [30], etc. Typically, a KGC model defines a score function to estimate the plausibility of triples; it learns embeddings of entities and relations by minimizing a global loss function over all the triples in a knowledge graph. The learned embeddings can be used to predict missing links in the knowledge graph. Here we train a Relation-view Transformer following KG-BERT [38] to encode relation-view features of concepts.

Let $\mathcal{G}_{rel} = \{C, R, T\}$ denote the relation-view of the concept graph; for a triple $t = (c, r, c')$, we generate a sequence "[CLS] c [SEP] r [SEP] c' [SEP]" as the input of the Relation-view Transformer. The final hidden state of [CLS] generated by the Relation-view Transformer is taken as the feature of t, denoted as $\mathbf{h}_t$, which is used to predicate the score of the triple. The Relation-view Transformer is trained by optimizing the following cross-entropy loss:

$$\mathcal{L}_{rel} = -\sum_{t\in T\cup T^-}\Big(y_t \log(s_t) + (1-y_t)\log(1-s_t)\Big) \tag{2}$$

where $s_t = \sigma\left(\mathbf{w}^\top \mathbf{h}_t + a\right)$ is the score of a triple t, T is the set of positive triples, T^- is the set of negative triples generated by replacing the head or tail entities in positive triples; $\mathbf{w}$ and a are the parameters, and σ represents the Sigmoid function.

3.3 Text-View Transformer

Let $\mathcal{G}_{text} = \{C, D\}$ denote the text-view of the concept graph $\mathcal{G}$, we train a Text-view Transformer to encode useful features from concept descriptions in $\mathcal{G}_{text}$. For a pair of concepts $p_i = (c, c')$, their descriptions $d, d' \in D$ are concatenated to generate a sequence of text tokens. More specifically, the sequence has the form of "[CLS] d

[SEP] d' [SEP]". The sequence of concatenated descriptions is fed to the Text-view Transformer model, the hidden state of [CLS] token is used as the text-view embedding of the concept pair $p_i = (c, c')$.

To get discriminative features of concept pairs, we use a set of training data to train the Text-view Transformer. Let $\{(p_i, y_i)\}_{i=1}^{N}$ be a set of N labeled concept pairs, $y_i = 1$ if the concept pair p_i is a positive sample, otherwise $y_i = 0$. The Text-view Transformer model is trained by optimizing the following cross-entropy loss function:

$$\mathcal{L}_{text} = -\sum_{k=1}^{N} \left(y_i \log f_i + (1 - y_i) \log(1 - f_i) \right) \tag{3}$$

f_i is computed as:

$$f_i = \sigma \left(\mathbf{u}^\top \mathbf{h}_i + b \right) \tag{4}$$

where $\mathbf{u}$ and b are parameters, $\mathbf{h}_i$ is the text-view embedding of concept pair p_i, σ is the sigmoid function.

4 Multi-view Feature Aggregation

The purpose of training multi-view transformers is to get useful features from multiple aspects. Therefore, features from multiple views are aggregated to predict prerequisite relations among concepts. We first pre-train the resource-view, relation-view, and text-view transformers separately. Then the features of concept pairs generated by multiple transformers are aggregated to predict the final prerequisite results.

4.1 Attention-Based Feature Aggregation

For a concept pair $p_i = (c, c')$, three sequences are generated as the inputs of resource-view, relation-view, and text-view transformers, respectively. Let d and d' be the descriptions of c and c', these sequences have the following forms:

- Resource-view: $\{[\text{CLS}], c, [\text{SEP}], c', [\text{SEP}]\}$
- Relation-view: $\{[\text{CLS}], c, [\text{SEP}], \textit{prerequisite}, [\text{SEP}], c', [\text{SEP}]\}$
- Text-view: $\{[\text{CLS}], d, [\text{SEP}], d', [\text{SEP}]\}$

The hidden states of [CLS] generated by three transformers are denoted as $\mathbf{h}_i^{(v)}$, where $v \in \{res, rel, text\}$. We design an attention-based feature aggregator to combine the features of different views for each concept pair. The idea of using an attention mechanism is to distinguish important features during the aggregation of features. For the embedding of concept pair $p_i = (c, c')$ in each view v, an attention coefficient $\alpha^{(v)}$ is first computed:

$$\alpha^{(v)} = \text{LeakyReLU} \left(\mathbf{v}^\top \mathbf{h}_i^{(v)} + d \right) \tag{5}$$

where $\mathbf{v}$ and d are parameters to be learned during model training. The coefficients of the three views are then normalized by the softmax function:

$$\beta^{(v)} = \frac{\exp\left(\alpha^{(v)}\right)}{\sum_{j \in \{res, rel, text\}} \exp\left(\alpha^{(j)}\right)} \tag{6}$$

Multi-view features of concepts are aggregated based on their attention:

$$\mathbf{h}_i = \sum_{v \in \{res, rel, text\}} \beta^{(v)} \mathbf{h}_i^{(v)} \tag{7}$$

The aggregated feature $\mathbf{h}_i$ will be used to predict prerequisite relation between c and c'.

4.2 Prerequisite Prediction

The aggregated feature $\mathbf{h}_i$ of a concept pair $p_i = (c, c')$ is passed to a feed-forward layer followed by a softmax classification layer, which predicts the probability distribution of being prerequisite or not:

$$g_i = \text{softmax}\left(\mathbf{u}^\top \mathbf{h}_i + z\right) \tag{8}$$

where $\mathbf{u}$ and z are parameters. Given a set of labeled concept pairs $\{(p_i, y_i)\}_{i=1}^N$ as training data, the prerequisite prediction model is trained by optimizing the cross-entropy loss function:

$$\mathcal{L} = -\sum_{i=1}^{N} \left(y_i \log g_i + (1 - y_i) \log \left(1 - g_i\right)\right) \tag{9}$$

5 Experiments

5.1 Datasets

We evaluate our approach on four datasets, which are built from different types of learning resources.

- **LectureBank**. It was built by Li et al. [14], which contains 3,119 lecture files in five different domains, including NLP, machine learning, artificial intelligence, deep learning and information retrieval. There are 208 concepts and 913 prerequisites in this dataset.
- **MOOC-DSA**. It was built by Pan et al. [23], which covers concepts about Data Structure and Algorithm (DSA). It contains video transcripts obtained from Coursera[2], course concepts in the transcripts are manually labeled. There are 200 concepts and 479 prerequisites in MOOC DSA.
- **MOOC-ML**. It was also created by Pan et al. [23], which covers concepts about Machine Learning (ML). There are 244 concepts and 1,735 prerequisites in MOOC ML.
- **University Course**. It was built by Chen et al. [18], which contains descriptions of 654 university courses, and covers 407 concepts in the domain of computer science. There are 1,008 prerequisites in this dataset (Table 1).

[2] https://www.coursera.org.

Table 1. Dataset Statistics.

Dataset	#Resources	#Concepts	#Prerequisites
LectureBank	3,119	208	913
MOOC-DSA	449	200	479
MOOC-ML	548	244	1,735
University Course	654	407	1,008

5.2 Concept Graphs

We build a concept graph for each dataset following the method introduced in Sect. 2. Firstly, concepts in the learning resources are identified by finding mentions of concept names in the texts in learning resources, which establishes links between concepts and resources. Because domain concepts are mostly mentioned using their formal names, this simple method can obtain desirable results for our approach. Secondly, concept descriptions are obtained by extracting introductory texts (i.e. the first sentence) in concepts' Wikipedia pages. To find the corresponding page of a concept in Wikipedia, we send a query of the concept's name to Wikipedia's search engine; if the top ranked page in the returned results has the same title as the concept, we take it as the corresponding page of the concept. Thirdly, concept relations are obtained from Wikidata, which has high coverage of concepts and relations. Most Wikipedia pages have links to their corresponding Wikidata pages, we can use these links to locate the equivalent items of the core concepts in Wikidata; then the one-hop neighbors of the core concepts can be further obtained.

Table 2 shows the statistics of concept graphs built for four datasets, which outlines the numbers of extended concepts, edges, concept descriptions and the average length of descriptions. It should be noted that we only extract descriptions for core concepts, there is a small number of them having no descriptions because their Wikipedia pages are not found; we use their names as the descriptions in such cases. Table 3 outlines all the relations in the concept graph. There are 9 relations in the concept graphs. *prerequisiteOf* relations between concepts are from annotations in the datasets; *hasConcept* and *hasDescription* relations are established by using our methods introduced above. The rest 6 relations are obtained from Wikidata.

Table 2. Statistics of Concept Graphs

Dataset	#Ext. Concepts	#Edges	#Descriptions(Avg. Length)
LectureBank	1,598	3,762	178 (27.0)
MOOC-DSA	971	2,315	185 (28.1)
MOOC-ML	1,925	4,239	216 (28.8)
University Course	9,167	22,278	372 (28.0)

Table 3. Relations in Concept Graphs

Relation	Explanation
prerequisiteOf	It states that one concept is a prerequisite of another;
hasConcept	It states that one resource contains a concept;
hasDescription	It states that one concept has a textual description;
subClassOf	It states that one concept is a subconcept of another;
partOf	It states that one concept is a part of another;
hasPart	It is an inverse relation of partOf;
instanceOf	It states that one concept is an instance of another;
facetOf	It states that one concept is an aspect of another;
hasQuality	It states that one concept has an inherent characteristic.

5.3 Baselines

To validate the performance and effectiveness of our approach, MTN, we compare it with six state-of-the-art prerequisite learning approaches and one highly relevant knowledge graph completion model. The compared prerequisite learning approaches are from formally published works, which provide source codes or have results in the same experimental setting as ours.

- **GAE** [14]. It trains a Doc2Vec [11] model to get concept embeddings, and uses graph auto-encoders to predict prerequisites.
- **VGAE** [14]. It is an extension of GAE, which uses variational auto-encoders to predict concept prerequisites.
- **PREREQ** [25]. It uses pairwise-link LDA to obtain concept representations and predicts prerequisites using a Siamese network.
- **CPRL** [10]. It uses R-GCN to learn concept embeddings, and predicts the prerequisite relations using a Siamese network.
- **MHAVGAE** [39]. It uses a multi-head attention variational graph auto-encoder for learning prerequisites in the concept-resource graph.
- **ConLearn** [29]. It is a contextual-knowledge-aware concept prerequisite relation learning approach.
- **KG-BERT** [38]. It is a knowledge graph completion model based on transformers. We include it in the baselines because the relation-view transformer in our approach is trained following the method in KG-BERT.

5.4 Experiment Settings

We conducted experiments in two settings: the *conventional setting*, used in previous works [10,29], allowing us to compare our results with those reported in the established works; and the *hard setting*, where we constructed a more challenging evaluation setting using unified cross-validations and more negative samples.

Conventional Setting. In the conventional setting, the proportions of the training, validation, and testing sets are 8:1:1 for the LectureBank dataset and 6:1:3 for the MOOC-DSA, MOOC-ML, and University Course datasets. Negative samples are generated by reversing each positive prerequisite pair and randomly sampling unrelated concept pairs. Reversing a positive sample (c, c') means exchanging the positions of the two concepts to generate a negative pair (c', c). Positive samples are oversampled to balance the number of positive and negative samples. In the conventional setting, the Precision, Recall, and F1 scores on the testing data are reported for all the compared methods; the results are averaged over five train-test splits.

Hard Setting. In the conventional setting, the train-test splits are not unified across all datasets, and the 1:1 ratio between positive and negative samples is overly simplistic compared to real-world problems. To enable more objective comparisons, we designed a harder evaluation setting with unified training and testing splits and a greater number of negative samples. In this setting, we conducted 5-fold cross-validation for all experiments. In each fold, 60%, 20%, and 20% of prerequisites are used for training, validation, and testing, respectively. Negative samples are generated by corrupting and reversing the positive ones. Corrupting a positive sample (c, c') involves replacing c or c' with randomly selected concepts. We generate eight negative samples for each positive sample, including seven corrupted concept pairs and one reversed concept pair. All compared approaches are run on the same splits of datasets, and the average Precision, Recall, F1, and AUC (Area Under the ROC Curve) over five train-test splits are reported.

Training Details. We implemented our approach using PyTorch[3] and conducted experiments on a workstation with an Intel Xeon CPU @ 2.50 GHz, 128 GB RAM, and a GPU with 24 GB VRAM. We used the pre-trained BERT model[4] to initialize the transformers in our approach. During training, we employed the Adam optimizer to train the three transformers with a batch size of 8. We considered the masking probability of the Resource-view Transformer among $\{0.05, 0.10, 0.15, 0.20, 0.25\}$ and the learning rates for the three transformers among $\{10^{-6}, 10^{-5}, 10^{-4}\}$. The best configurations of these hyper-parameters were selected based on the F1 score. For the baseline approaches, we followed their respective papers and tuned their parameters according to the F1 scores.

5.5 Experimental Results

Results in Conventional Setting. Table 4 presents the results of the compared approaches in the conventional setting. The best and second-best results in each row are highlighted in boldface and with an underline, respectively. The results of GAE, VGAE, PREREQ, CPRL, and ConLearn are cited from [29], as we use the same datasets and experimental setting. The results of MHAVGAE and KG-BERT in this conventional setting are not available in previous works, so their results are obtained by running their source codes. Our approach, MTN, achieves the highest F1 scores on three datasets and the second-highest F1 score on one dataset. Among all the compared approaches,

[3] https://pytorch.org.

[4] https://huggingface.co/bert-base-uncased.

Table 4. Results of compared approaches in the conventional setting.

Dataset	Metric	GAE	VGAE	PREREQ	CPRL	MHAVGAE	ConLearn	KG-BERT	MTN
LectureBank	P	0.462	0.417	0.590	<u>0.861</u>	0.421	0.831	0.551	**0.915**
	R	0.811	0.575	0.502	0.858	0.654	**0.960**	<u>0.899</u>	0.871
	F1	0.589	0.484	0.543	0.860	0.512	<u>0.891</u>	0.683	**0.893**
MOOC-DSA	P	0.294	0.269	0.492	0.641	0.392	<u>0.823</u>	0.558	**0.853**
	R	0.715	0.657	0.462	0.619	0.626	**0.816**	<u>0.801</u>	0.778
	F1	0.417	0.382	0.476	0.630	0.482	**0.819**	0.658	<u>0.814</u>
MOOC-ML	P	0.293	0.266	0.448	0.800	0.364	**0.895**	0.643	<u>0.894</u>
	R	0.733	0.647	0.592	0.642	0.713	<u>0.850</u>	0.820	**0.905**
	F1	0.419	0.377	0.510	0.712	0.482	<u>0.872</u>	0.721	**0.900**
University Course	P	0.450	0.470	0.468	<u>0.689</u>	0.449	0.611	0.558	**0.874**
	R	0.886	0.694	0.916	0.760	0.822	**0.966**	<u>0.947</u>	0.851
	F1	0.597	0.560	0.597	0.723	0.581	<u>0.749</u>	0.703	**0.862**

ConLearn is the most competitive one. In terms of F1, ConLearn gets the best F1 on MOOC-DSA, with a 0.5% improvement over MTN. However, our approach outperforms ConLearn by 0.2%, 2.8% and 11.3% on LectureBank, MOOC-ML, and University Course datasets.

The performance of GAE-based approaches is suboptimal compared to ConLearn and MTN. We believe this is due to their decoding methods' inability to effectively distinguish between positive concept pairs and their reversed pairs. For instance, VGAE and MHAVGAE predict prerequisite relationships between two concepts based on the inner product of their latent vectors. Reversing the order of the two concepts does not affect the results. Since a large portion of negative samples in the training and testing datasets are reversals of positive ones, it is difficult for GAE-based approaches to achieve high precision.

The results of KG-BERT demonstrate that prerequisite relationships between concepts can be predicted based on known triples in the concept graph. KG-BERT outperforms GAE-based approaches, highlighting its effectiveness in prerequisite learning tasks. However, its performance falls short of MTN, which incorporates additional information from resources and concept descriptions.

Results in Hard Setting. Table 5 presents the results of the compared approaches in the hard setting. As in Table 4, the best and second best result in each row are highlighted in boldface and with an underline, respectively. In the hard setting, the results of all the compared approaches are produced with their source codes. Experiments are conducted on the same 5-fold cross-validations. Because CPRL does not provide source code, we are not able to compare it in the hard setting. According to the results, our approach MTN gets the best F1 and AUC scores on all of the four datasets. ConLearn is still the most competitive baseline, however, our approach gets 1.0%, 17.8%, 8.6% and 8.6% improvements of F1 over ConLearn on four datasets, respectively. In terms of AUC, our approach gets 2.7%, 7.9%, 5.1% and 2.5% improvements over ConLearn.

Table 5. Results of compared approaches in the hard setting.

Dataset	Metric	GAE	VGAE	PREREQ	MHAVGAE	ConLearn	KG-BERT	MTN
LectureBank	P	0.365	0.366	0.403	0.371	**0.811**	0.255	0.758
	R	0.604	0.612	0.450	0.648	0.671	0.552	**0.732**
	F1	0.455	0.458	0.425	0.472	0.734	0.348	**0.744**
	AUC	0.779	0.789	0.684	0.803	0.909	0.740	**0.936**
MOOC-DSA	P	0.334	0.335	0.240	0.351	0.541	0.262	**0.678**
	R	0.585	0.577	0.399	0.553	0.408	0.514	**0.611**
	F1	0.425	0.424	0.299	0.430	0.465	0.347	**0.643**
	AUC	0.788	0.785	0.556	0.798	0.813	0.756	**0.892**
MOOC-ML	P	0.301	0.301	0.318	0.307	**0.698**	0.249	0.696
	R	0.557	0.561	0.606	0.601	0.566	0.694	**0.726**
	F1	0.391	0.392	0.417	0.406	0.625	0.367	**0.711**
	AUC	0.777	0.770	0.728	0.792	0.897	0.782	**0.948**
University Course	P	0.307	0.307	0.485	0.346	0.620	0.252	**0.672**
	R	0.436	0.435	0.533	0.536	0.557	**0.813**	0.675
	F1	0.360	0.360	0.508	0.421	0.587	0.385	**0.673**
	AUC	0.685	0.683	0.793	0.776	0.903	0.823	**0.928**

In the hard setting, the training and testing datasets contain more negative samples. The GAE-based approaches (GAE, VGAE, and MHAVGAE) still perform poorly. KG-BERT also performs worse in the hard setting, indicating that relying solely on triples in concept graphs does not yield desirable results when there are more negative samples than positive ones.

5.6 Contributions of Component Models

To get better insight into the effectiveness of component models, we conduct an ablation study of MTN. Table 6 presents the ablation study of MTN's component models on four datasets in the hard setting. MTN(-w.o. Res.), MTN(-w.o. Rel.), and MTN(-w.o. Text.) are variations of MTN by removing resource-view, relation-view, and text-view embedding models, respectively. The results outlined in Table 6 are F1 values, the numbers in brackets are the differences of F1 values compared with MTN. It is observed that removing any models in MTN leads to decreases in F1 values. According to the F1 decreases, we find that the relation-view embedding model contributes the most to MTN, with a decrease of 0.040 in LectureBank, 0.059 in MOOC-DSA, 0.016 in MOOC-ML, and 0.047 in University Course. This suggests that the relation-view model is a key factor in the success of MTN and has a substantial impact on its ability to perform the task effectively. It shows that transformers of three views all encode useful features for predicting prerequisites. When features from three views are aggregated, better results are obtained.

Table 6. Results of Ablation Study of MTN's Component Models (F1).

Dataset	MTN(-w.o. Res.)	MTN(-w.o. Rel.)	MTN(-w.o. Text.)	MTN
LectureBank	0.736 (−0.008)	0.704 (−0.040)	0.737 (−0.007)	0.744
MOOC DSA	0.636 (−0.007)	0.584 (−0.059)	0.623 (−0.020)	0.643
MOOC ML	0.706 (−0.005)	0.695 (−0.016)	0.705 (−0.006)	0.711
University Course	0.648 (−0.025)	0.626 (−0.047)	0.651 (−0.022)	0.673

5.7 Effect of Embedding Aggregation Method

To evaluate the effectiveness of the attention-based embedding aggregation method in our approach, we compared it with two simple aggregation methods, embedding addition and concatenation. Embedding addition directly adds concept embeddings from three views, embedding concatenation aggregates concept embeddings by concatenating them. Figure 3 compares the results of different aggregation methods on four datasets in the hard setting. It is observed that embedding addition gets the lowest F1 values on all the datasets. Attention-based embedding aggregation and embedding concatenation have close results, while the attention-based method performs slightly better on the four datasets, with 0.4% to 2.4% improvements of F1. Comparing with embedding concatenation method, our attention-based method can promote the results in most cases.

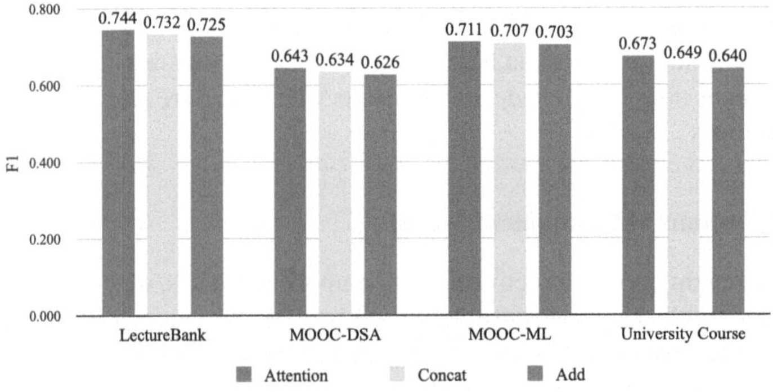

Fig. 3. Results comparison of Different Aggregation Methods (F1).

6 Related Work

6.1 Feature Engineering Approaches

To determine whether one concept is a prerequisite of another concept, researchers have investigated various features of concept pairs. These features are computed based on different kinds of resources, including Wikipedia, MOOCs, Textbooks, Scientific Corpus, Knowledge Graphs, etc.

Links and textual contents in Wikipedia are commonly used in early prerequisite learning approaches. Talukdar and Cohen [31] investigated reliable features based on hyperlinks, edits, and page contents in Wikipedia for discovering prerequisite relations. Liang et al. [16] proposed a link-based metric called reference distance (RefD), which measures the prerequisite relations between concepts. RefD measures how differently two concepts refer to each other to predict prerequisite relations. Liang et al. [17, 19] compared various features in the active learning framework for prerequisite learning, including graph-based features and text-based features. Clickstream data of Wikipedia is also used to generate features of concepts, which are fed to binary classifiers to predict prerequisite relations [26]. Xiao et al. [36] explored more comprehensive features from Wikipedia for prerequisite learning, including link-based, clickstream-based, category-based, content-based and time-based features.

With the quick growth of MOOCs, lecture transcripts, video playlists and course descriptions in MOOCs are explored for prerequisite learning. Pan et al. [23] defined concept relatedness, contextual features and structure features based on MOOCs, including video references, sentence references and average position distance, etc. ALSaad et al. [2] proposed BEM (Bridge Ensemble Measure) and GDM (Global Direction Measure) based on lecture transcripts of MOOCs for prerequisite prediction. BEM captures concept dependencies based on lecture bridging concepts, sliding windows, and the first lecture indicator; GDM incorporates time directly by analyzing the concept time ordering both globally and within lectures. Xiao et al. [35] designed features based on the concept frequencies and positions in course descriptions for prerequisite learning.

Features from Textbooks, scientific corpus, and university course curriculums are also studied for identifying prerequisite relations. Wang et al. [34] proposed a concept map extraction model that jointly extracts key concepts and identifies prerequisite relations from textbooks. Gordon et al. [8] used a LDA model to identify concepts from scientific papers, and employed cross-entropy and information flow methods to discover prerequisite relations. CPR-Recover [18] recovers concept prerequisite relations from course dependencies by using an optimization based framework. Information and dependencies of courses are collected from different universities, which are consumed by CPR-Recover to get the concept-level prerequisite relations. EMRCM [9] builds a concept map containing multiple relations between concepts including the prerequisite relations. Student question logs, textbooks, and Wikipedia are used by EMRCM to infer prerequisite relations.

Open knowledge graphs contain rich structure information about concepts, which also have been explored for prerequisite learning. Manrique et al. [20, 21] proposed an approach which uses the structural knowledge in DBpedia to search prerequisite candidates; features of concept pairs are computed from DBpedia and a document corpus to train a binary classifier for prerequisite learning. To avoid generating too many candidates, they set a maximum length of the paths that link concepts. Our approach also uses a similar filtering method to control the size of concept graphs.

The above studies mainly focus on computing useful features of concept pairs from different types of resources. Features are manually designed and cannot be easily transferred to new resources. Our approach gathers information from various resources into a multi-relational concept graph, and then employs deep models to learn latent features of concepts.

6.2 Deep Learning Approaches

Roy et al. [25] proposed PREREQ, which predicts prerequisites from labeled prerequisite relations of concepts, courses, or video playlists. It uses a pairwise-link LDA model to get vector representations of concepts, and uses a Siamese network to predict new concept prerequisites. Li et al. [12] used pre-trained language model and graph embedding model to get concept representations, which are used for predicting prerequisites.

Several approaches solved the prerequisite learning problem as link prediction within a graph, which consists of concept and resource nodes. Li et al. [13] used a relational-variational graph auto-encoder (R-VGAE) to predict prerequisite relations in the concept-resource graph. Following similar framework, Li et al. further proposed an unsupervised cross-domain prerequisite learning model, which learns to transfer concept prerequisite relations from an information-rich domain to an information-poor domain [15]. Jia et al. [10] proposed to use a relational graph convolutional network (R-GCN) to learning representations of concepts and resources. Prerequisites were predicted by a Siamese network which takes the learned concept representations as inputs. Zhang et al. [39] proposed a multi-head attention variational graph auto-encoders for learning prerequisites in a concept-resource graph, which employs a resource prerequisite reference distance metric to generate weak supervision labels. The work in [24] proposed a directed graph neural network based on the Weisfeiler-Leman algorithm for prerequisite learning. ConLearn [29] used gated GNN to generate representations of concepts, and applied Siamese network to predict prerequisites. The work in [40] proposed a novel alternating knowledge distillation approach to take advantage of both content-based and graph-based models for prerequisite learning. TCPL [32] also combines textual and structural features of concepts for prerequisite learning.

7 Conclusion

This paper presents a Multi-view Transformer-based Network (MTN) for prerequisite learning. To fully explore various information for discovering prerequisites, our approach learns resource-view, relation-view, and text-view concept representations from a concept graph. Features from multiple views are aggregated as the input for a prediction model, which determines whether given concept pairs have prerequisite relationships. We evaluate our approach on four datasets built from different resources. Compared to recently published approaches, our method achieves state-of-the-art results in both conventional setting and hard setting.

The main limitation of this work is that transformers in different views are trained separately, and the features from each view are frozen before passing them to the feature aggregator. As a result, the component models in MTN are not optimized jointly during training. Exploring efficient methods for the joint learning of multi-view transformers is worthwhile in the future work, which is likely to enhance the results.

Acknowledgement. This work was partially supported by the National Science and Technology Major Project (No. 2021ZD0113004) and National Natural Science Foundation of China (No. 62276026).

Supplemental Material Statement. Our source code, experimental data, and instructions for repeating all experiments are available at https://github.com/kg-bnu/MTN.

References

1. Agrawal, R., Golshan, B., Papalexakis, E.: Toward data-driven design of educational courses: a feasibility study. J. Educ. Data Min. **8**(1), 1–21 (2016). https://doi.org/10.5281/zenodo.3554601
2. ALSaad, F., Boughoula, A., Geigle, C., Sundaram, H., Zhai, C.: Mining MOOC lecture transcripts to construct concept dependency graphs. International Educational Data Mining Society (2018)
3. Bordes, A., Usunier, N., Garcia-Durán, A., Weston, J., Yakhnenko, O.: Translating embeddings for modeling multi-relational data. In: Proceedings of the 26th International Conference on Neural Information Processing Systems - Volume 2. NIPS'13, Red Hook, NY, USA, pp. 2787—2795. Curran Associates Inc. (2013). https://doi.org/10.5555/2999792.2999923
4. Chanaa, A., El Faddouli, N.E.: Prerequisites-based course recommendation: recommending learning objects using concept prerequisites and metadata matching. Smart Learn. Environ. **11**(1), 16 (2024). https://doi.org/10.1186/s40561-024-00301-0
5. Chen, P., Lu, Y., Zheng, V.W., Pian, Y.: Prerequisite-driven deep knowledge tracing. In: 2018 IEEE International Conference on Data Mining (ICDM), pp. 39–48 (2018). https://doi.org/10.1109/ICDM.2018.00019
6. Devlin, J., Chang, M.W., Lee, K., Toutanova, K.: BERT: pre-training of deep bidirectional transformers for language understanding. In: Proceedings of the 2019 Conference of the North American Chapter of the Association for Computational Linguistics: Human Language Technologies, Volume 1 (Long and Short Papers), Minneapolis, Minnesota, pp. 4171–4186. Association for Computational Linguistics (2019). https://doi.org/10.18653/v1/N19-1423
7. Gordon, J., Aguilar, S., Sheng, E., Burns, G.: Structured generation of technical reading lists. In: Tetreault, J., Burstein, J., Leacock, C., Yannakoudakis, H. (eds.) Proceedings of the 12th Workshop on Innovative Use of NLP for Building Educational Applications, Copenhagen, Denmark, pp. 261–270. Association for Computational Linguistics (2017). https://doi.org/10.18653/v1/W17-5029
8. Gordon, J., Zhu, L., Galstyan, A., Natarajan, P., Burns, G.: Modeling concept dependencies in a scientific corpus. In: Proceedings of the 54th Annual Meeting of the Association for Computational Linguistics (Volume 1: Long Papers), Berlin, Germany, pp. 866–875. Association for Computational Linguistics (2016). https://doi.org/10.18653/v1/P16-1082
9. Huang, X., et al.: Constructing educational concept maps with multiple relationships from multi-source data. In: 2019 IEEE International Conference on Data Mining (ICDM), pp. 1108–1113 (2019). https://doi.org/10.1109/ICDM.2019.00132
10. Jia, C., Shen, Y., Tang, Y., Sun, L., Lu, W.: Heterogeneous graph neural networks for concept prerequisite relation learning in educational data. In: Proceedings of the 2021 Conference of the North American Chapter of the Association for Computational Linguistics: Human

Language Technologies, pp. 2036–2047. Association for Computational Linguistics (2021). https://doi.org/10.18653/v1/2021.naacl-main.164

11. Le, Q., Mikolov, T.: Distributed representations of sentences and documents. In: Xing, E.P., Jebara, T. (eds.) Proceedings of the 31st International Conference on Machine Learning. Proceedings of Machine Learning Research, vol. 32, Beijing, China, pp. 1188–1196. PMLR (2014). https://proceedings.mlr.press/v32/le14.html
12. Li, B., Peng, B., Shao, Y., Wang, Z.: Prerequisite learning with pre-trained language and graph embedding models. In: Wang, L., Feng, Y., Hong, Yu., He, R. (eds.) NLPCC 2021. LNCS (LNAI), vol. 13029, pp. 98–108. Springer, Cham (2021). https://doi.org/10.1007/978-3-030-88483-3_8
13. Li, I., Fabbri, A., Hingmire, S., Radev, D.: R-VGAE: relational-variational graph autoencoder for unsupervised prerequisite chain learning. In: Proceedings of the 28th International Conference on Computational Linguistics, pp. 1147–1157. International Committee on Computational Linguistics (2020). https://doi.org/10.18653/v1/2020.coling-main.99
14. Li, I., Fabbri, A.R., Tung, R.R., Radev, D.R.: What should I learn first: introducing lecturebank for NLP education and prerequisite chain learning. In: Proceedings of the AAAI Conference on Artificial Intelligence **33**, 6674–6681 (2019). https://doi.org/10.1609/aaai.v33i01.33016674
15. Li, I., Yan, V., Li, T., Qu, R., Radev, D.: Unsupervised cross-domain prerequisite chain learning using variational graph autoencoders. In: Proceedings of the 59th Annual Meeting of the Association for Computational Linguistics and the 11th International Joint Conference on Natural Language Processing (Volume 2: Short Papers), pp. 1005–1011. Association for Computational Linguistics (2021). https://doi.org/10.18653/v1/2021.acl-short.127
16. Liang, C., Wu, Z., Huang, W., Giles, C.L.: Measuring prerequisite relations among concepts. In: Proceedings of the 2015 Conference on Empirical Methods in Natural Language Processing, Lisbon, Portugal, pp. 1668–1674. Association for Computational Linguistics (2015). https://doi.org/10.18653/v1/D15-1193
17. Liang, C., Ye, J., Wang, S., Pursel, B., Giles, C.L.: Investigating active learning for concept prerequisite learning. In: Proceedings of the AAAI Conference on Artificial Intelligence **32**(1) (2018). https://doi.org/10.1609/aaai.v32i1.11396
18. Liang, C., Ye, J., Wu, Z., Pursel, B., Giles, C.: Recovering concept prerequisite relations from university course dependencies. In: Proceedings of the AAAI Conference on Artificial Intelligence **31**(1) (2017). https://doi.org/10.1609/aaai.v31i1.10550
19. Liang, C., Ye, J., Zhao, H., Pursel, B., Giles, C.: Active learning of strict partial orders: a case study on concept prerequisite relations. In: Lynch, C., Merceron, A., Desmarais, M., Nkambou, R. (eds.) EDM 2019 - Proceedings of the 12th International Conference on Educational Data Mining. pp. 348–353. EDM 2019 - Proceedings of the 12th International Conference on Educational Data Mining, International Educational Data Mining Society (2019)
20. Manrique, R., Pereira, B., Mariño, O.: Exploring knowledge graphs for the identification of concept prerequisites. Smart Learn. Environ. **6**(1), 1–18 (2019). https://doi.org/10.1186/s40561-019-0104-3
21. Manrique, R., Pereira, B., Marino, O., Cardozo, N., Wolfgand, S.: Towards the identification of concept prerequisites via knowledge graphs. In: 2019 IEEE 19th International Conference on Advanced Learning Technologies (ICALT), vol. 2161-377X, pp. 332–336 (2019). https://doi.org/10.1109/ICALT.2019.00101
22. Nallapati, R.M., Ahmed, A., Xing, E.P., Cohen, W.W.: Joint latent topic models for text and citations. In: Proceedings of the 14th ACM SIGKDD International Conference on Knowledge Discovery and Data Mining. KDD '08, New York, NY, USA, pp. 542–550. Association for Computing Machinery (2008). https://doi.org/10.1145/1401890.1401957

23. Pan, L., Li, C., Li, J., Tang, J.: Prerequisite relation learning for concepts in MOOCs. In: Proceedings of the 55th Annual Meeting of the Association for Computational Linguistics (Volume 1: Long Papers), Vancouver, Canada, pp. 1447–1456. Association for Computational Linguistics (2017). https://doi.org/10.18653/v1/P17-1133
24. Qu, X., Shang, X., Zhang, Y.: Concept prerequisite relation prediction by using permutation-equivariant directed graph neural networks (2024). https://arxiv.org/abs/2312.09802
25. Roy, S., Madhyastha, M., Lawrence, S., Rajan, V.: Inferring concept prerequisite relations from online educational resources. In: Proceedings of the AAAI Conference on Artificial Intelligence, vol. 33(01), pp. 9589–9594 (2019). https://doi.org/10.1609/aaai.v33i01.33019589
26. Sayyadiharikandeh, M., Gordon, J., Ambite, J.L., Lerman, K.: Finding prerequisite relations using the wikipedia clickstream. In: Companion Proceedings of The 2019 World Wide Web Conference. WWW '19, New York, NY, USA, pp. 1240—1247. Association for Computing Machinery (2019). https://doi.org/10.1145/3308560.3316753
27. Shen, T., Zhang, F., Cheng, J.: A comprehensive overview of knowledge graph completion. Knowl.-Based Syst. **255**, 109597 (2022). https://doi.org/10.1016/j.knosys.2022.109597
28. Speer, R., Chin, J., Havasi, C.: Conceptnet 5.5: an open multilingual graph of general knowledge. In: Proceedings of the Thirty-First AAAI Conference on Artificial Intelligence. AAAI'17, pp. 4444—4451. AAAI Press (2017). https://doi.org/10.5555/3298023.3298212
29. Sun, H., Li, Y., Zhang, Y.: ConLearn: contextual-knowledge-aware concept prerequisite relation learning with graph neural network, pp. 118–126. https://doi.org/10.1137/1.9781611977172.14
30. Sun, Z., Deng, Z.H., Nie, J.Y., Tang, J.: Rotate: knowledge graph embedding by relational rotation in complex space. In: International Conference on Learning Representations (2019)
31. Talukdar, P., Cohen, W.: Crowdsourced comprehension: Predicting prerequisite structure in Wikipedia. In: Proceedings of the Seventh Workshop on Building Educational Applications Using NLP, Montréal, Canada, pp. 307–315. Association for Computational Linguistics (2012). https://doi.org/10.5555/2390384.2390423
32. Tang, X., Liu, K., Xu, H., Xiao, W., Tan, Z.: Continual pre-training of language models for concept prerequisite learning with graph neural networks. Mathematics **11**(12) (2023). https://doi.org/10.3390/math11122780
33. Vrandečić, D.: Wikidata: A new platform for collaborative data collection. In: Proceedings of the 21st International Conference on World Wide Web. pp. 1063—1064. WWW '12 Companion, Association for Computing Machinery, New York, NY, USA (2012). https://doi.org/10.1145/2187980.2188242
34. Wang, S., Ororbia, A., Wu, Z., Williams, K., Liang, C., Pursel, B., Giles, C.L.: Using prerequisites to extract concept maps fromtextbooks. In: Proceedings of the 25th ACM International on Conference on Information and Knowledge Management. CIKM '16, New York, NY, USA, pp. 317—326. Association for Computing Machinery (2016). https://doi.org/10.1145/2983323.2983725
35. Xiao, K., Bai, Y., Wang, Z.: Extracting prerequisite relations among concepts from the course descriptions. Int. J. Software Eng. Knowl. Eng. **32**(04), 503–523 (2022). https://doi.org/10.1142/S0218194022400034
36. Xiao, K., Fu, Y., Deng, Y., Xia, L.: Identifying prerequisite relations between concepts in Wikipedia. In: 2022 International Conference on Service Science (ICSS), pp. 271–276 (2022). https://doi.org/10.1109/ICSS55994.2022.00049
37. Yang, B., Yih, S.W.t., He, X., Gao, J., Deng, L.: Embedding entities and relations for learning and inference in knowledge bases. In: Proceedings of the International Conference on Learning Representations (ICLR) 2015 (2015)
38. Yao, L., Mao, C., Luo, Y.: KG-BERT: Bert for knowledge graph completion (2019)

39. Zhang, J., Lan, H., Yang, X., Zhang, S., Song, W., Peng, Z.: Weakly supervised setting for learning concept prerequisite relations using multi-head attention variational graph auto-encoders. Knowl.-Based Syst. **247**, 108689 (2022). https://doi.org/10.1016/j.knosys.2022.108689
40. Zhu, Y., Zamani, H.: Predicting prerequisite relations for unseen concepts. In: Proceedings of the 2022 Conference on Empirical Methods in Natural Language Processing, Abu Dhabi, United Arab Emirates, pp. 8542–8548. Association for Computational Linguistics (2022). https://aclanthology.org/2022.emnlp-main.585

Knowledge Graph Structure as Prompt: Improving Small Language Models Capabilities for Knowledge-Based Causal Discovery

Yuni Susanti[1(✉)] and Michael Färber[2(✉)]

[1] Artificial Intelligence Lab., Fujitsu Ltd., Kanagawa, Japan
yuni.susanti@fujitsu.com
[2] ScaDS.AI & TU Dresden, Dresden, Germany
michael.faerber@tu-dresden.de

Abstract. Causal discovery aims to estimate causal structures among variables based on observational data. Large Language Models (LLMs) offer a fresh perspective to tackle the causal discovery problem by reasoning on the metadata associated with variables rather than their actual data values, an approach referred to as *knowledge-based causal discovery*. In this paper, we investigate the capabilities of Small Language Models (SLMs, defined as LLMs with fewer than 1 billion parameters) with prompt-based learning for knowledge-based causal discovery. Specifically, we present "`KG Structure as Prompt`", a novel approach for integrating structural information from a knowledge graph, such as *common neighbor nodes* and *metapaths*, into prompt-based learning to enhance the capabilities of SLMs. Experimental results on three types of biomedical and open-domain datasets under few-shot settings demonstrate the effectiveness of our approach, surpassing most baselines and even conventional fine-tuning approaches trained on full datasets. Our findings further highlight the strong capabilities of SLMs: in combination with knowledge graphs and prompt-based learning, SLMs demonstrate the potential to surpass LLMs with larger number of parameters. Our code and datasets are available on GitHub.[1](https://github.com/littleflow3r/kg-structure-as-prompt)

Keywords: causal relation · language model · knowledge graph

1 Introduction

One of the fundamental tasks in various scientific disciplines is to find underlying causal relationships and eventually utilize them [10]. Causal discovery is a branch of causality study which estimates causal structures from observational data and

Y. Susanti—This work was conducted during a research stay at KIT and ScaDS.AI/TU Dresden, Germany.

G. Demartini et al. (Eds.): ISWC 2024, LNCS 15231, pp. 87–106, 2025.
https://doi.org/10.1007/978-3-031-77844-5_5

generates a causal graph as a result. A causal graph, as illustrated in Fig. 1, is a directed graph modeling the causal relationships between observed variables; a node represents a variable and an edge represents a causal relationship.

Conventionally, causal discovery involves learning causal relations from observational data by measuring how changes in one variable are associated with changes in another variable, an approach referred to as *covariance-based causal discovery* [21]. Driven by the recent advancements in LLMs, recent work has explored the causal capabilities of LLMs using metadata (e.g., variable names) rather than their actual data values. In other words, the causal relation is queried in natural language directly to the LLMs. This paper focuses on the latter, and to differentiate with *covariance-based causal discovery*, we refer to this approach as ***knowledge-based causal discovery***, following the definition of [21].

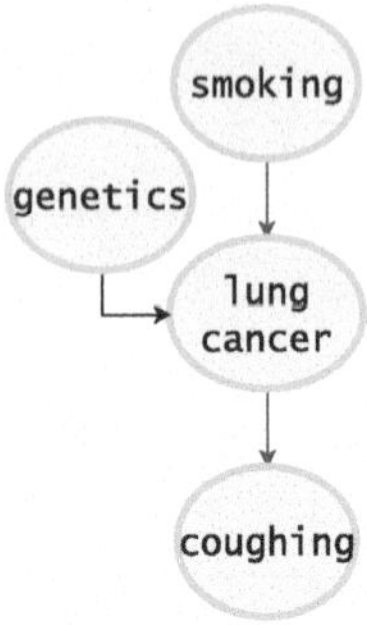

Fig. 1. Example of a causal graph.

Typically, such metadata-based causal reasoning is performed by Subject Matter Experts (SMEs) as they construct a causal graph, drawing from their expertise in domain-specific subjects and common sense [21], or based on literature surveys on subjects related to the variables. The advancement in LLMs has simplified this formerly challenging process, as LLMs are now capable of providing the knowledge that previously can only be provided by SMEs. Recent works [18,39,42,45] also show promising results, notably, [21] explores causal capabilities of LLMs by experimenting on cause-effect pairs. Their finding suggests that LLM-based methods achieved state-of-the-art performance on several causal benchmarks. Similarly, [45] investigated the causal capability of LLMs by analyzing their behavior given a certain causal question. However, in contrast to [21], their result suggests that LLMs currently lack the capability to offer satisfactory answers for discovering new knowledge. Meanwhile, a work by [18] focused on investigating the LLMs' capability for causal association among events expressed in natural language. Thus, their study is more oriented towards extracting a causal diagram (e.g., a chain of events) from unstructured text instead of discovering new causal relations.

In this paper, we investigate the capabilities of language models for knowledge-based causal discovery between variable pairs given a textual context from text sources. Specifically, given a pair of variables e_1 and e_2, the task is to predict if a causal relation can be inferred between the variables. Therefore, similar to [18], our focus also lies in inferring causal relations from text rather than discovering new causal relations. In particular, we present "`KG Structure as Prompt`," a novel approach for integrating structural information from a Knowledge Graph (KG) into *prompt-based learning* with Small Language Models (SLMs). Prompt-based learning adapts LMs for specific tasks by incorporating prompts-task-specific instruction combined with the text input-to guide the models' output for the downstream tasks. Our approach enhances this method by incorporating additional information from KGs, leveraging the strengths of KGs in providing context and background knowledge. We opted for SLMs because a smaller model that can outperform larger models is more cost-effective and therefore preferable. We conduct experiments on three types of biomedical and an open-domain datasets, and further evaluate the performance of the proposed approach under three different architectures of language models.

To summarize, our main contributions are as follows:

1. We present "KG Structure as Prompt", a novel approach for injecting structural information from KGs into prompt-based learning. In experiments under few-shot settings, we demonstrate that our approach outperforms most of the no-KG baselines and achieves performance comparable to the conventional fine-tuning using a full dataset, even with limited samples.
2. We show that our approach is effective with different types of language model architectures and knowledge graphs, showcasing its flexibility and adaptability across various language models and knowledge graphs.
3. We demonstrate the robust capabilities of SLMs: fused with prompt-based learning and an access to a knowledge graph, SLMs are able to surpass an LLM with much larger number of parameters.[1]

2 Background and Related Work

Small Language Models. Small Language Models (SLMs) refer to language models with fewer parameters, resulting in a reduced capacity to process text compared to larger-parameter LLMs. However, SLMs typically require less computation resources, making them faster to train and deploy, and maintaining them is generally more cost-effective. On the contrary, LLMs are trained on vast amounts of diverse data, thus have significantly more parameters and are capable of handling more complex language tasks than SLMs. Nevertheless, LLMs are expensive and difficult to train and deploy as they typically require more computational resource. For instance, GPT-3 [4], which consists of 175 billion parameters, is impractical to run on hardware with limited resources.

In this work, we define SLMs as LMs with less than 1 billion parameters. We explore the causal capability of SLMs with different architectures: (1) Masked Language Model (MLM) especially the encoder-only model, (2) Causal Language Model (CLM) or decoder-only language model, and (3) Sequence-to-Sequence Language Model (Seq2SeqLM) or encoder-decoder model. We provide an overview of each type of architecture below.

MLMs, especially encoder-only models such as BERT [8], are a type of LM that utilizes encoder blocks within the transformer architecture and are trained to predict masked tokens based on the context provided by surrounding words. They excel in natural language understanding (NLU) tasks, e.g., text classification, as they are able to capture relationships between words in a text sequence. CLMs, such as GPT-3 [4], use the decoder blocks within the transformer architecture and are trained to generate text one token at a time, by conditioning each token on the preceding tokens in the sequence. Meanwhile, Seq2SeqLMs,

[1] GPT 3.5 turbo model [31] with ICL [4] prompting method.

such as T5 [32], consist of both encoder and decoder blocks. The encoder transforms the input sequence into vector representation, while the decoder produces the output based on the encoded vector. CLMs and Seq2SeqLMs generally work well for natural language generation (NLG) and NLU tasks such as translation and summarization, as they can produce coherent and grammatically accurate sentences. We list our choice of language models in Sect. 5.

Prompt-Based Learning and Knowledge Injection. Research on classifying causal relations from text has predominantly occurred within supervised settings, utilizing classical machine learning (ML) approaches [3,5,6,19,20,28] or *fine-tuning* pre-trained language models [11,18,33,36,38]. Classical ML techniques often require extensive feature engineering and have shown inferior performance compared to fine-tuning language models such as BERT [8]. Therefore, we evaluate our method against fine-tuning methods as baselines.

Meanwhile, ***prompt-based learning***, also known as *prompt-tuning*, has recently emerged as a promising alternative to the conventional fine-tuning approach for a variety of Natural Language Processing (NLP) tasks [1,26,34,35]. Typically, a *prompt* is composed of discrete text (*hard* prompt); however, recent work has introduced *soft prompt*, a continuous vector that can be optimized through backpropagation [23,25]. In the relation classification task, prompt-based learning often involves inserting a prompt template containing masked tokens into the input, essentially converting the task into *masked language modeling* or *text generation* problems [7,13,14]. This approach is particularly well-suited for few-shot or zero-shot scenarios, where only limited labeled data is available [9,35]. This motivates us to investigate such prompt-based learning under few-shot settings, given the scarcity of datasets for our causal relation classification task.

Other works explore **knowledge injection** for the prompt construction, for instance, KnowPrompt [7] injects latent knowledge contained in relation labels into prompt construction with learnable virtual words. KAPING [2] retrieves top-K similar triples of the target entities from Wikidata and further augments them as a prompt. KiPT [24] uses WordNet to calculate semantic correlation between the input and manually constructed core concepts to construct the prompts. Our work differs from them since we focus on leveraging *structural information* of knowledge graphs to construct the prompt (see Sect. 4).

3 Task Formulation

In this work, we focus on *pairwise* knowledge-based causal discovery: given a pair of entities e_1 and e_2, i.e., variable or node pairs such as `FGF6` and `prostate cancer`, the task is to predict if a causal relation can be inferred between the pair. We formulate the task as a *binary classification task*, classifying the relation as *causal* or *non-causal*. We evaluate our approach on a dataset $\mathcal{D} = \{\mathcal{X}, \mathcal{Y}\}$, where $\mathcal{X}$ is a set of training instances and $\mathcal{Y} = \{causal, non\text{-}causal\}$ is a set of relation labels. Each instance $x \in \mathcal{X}$ consists of a token sequence $x = \{w_1, w_2, ...w_{|n|}\}$ and the spans of a marked variable pair, and is annotated with a label $y_x \in \mathcal{Y}$.

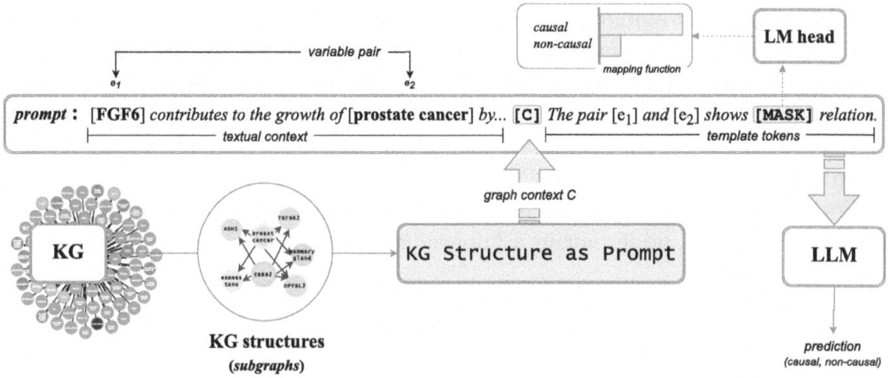

Fig. 2. Overall framework of our KG Structure as Prompt with prompt-based learning

4 Approach

We illustrate our proposed approach in Fig. 2. First, we generate a **graph context**, which is derived from the structural information of a knowledge graph with our KG Structure as Prompt method. Next, we feed the generated graph context and the inputs, i.e., the **variable pair** and its **textual context**, into the SLMs to train a prompt-based learning model.

We elaborate our proposed approach in the following subsections. We start with preliminaries (Sect. 4.1), followed by the design of the KG structure as Prompt for generating the graph context (Sect. 4.2), and the incorporation of the generated graph context into the SLMs architecture with prompt-based learning (Sect. 4.3).

4.1 Preliminaries

Formally, we define a directed graph $\mathcal{G} = (\mathcal{V}, \mathcal{E})$ where $\mathcal{V}$ is a set of vertices or nodes, and $\mathcal{E} \subseteq \mathcal{V} \times \mathcal{V}$ is a set of directed edges. A knowledge graph is a specific type of directed graph representing a network of entities and the relationships between them. Formally, we define a knowledge graph as a directed *labeled* graph $\mathcal{KG} = (N, E, R, \mathcal{F})$ where N is a set of nodes (entities), $E \subseteq N \times N$ is a set of edges (relations), R is a set of relation labels, and $\mathcal{F} : E \to R$, is a function assigning edges to relation labels. For instance, assignment label r to an edge $e = (x, y)$ can be viewed as a triple (x, r, y), e.g., (Tokyo, IsCapitalOf, Japan).

4.2 Knowledge Graph Structure as Prompt

In the field of Graph Neural Networks (GNNs), [44] explores whether LLMs can replace GNNs as the foundation model for graphs by using natural language to describe the geometric structure of the graph. Their results on several graph datasets surpass traditional GNN-based methods, showing the potential of LLMs as a new foundational model for graphs. Inspired by their success, we similarly leverage the structural information of a specific type of graph, i.e., a knowledge graph, to infer causal relationships between variable pairs. We select knowledge graphs due to their rich structured information and their capability to express interconnected relationships. We call our approach **"Knowledge Graph Structure as Prompt"**.

For instance, we may infer a causal relationship by looking at multi-hop relations between a node pair in a knowledge graph, as illustrated in Fig. 3.

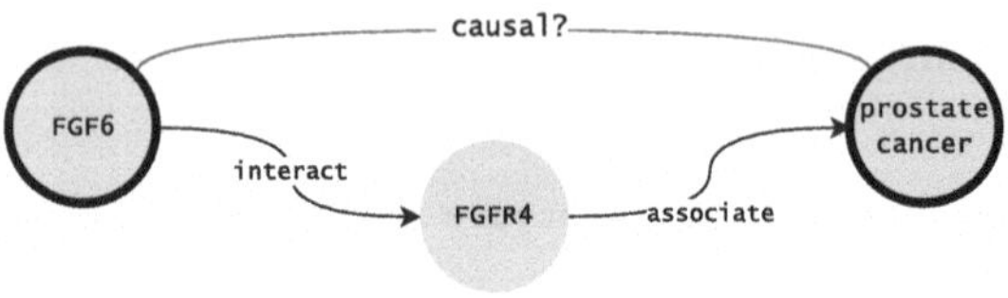

Fig. 3. Illustration of inferring a causal relationship in KG.

In Fig. 3, the node `FGF6` is *indirectly* connected to the node `prostate cancer` within one hop via the node `FGFR4`. As verified by a human expert, there is indeed a causal relation between the nodes `FGF6` and `prostate cancer`. We argue that such graph structural information, in this example a *path*, adds background knowledge on top of internal knowledge of LMs, effectively assisting LMs in inferring causal relation between the variable pair. Specifically, we aim to use a natural language description of the structural information from the knowledge graph to be used as a prompt for prompt-based learning. We refer to such a description of knowledge graph structure as a ***graph context***.

In this work, we specifically examine three kinds of vital structural information of a KG to be used as the graph context, namely **(1) neighbor nodes, (2) common neighbor nodes, (3)** ***metapath***, described in detail as follows.

(1) Neighbor Nodes ($\mathcal{NN}$). The essence of GNNs lies in applying different aggregate functions to the graph structure, i.e., passing node features to *neighboring nodes*, where each node aggregates the feature vectors of its neighbors to further update its feature vector. Thus, it is evident that the neighbor nodes are the most crucial feature within a graph. Inspired by that, we examine the neighboring nodes of the target node pairs to infer their causal relationship.

Formally, a node x is a **neighbor** of a node y in a knowledge graph $\mathcal{KG} = (V, E)$ if there is an edge $\{x, y\} \in E$. We provide an example of neighbor nodes from Wikidata [40] in Fig. 4. According to the provided example, the node `prostate cancer` has `urology` as one of its neighbor nodes, while `FGF6` has `urinary bladder` as one of its neigbors. Thus, it is likely that a connection exists between the node pair (`FGF6, prostate cancer`) due to their respective neighboring nodes: `urinary bladder` $\leftrightarrow$ `urology`.

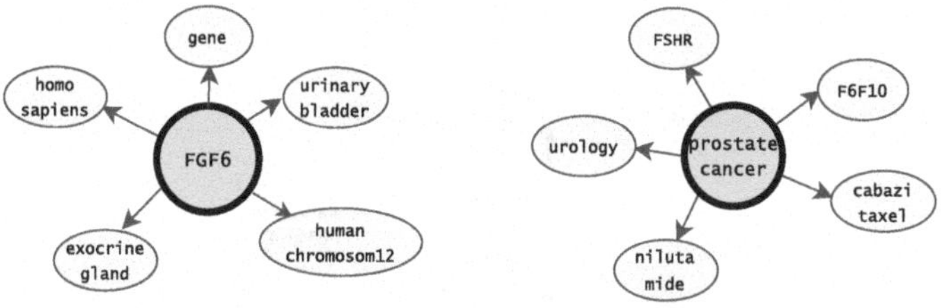

Fig. 4. Example of neighbor nodes for `FGF6` (*left*) and `prostate cancer` (*right*).

For utilizing the neighbor nodes structure in the prompt, we describe it in natural language to form a graph context $\mathcal{C}$, which we formally denote as:

$$\mathcal{C}(x, V, E) = \{x\} \text{“is connected to”} \{[x_2]_{x_2 \in V_2^x}\} \tag{1}$$

We also create a variation of $\mathcal{C}$ where we include the edge description/relation labels E, formally denoted as follows:

$$\mathcal{C}(x, V, E) = \{x\} \text{“has”} \{E_{x,x_2}\} \text{“relation with”} \{[x_2]_{x_2 \in V_2^x}\} \tag{2}$$

where V_k^x represents the list of node x's k-hop neighbor nodes and E_{x,x_2} represents the relation or edge description between the node x and its neighbor nodes. The additional template words such as *“is connected to”* and *“has relation with”* are optional, and can be replaced by any other fitting words. Then, with Eq. 1, the generated graph context C for the node `prostate cancer` in Fig. 4 is shown in the following Example 1.

Example 1. `prostate cancer` is connected to *nilutamide, cabazitaxel, urology, FSHR, F6F10*

When including the relation labels (Eq. 2), the graph context would be:

Example 2. `prostate cancer` has *drug or therapy used for treatment* relation with *nilutamide and cabazitaxel*, has *genetic association* with *FSHR and F6F10*

(2) Common Neighbor Nodes ($\mathcal{CNN}$). Unlike neighbor nodes, **common neighbor nodes** capture the idea that the more neighbors a pair of nodes (x, y) shares, the more likely it is for the pair to be connected, i.e., there exists an edge $e = x, y$ between them. We argue that common neighbors between two nodes help infer their relationship, so we examine the common neighbors information between the node pair as graph context, as well. Figure 5 shows an example of common neighbor nodes for the pair `(breast cancer, ERBB2)`, taken from Hetionet knowledge graph [17]. According to the provided example, the pair has in total 95 common neighbors, confirming a close relationship between them.

Formally, common neighbors between the nodes x and y can be defined as:

$$\mathcal{CN}\{x, y\} = N(x) \cap N(y) \tag{3}$$

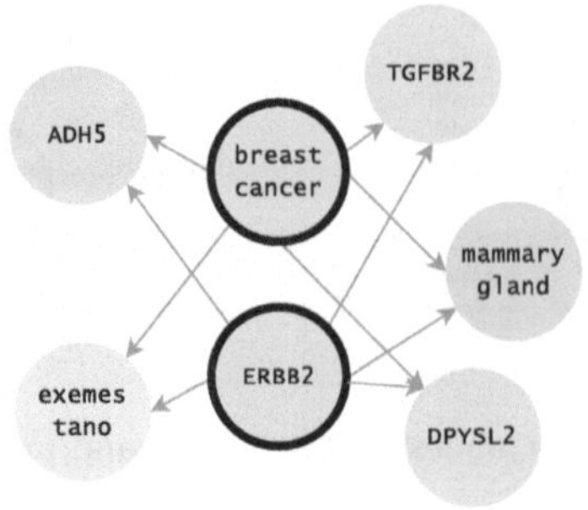

Fig. 5. Example of common neighbor nodes for the pair `(ERBB2, breast cancer)`. Different colors of the nodes represent different node types.

where $N(x)$ is the set of nodes adjacent to node x (the neighbors of x), and $N(y)$ is the set of nodes adjacent to node y (the neighbors of y). Subsequently, the graph context $\mathcal{C}$ for describing the common neighbors between the pairs x and y can be formed as follows:

$$\mathcal{C}(x, \mathcal{CN}, y) = \text{“Common neighbor nodes of } \{x\} \text{ and } \{y\} \text{ are”} : \{[n]_{n \in \mathcal{CN}}\} \quad (4)$$

where $\mathcal{CN}$ represents the list of common neighbor nodes of the pair x and y as defined in Eq. 3. Again, the additional template words *"Common neighbor nodes of..."* are optional and can be replaced by other words. Then, we can generate the graph context $\mathcal{C}$ including the common neighbor nodes information for the pair in Fig. 5, as follows:

Example 3. Common neighbor nodes of `breast cancer` and `ERBB2` are: *ADH5, mammary gland, exemestane, TGFBR2, DPYSL2*

(3) Metapath ($\mathcal{MP}$). *Metapaths*, or *meta-paths* are sequences of node types which define a walk from an origin node to a destination node [37]. The term "metapath" in this work is borrowed from the biomedical domain, referring to specific node type combinations thought to be informative [30]. Due to its importance in biomedical network analysis [41,43], we investigate the metapaths of two nodes for inferring their causal relationship. Moreover, causal relationships are frequently observed in the biomedical domain. Figure 6 shows examples of metapaths of the pair `prostate cancer` and `FGF6`.

Formally, a metapath $\mathcal{MP}$ can be defined as a path $Z_1 \xrightarrow{R_1} Z_2 \xrightarrow{R_2} ... \xrightarrow{R_n} Z_{n+1}$ describing a relation R between node types Z and Z_{n+1}. The following examples illustrate metapaths of different path length n from Fig. 6.

$\mathcal{MP}$ = `(FGF6, FGFR4, prostate cancer)`, composed of node types *{gene, gene, disease}*, with $n = 3$

$\mathcal{MP}$ = `(FGF6, tendon, SDRDL, FGFR2, prostate cancer)`, composed of node types *{gene, anatomy, gene, gene, disease}*, with $n = 5$

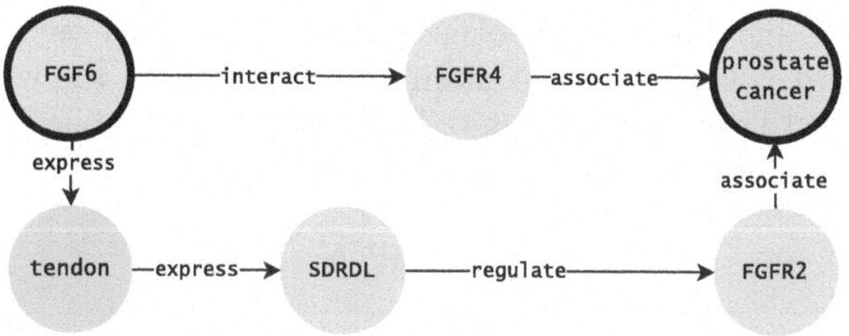

Fig. 6. Example of metapaths for the pair (FGF6, prostate cancer). Different colors of the nodes represent different node types.

As explained by the example provided in Fig. 3, we argue that an *indirect path* between two nodes can be useful for inferring a causal relation between two pairs, even when the edge itself does not describe a causal relation. Thus, an *indirect metapath*, or combination of meaningful node types could be *latent* evidence of causality between a pair of variables. We describe the metapath structure from KG in natural language to form a graph context $\mathcal{C}$, as follows:

$$\mathcal{C}(x, y, \mathcal{MP}\{V, E\}) = \{x\} \text{“is connected to”} \{y\} \text{“via the following path: ''} \{v\} \{E_{v,v_2}\} \{v_2\} \tag{5}$$

where $\mathcal{MP}\{V, E\}$ is a metapath $\mathcal{MP}$ with length n containing a set of nodes $V(v_1, v_2, ...v_{|n|})$ and a set of edges $E(v_1, v_{1+n})$. Additional tokens *"is connected to..."* are optional and can be replaced by other tokens. Then, the graph context $\mathcal{C}$ with metapath information for the example in Fig. 6 would be:

Example 4. FGF6 is connected to prostate cancer via the following paths: *FGF6 expressed in tendon, tendon expresses SQRDL, FGFR2 regulates SQRDL, FGFR2 associates with prostate cancer*

To prevent bias in prediction by the LMs, we avoid the *direct* path. For instance, for the pair (x, y), we avoid the path $\mathcal{MP} = (x, y)$ and $\mathcal{MP} = (y, x)$, when such path exists in the KG.

4.3 Prompt-Based Learning with *graph Context*

As illustrated in the model architecture in Fig. 2, we feed the **textual context** into SLMs together with the **graph context** generated with KG Structure as Prompt. We further design a prompt-based learning approach utilizing both contexts elaborated in this section. To get a clear distinction between conventional fine-tuning and our proposed prompt-based learning approach, we first provide a short overview of the conventional fine-tuning approach, as follows.

Given a pre-trained LM $\mathcal{L}$ to fine-tune on a dataset $\mathcal{D}$, the **conventional fine-tuning** method encodes the training sequence $x = \{w_1, w_2, ...w_{|n|}\}$ into the corresponding output hidden vectors of the LMs $h = \{h_1, h_2, ...h_{|n|}\}$. For MLMs such as BERT [8], the special token "[CLS]" is inserted at the beginning of the sequence, and this special token is used as the final sequence representation h', since it is supposed to contain information from the whole sequence. A fully-connected layer and a softmax layer are further applied on top of this representation to calculate the probability distribution over the class set $\mathcal{Y}$, as follows.

$$p = softmax(W_f h' + b_f) \tag{6}$$

Prompt-based learning, on the other hand, adapts the pre-trained LMs for the downstream task via priming on natural language ***prompts***–pieces of text that are combined with the input and fed to the LMs to produce an output for downstream tasks [1]. Concretely, we first convert each input sequence x with a template $\mathcal{T}$ to form a prompt x': $\mathcal{T} : x \mapsto x'$. In addition, a mapping function $\mathcal{M}$ is used to map the downstream task class set $\mathcal{Y}$ to a set of label words $\mathcal{V}$ constituting all vocabularies of the LM $\mathcal{L}$, i.e., $\mathcal{M} : \mathcal{Y} \mapsto \mathcal{V}$. As in the pre-training of LMs, we further insert the special token "`[MASK]`" into x' for $\mathcal{L}$ to fill with the label words $\mathcal{V}$. We provide an example of the prompt formulation below.

Given x ="Smoking causes cancer in adult male.", we set a template $\mathcal{T}$, e.g.,

$\mathcal{T}$ = $[x]$ "It shows `[MASK]` relation."

Then, the prompt x' would be:

x' = "Smoking causes cancer in adult male. It shows `[MASK]` relation."

We further feed the prompt x' into $\mathcal{L}$ to obtain the hidden vector $h_{\texttt{[MASK]}}$ of `[MASK]`. Next, with the mapping function $\mathcal{M}$ connecting the class set $\mathcal{Y}$ and the label words, we formalize the probability distribution over $\mathcal{Y}$ at the masked position, i.e., $p(y|x) = p(\texttt{[MASK]} = \mathcal{M}(y)|x')$. Here, the mapping function can also be set manually e.g., $\mathcal{M}(true)$ = "*causal*" and $\mathcal{M}(false)$ = "*non-causal*". Note that depending on the task, dataset, and the prompt design, the class labels themselves can be used directly without any mapping function $\mathcal{M}$.

In this study, our prompt-based learning combines the input sequence x with the graph context $\mathcal{C}$ into the prompt x', as illustrated in Fig. 2. Specifically, we formulate the prompt x' to include the following elements:

(1) textual context: input sequence x containing the pair,
(2) graph context $\mathcal{C}$: context generated from KG structures as described in Sect. 4.2,
(3) target pair: pair e_1 and e_2 as the target, e.g., `(FGF6, prostate cancer)`,
(4) `[MASK]` token,
(5) (*optional*) template tokens.

Subsequently, our final prompt x' as the input to the LM for the pair e_1 and e_2 can be formally defined as:

$$x' = [x]\ [\mathcal{C}]\ \text{The pair } [e_1] \text{ and } [e_1] \text{ shows a } \texttt{[MASK]} \text{ relation.} \tag{7}$$

In this study, we select three SLMs, one for each of the three architectures: MLM, CLM, Seq2SeqLM. Since each type of SLMs is trained differently, we design the prompt x' differently across each type of SLMs. For instance, the prompt x' in Eq. 7, which is a *cloze-style task* prompt, suits the MLM architecture, since this model is trained to be able to see the preceding and succeeding words in texts. As for CLM and Seq2SeqLM, we cast the task as a *generation*-type, with prompt x' such as:

$$x' = [x]\ [\mathcal{C}]\ \text{The pair}\ [e_1]\ \text{and}\ [e_2]\ \text{shows a causal relation:}\ \texttt{[MASK]}. \quad (8)$$

As mentioned earlier, the design of the mapping function $\mathcal{M}$ to map the output into the downstream task labels varies depending on the task, dataset, and the prompt design. For instance, with the prompt x' as in Eq. 7, we can directly use the class labels set $\mathcal{Y} = \{causal, non\text{-}causal\}$ without any mapping function. Meanwhile, for prompt x' in Eq. 8, we manually define a mapping function, e.g., $\mathcal{M}(causal)$ = "*true*" and $\mathcal{M}(non\text{-}causal)$ = "*false*". Note that the template "*The pair shows...*" is optional and can be replaced with other text.

5 Evaluation

Experiment Settings. We evaluate the proposed approach under few-shot settings, using $k = 16$ training samples across all experiments. Precision (P), Recall (R), and F1-score (F1) metrics are employed to evaluate the performance. Since fine-tuning on low resources often suffers from instability and results may change given a different split of data [35], we apply 5-fold cross-validation and the metric scores are averaged. We restrict the number of contents from the KG structures to be included in the prompt since the length of the prompt for SLMs is limited, and we restrict the number of hops when querying the KG, as well. We experimented with different settings and reported the best performing models. Additional technical details are provided online as supplementary materials.

Datasets. The evaluation datasets are summarized in Table 1. Causality is often observed in the biomedical domain, thus we primarily evaluate our approach within this field, supplemented by an open-domain dataset. Each instance in the dataset comprises textual context where a variable pair co-occurs in a text (see Example 5 & 6), and is annotated by human experts to determine if there is a causal relation between the variables.

Example 5. ***FGF6*** *contributes to the growth of* ***prostate cancer*** *by activating...*

Example 6. The deadly train ***crash*** *was caused by a terrorist* ***attack****.*

Table 1. Dataset sizes and types.

dataset	domain	total instances	description
GENEC (ours)	biomedical	789	gene-gene causality
DDI [16]	biomedical	33,508	drug-drug causality
COMAGC [22]	biomedical	820	gene-disease causality
SEMEVAL-2010 Task 8 [15]	open-domain	10,717	general domain causality

Choice of SLMs. In this work, we define SLMs as LMs with **less than 1 billion** of total parameters. We experimented with SLMs with three different architectures, as follows.

(a) MLM: `roberta` [27] model adapted to the biomedical domain, with 125 million parameters (`biomed-roberta-base-125m` [12]),
(b) CLM: `bloomz-560m` [29] with 560 million parameters,
(c) Seq2SeqLM: `T5-base-220m` [32] model with 220 million parameters

Choice of KGs. We selected the following two KGs for the experiments:

(a) Wikidata [40], as a representation of the general-domain KG,
(b) Hetionet [17], a domain-specific KG assembled from 29 different databases, covering genes, compounds, and diseases.

We selected Wikidata for its broad coverage of numerous subjects and topics. As a comparison, we selected biomedical-KG Hetionet since we primarily evaluate our approach on the datasets from this particular domain.

Model Comparison. We compare the following models: Models (1) to (4) represent the models trained without the graph context, i.e., the baselines, while models marked with "PBL" (model 5 to 7) are our proposed prompt-based learning method injected with graph context information from KGs.

(1) ICL: In-Context Learning refers to a prompting method where few demonstrations of the task are provided to the LLMs as part of the prompt [4]. For this method, we selected `GPT-3.5-turbo-instruct` model by OpenAI, and provided $k = 16$ samples as demonstrations to query the model.
(2) FT_{full}: Conventional Fine-Tuning models trained using the full datasets.
(3) $\text{FT}_{\text{few-shot}}$: Conventional Fine-Tuning models under few-shot $k = 16$ setting.
(4) $\text{PT}_{\text{few-shot}}$: Original Prompt Tuning [23] as a baseline, which is essentially prompt-based learning without any graph context.
(5) $\text{PBL}_{\mathcal{NN}\text{-Wiki-few-shot}}$:
Our proposed Prompt-based Learning + `KG Structure as Prompt` using the neighbor nodes $\mathcal{NN}$ structure from Wikidata.
(6) $\text{PBL}_{\mathcal{CNN}\text{-Het-few-shot}}$:
Our proposed Prompt-based Learning + `KG Structure as Prompt` using the common neighbor nodes $\mathcal{CNN}$ structure from Hetionet.

(7) $\text{PBL}_{\mathcal{MP}\text{-Het-few-shot}}$: Our proposed Prompt-based Learning + KG Structure as Prompt using the metapaths $\mathcal{MP}$ structure from Hetionet.

Some variants of the proposed approach, such as $\text{PBL}_{\mathcal{MP}\text{-Wiki-few-shot}}$, were omitted due to the computational expense of multi-hop querying in Wikidata, which often results in no usable metapaths for many pairs. In addition, to focus the discussion on the more effective models, we have omitted the results of less effective models, such as $\text{PBL}_{\mathcal{NN}\text{-Het-few-shot}}$. We provide the more complete results, including zero-shot prompting and classical ML experiment results, online as supplementary materials.

6 Results and Discussion

Tables 2 and 3 summarize the results. We report the averaged Precision (P), Recall (R), and F1 scores, including the standard deviation values of the F1 scores over the 5-folds cross-validation. We provide a summary of the primary findings (Sect. 6.1), followed by analysis and discussion of the results (Sect. 6.2).

6.1 Primary Findings

We listed the summary of the main results from Table 2 below.

(a) Our proposed approach outperforms the no-graph context baseline models, in most of the experiments across different dataset domains: up to 15.1 points of improvement of F1 scores on biomedical datasets (55.5 $\rightarrow$ 70.6, GENEC dataset) and 6.8 points of improvement on open-domain dataset (61.1 $\rightarrow$ 67.9, SEMEVAL dataset).
(b) Under few-shot settings with $k = 16$ training samples, our proposed approach generally achieves the second-best performance compared to FT_{full} model, which is the conventional fine-tuning models trained with full datasets. Few even surpassed them, such as $\text{PBL}_{\mathcal{NN}\text{-Wiki-few-shot}}$ model with MLM architecture (63.0 vs. 61.5) and $\text{PBL}_{\mathcal{CNN}\text{-Het-few-shot}}$ model with CLM architecture, on GENEC dataset (69.1 vs. 60.7).
(c) Our models based on SLMs with less that 1 billion parameters surpassed the ICL prompting method on much larger model across all datasets in most experiments, underlining the importance of KGs to support the constrained internal knowledge of smaller LMs.

6.2 Analysis and Discussion

$\mathcal{NN}$ vs. $\mathcal{CNN}$ vs. $\mathcal{MP}$ In our experiments, the KG structure *metapath* $\mathcal{MP}$ contributed the most to the top-performing models, while the neighbors nodes $\mathcal{NN}$ and common neighbors nodes $\mathcal{CNN}$ roughly exhibited comparable performance across models and datasets. The effectiveness of $\mathcal{MP}$ likely depends on the hop count between entity pairs in the dataset, i.e., the hop count is

Table 2. Evaluation results on biomedical-domain datasets. Values in parenthesis are the standard deviations of F1 scores over 5-cv test folds. $\mathcal{NN}$, $\mathcal{CNN}$, $\mathcal{MP}$ indicate the KG structures used as *graph context*: *neighbors nodes*, *common neighbors nodes*, and *metapath*, respectively. **bold**: highest F1 scores per LMs architecture and per dataset, underline: F1 scores of the highest-performed models per dataset.

	COMAGC			GENEC			DDI		
	P	R	F1	P	R	F1	P	R	F1
(baseline) ICL$_{\text{(GPT-3.5-turbo)}}$	64.1	67.7	65.5$_{(.18)}$	55.4	77.2	62.6$_{(.16)}$	53.2	99.0	68.9$_{(.08)}$
MLM architecture (`biomed-roberta-base-125m`)									
FT$_{\text{full}}$	90.0	86.8	88.2$_{(.02)}$	61.0	61.0	61.5$_{(.03)}$	84.0	98.9	90.7$_{(.04)}$
(baseline) FT$_{\text{few-shot}}$	87.0	71.0	76.8$_{(.02)}$	52.0	52.0	52.0$_{(.02)}$	64.9	87.0	73.9$_{(.07)}$
(baseline) PT$_{\text{few-shot}}$	87.0	77.2	80.6$_{(.03)}$	58.0	58.0	58.0$_{(.02)}$	69.6	83.0	75.4$_{(.03)}$
(ours) PBL$_{\mathcal{NN}\text{-Wiki-few-shot}}$	82.0	85.0	83.5$_{(.02)}$	63.0	63.0	**63.0**$_{(.03)}$	70.2	85.0	**$\underline{76.6}$**$_{(.03)}$
(ours) PBL$_{\mathcal{CNN}\text{-Het-few-shot}}$	77.4	89.5	82.7$_{(.05)}$	54.5	54.4	54.4$_{(.02)}$	65.1	89.9	74.6$_{(.05)}$
(ours) PBL$_{\mathcal{MP}\text{-Het-few-shot}}$	80.0	89.3	**$\underline{83.9}$**$_{(.03)}$	60.5	60.5	60.5$_{(.02)}$	67.0	87.6	75.4$_{(.02)}$
CLM architecture (`bloomz-560m`)									
FT$_{\text{full}}$	58.0	91.8	71.3$_{(.07)}$	53.8	73.0	60.7$_{(.07)}$	83.0	91.4	86.7$_{(.06)}$
(baseline) FT$_{\text{few-shot}}$	73.4	85.0	77.6$_{(.04)}$	48.2	86.0	61.7$_{(.01)}$	72.0	61.5	66.1$_{(.04)}$
(baseline) PT$_{\text{few-shot}}$	64.1	95.0	76.3$_{(.01)}$	51.3	97.0	67.6$_{(.01)}$	60.2	92.0	72.7$_{(.02)}$
(ours) PBL$_{\mathcal{NN}\text{-Wiki-few-shot}}$	71.7	90.9	79.0$_{(.02)}$	54.1	90.0	67.4$_{(.01)}$	63.3	88.0	72.6$_{(.02)}$
(ours) PBL$_{\mathcal{CNN}\text{-Het-few-shot}}$	65.7	94.7	77.2$_{(.05)}$	52.8	100	**69.1**$_{(.00)}$	60.4	93.9	72.8$_{(.05)}$
(ours) PBL$_{\mathcal{MP}\text{-Het-few-shot}}$	76.9	89.0	**81.8**$_{(.04)}$	52.8	91.0	68.5$_{(.03)}$	65.5	90.8	**74.8**$_{(.05)}$
Seq2SeqLM architecture (`T5-base-220m`)									
FT$_{\text{full}}$	88.5	78.0	82.6$_{(.07)}$	60.6	43.0	50.0$_{(.11)}$	96.3	83.0	88.8$_{(.04)}$
(baseline) FT$_{\text{few-shot}}$	68.8	81.0	72.7$_{(.06)}$	48.3	67.0	55.5$_{(.01)}$	55.6	94.0	69.6$_{(.04)}$
(baseline) PT$_{\text{few-shot}}$	64.5	91.0	75.0$_{(.05)}$	63.0	83.0	69.3$_{(.06)}$	63.3	82.0	70.3$_{(.04)}$
(ours) PBL$_{\mathcal{NN}\text{-Wiki-few-shot}}$	65.3	90.0	74.7$_{(.01)}$	66.5	76.0	70.3$_{(.02)}$	57.5	95.0	70.9$_{(.03)}$
(ours) PBL$_{\mathcal{CNN}\text{-Het-few-shot}}$	65.4	86.3	73.4$_{(.02)}$	56.0	95.8	**$\underline{70.6}$**$_{(.01)}$	56.2	96.0	70.6$_{(.02)}$
(ours) PBL$_{\mathcal{MP}\text{-Het-few-shot}}$	73.3	82.0	**75.6**$_{(.03)}$	56.5	91.0	69.7$_{(.02)}$	60.6	92.9	**72.9**$_{(.03)}$

Table 3. Evaluation results for open-domain dataset: SEMEVAL-2010 Task 8

	P	R	F1	P	R	F1	P	R	F1
(baseline) ICL$_{\text{GPT-3.5-turbo}}$	52.2	97.2	67.5$_{(.07)}$						
	MLM			CLM			Seq2SeqLM		
FT$_{\text{full}}$	94.8	88.7	91.6$_{(.02)}$	73.0	74.0	71.3$_{(.07)}$	82.8	77.0	79.4$_{(.02)}$
(baseline) FT$_{\text{few-shot}}$	57.2	83.0	67.2$_{(.04)}$	50.2	99.0	66.6$_{(.01)}$	52.1	90.9	61.1$_{(.04)}$
(baseline) PT$_{\text{few-shot}}$	51.9	94.0	66.9$_{(.00)}$	51.7	98.0	**67.6**$_{(.02)}$	52.5	93.0	66.7$_{(.02)}$
(ours) PBL$_{\mathcal{NN}\text{-Wiki-few-shot}}$	55.7	93.0	**$\underline{69.7}$**$_{(.01)}$	53.4	91.2	67.4$_{(.00)}$	53.7	93.0	**67.9**$_{(.01)}$

relatively high (2.8) for the COMACG dataset, where $\mathcal{MP}$ gave the best performance. Conversely, for the GENEC dataset, where the average $\mathcal{MP}$ hop is low (1.8), $\mathcal{CNN}$ and $\mathcal{NN}$ outperformed $\mathcal{MP}$. To train a robust model that is able to generalize well given any KG structure, we opted to not optimize the content selection of the KG structures in the current experiments. For instance, when there are more than m metapaths for a pair, we *randomly* select m of them, m being a *hyperparameter* of the number of metapaths to be included as prompt. In spite of that, our proposed approach achieved a relatively satisfactory performance, suggesting that rather than the content of the structure, the **type of the structural information**, i.e., $\mathcal{NN}$ vs. $\mathcal{CNN}$ vs. $\mathcal{MP}$, is arguably more important based on the experiments.

MLM Vs. CLM Vs. Seq2SeqLM. For classification tasks, language models trained with MLM architecture are often preferred. This preference comes from the fact that MLMs are trained to consider both preceding and succeeding words, a crucial aspect for accurately predicting the correct class in a classification model. In line with this, the top-performing models trained on both full and few-shot datasets are based on the MLM architecture. The second best-performing models using full dataset are based on the Seq2SeqLM architecture, followed by those based on the CLM architecture. This is most likely because, similar to MLMs, Seq2SeqLMs also include encoder blocks and are trained to recognize the surrounding words [32]. However, this trend slightly differs in experiments under few-shot settings, as the models based on CLM architecture outperformed those based on Seq2SeqLM architecture. Thus, selecting an appropriate architecture, specifically how the LMs are trained, is crucial when adapting the LMs for downstream tasks. As demonstrated by the outcomes of our experiments, LMs trained with the MLM architecture are generally more suitable for classification tasks than those with Seq2SeqLM and CLM architectures.

Wikidata Vs. Hetionet. In the biomedical domain, the proposed approach injected with structural information from Hetionet demonstrates better performance in most experiments. This is expected considering the domain-specific nature of the dataset. Nevertheless, both Wikidata and Hetionet performed relatively well; the top-performing models for COMAGC and GENEC datasets are attained with Hetionet, while for DDI dataset are achieved with Wikidata. We also achieved 6.8 points of F1 score improvement on SEMEVAL dataset with Wikidata. This suggests that the proposed approach is rather flexible regarding the choice of KGs.

SLMs Vs. LLMs. We selected OpenAI's `GPT-3.5-turbo-instruct` [31] as a representative of larger parameter-LLMs. However, OpenAI does not provide technical details such as the numbers of parameters; except the context windows which is 4,096 tokens in size for this model [31]. This is much larger than our choice of SLMs with a maximum token length ranging from 128 to 512. To summary, the results demonstrate that the SLMs outperformed this model across all datasets in most experiment. This further shows the potential of SLMs: combined with prompt-based learning and access to KGs, the proposed approach outperforms LLMs with considerably larger size and parameters, with minimal training effort (few-shot). Note that we also provided $k = 16$ training samples as task demonstration to query the GPT model for a more fair comparison with the experiments under few-shot settings.

Typically, SLMs are trained on significantly less data compared to LLMs, which leads to reduced capacity and inferior performance in downstream tasks. Therefore, the graph context derived from the structural information of KG by our proposed `KG Structure as Prompt` approach effectively serves as an additional *evidence of causality*; in other words, it assists the SLMs to rely not only on their constrained internal knowledge, but also by enhancing their capacity through denser information sourced from the KGs.

7 Conclusion

In this paper, we presented "`KG Structure as Prompt`", a novel approach for integrating structural information from KGs into prompt-based learning, to further enhance the capability of Small Language Models (SLMs). We evaluated our approach on knowledge-based causal discovery tasks. Extensive experiments under few-shot settings on biomedical and open-domain datasets highlight the effectiveness of the proposed approach, as it outperformed most of the no-KG baselines, including the conventional fine-tuning method with a full dataset. We also demonstrated the robust capabilities of SLMs: in combination with prompt-based learning and KGs, SLMs are able to surpass a language model with larger parameters. Our proposed approach has proven to be effective with different types of LMs architectures and KGs, as well, showing its flexibility and adaptability across various LMs and KGs.

Our work has been centered on discovering causal relationships between pairs of variables. In future work, we aim to tackle more complex scenarios by developing methods to analyze causal graphs with multiple interconnected variables, which will offer a deeper understanding of causalities.

Supplemental Material Statement: Datasets, source code, and other details are available online at https://github.com/littleflow3r/kg-structure-as-prompt

References

1. Agrawal, M., Hegselmann, S., Lang, H., Kim, Y., Sontag, D.: Large language models are few-shot clinical information extractors. In: Proceedings of the 2022 Conference on Empirical Methods in Natural Language Processing. pp. 1998–2022. Association for Computational Linguistics, Abu Dhabi, United Arab Emirates (Dec 2022). https://aclanthology.org/2022.emnlp-main.130

2. Baek, J., Aji, A.F., Saffari, A.: Knowledge-augmented language model prompting for zero-shot knowledge graph question answering. In: Dalvi Mishra, B., Durrett, G., Jansen, P., Neves Ribeiro, D., Wei, J. (eds.) Proceedings of the 1st Workshop on Natural Language Reasoning and Structured Explanations (NLRSE), pp. 78–106. Association for Computational Linguistics, Toronto, Canada (Jun 2023), https://aclanthology.org/2023.nlrse-1.7
3. Blanco, E., Castell, N., Moldovan, D.I.: Causal relation extraction. In: Proceedings of the International Conference on Language Resources and Evaluation, LREC 2008, 26 May - 1 June 2008, Marrakech, Morocco. European Language Resources Association (2008). http://www.lrec-conf.org/proceedings/lrec2008/summaries/87.html
4. Brown, T.B., et al.: Language models are few-shot learners. In: Larochelle, H., Ranzato, M., Hadsell, R., Balcan, M., Lin, H. (eds.) Advances in Neural Information Processing Systems 33: Annual Conference on Neural Information Processing Systems 2020, NeurIPS 2020, December 6-12, 2020, virtual (2020). https://proceedings.neurips.cc/paper/2020/hash/1457c0d6bfcb4967418bfb8ac142f64a-Abstract.html
5. Bui, Q.C., Nualláin, B.Ó., Boucher, C.A., Sloot, P.M.: Extracting causal relations on hiv drug resistance from literature. BMC Bioinform. **11**(1), 101 (Feb 2010). https://doi.org/10.1186/1471-2105-11-101
6. Chang, D.S., Choi, K.S.: Incremental cue phrase learning and bootstrapping method for causality extraction using cue phrase and word pair probabilities. Inform. Process. Manage. **42**(3), 662–678 (2006). https://www.sciencedirect.com/science/article/pii/S0306457305000580
7. Chen, X., et al.: Knowprompt: Knowledge-aware prompt-tuning with synergistic optimization for relation extraction. In: Proceedings of the ACM Web Conference 2022, p. 2778-2788. WWW '22, Association for Computing Machinery, New York, NY, USA (2022). https://doi.org/10.1145/3485447.3511998
8. Devlin, J., Chang, M.W., Lee, K., Toutanova, K.: BERT: Pre-training of deep bidirectional transformers for language understanding. In: Proceedings of the 2019 Conference of the North American Chapter of the Association for Computational Linguistics: Human Language Technologies, Volume 1 (Long and Short Papers), pp. 4171–4186. Association for Computational Linguistics, Minneapolis, Minnesota (Jun 2019). https://aclanthology.org/N19-1423
9. Gao, T., Fisch, A., Chen, D.: Making pre-trained language models better few-shot learners. In: Zong, C., Xia, F., Li, W., Navigli, R. (eds.) Proceedings of the 59th Annual Meeting of the Association for Computational Linguistics and the 11th International Joint Conference on Natural Language Processing (Volume 1: Long Papers), pp. 3816–3830. Association for Computational Linguistics, Online (Aug 2021). https://aclanthology.org/2021.acl-long.295
10. Glymour, C., Zhang, K., Spirtes, P.: Review of causal discovery methods based on graphical Models. Front. Genetics **10**(524) (2019). https://doi.org/10.3389/fgene.2019.00524
11. Gu, J., Qian, L., Zhou, G.: Chemical-induced disease relation extraction with various linguistic features. Database **2016** (04 2016). https://doi.org/10.1093/database/baw042, baw042
12. Gururangan, S., et al.: Don't stop pretraining: Adapt language models to domains and tasks. In: Jurafsky, D., Chai, J., Schluter, N., Tetreault, J. (eds.) Proceedings of the 58th Annual Meeting of the Association for Computational Linguistics, pp.

8342–8360. Association for Computational Linguistics, Online (Jul 2020). https://aclanthology.org/2020.acl-main.740
13. Han, J., Zhao, S., Cheng, B., Ma, S., Lu, W.: Generative prompt tuning for relation classification. In: Goldberg, Y., Kozareva, Z., Zhang, Y. (eds.) Findings of the Association for Computational Linguistics: EMNLP 2022, pp. 3170–3185. Association for Computational Linguistics, Abu Dhabi, United Arab Emirates (Dec 2022). https://aclanthology.org/2022.findings-emnlp.231
14. Han, X., Zhao, W., Ding, N., Liu, Z., Sun, M.: Ptr: prompt tuning with rules for text classification. AI Open **3**, 182–192 (2022). https://www.sciencedirect.com/science/article/pii/S2666651022000183
15. Hendrickx, I., et a.: SemEval-2010 task 8: multi-way classification of semantic relations between pairs of nominals. In: Proceedings of the 5th International Workshop on Semantic Evaluation, pp. 33–38. Association for Computational Linguistics, Uppsala, Sweden (Jul 2010). https://aclanthology.org/S10-1006
16. Herrero-Zazo, M., Segura-Bedmar, I., Martínez, P., Declerck, T.: The ddi corpus: An annotated corpus with pharmacological substances and drug-drug interactions. J. Biomed. Inform. **46**(5), 914–920 (2013). https://www.sciencedirect.com/science/article/pii/S1532046413001123
17. Himmelstein, D.S., et al.: Systematic integration of biomedical knowledge prioritizes drugs for repurposing. eLife **6**, e26726 (sep 2017). https://doi.org/10.7554/eLife.26726
18. Khetan, V., Rizvi, M.I., Huber, J., Bartusiak, P., Sacaleanu, B., Fano, A.: MIMICause: representation and automatic extraction of causal relation types from clinical notes. In: Findings of the Association for Computational Linguistics: ACL 2022, pp. 764–773. Association for Computational Linguistics, Dublin, Ireland (May 2022). https://aclanthology.org/2022.findings-acl.63
19. Khoo, C.S.G., Chan, S., Niu, Y.: Extracting causal knowledge from a medical database using graphical patterns. In: Proceedings of the 38th Annual Meeting on Association for Computational Linguistics, pp. 336-343. ACL '00, Association for Computational Linguistics, USA (2000). https://doi.org/10.3115/1075218.1075261
20. Khoo, C.S.G., Kornfilt, J., Oddy, R.N., Myaeng, S.H.: Automatic extraction of cause-effect information from newspaper text without knowledge-based inferencing. Literary Linguist. Comput. **13**(4), 177–186 (12 1998). https://doi.org/10.1093/llc/13.4.177
21. Kiciman, E., Ness, R., Sharma, A., Tan, C.: Causal reasoning and large language models: Opening a new frontier for causality. CoRR **abs/2305.00050** (2023). https://doi.org/10.48550/arXiv.2305.00050
22. Lee, H.J., Shim, S.H., Song, M.R., Lee, H., Park, J.C.: Comagc: a corpus with multi-faceted annotations of gene-cancer relations. BMC Bioinformatics **14**(1), 323 (Nov 2013). https://doi.org/10.1186/1471-2105-14-323
23. Lester, B., Al-Rfou, R., Constant, N.: The power of scale for parameter-efficient prompt tuning. In: Moens, M.F., Huang, X., Specia, L., Yih, S.W.t. (eds.) Proceedings of the 2021 Conference on Empirical Methods in Natural Language Processing, pp. 3045–3059. Association for Computational Linguistics, Online and Punta Cana, Dominican Republic (Nov 2021). https://aclanthology.org/2021.emnlp-main.243
24. Li, H., et al.: KiPT: Knowledge-injected prompt tuning for event detection. In: Proceedings of the 29th International Conference on Computational Linguistics, pp. 1943–1952. International Committee on Computational Linguistics, Gyeongju, Republic of Korea (Oct 2022). https://aclanthology.org/2022.coling-1.169

25. Li, X.L., Liang, P.: Prefix-tuning: optimizing continuous prompts for generation. In: Zong, C., Xia, F., Li, W., Navigli, R. (eds.) Proceedings of the 59th Annual Meeting of the Association for Computational Linguistics and the 11th International Joint Conference on Natural Language Processing (Volume 1: Long Papers), pp. 4582–4597. Association for Computational Linguistics, Online (Aug 2021), https://aclanthology.org/2021.acl-long.353
26. Liu, P., Yuan, W., Fu, J., Jiang, Z., Hayashi, H., Neubig, G.: Pre-train, prompt, and predict: A systematic survey of prompting methods in natural language processing. ACM Comput. Surv. **55**(9) (2023). https://doi.org/10.1145/3560815
27. Liu, Y., et al.: Roberta: A robustly optimized BERT pretraining approach. CoRR **abs/1907.11692** (2019). http://arxiv.org/abs/1907.11692
28. Mihăilă, C., Ananiadou, S.: Semi-supervised learning of causal relations in biomedical scientific discourse. BioMedical Engineering OnLine **13**(2), S1 (Dec 2014). https://doi.org/10.1186/1475-925X-13-S2-S1
29. Muennighoff, N., et al.: Crosslingual generalization through multitask finetuning. In: Rogers, A., Boyd-Graber, J.L., Okazaki, N. (eds.) Proceedings of the 61st Annual Meeting of the Association for Computational Linguistics (Volume 1: Long Papers), ACL 2023, Toronto, Canada, July 9-14, 2023, pp. 15991–16111. Association for Computational Linguistics (2023), https://doi.org/10.18653/v1/2023.acl-long.891
30. Noori, A., Li, M.M., Tan, A.L.M., Zitnik, M.: Metapaths: similarity search in heterogeneous knowledge graphs via meta-paths. Bioinformatics **39**(5), btad297 (2023). https://doi.org/10.1093/bioinformatics/btad297
31. OpenAI: Gpt-3.5-turbo. https://platform.openai.com/docs/models/gpt-3-5-turbo. Accessed 11 Apr 2024
32. Raffel, C., et al.: Exploring the limits of transfer learning with a unified text-to-text transformer. J. Mach. Learn. Res. **21**(140), 1–67 (2020). http://jmlr.org/papers/v21/20-074.html
33. Reklos, I., Meroño-Peñuela, A.: Medicause: causal relation modelling and extraction from medical publications. In: Tiwari, S., Mihindukulasooriya, N., Osborne, F., Kontokostas, D., D'Souza, J., Kejriwal, M., Bozzato, L., Carriero, V.A., Hahmann, T., Zimmermann, A. (eds.) Proceedings of the 1st International Workshop on Knowledge Graph Generation From Text and the 1st International Workshop on Modular Knowledge co-located with 19th Extended Semantic Conference (ESWC 2022), Hersonissos, Greece, May 30th, 2022. CEUR Workshop Proceedings, vol. 3184, pp. 1–18. CEUR-WS.org (2022). https://ceur-ws.org/Vol-3184/TEXT2KG_Paper_1.pdf
34. Schick, T., Schütze, H.: Exploiting cloze-questions for few-shot text classification and natural language inference. In: Merlo, P., Tiedemann, J., Tsarfaty, R. (eds.) Proceedings of the 16th Conference of the European Chapter of the Association for Computational Linguistics: Main Volume, pp. 255–269. Association for Computational Linguistics, Online (Apr 2021). https://aclanthology.org/2021.eacl-main.20
35. Schick, T., Schütze, H.: It's not just size that matters: Small language models are also few-shot learners. In: Toutanova, K., et al. (eds.) Proceedings of the 2021 Conference of the North American Chapter of the Association for Computational Linguistics: Human Language Technologies, pp. 2339–2352. Association for Computational Linguistics, Online (Jun 2021). https://aclanthology.org/2021.naacl-main.185

36. Su, P., Vijay-Shanker, K.: Investigation of improving the pre-training and fine-tuning of bert model for biomedical relation extraction. BMC Bioinform. **23**(1), 120 (Apr 2022). https://doi.org/10.1186/s12859-022-04642-w
37. Sun, Y., Han, J., Yan, X., Yu, P.S., Wu, T.: Pathsim: meta path-based top-k similarity search in heterogeneous information networks. Proc. VLDB Endow. **4**(11), 992–1003 (2011). https://doi.org/10.14778/3402707.3402736
38. Susanti, Y., Uchino, K.: Causal-evidence graph for causal relation classification. In: Hong, J., Park, J.W. (eds.) Proceedings of the 39th ACM/SIGAPP Symposium on Applied Computing, SAC 2024, Avila, Spain, April 8-12, 2024, pp. 714–722. ACM (2024). https://doi.org/10.1145/3605098.3635894
39. Tu, R., Ma, C., Zhang, C.: Causal-discovery performance of chatgpt in the context of neuropathic pain diagnosis. CoRR **abs/2301.13819** (2023). https://doi.org/10.48550/arXiv.2301.13819
40. Vrandečić, D., Krötzsch, M.: Wikidata: a free collaborative knowledgebase. Commun. ACM **57**(10), 78–85 2014). https://doi.org/10.1145/2629489
41. Wang, H., Wang, X., Liu, W., Xie, X., Peng, S.: deepdga: biomedical heterogeneous network-based deep learning framework for disease-gene association predictions. In: Adjeroh, D.A., et al. (eds.) IEEE International Conference on Bioinformatics and Biomedicine, BIBM 2022, Las Vegas, NV, USA, December 6-8, 2022, pp. 601–606. IEEE (2022), https://doi.org/10.1109/BIBM55620.2022.9995651
42. Willig, M., Zecevic, M., Dhami, D.S., Kersting, K.: Can foundation models talk causality? CoRR **abs/2206.10591** (2022). https://doi.org/10.48550/arXiv.2206.10591
43. Yao, W., Zhao, W., Jiang, X., Shen, X., He, T.: MPGNN-DSA: A meta-path-based graph neural network for drug-side effect association prediction. In: Adjeroh, D.A., et al. (eds.) IEEE International Conference on Bioinformatics and Biomedicine, BIBM 2022, Las Vegas, NV, USA, December 6-8, 2022, pp. 627–632. IEEE (2022), https://doi.org/10.1109/BIBM55620.2022.9995486
44. Ye, R., Zhang, C., Wang, R., Xu, S., Zhang, Y.: Language is all a graph needs. In: Graham, Y., Purver, M. (eds.) Findings of the Association for Computational Linguistics: EACL 2024, pp. 1955–1973. Association for Computational Linguistics, St. Julian's, Malta (Mar 2024). https://aclanthology.org/2024.findings-eacl.132
45. Zhang, C., et al.: Understanding causality with large language models: Feasibility and opportunities. CoRR **abs/2304.05524** (2023). https://doi.org/10.48550/arXiv.2304.05524

Repairing Networks of $\mathcal{EL}_{\perp}$ Ontologies Using Weakening and Completing

Ying Li[1,2(✉)] and Patrick Lambrix[1,2(✉)]

[1] Linköping University, Linköping, Sweden
{Ying.Li,Patrick.Lambrix}@liu.se
[2] The Swedish e-Science Research Centre, Linköping, Sweden

Abstract. The quality of ontologies and their alignments is crucial for developing high-quality semantics-based applications. Traditional debugging techniques repair ontology networks by removing unwanted axioms and mappings, but may thereby remove consequences that are correct in the domain of the ontology network. In this paper we propose a framework for repairing ontology networks that deals with this issue. It defines basic operations such as debugging, weakening and completing. Further, it defines combination operators that reflect choices in how and when to use the basic operators, as well as choices regarding the autonomy level of the ontologies and alignments in the ontology network. We show the influence of the combination operators on the quality of the repaired network and present an implemented tool. By using our framework together with existing algorithms for debugging, weakening and completing, we essentially provide a blueprint for extending previous work and systems.

1 Introduction

Ontologies and ontology networks, i.e., a set of ontologies connected through alignments, are core components in application scenarios that involve searching, integrating, managing and extracting value from diverse sources of data at large scale. In the latter case they are the input for machine learning and data mining applications in diverse fields such as business analytics, health, crime analysis, and materials design. They are also the structural part of knowledge graphs which are used by, e.g., major data and database providers such as Google, Amazon, Meta, and Neo4j. The quality of ontologies, ontology networks and knowledge graphs is crucial for developing high-quality semantics-based applications. However, ensuring their quality, in particular regarding completeness (or coverage, all relevant information is modeled) and correctness (no wrong information is modeled), is a major challenge [4,9,18,31,32].

Repairing ontology networks is a natural requirement for any application that would need to use several ontologies. We have, for instance, experience in a number of settings where an ontology network is repaired. A first example is the case of ontologies in the Ontology Alignment Evaluation Initiative (OAEI) where the ontologies to be aligned and a partial alignment were used to detect and repair defects [21] (and the results were sent to the ontology owners). Another example is the development of modular ontologies where the modules and connections

G. Demartini et al. (Eds.): ISWC 2024, LNCS 15231, pp. 107–125, 2025.
https://doi.org/10.1007/978-3-031-77844-5_6

between the modules have been repaired (e.g., [19]). Further, we have worked with companies that used publicly available ontologies as well as concern-wide ontologies and where the network of these were repaired (e.g., [10]).

The workflow for dealing with unwanted axioms in ontologies or networks consists of several steps including the detection and localization of the defects and the repairing. In this paper we assume we have detected defects and we now need to repair the ontologies and networks. In the classical approaches the end result is a set of axioms to remove from the ontology or network that is obtained after detection and localization, and the repairing consists solely of removing the suggested axioms. However, more knowledge than needed may be removed and approaches that alleviate the effect of removing unwanted axioms using weakening and completing have been proposed. In [24] a framework for repairing $\mathcal{EL}$ ontologies, based on the basic operations removing, weakening and completing, was proposed. Further, different combination operators were introduced that relate to choices that can be made when combining the basic operations (e.g., in which order to perform the operations, and when to update the ontologies). It was shown that the choice of combination has an influence on the amount of validation work by a domain expert and the completeness of the final ontology. It was also shown that earlier work on weakening (without completing) only considered one of the possible combinations. Similarly, earlier work on completing (without weakening) also considered only one of the possible combinations.

Our contributions in this paper relate to different ways in which we extend this framework. (i) A first extension is that we add the basic operation of debugging into the framework of [24]. We introduce combination operators for debugging and show the influence of the choice with respect to completeness, incorrectness and validation work (Sect. 2.3). (ii) As our first main contribution, we extend the framework in [24] to deal with ontology *networks*, formalize the problem, and show that new choices appear in addition to the choices for ontologies, when ontologies are connected with alignments (Sect. 3) (iii) As our second main contribution, we introduce different levels of autonomy for the ontologies and the alignments in the ontology network, reflecting the policies of the ontology and alignment owners regarding updating and computing for their ontologies and alignments (Sect. 3). We define combination operators based on these autonomy levels and show the influences on the quality of the repair and the validation work (Sect. 4). In general, there is a trade-off between the quality of the repaired ontologies on the one hand, and the amount of validation work for the oracle (e.g., domain experts) and the autonomy level for the ontologies and alignments on the other hand. We also give recommendations about which combinations to use in different cases, and we show that current systems for alignment repair (a special case of ontology network repair) use one particular combination of choices. In Sect. 5 we give examples of repairing existing ontology networks and (iv) in Sect. 6 we briefly describe an implemented tool that allows users to make different choices for the combination operators.

The only other work that discusses the combination of basic operations for repairing is [24] where the focus is on ontologies and the basic operations are removing, weakening and completing. For the basic operations different approaches can be used. As this paper is not about possible approaches for the basic operations, but rather about their combinations, we mention these approaches in Sect. 2.3 and refer for an overview that compares these approaches to [18]. This paper essentially treats the basic operations of debugging, weakening and completing as black boxes and does not put requirements on the actual implementation of these operations. Therefore, by using our framework and the combination operators together with existing algorithms for debugging, weakening and completing, we essentially provide a blueprint for extending previous work and systems.

Table 1. $\mathcal{EL}_\bot$ syntax and semantics.

Name	Syntax	Semantics
top	$\top$	$\Delta^\mathcal{I}$
bottom	$\bot$	$\emptyset$
conjunction	$P \sqcap Q$	$P^\mathcal{I} \cap Q^\mathcal{I}$
existential restriction	$\exists r.P$	$\{x \in \Delta^\mathcal{I} \mid \exists y \in \Delta^\mathcal{I} :$ $(x,y) \in r^\mathcal{I} \wedge y \in P^\mathcal{I}\}$
GCI	$P \sqsubseteq Q$	$P^\mathcal{I} \subseteq Q^\mathcal{I}$

2 Preliminaries

2.1 Description Logics

Description logics (DL) [2] are knowledge representation languages where concept descriptions are constructed inductively from a set N_C of atomic concepts and a set N_R of atomic roles and (possibly) a set N_I of individual names. Different DLs allow for different constructors for defining complex concepts and roles. An interpretation $\mathcal{I}$ consists of a non-empty set $\Delta^\mathcal{I}$ and an interpretation function $\cdot^\mathcal{I}$ which assigns to each atomic concept $P \in N_C$ a subset $P^\mathcal{I} \subseteq \Delta^\mathcal{I}$, to each atomic role $r \in N_R$ a relation $r^\mathcal{I} \subseteq \Delta^\mathcal{I} \times \Delta^\mathcal{I}$, and to each individual name[1] $i \in N_I$ an element $i^\mathcal{I} \in \Delta^\mathcal{I}$. The interpretation function is straightforwardly extended to complex concepts. A TBox is a finite set of axioms which in $\mathcal{EL}_\bot$ are *general concept inclusions* (GCIs). The syntax and semantics for $\mathcal{EL}_\bot$ are shown in Table 1.

An interpretation $\mathcal{I}$ is a *model* of a TBox $\mathcal{T}$ if for each GCI in $\mathcal{T}$, the semantic conditions are satisfied. We say that a TBox $\mathcal{T}$ is *inconsistent* if there is no model for $\mathcal{T}$. Further, a concept P in a TBox $\mathcal{T}$ is *unsatisfiable* if for all models $\mathcal{I}$ of $\mathcal{T}$:

[1] As we do not deal with individuals in this paper, we do not use individuals in the later sections.

$P^{\mathcal{I}} = \emptyset$. We say that a TBox is *incoherent* if it contains an unsatisfiable concept. One of the main reasoning tasks for DLs is subsumption checking[2] in which the problem is to decide for a TBox $\mathcal{T}$ and concepts P and Q whether $\mathcal{T} \models P \sqsubseteq Q$, i.e., whether $P^{\mathcal{I}} \subseteq Q^{\mathcal{I}}$ for every model $\mathcal{I}$ of TBox $\mathcal{T}$. In this paper we update the TBox during the repairing and we always use subsumption with respect to the current TBox.

2.2 Ontology Networks

In this paper we assume that ontologies are represented using DL TBoxes. An alignment between two ontologies is a set of mappings between the ontologies. A mapping between two ontologies is represented by $P \sqsubseteq Q$ where P is a concept in the first ontology and Q is a concept in the second ontology. Note that equivalence mappings (e.g., P is equivalent to Q) are represented by two subsumption mappings ($P \sqsubseteq Q$ and $Q \sqsubseteq P$). Although we base our work and examples on $\mathcal{EL}_{\perp}$, the discussions hold for ontologies represented by DLs in general. An ontology network is a collection of ontologies together with their alignments and can be represented by a TBox (Definition 1).[3] In the remainder we use the term axiom for the axioms in the ontologies and the mappings. When we mean axioms in the ontologies, we will explicitly state this.

Definition 1. Let $\mathcal{T}_1$, ...,$\mathcal{T}_n$ be TBoxes representing ontologies $\mathcal{O}_1$, ..., $\mathcal{O}_n$, respectively. For $i, j \in [1..n]$ with $i < j$, let $\mathcal{A}_{ij}$ be an alignment between ontology $\mathcal{O}_i$ and $\mathcal{O}_j$. The network of the ontologies and their alignments is then represented by TBox $\mathcal{T} = (\bigcup_{i=1..n} \mathcal{T}_i) \cup (\bigcup_{i,j=1..n, i<j} \mathcal{A}_{ij})$.

Our aim is to find repairs that remove as much wrong knowledge and add as much correct knowledge (back) to our ontology network as possible. Therefore, we use the preference relations *more complete* and *less incorrect* between TBoxes (Definitions 2 and 3) that formalize these intuitions [18]. Further, if a TBox representing an ontology (network) is more complete/less incorrect than the Tbox of an other ontology (network), then we say that the first ontology (network) is more complete/less incorrect than the second ontology (network). The definitions assume the existence of an oracle (representing a domain expert) that, when given an axiom, can answer whether this axiom is correct or wrong in the domain of interest of the ontology network.

Definition 2 (more complete). TBox $\mathcal{T}_1$ is *more complete* than TBox $\mathcal{T}_2$ (or $\mathcal{T}_2$ is *less complete* than $\mathcal{T}_1$) according to oracle Or iff $(\forall\psi : (\mathcal{T}_2 \models \psi \land Or(\psi) = true) \rightarrow \mathcal{T}_1 \models \psi)) \land (\exists\psi : Or(\psi) = true \land \mathcal{T}_1 \models \psi \land \mathcal{T}_2 \not\models \psi)$. They are *equally complete* iff $\forall\psi : Or(\psi) = true \rightarrow (\mathcal{T}_1 \models \psi \leftrightarrow \mathcal{T}_2 \models \psi)$

[2] Note that unsatisfiability checking in $\mathcal{EL}_{\perp}$ can be performed using subsumption checking. A concept P is unsatisfiable if $P \sqsubseteq \perp$. Further, we can express that two concepts P and Q are disjoint by requiring that $P \sqcap Q \sqsubseteq \perp$.

[3] We do not require that the ontologies in the network have the same signature.

Definition 3 (less incorrect). TBox $\mathcal{T}_1$ is *less incorrect* than TBox $\mathcal{T}_2$ ($\mathcal{T}_2$ is *more incorrect* than $\mathcal{T}_1$) according to oracle Or iff $(\forall\psi : (\mathcal{T}_1 \models \psi \wedge Or(\psi) = false) \rightarrow \mathcal{T}_2 \models \psi)) \wedge (\exists\psi : Or(\psi) = false \ \wedge \mathcal{T}_1 \not\models \psi \wedge \mathcal{T}_2 \models \psi)$. $\mathcal{T}_1$ and $\mathcal{T}_2$ are *equally incorrect* iff $\forall\psi : Or(\psi) = false \rightarrow (\mathcal{T}_1 \models \psi \leftrightarrow \mathcal{T}_2 \models \psi)$.

2.3 Basic Operations

To repair ontologies, algorithms can be developed using a number of basic operations such as removing, weakening and completing, and combining these in different ways [24]. In this paper we add a basic operation, debugging, and use variants of these operations to repair ontology networks.

Given a set of wrong axioms W, *debugging* aims to find a set of wrong `asserted` axioms D that when all axioms in D are removed from the network, the axioms in W cannot be derived anymore. Many debugging approaches have been proposed (e.g., [1,7,11,15–17,23,27–30,35,37–41], overview in [18])[4]. A basic approach is based on the computation of justifications for the wrong axioms and then computing a Hitting set over the set of justifications. As an example, in Fig. 1 derived wrong axiom A $\sqsubseteq$ C needs to be removed. This can be done by removing asserted axiom A $\sqsubseteq$ B or asserted axiom B $\sqsubseteq$ C. *Removing* deletes all the wrong asserted axioms in a given set D from the ontology network. Removing makes a network less or equally incorrect than it was before the operation. Given an axiom, *weakening* aims to find other axioms that are weaker than the given axiom, i.e., the given axiom logically implies the other axioms within the network. For the repairing this means that a wrong axiom $\alpha \sqsubseteq \beta$ can be replaced by a correct weaker axiom $sb \sqsubseteq sp$ such that sb is a sub-concept of α and sp is a super-concept of β, thereby mitigating the effect of removing the wrong axiom (Fig. 1). Algorithms for weakening have been provided in e.g., [3,5,24,42]. *Completing* aims to find correct axioms that are not derivable from the ontology yet and that would make a given axiom derivable. For a given axiom $\alpha \sqsubseteq \beta$, it finds correct axioms $sp \sqsubseteq sb$ such that sp is a super-concept of α and sb is a sub-concept of β (Fig. 1). This means that if $sp \sqsubseteq sb$ is added to $\mathcal{T}$, then $\alpha \sqsubseteq \beta$ would be derivable. Completing is performed on correct axioms, and in repairing, it is applied to weakened axioms. Completing algorithms are proposed in, e.g., [6,8,20,24,43]. Note that weakening and completing are dual operations where the former finds weaker axioms and the latter stronger axioms. Both these operations make an ontology network more or equally complete.

These basic operations can be combined in different ways and there are choices to be made in terms of, e.g., the order in which the operations are performed, the order in which the axioms are processed, whether one axiom is dealt with at a time or all at once, and when the TBox is updated. For removing, weakening and completing, the different combinations were classified in Hasse diagrams [24], and here we add a Hasse diagram for debugging (Fig. 2). Explanations for removing, weakening and completing are from [24] and are given in the

4 Many of these approaches use axiom pinpointing [33]. Further, there are other approaches that take ABoxes into account.

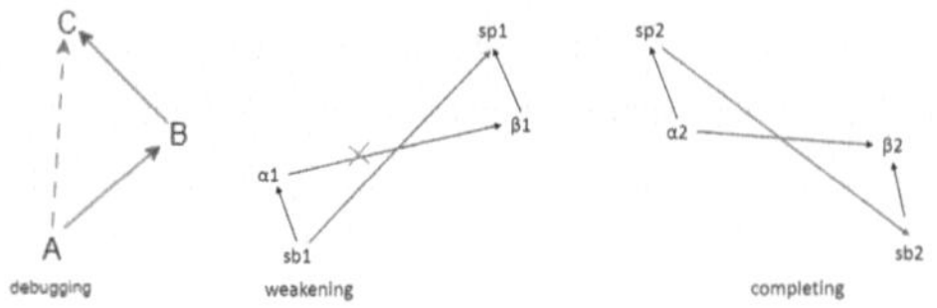

Fig. 1. Debugging, weakening and completing.

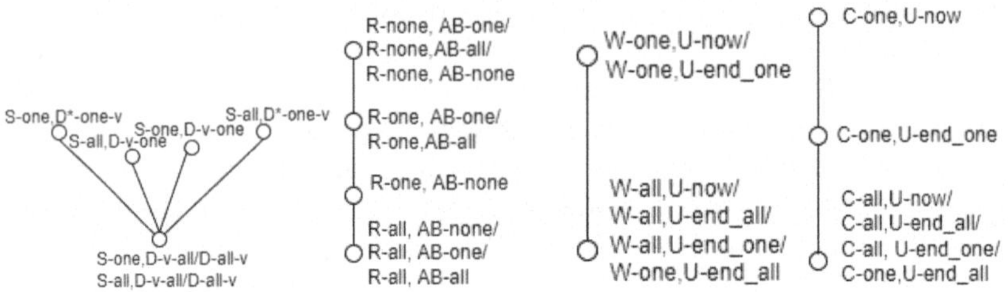

(a) Debugging (b) Removing (c) Weakening (d) Completing

Fig. 2. Hasse diagrams (b-d from [24]). (a) selecting and debugging; (b) removing and adding back wrong axioms; (c) weakening and updating; (d) completing and updating.

supplemental material. For debugging, we introduce the combination operators S-one, S-all, D-one-v, D-v-one and D-all-v/D-v-all. S-one and S-all represent the choices to calculate the justifications for one wrong axiom at the time or for all at once, respectively. The operations with a name starting with D concern choices regarding using the justifications to generate asserted wrong axioms to remove from the ontology. When using D-one-v, one Hitting set is generated from the justifications, and then the asserted axioms in the generated Hitting set are validated. With D-v-one, one valid Hitting set in the justifications is validated. Using D-all-v/D-v-all, all asserted axioms from the justifications are validated. Note that using D-one-v may not guarantee that a repair is found as axioms in the Hitting set may be correct and therefore should not be removed. The proof of the Hasse diagram for debugging is given in the supplemental material.[5]

In general, operations higher up in the diagrams use more (but also more possibly wrong) information during the computations and lead to more (or equally) complete ontologies, more (or equally) incorrect ontologies as well as more validation work for the domain expert. Algorithms for repairing can be defined by which of the operators are used and in which order. These algorithms can then be compared using the Hasse diagrams. In general, if the sequence of operators for one algorithm can be transformed into the sequence of operators of a second

[5] Note that the discussions and proofs for all Hasse diagrams in this paper hold for ontologies and ontology networks represented by DL TBoxes in general, and thus the results regarding the combination operators are language agnostic. When the framework is instantiated to create actual systems, then choices need to be made regarding which algorithms to use for the different basic operations, and the choice of these algorithms will, of course, also influence the completeness and correctness of an ontology or ontology network (but this is not the topic of this paper).

algorithm, by replacing some operators of the first algorithm using operators higher up in the Hasse diagrams in Fig. 2, then the ontologies repaired using the second algorithm are more or equally complete and incorrect than the ontologies repaired using the first algorithm. The work in [24] was the first to identify these different combinations. It also showed that previous work on combining removing with weakening used the combination (R-one, AB-none) with (W-one, U-now). Previous work on completing used (C-one, U-end-all). There was no work that used other combinations and no work that combined all basic operations.

Algorithm 1. Generate the justifications of each wrong axiom and validate all wrong asserted axioms from the generated justifications, weaken all wrong asserted axioms, complete all weakened axioms, add all completed axioms and remove all wrong asserted axioms at the end (S-one, D-v-all/R-none, AB-none/W-all, U-end_all/C-all, U-end_all).

```
Input: TBox T, Oracle Or, set of unwanted axioms W
Output: A repaired TBox
D ← ∅
for each α ⊑ β ∈ W do
    for each J ∈ Justifications(α ⊑ β) do
        for each axiom ∈ J do
            if Validate_axiom(axiom, Or) = false then
                D ← D ∪ {axiom}
            end if
        end for
    end for
end for
for each α ⊑ β ∈ D do
    w_{α⊑β} ← weakened-axiom-set(α ⊑ β, T, Or)
end for
c_{α⊑β} ← ∅
for each α ⊑ β ∈ D do
    for each sb ⊑ sp ∈ w_{α⊑β} do
        c_{sb⊑sp} ← completed-axiom-set(sb ⊑ sp, T, Or)
        c_{α⊑β} ← c_{α⊑β} ∪ c_{sb⊑sp}
    end for
end for
T_r ← Add-axioms(T, ⋃_{α⊑β} c_{α⊑β})
T_r ← Remove-axioms(T_r, D)
return T_r
```

For the examples in this paper we have used Algorithm 1 as a basis for discussing repairing of ontology networks. It uses a particular combination of debugging, removing, weakening and completing with specific algorithms for the basic operations. Our discussion regarding the choices for *ontology networks* (Sect. 3) would still hold if we used other algorithms for the basic operations, or different combination operators for the basic operators.

3 Repairing Ontology Networks Problem Definition

In this section we define the repairing problem for ontology networks. Definition 4 is an extension of the definition of repair for single ontologies as defined in [24]. We are given a set of wrong axioms W that we want to remove from the ontology network, and when they are removed, they cannot be derived from the TBox representing the ontology network anymore. These axioms in W can be axioms in the ontologies or mappings. Further, to guarantee a high level of quality of the ontology (i.e., so that no correct information is removed or no incorrect information is added), domain expert validation is a necessity (e.g., [24,34]). Therefore, we assume an oracle (representing a domain expert) that, when given an axiom, can answer whether this axiom is correct or wrong in the domain of interest of the ontology network. A repair (A, D) for the ontology network given the TBox $\mathcal{T}$, oracle Or, and a set of wrong axioms W, is a tuple containing two sets: a set A of axioms that are correct according to the oracle and should be added to the TBox, and a set D of asserted axioms that are not correct according to the oracle and should be removed from the TBox. We require that when the axioms in D are removed and the axioms in A are added, the wrong axioms in W cannot be derived anymore.

Definition 4 (Repair). Let TBox $\mathcal{T} = (\bigcup_{i=1..n} \mathcal{T}_i) \cup (\bigcup_{i,j=1..n,i<j} \mathcal{A}_{ij})$ represent a network of ontologies $\mathcal{O}_i$ represented by TBoxes $\mathcal{T}_i$, and their alignments $\mathcal{A}_{ij}$. Let Or be an oracle that given a TBox axiom returns true or false. Let W be a finite set of TBox axioms in $\mathcal{T}$ such that $\forall\ \psi \in W$: $Or(\psi)$ = false. Then, a repair for Debug-Problem DP($\mathcal{T}, Or, W$) is a tuple (A, D) where A and D are finite sets of TBox axioms such that
(i) $\forall\ \psi \in A$: $Or(\psi)$ = true;
(ii) D is a finite set of *asserted* axioms in $\mathcal{T}$;
(iii) $\forall\ \psi \in D$: $Or(\psi)$ = false;
(iv) $\forall\ \psi \in W$: $(\mathcal{T} \cup A) \setminus D \not\models \psi$.

From a theoretical point of view, as we have represented the ontology network as a TBox, and previous work has represented ontologies as TBoxes, we could reuse the algorithms and approaches in, e.g., [24]. However, from a practical point of view, the situation is more complex. When working with single ontologies, it is in the interest and mandate of the ontology owners to repair their ontologies. However, when ontologies are connected in a network, the ontology and alignment owners may want to retain different levels of autonomy and not necessarily allow others to change or propose changes to their ontologies and alignments. Also, computation time and validation work for repairing may be issues. In this case, computation time and validation work may be lower within an ontology or alignment than for the whole network. In this paper we discuss three levels of autonomy and show the influence of these different choices.

The first level consists of the cases 'O' (ontology) and 'M' (mappings). 'O' represents the choice where ontologies are completely autonomous. Essentially, this means that ontologies act on their own regarding detection and repairing of defects. W in Definition 4 contains only axioms in the ontology, only the axioms within the ontology itself can be used for the computation of repairs, and solutions can only include axioms in the ontology itself. A dual case is 'M' where the owners of an alignment are autonomous. In this case W contains only mappings, and the alignment is repaired using only the mappings in the alignment. The second level consists of the cases 'MO' (materialized ontology) and 'MM' (materialized mappings). 'MO' uses the network to derive new axioms within the ontology and materializes these axioms.[6] W contains only axioms in the ontology. For the computation of repairs the materialized ontology is used, and solutions contain only axioms within the ontology. This level accepts the fact that the network provides more knowledge about the own ontology than is represented by the ontology itself, and accepts this knowledge, but it does not use the network in repairing. 'MM', the dual case for mappings, computes derived mappings for the alignment, but then acts autonomously. W contains only mappings. The third level 'ON' (ontology network) considers the ontologies and alignments as integral parts of the network, uses the full network for the computation of repairs, and repairs defects using axioms within all ontologies and alignments. W can contain ontology axioms and mappings. We note that different ontology and alignment owners may make different choices regarding their level of autonomy.

These choices have an influence on the detection and repairing of effects. We give an example for the detection here, and focus on the repairing in further sections. For the network in Fig. 3 we have the following situation. Using the full network (level 'ON'), we can derive that concepts E, F, e, and f are unsatisfiable.[7] Using level 'MO' for both ontologies, we materialize $\mathrm{E} \sqsubseteq \mathrm{D}$ and $\mathrm{F} \sqsubseteq \mathrm{E}$ in the first ontology, and $\mathrm{e} \sqcap \mathrm{b} \sqsubseteq \bot$ in the second ontology. This allows us to obtain the same unsatisfiable concepts as in the 'ON' level (although the repairing will be different). When using level 'O' for both ontologies, we cannot detect any unsatisfiable concepts.

In general, there is a trade-off between the quality of the repaired ontologies on the one hand, and the amount of validation work for the oracle and the autonomy level for the ontologies and alignments on the other hand. In the next sections we define and exemplify these notions.

4 Repairing Ontology Networks Combination Operators

During the repairing process different levels of autonomy can be used at different stages. The choice has an influence on the quality of the repair. Here we show this influence for different stages.

[6] We note that a choice may be made regarding which axioms to materialize. For taxonomies it may be feasible to materialize all. However, for $\mathcal{EL}_\bot$ there is an infinite number of derivable axioms. In our experiments we restrict the space to axioms with concepts at the left- and right-hand side with non-nested operators (SCC in [24]).

[7] E unsatisfiable because $\mathrm{D} \sqcap \mathrm{E} \sqsubseteq \bot$, $\mathrm{E} \sqsubseteq \mathrm{e}$, $\mathrm{e} \sqsubseteq \mathrm{b}$, $\mathrm{b} \sqsubseteq \mathrm{D}$. e unsatisfiable because E unsatisfiable and $\mathrm{e} \sqsubseteq \mathrm{E}$. f unsatisfiable because e unsatisfiable and $\mathrm{f} \sqsubseteq \mathrm{e}$. F unsatisfiable because f unsatisfiable and $\mathrm{F} \sqsubseteq \mathrm{f}$.

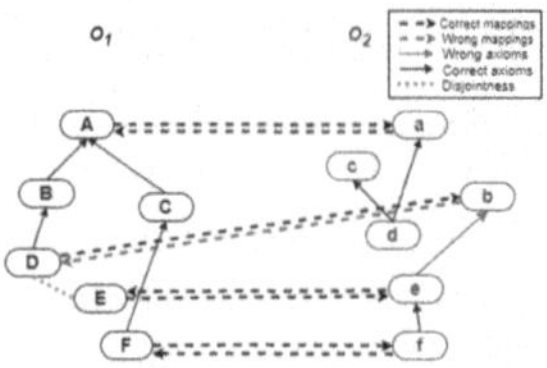

(a)

$N_{C_{O1}}$ = { A, B, C, D, E, F }; $N_{C_{O2}}$ = { a, b, c, d, e, f };
$\mathcal{T}_{O1}$ = { B ⊑ A, D ⊑ B, C ⊑ A, F ⊑ C, D ⊓ E ⊑ ⊥ }
$\mathcal{T}_{O2}$ = { d ⊑ a, d ⊑ c, e ⊑ b, f ⊑ e }
$\mathcal{A}$ = { A ⊑ a, a ⊑ A, D ⊑ b, b ⊑ D, E ⊑ e, e ⊑ E, F ⊑ f, f ⊑ F }
W = { e ⊑ b, b ⊑ D }
Or returns *true* for:
B ⊑ A, D ⊑ B, C ⊑ A, D ⊑ A, F ⊑ C, F ⊑ E, E ⊑ C, E ⊑ A, F ⊑ A,
d ⊑ a, d ⊑ c, f ⊑ e, f ⊑ b, e ⊑ d, e ⊑ c, e ⊑ a, f ⊑ d, f ⊑ c, f ⊑ a, b ⊑ a,
A ⊑ a, a ⊑ A, E ⊑ e, e ⊑ E, F ⊑ f, f ⊑ F, D ⊑ b, b ⊑ B, B ⊑ b, F ⊑ e,
f ⊑ E, f ⊑ C, f ⊑ B, f ⊑ A, e ⊑ A, F ⊑ b, F ⊑ c, F ⊑ d, F ⊑ a, E ⊑ c,
E ⊑ d, E ⊑ a, e ⊑ C, b ⊑ A, d ⊑ A, B ⊑ a, C ⊑ a, D ⊑ a
For other non-trivial axioms P ⊑ Q with P, Q ∈ N_C, *Or*(P ⊑ Q) = false.

(b)

Fig. 3. The network contains unsatisfiable concepts E, F, e, and f. Asserted axiom e ⊑ b in O_2, and mapping b ⊑ D between O_2 and O_1 lead to network incoherence.

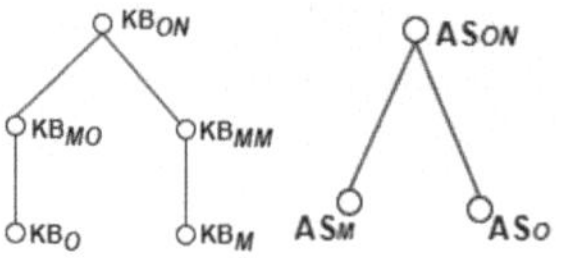

(a) (b)

Fig. 4. Hasse diagrams regarding (a) the use of different knowledge bases during repairing (KB); (b) different restrictions on the add set (AS);

4.1 Use of Background

As discussed earlier, we can use different autonomy levels during the computation of repairs. In our algorithms, this is reflected by which TBox is used. We can combine particular choices for debugging, removing, weakening and completing algorithms with different autonomy levels. As an example, assume we have made the choices for the basic operations as in Algorithm 1. Then, for autonomy level 'ON' we can use Algorithm 1 with as input the TBox representing the whole network. For levels 'O' and 'MO' we can use Algorithm 1 repeatedly using each of the TBoxes of the ontologies or materialized ontologies, respectively. (Another possibility is to use as input the union of these TBoxes, i.e., there will be no axioms representing mappings in the network.) For 'M' and 'MM' we use the alignments or materialized alignments as TBoxes. The choices are explained in Table 2 where KB stands for 'knowledge base'. Note that the choices can be performed on each of the basic operations. For instance, it is possible to debug using 'ON' and then weaken and complete using 'MO'. We can organize the choices in a Hasse diagram as in Fig. 4(a). The proofs for the Hasse diagram are given in the supplemental material. In general, using more background knowledge leads to more (or equally) complete and more (or equally) incorrect networks, and more validation work by the oracle.

As an example, assume we have used 'ON' in the debugging step where we validate all axioms in the justifications, for the network in Fig. 3. This results in wrong axioms e ⊑ b and b ⊑ D. We now look at the weakening step for the different autonomy levels. When weakening e ⊑ b in the second ontology, we use sub-concepts of e and super-concepts of b to find weakened axioms. These sets

Table 2. Choices for background knowledge (KB) and add sets (AS).

Choices	Description
KB_{ON}	Use the whole ontology network as the background knowledge base to compute the sub/sup-concepts when weakening and completing an axiom.
KB_{MO}	Materialize each ontology in the network. Disconnect each ontology from the ontology network. Use only the axioms within the materialized ontologies to compute the sub/sup-concepts when weakening and completing an axiom.
KB_{O}	Disconnect each ontology from the ontology network. Use the axioms within the respective ontologies to compute the sub/sup-concepts when weakening and completing an axiom.
KB_{MM}	Materialize each alignment in the network. Disconnect each alignment from the ontology network. Use only the mappings within the materialized alignments to compute the sub/sup-concepts when weakening and completing an axiom.
KB_{M}	Disconnect each alignment from the ontology network. Use the mappings within the respective alignments to compute the sub/sup-concepts when weakening and completing an axiom.
AS_{ON}	Add all axioms.
AS_{O}	Add only axioms within the respective ontologies.
AS_{M}	Add only mappings between the ontologies.

are different for different autonomy levels. We have Sub(e, KB_O) = {e, f}, Sub(e, KB_{MO})={e, f}, Sub(e, KB_{ON})={e, f, E, F}, and Sup(b, KB_O)={b}, Sup(b, KB_{MO})={b, a}, Sup(b, KB_{ON})={b, a, D, B, A}. Therefore, there are 2, 4 and 20 candidates for the weakened axioms for 'O', 'MO' and 'ON', respectively. After validation we have as weakened axioms f $\sqsubseteq$ b for 'O', f $\sqsubseteq$ b and e $\sqsubseteq$ a for 'MO', and f $\sqsubseteq$ b, e $\sqsubseteq$ a, and E $\sqsubseteq$ A for 'ON' (Table 3). As expected from the Hasse diagram, 'ON' leads to the most complete network, followed by 'MO' and then 'O'. When weakening the wrong mapping b $\sqsubseteq$ D, we can choose between 'M', 'MM' and 'ON'. We have Sub(b, KB_M)={b, D}, Sub(b, KB_{MM}) = Sub(b, KB_{ON})={e, f, b, D, E, F}, Sup(D, KB_M)={D, b}, and Sup(D,KB_{MM}) = Sup(D, KB_{ON})={D, A, B, b, a}.[8] For 'M' there are no weakened axioms. For 'MM' we find b $\sqsubseteq$ B. For 'ON' we find b $\sqsubseteq$ B and e $\sqsubseteq$ a. The latter includes both mappings and ontology axioms. Table 3 also shows the results after completing the weakened axioms using the same autonomy level as for weakening. The network is repaired by removing the wrong axioms and adding the completed axioms.

[8] All algorithms for debugging, weakening and completing use heuristics when computing the sub-concepts and super-concepts to prune the search space of solutions [18,24]. Also for the networks different heuristics can be used. For instance, when computing the sub- and super-concepts for the concepts in mappings, one heuristic is to only allow sub- and super-concepts in the same ontology. In the example we have allowed sub- and super-concepts to belong to other ontologies as long as they are involved in mappings.

Table 3. Weakening and completing the wrong axioms e $\sqsubseteq$ b and b $\sqsubseteq$ D.

Background knowledge base	KB_O e $\sqsubseteq$ b	KB_{MO} e $\sqsubseteq$ b	KB_{ON} e $\sqsubseteq$ b	KB_M b $\sqsubseteq$ D	KB_{MM} b $\sqsubseteq$ D	KB_{ON} b $\sqsubseteq$ D
$\lvert Sub(\alpha,\mathcal{T})\rvert$	2	2	4	2	6	6
$\lvert Sup(\beta,\mathcal{T})\rvert$	1	2	5	2	5	5
Weakened	f $\sqsubseteq$ b	f $\sqsubseteq$ b, e $\sqsubseteq$ a	f $\sqsubseteq$ b, e $\sqsubseteq$ a, E $\sqsubseteq$ A		b $\sqsubseteq$ B	b $\sqsubseteq$ B, e $\sqsubseteq$ a
$\lvert Sup(\alpha,\mathcal{T})\rvert$	2	4 3	10 7 7		5	5 7
$\lvert Sub(\beta,\mathcal{T})\rvert$	1	3 5	6 11 11		7	7 11
Completed	f $\sqsubseteq$ b	f $\sqsubseteq$ b, e $\sqsubseteq$ d	f $\sqsubseteq$ b, e $\sqsubseteq$ d, E $\sqsubseteq$ C		b $\sqsubseteq$ B, B $\sqsubseteq$ b	b $\sqsubseteq$ B, B $\sqsubseteq$ b

4.2 Add Sets

Another stage where the choice of autonomy level influences the quality of the repair is when deciding what repairing solutions to retain for the final repair, i.e. A in Definition 4. The choices are summarized in Table 2 under 'AS' (Add Set). Choice AS_{ON} is the most general case and allows all kinds of axioms to be added to the network. This means that regardless which choice was used during the computation of the repairs, these repairs can be used without any adaptions. Choice AS_O only allows to add axioms within ontologies. This represents the case where ontology owners only focus on repairing their own ontologies. Similarly, choice AS_M only allows to add mappings and represents the case where alignment owners only focus on repairing their own mappings. In AS_O and AS_M, not all repairing suggestions may be retained for the final solution. Therefore, when 'ON' was used during the computation of repairs and 'O' or 'M' is used during this stage, this may lead to a lower level of completeness for the network than if 'ON' is used for this stage. The Hasse diagram for these choices is given in Fig. 4(b) and the proofs are given in the supplemental material.

4.3 Finalizing

In the case of 'ON' the repairing solutions may contain axioms in different ontologies as well as mappings. In this case the ontology and alignment owners may decide to materialize the knowledge derived from the network which regards their ontology or alignment. From the network point of view the network does not change logically as the same axioms can be derived. From the ontology or alignment point of view, the difference appears when they are disconnected from the network. The materialized versions are more (or equally) complete.

4.4 Discussion

When the network is owned by one entity (e.g., in the case of modular ontologies with mappings) or there is a tight cooperation between the owners of the individual parts of the network (e.g., in a consortium such as EMMO (https://github.com/emmo-repo/EMMO) or OBO (https://obofoundry.org/)), and computation time and domain expert staff is not an issue, the recommended combination is to use (KB_{ON}, AS_{ON}, final materialization). This ensures the highest level of completeness for the network as well as for the ontologies and alignments when they are disconnected from the network.

The least complete networks come from the combinations (KB_O, AS_O) and (KB_M, AS_M). Essentially, this means that mappings between the ontologies exist, but the network is not taken into account at all during repairing. The repairs are the same as when repairing is done without the network, and this seems to be a common case in practice.

When ontology or alignment owners require full control over the computation resources, while still taking into account the knowledge in the network, then the combinations with KB_{MO} and KB_{MM} may be a good choice. Maintaining full control about what is added leads to choices with AS_O and AS_M.

In the ontology alignment field there are alignment systems that also repair the alignment. The current systems require that the repair only contains mappings and thus use AS_M. Examples of such systems are ALCOMO [26], LogMap [13,14], AgreementMakerLight [36]. Regarding the background knowledge, they all use the choice KB_{ON}. RaDON [12] is a system focusing on network repair, but makes the same choices as the alignment systems with repair functionality.

5 Experiments

As examples of the use of different choices for the combination operators, we performed experiments on 5 ontology networks. The ontologies (ekaw, sigkdd, iasted, cmt) used in these networks are from the conference track of the OAEI[9]. We have used the parts of these ontologies that are expressible in $\mathcal{EL}_\perp$ in the sense that we removed the parts of axioms that used constructors not in $\mathcal{EL}_\perp$. We introduced wrong axioms in the ontologies and mappings between ontologies by replacing existing axioms with axioms where the left-hand or right-hand side concepts of the existing axioms were changed. Further, we also flagged some existing axioms as wrong in our full experiment set. All axioms were validated manually. The characteristics of the ontologies and the wrong axioms are shown in the supplemental material.

We repaired the networks using all choices regarding the use of background knowledge together with Algorithm 1. To repair ontology axioms we used KB_O, KB_{MO} and KB_{ON}. To repair mappings we used KB_M, KB_{MM} and KB_{ON}. We computed the sizes of the sets of sub-concepts and super-concepts used in weakeing and completing. The sizes of these sets reflect the number of axioms that need to be validated by the oracle. We note, however, that using the visualization in our system (see below) these sets are shown together and thus the validation of many axioms can be done at the same time.

[9] http://oaei.ontologymatching.org/2023/conference/index.html.

The full results for the experiments are shown in the supplemental material. In the experiments, the number of axioms to be validated for KB_{ON} is between 3 and 5 times higher than for KB_O/KB_M. The validation work for the materialized versions KB_{MO}/KB_{MM} is between 6% and 40% higher than for KB_O/KB_M. For all networks there were axioms for which the repairing with an operator higher up in the Hasse diagram led to a strictly more complete ontology network.

6 Implemented System

We implemented a Java-based system which extends the $\mathcal{EL}$ version of the RepOSE system ([22,24,43]) with full debugging, weakening and completing for $\mathcal{EL}_\perp$ ontology network repairing. The system allows the user to choose different combinations, thereby giving a choice in the trade-off between validation work, incorrectness and completeness.

The system uses an interactive way to repair the ontology network. It takes as input the ontologies and alignments in the network as well as a set of wrong axioms. It is also possible to not give a set of wrong axioms but let the system deduce unsatisfiable concepts in the network. As basic algorithms, we have used the black-box algorithm in [15] for debugging, and the weakening and completing algorithms in [24]. With respect to the combination operators in the Hasse diagrams, the system supports (S-one, D-v-all) and (S-one, D-one-v) thereby providing the choice to validate all axioms in the justifications or to validate Hitting sets. Regarding weakening the combinations are (R-none, AB-none/W-all, U-end_all), (R-all, AB-none/W-all, U-end_all) and (R-one, AB-one/W-one, U-end_all). The first combination does not remove wrong axioms during the computation, weakens all axioms at once and updates at the end. The second removes all wrong axioms before the computation, weakens all axioms at once and updates at the end. The third removes wrong axioms one at a time during the computation and puts them back before dealing with the next wrong axiom. It weakens axioms one at a time and updates at the end. For completing, the choices are (C-all, U-end_all) and (C-one, U-end_one). The first combination completes all weakened axioms at once and updates at the end. The second completes the weakened axioms one at a time and updates the ontology after the weakened axiom set is handled for each wrong axiom. Regarding the choices for the combinations for the network, all choices for KB are implemented. The AS choices are supported using visual clues. The concepts in the axioms to be validated are labeled with the ontology source, such that the user can distinguish mappings from axioms within the ontologies. We also use different colors to represent the concepts which belong to different ontologies. At the appropriate times the system shows the different combinations that can be chosen and the user can select the desired choice.

For the basic operations the user interactions are adapted to the task at hand and different panels are used. For debugging the user requests the generation of the justifications. Then, the user can validate the axioms in the justifications or ask the system to compute Hitting sets and validate the axioms in those.

The axioms to be validated are shown in a list. During weakening, after choosing the preferred combination strategy, the user requests the system to generate the candidate weakened axioms for each axiom $\alpha \sqsubseteq \beta$ in the wrong asserted axioms set. The system computes the set of sub-concepts of α (sub) and the set of super-concepts of β (sup), thereby representing the possible choices for weaker axioms. These weaker axioms can be visualized in two ways: (i) as a list of axioms and (ii) by two panes representing the sub and sup sets with their subsumption relations (Fig. 5), respectively. In the latter case the user can choose weakened axioms by clicking on a concept in the sub set and a concept in the sup set and select the axiom as a weakened axiom. The advantage of this case is that these axioms are validated with the context in the domain of the ontology (showing the partial ontology through visualization). The set-up for completing is similar as for the weakening. For an axiom $\alpha \sqsubseteq \beta$ to be completed, the set of super-concepts of α and the set of sub-concepts of β are computed and visualized as lists or using two panes (Fig. 6). Validation is performed in a similar way as for weakening.

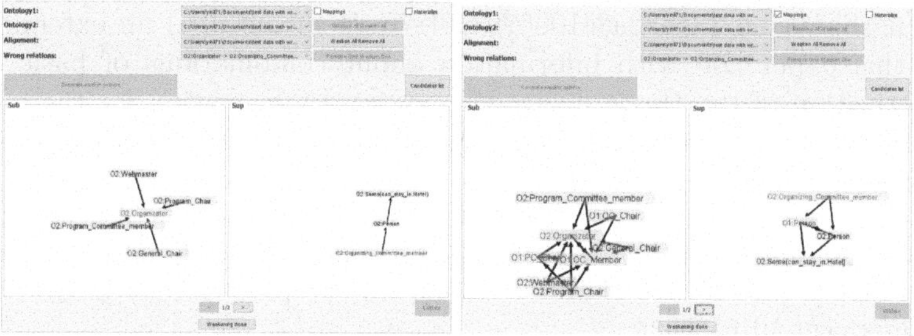

(a) (b)

Fig. 5. Sub and sup when weakening wrong axiom Organizator $\sqsubseteq$ Organizing_Committee_Member in ontology network ekaw-sigkdd using (a) KB_O; (b) KB_{ON}. Concepts in wrong axiom in red, concepts in ekaw in blue, concepts in sigkdd in black. (Color figure online)

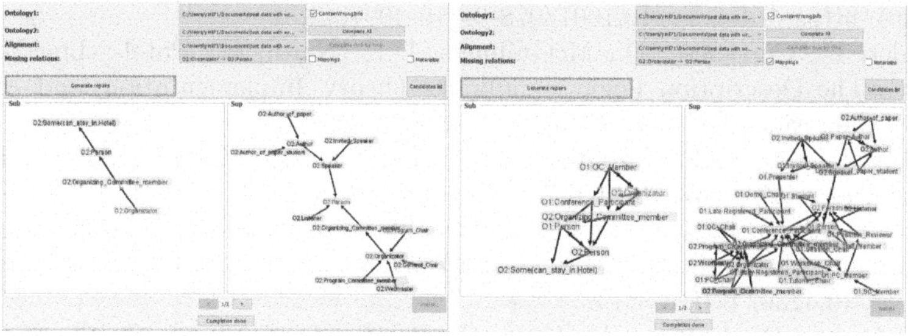

(a) (b)

Fig. 6. Sub and sup when completing weakened axiom Organizator $\sqsubseteq$ Person in ontology network ekaw-sigkdd using (a) KB_O; (b) KB_{ON}. Concepts in weakened axiom in red, concepts in ekaw in blue, concepts in sigkdd in black. (Color figure online)

7 Conclusion

In this paper we presented a framework for repairing ontology networks that alleviates the problem of removing correct knowledge when removing unwanted axioms from the network. It uses the basic operators of debugging, removing, weakening and completing for which there exist different approaches. We defined combination operators that represent choices to be made when combining the basic operations. We introduced different levels of autonomy for the ontologies and alignments in the networks and defined combination operators based on these levels and the use of background knowledge during the computation of repairs and the selection of the final solution. We have shown the influence of the combination operators on the quality of the repaired network. The framework gives flexibility to the ontology and alignment owners regarding their use and update policies. The framework also provides a blueprint to extend existing systems to more general systems for repairing ontologies and ontology networks.

Supplemental Material Statement: The supplemental material is available at https://figshare.com/s/e652a8e100579316f876. It includes (i) an extended version of this paper [25] with information about combinations of basic operations, derivation of the Hasse diagrams, extended information for the example in Sect. 4, and full experiment results, (ii) ontology versions used in the experiments and (iii) implemented system.

Acknowledgements. This work is financially supported by the Swedish e-Science Research Centre (SeRC) and the EU Horizon Europe project Onto-DESIDE under Grant Agreement 101058682.

References

1. Arif, M.F., Mencía, C., Ignatiev, A., Manthey, N., Peñaloza, R., Marques-Silva, J.: BEACON: an efficient SAT-based tool for debugging $\mathcal{EL}^+$ ontologies. In: Creignou, N., Le Berre, D. (eds.) SAT 2016. LNCS, vol. 9710, pp. 521–530. Springer, Cham (2016). https://doi.org/10.1007/978-3-319-40970-2_32
2. Baader, F., Calvanese, D., McGuinness, D.L., Nardi, D., Patel-Schneider, P.F. (eds.): The Description Logic Handbook: Theory, Implementation, and Applications. Cambridge University Press, Cambridge (2003)
3. Baader, F., Kriegel, F., Nuradiansyah, A., Peñaloza, R.: Making repairs in description logics more gentle. In: KR, pp. 319–328 (2018)
4. Chen, J., et al.: Knowledge graphs for the life sciences: recent developments, challenges and opportunities. Trans. Graph Data Knowl. **1**(1), 5:1–33 (2023). https://doi.org/10.4230/TGDK.1.1.5
5. Confalonieri, R., Galliani, P., Kutz, O., Porello, D., Righetti, G., Troquard, N.: Towards even more irresistible axiom weakening. In: DL (2020)
6. Du, J., Wan, H., Ma, H.: Practical TBox abduction based on justification patterns. In: AAAI, pp. 1100–1106 (2017)

7. Fleischhacker, D., Meilicke, C., Völker, J., Niepert, M.: Computing incoherence explanations for learned ontologies. In: Faber, W., Lembo, D. (eds.) RR 2013. LNCS, vol. 7994, pp. 80–94. Springer, Heidelberg (2013). https://doi.org/10.1007/978-3-642-39666-3_7
8. Haifani, F., Koopmann, P., Tourret, S., Weidenbach, C.: Connection-minimal abduction in $\mathcal{EL}$ via translation to fol. In: Blanchette, J., Kovács, L., Pattinson, D. (eds.) IJCAR 2022. LNCS, vol. 13385, pp. 188–207. Springer, Cham (2022). https://doi.org/10.1007/978-3-031-10769-6_12
9. Hogan, A., et al.: Knowledge graphs. ACM Comput. Surv. **54**(4), 71:1–37 (2022). https://doi.org/10.1145/3447772
10. Ivanova, V., Laurila Bergman, J., Hammerling, U., Lambrix, P.: Debugging Taxonomies and their Alignments: the ToxOntology - MeSH Use Case. In: WoDOOM. LECP, vol. 79, pp. 25–36 (2012)
11. Ji, Q., Gao, Z., Huang, Z., Zhu, M.: An efficient approach to debugging ontologies based on patterns. In: Pan, J.Z., et al. (eds.) JIST 2011. LNCS, vol. 7185, pp. 425–433. Springer, Heidelberg (2012). https://doi.org/10.1007/978-3-642-29923-0_33
12. Ji, Q., Haase, P., Qi, G., Hitzler, P., Stadtmüller, S.: RaDON — repair and diagnosis in ontology networks. In: Aroyo, L., et al. (eds.) ESWC 2009. LNCS, vol. 5554, pp. 863–867. Springer, Heidelberg (2009). https://doi.org/10.1007/978-3-642-02121-3_71
13. Jiménez-Ruiz, E., Cuenca Grau, B.: LogMap: logic-based and scalable ontology matching. In: Aroyo, L., et al. (eds.) ISWC 2011. LNCS, vol. 7031, pp. 273–288. Springer, Heidelberg (2011). https://doi.org/10.1007/978-3-642-25073-6_18
14. Jiménez-Ruiz, E., Grau, B.C., Zhou, Y., Horrocks, I.: Large-scale interactive ontology matching: Algorithms and implementation. In: ECAI, pp. 444–449 (2012). https://doi.org/10.3233/978-1-61499-098-7-444
15. Kalyanpur, A., Parsia, B., Horridge, M., Sirin, E.: Finding all justifications of OWL DL entailments. In: Aberer, K., et al. (eds.) ASWC/ISWC -2007. LNCS, vol. 4825, pp. 267–280. Springer, Heidelberg (2007). https://doi.org/10.1007/978-3-540-76298-0_20
16. Kalyanpur, A., Parsia, B., Sirin, E., Cuenca-Grau, B.: Repairing unsatisfiable concepts in OWL ontologies. In: Sure, Y., Domingue, J. (eds.) ESWC 2006. LNCS, vol. 4011, pp. 170–184. Springer, Heidelberg (2006). https://doi.org/10.1007/11762256_15
17. Kazakov, Y., Skočovský, P.: Enumerating justifications using resolution. In: Galmiche, D., Schulz, S., Sebastiani, R. (eds.) IJCAR 2018. LNCS (LNAI), vol. 10900, pp. 609–626. Springer, Cham (2018). https://doi.org/10.1007/978-3-319-94205-6_40
18. Lambrix, P.: Completing and debugging ontologies: State of the art and challenges in repairing ontologies. ACM J. Data Inf. Qual. **15**(4), 41:1–38 (2023). https://doi.org/10.1145/3597304
19. Lambrix, P., Armiento, R., Li, H., Hartig, O., Abd Nikooie Pour, M., Li, Y.: The materials design ontology. Semantic Web **15**(2), 481–515 (2024). https://doi.org/10.3233/SW-233340
20. Lambrix, P., Dragisic, Z., Ivanova, V.: Get my pizza right: repairing missing is-a relations in $\mathcal{ALC}$ ontologies. In: Takeda, H., Qu, Y., Mizoguchi, R., Kitamura, Y. (eds.) JIST 2012. LNCS, vol. 7774, pp. 17–32. Springer, Heidelberg (2013). https://doi.org/10.1007/978-3-642-37996-3_2

21. Lambrix, P., Ivanova, V.: A unified approach for debugging is-a structure and mappings in networked taxonomies. J. Biomed. Semant. **4**, 10 (2013). https://doi.org/10.1186/2041-1480-4-10
22. Lambrix, P., Wei-Kleiner, F., Dragisic, Z.: Completing the is-a structure in light-weight ontologies. J. Biomed. Semant. **6**(12), 1–26 (2015). https://doi.org/10.1186/s13326-015-0002-8
23. Lehmann, J., Bühmann, L.: ORE - a tool for repairing and enriching knowledge bases. In: Patel-Schneider, P.F., et al. (eds.) ISWC 2010. LNCS, vol. 6497, pp. 177–193. Springer, Heidelberg (2010). https://doi.org/10.1007/978-3-642-17749-1_12
24. Li, Y., Lambrix, P.: Repairing $\mathcal{EL}$ ontologies using weakening and completing. In: Pesquita, C., et al. (eds.) ESWC 2023. LNCS, vol. 13870, pp. 298–315. Springer, Cham (2023). https://doi.org/10.1007/978-3-031-33455-9_18
25. Li, Y., Lambrix, P.: Repairing networks of $\mathcal{EL}_\perp$ ontologies using weakening and completing - extended version (2024). arXiv:2407.18848
26. Meilicke, C.: Alignment Incoherence in Ontology Matching. Ph.D. thesis, University of Mannheim (2011)
27. Meyer, T., Lee, K., Booth, R., Pan, J.: Finding maximally satisfiable terminologies for the description logic $\mathcal{ALC}$. In: AAAI, pp. 269–274 (2006)
28. Moodley, K., Meyer, T., Varzinczak, I.J.: Root justifications for ontology repair. In: Rudolph, S., Gutierrez, C. (eds.) RR 2011. LNCS, vol. 6902, pp. 275–280. Springer, Heidelberg (2011). https://doi.org/10.1007/978-3-642-23580-1_24
29. Méndez, J., Alrabbaa, C., Koopmann, P., Langner, R., Baader, F., Dachselt, R.: Evonne: a visual tool for explaining reasoning with OWL ontologies and supporting interactive debugging. Computer Graphics forum **42**(6), e14730:1–15 (2023). https://doi.org/10.1111/cgf.14730
30. Nikitina, N., Rudolph, S., Glimm, B.: Interactive ontology revision. J. Web Semant. **12**, 118–130 (2012). https://doi.org/10.1016/j.websem.2011.12.002
31. Noy, N., Gao, Y., Jain, A., Narayanan, A., Patterson, A., Taylor, J.: Industry-scale knowledge graphs: lessons and challenges. Commun. ACM **62**(8), 36–43 (2019). https://doi.org/10.1145/3331166
32. Paulheim, H.: Knowledge graph refinement: a survey of approaches and evaluation methods. Semantic Web J. **8**(3), 489–508 (2017). https://doi.org/10.3233/SW-160218
33. Peñaloza, R.: Axiom pinpointing. In: Cota, G., Daquino, M., Pozzato, G.L. (eds.) Applications and Practices in Ontology Design, Extraction, and Reasoning, Studies on the Semantic Web, vol. 49, pp. 162–177. IOS Press (2020). https://doi.org/10.3233/SSW200042
34. Pesquita, C., Faria, D., Santos, E., Couto, F.M.: To repair or not to repair: reconciling correctness and coherence in ontology reference alignments. In: OM, pp. 13–24 (2013)
35. Rodler, P., Schmid, W.: On the impact and proper use of heuristics in test-driven ontology debugging. In: Benzmüller, C., Ricca, F., Parent, X., Roman, D. (eds.) RuleML+RR 2018. LNCS, vol. 11092, pp. 164–184. Springer, Cham (2018). https://doi.org/10.1007/978-3-319-99906-7_11
36. Santos, E., Faria, D., Pesquita, C., Couto, F.M.: Ontology alignment repair through modularization and confidence-based heuristics. PLoS ONE **10**(12), e0144807), 1–19 (2015). https://doi.org/10.1371/journal.pone.0144807

37. Schekotihin, K., Rodler, P., Schmid, W.: OntoDebug: interactive ontology debugging plug-in for Protégé. In: Ferrarotti, F., Woltran, S. (eds.) FoIKS 2018. LNCS, vol. 10833, pp. 340–359. Springer, Cham (2018). https://doi.org/10.1007/978-3-319-90050-6_19
38. Schlobach, S.: Debugging and semantic clarification by pinpointing. In: Gómez-Pérez, A., Euzenat, J. (eds.) ESWC 2005. LNCS, vol. 3532, pp. 226–240. Springer, Heidelberg (2005). https://doi.org/10.1007/11431053_16
39. Schlobach, S., Cornet, R.: Non-standard reasoning services for the debugging of description logic terminologies. In: IJCAI, pp. 355–360 (2003)
40. Schlobach, S., Huang, Z., Cornet, R., van Harmelen, F.: Debugging Incoherent Terminologies. J. Automated Reasoning **39**(3), 317–349 (2007). https://doi.org/10.1007/s10817-007-9076-z
41. Shchekotykhin, K.M., Friedrich, G., Fleiss, P., Rodler, P.: Interactive ontology debugging: two query strategies for efficient fault localization. J. Web Semantics **12**, 88–103 (2012). https://doi.org/10.1016/j.websem.2011.12.006
42. Troquard, N., Confalonieri, R., Galliani, P., Peñaloza, R., Porello, D., Kutz, O.: Repairing ontologies via axiom weakening. In: AAAI, pp. 1981–1988 (2018)
43. Wei-Kleiner, F., Dragisic, Z., Lambrix, P.: Abduction framework for repairing incomplete $\mathcal{EL}$ ontologies: complexity results and algorithms. In: AAAI, pp. 1120–1127 (2014)

Do LLMs Really Adapt to Domains? An Ontology Learning Perspective

Huu Tan Mai[1,2(✉)], Cuong Xuan Chu[2(✉)], and Heiko Paulheim[1(✉)]

[1] University of Mannheim, Data and Web Science Group, 68131 Mannheim, Germany
{huu.tan.mai,heiko.paulheim}@uni-mannheim.de
[2] Bosch Center for AI, 71272 Renningen, Germany
{huutan.mai,cuongxuan.chu}@de.bosch.com

Abstract. Large Language Models (LLMs) have demonstrated unprecedented prowess across various natural language processing tasks in various application domains. Recent studies show that LLMs can be leveraged to perform lexical semantic tasks, such as Knowledge Base Completion (KBC) or Ontology Learning (OL). However, it has not effectively been verified whether their success is due to their ability to reason over unstructured or semi-structured data, or their effective learning of linguistic patterns and senses alone. This unresolved question is particularly crucial when dealing with domain-specific data, where the lexical senses and their meaning can completely differ from what a LLM has learned during its training stage. This paper investigates the following question: *Do LLMs really adapt to domains and remain consistent in the extraction of structured knowledge, or do they only learn lexical senses instead of reasoning?* To answer this question and, we devise a controlled experiment setup that uses WordNet to synthesize parallel corpora, with English and gibberish terms. We examine the differences in the outputs of LLMs for each corpus in two OL tasks: relation extraction and taxonomy discovery. Empirical results show that, while adapting to the gibberish corpora, off-the-shelf LLMs do not consistently reason over semantic relationships between concepts, and instead leverage senses and their frame. However, fine-tuning improves the performance of LLMs on lexical semantic tasks even when the domain-specific terms are arbitrary and unseen during pre-training, hinting at the applicability of pre-trained LLMs for OL.

Keywords: ontology learning · LLMs · domain adaptation

1 Introduction

Knowledge Bases (KB) and ontologies play a key role in structuring and organizing knowledge across domains, and offer powerful solutions to link data that would otherwise remain unstructured (such as text). As of now, many sources of data can be used as ontologies, of varying specificity. For instance, WordNet [17], ConceptNet [14] and WebIsA [23] contain common knowledge, whereas KBs such

G. Demartini et al. (Eds.): ISWC 2024, LNCS 15231, pp. 126–143, 2025.
https://doi.org/10.1007/978-3-031-77844-5_7

as Unified Medical Language System (UMLS) [2] and GeoNames [6] have their own domain specificities (respectively, medical and geographic). For knowledge-intensive applications, access to structured data is of utmost importance, but creating it is a very tedious and time-consuming process that inevitably demands domain expertise. Ontology Learning (OL) is a field of artificial intelligence that concerns itself with automatically identifying terms, types and axioms between them from unstructured or structured information sources such as text or KBs. In particular, OL deals with identifying hyponymy (resp. hypernymy) relations in a KB. That is, for pairs of concepts (A, B) in the KB, one wants to infer whether or not Concept A is a subclass (resp. a superclass) of Concept B.

In the past few years, Large Language Models (LLMs), such as GPT-3 [3], GPT-4, LLaMa2 [26] or Falcon-40B [1] have displayed unprecedented prowess in many NLP applications across various domains. LLMs are language models with a very large parameter count that are trained with enormous amounts of textual data. Hence, they are equipped with common knowledge and have shown remarkable success in generating text. Furthermore, LLMs have made it possible to capture the meaning of text and reason about it, providing a promising alternative for knowledge-intensive tasks such as KB completion and ontology-related tasks like OL and OM (Ontology Matching). Recent studies have shown that LLMs could be viewed as Knowledge Bases [22], storing knowledge incorporated in their parameters (e.g. factual knowledge [25], event knowledge [11], commonsense knowledge [13,33], etc.). In particular, LLMs4OL [7] introduces a novel approach to OL using LLMs: the work provides comprehensive empirical evidence that, although requiring fine-tuning for better performance, LLMs can work as effective ontology learners on specialized datasets.

However, there are several challenges that come with LLMs, and that have been left relatively unexplored in the frame of ontology learning. They include: (1) LLMs are susceptible to hallucinate [12], i.e. provide generate text that is syntactically sound but factually incorrect. (2) LLMs are trained on massive corpora of textual data and acquire common knowledge, but their few - or zero - shot generalizability and adaptability to unknown domains remains relatively undiscussed. Studying these two aspects is crucial to better understand the current limits of LLMs, and is ever so needed since they are being become increasingly prominent for domain-specific uses. On the one hand, it is effectively possible to get LLMs to *adapt* to a domain by fine-tuning, but such a process requires labeled data in this domain and can be computationally expensive. On the other hand, *generalizability* is also an extremely valuable quality for OL in domain-specific settings. To illustrate this, consider the Examples 1 and 2.

In OL, a LLM may be able to identify that a *macaron* is a subclass of *confection* that is made from many ingredients such as *egg white*, *icing sugar*, *granulated sugar*, and so on. Given Example 2, obtained by turning the words of Example 1 into gibberish, a model capable of *generalization* should retrieve the analogous concepts as hypernyms or meronyms (i.e., *twiglomptoroa* is a subclass of *becsverdecoroal* etc.). However, it was not explicitly verified if LLMs would do so, or more broadly, if they are able to generalize taxonomic axioms over text

Example 1 (macaron). a sweet meringue-based confection made with egg white, icing sugar, granulated sugar, almond powder or ground almond, and food colouring.

Example 2 (twiglomptoroa). a becsverdecoroa meringue-based becsverdecoroal made with egg white, icing shifbousadu stintsobroa, granulated shifbousadu stintsobroa, almond powder or ground almond, and food colouring.

(e.g. textual patterns indicating that A is a subclass of B) rather than learn the concepts themselves during the pre-training process.

This paper presents comprehensive experiments to study the generalizability and domain adaptability of LLMs, with perspective of ontology learning. By synthesizing three new domain corpora from the Open English WordNet, and creating a gibberish counterpart each, we assess the performance of LLMs on two main tasks: relation extraction and taxonomy discovery. We conduct the experiments on popular LLMs, including closed- and open-source, off-the-shelf and fine-tuned, and evaluate them on both in-domain and across-domain setups. The novel contributions of this paper are as follows:

- We create three synthetic datasets as parallel corpora from the Open English WordNet, by turning domain-specific terms into gibberish.
- We conduct experiments to simulate the adaptability and generalizability of LLMs in unseen domains, with or without backpropagation.
- We provide empirical evidence that there is a limit to the generalization capability of off-the-shelf LLMs, with OL tasks that leverage lexical semantics such as relation extraction and taxonomy discovery.
- We show that in-domain fine-tuning improves in-domain task-specific performance, and that the improvements are transferable to new domains.

2 Related Work

Ontology Learning with LLMs. OL is the (semi)automatic acquisition of T-Box and/or A-Box data from various data sources. In the context of this work, we look at OL from unstructured text or semi-structured data such as Knowledge Graphs paired with textual descriptions. More generally, recent studies show that LLMs can be leveraged to perform ontology related tasks, such as OM (Ontology Matching) or OL. For instance, Norouzi et al. [20] use a naive approach that uses ChatGPT for ontology alignment, by providing the entire source and target ontologies. Mateiu et al. [15] use a fine-tuned GPT-3 to convert natural language into OWL Functional Syntax for ontology enrichment. Hertling et al. [9] use few-shot prompting to enhance the performance of open-source LLMs on OM tasks.

In LLMs4OL [7], the authors argue that with sufficient formulation, all tasks pertinent to OL fall within one of the three categories: A) Term Typing (determining a generalized type for a lexical term), B) Taxonomy Discovery (determining the hierarchy between a pair of concepts), C) Non-Taxonomic

Relation Extraction (finding non-hierarchic relations between concepts). This task paradigm allows them to evaluate LLMs in OL with a zero-shot prompting method. In the work, the authors show that although LLMs may not be suitable for OL as is, they may still be helpful when effectively fine-tuned for ontology construction.

SPIRES [4] is a successful application of LLMs to populate ontologies. It leverages Zero-Shot Learning to extract relations between concepts in textual corpora, then grounds the concepts using other existing ontologies in the target domain (e.g. FoodOn or Wikidata). However, in a domain-specific setting, it is not granted that public ontologies of the domain exist and are of high quality.

Moskvoretskii et al. [19] use LLaMa [26] fine-tuned on WordNet, to perform OL tasks such as taxonomy discovery, taxonomy enrichment, taxonomy construction and lexical entailment. Specifically, they provide further empirical evidence that fine-tuning LLMs for taxonomy discovery on domains drastically increases their performance, making them suitable for the task. The method was tested on real domains such as the food, music and medical domains. In comparison, our work seeks to establish whether or not domain adaptation would hold in arbitrary domains, where the terminology is unknown to the model.

In-Context Learning with LLMs. It was previously observed and verified that LLMs can learn from a few in-context examples in the form of demonstration. In fact, to better answer a given query, a LLM can leverage previous examples to estimate the distribution of input-output pairs. This emergent behavior of LLMs [29] has become a successful learning paradigm because it no longer requires the expensive optimization of model parameters. With respect to our paper, four particular works pertaining to In-Context Learning (ICL) are of high interest. Firstly, Chain-of-Thought prompting [30] forces the model to generate intermediate steps before returning an output, which was shown to elicit reasoning in very large language models and improve their symbolic reasoning performance. Secondly, Min et al. [18] show that ground-truth labels do not significantly hurt the performance of LLMs on downstream tasks, suggesting that models implicitly learn input-label mappings from the language modelling objective alone. Thirdly, symbol tuning [31], the process of fine-tuning by replacing original labels to semantically unrelated ones, was shown to improve the in-context learning performance of very large LMs, and effectively override prior semantic knowledge. Finally, Wei et al. [32] show that "smaller" LLMs greatly suffer from semantically unrelated labels in comparison to larger ones, heavily implying that they overly rely on semantic priors of targets instead of effectively reasoning over them. The contributions of these works justify our necessity to verify the in-context adaptation of LLMs to domains by extending this verification to semantically unrelated inputs (e.g. gibberish input-label mapings).

Domain Adaptation with LLMs. Few works of interest deal with the performance of Large Language Models given domain-specific training corpora. Wan et al. [28] propose a domain adaptation framework for very large language models (GPT-4 [21]) to address the scarcity of Chinese legal domain texts, using an adapt-retrieve-revise process. With a smaller LLM trained on in-domain cor-

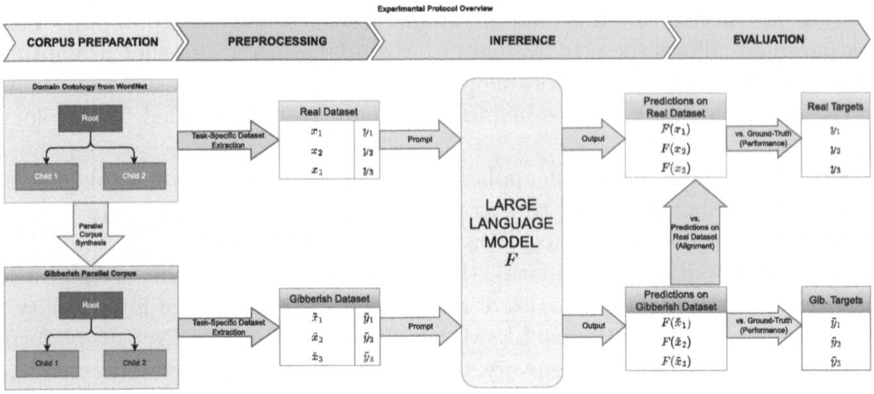

Fig. 1. Overview of the off-the-shelf evaluation pipeline. The dataset extraction and the prompt depend on the task to perform.

pora, the authors generate a draft answer to retrieve evidence from an external knowledge base, both of which are given to GPT-4 to generate a final answer. Gururangan et al. [8] show that domain-adaptive pretraining (DAPT), i.e. continued pre-training on domain-specific text, allows one to adapt a language model to a domain at reduced cost. However, Cheng et al. [5] argue that while DAPT may improve specific task performance after fine-tuning, it overall hurts the ability of LLMs to perform question answering. Instead, they propose AdaptLLM, a scalable approach that aims to train a LLM on reading comprehension texts created from the raw domain-specific corpora. Finally, Shin et al. [24] show that the in-context learning ability of a LLM heavily depends on the corpus sources, and may emerge by combining multiple corpora, but the domain relevance of the corpus may not be indicative of the few-shot performance of the model.

3 Approach

Figure 1 illustrates an overview of the pipeline we employ to test the *adaptability* and *generalizability* of off-the-shelf LLMs (pretrained, and as is), which includes two main steps: corpus preparation and LLMs evaluation.

In particular, we use the English WordNet (2023 Edition) [16] to generate a parallel corpus of terms and definitions in the form of gibberish, which serve as our reference domain-specific setting. The process begins by choosing root concepts (for instance, sweets and desserts) in the WordNet taxonomy, then explores the graph through hyponymy, derivation and other (e.g. topic) relationships across concepts (with a set maximal exploration depth). The explored concepts form a domain in the real WordNet (e.g. sweets domain) that can be used to create a parallel corpus by propagating gibberish representations and definitions. More details about the algorithm can be found in Sect. 3.1.

After obtaining a parallel corpus of a particular domain, we evaluate a LLM on two different tasks: *relation extraction* and *taxonomy discovery*, each on both versions of the corpus. Naturally, since the concepts remain the same up to an input-label mapping, we ideally expect the results to be analogous. More details can be found in Subsect. 3.2. Additionally, we investigate the effect of fine-tuning on the in-domain performance of LLMs, as described in Subsect. 3.3.

3.1 Parallel Corpus Synthesis

To simulate a domain that is unseen for the LLM, we generate another KG where the domain concepts have gibberish representations and definitions that do not collide (e.g. if "sugar" is turned into "arghl" then any definition that contains the word "sugar" will see it turned into the word "arghl" instead). For this purpose, we devise a procedure which includes three steps: concept mining, concept linking and gibberish generation. The code can be found online.[1]

Concept Mining. The concept mining algorithm is a simple Breadth-First Search algorithm, starting from each of the root concepts C_0 and only going through user-selected relationships (hypernymy, sense derivation, and concept topic). We set a maximal exploration depth D, which is set to 5 during experiments. The explored concepts form a dataset $\mathcal{D}$.

Concept Linking. The next step of this process is to establish the dependencies between concept definitions and other concepts. For example, if "sugar" is mentioned in the definition of concept c, then we will link all the concepts c_{sugar} which have "sugar" as a representation with c by introducing a blank node as follows, where {c_id} denotes the WordNet ID of c:

```
c       sct:definitionWord    _:_sugar_{c_id} .
_:_sugar_{c_id} rdf:value     "sugar"@en .
_:_sugar_{c_id} sct:references   c_sugar .
```

Listing 1.1. Example of linking triples.

Gibberish Generation. We assume that we have an algorithm T that creates a gibberish representation $T(c)$ from a concept c based on its initial representation, definition and part-of-speech. A concept is fully processed when it has a gibberish definition AND a gibberish representation. A concept is partially processed when it has a gibberish representation (fully processed implies partially processed).

Denote $\mathcal{D}_0$ the set of concepts in $\mathcal{D}$ that have no internal dependencies (i.e. for any c in $\mathcal{D}_0$, the definition of c does not refer to any concept in $\mathcal{D}$), as shown in Fig. 2a. We create an initial representation $T(c)$ for any c in $\mathcal{D}_0$, and give them a gibberish definition identical to their original one. We will additionally

[1] https://github.com/boschresearch/llm-vs-gibberish-ontologies.

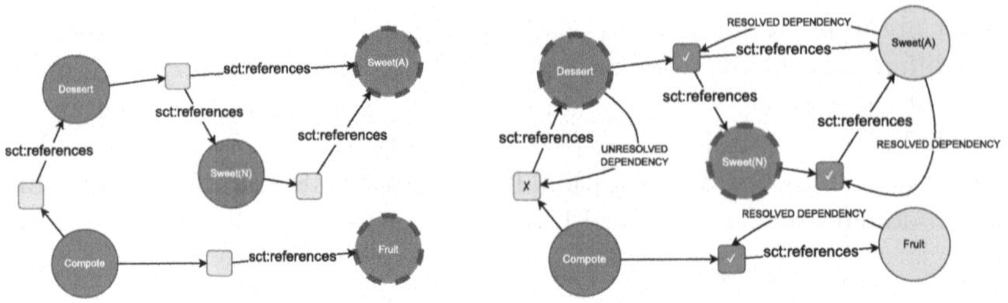

(a) Step 0 : Make a gibberish representation and (unchanged) definition for concepts with no dependencies.

(b) Step $n+1$: Use at least partially processed concepts to resolve dependencies and create new gibberish representations and definitions.

Fig. 2. Algorithm to propagate gibberish representations and definitions. Squares are blank nodes that indicate that the preceding concept has a word that refers to one of the node's successors. Dashed circles represent the concepts eligible to be fully processed. Green circles represent (at least partially) processed concepts.

add the homonyms of the previously processed concepts in $\mathcal{D}_0$, with no gibberish representation. Moreover, set $\mathcal{D}_{-1} = \emptyset$. We then repeat the following loop until we have fully processed all the concepts in $\mathcal{D}$, as illustrated in Fig. 2b.

Suppose we have obtained $\mathcal{D}_{n-1}$ and $\mathcal{D}_{n-2}$. If $|\mathcal{D}_{n-1}| > |\mathcal{D}_{n-2}|$, we proceed as follows: obtain concepts c that are not fully labeled and which dependencies can all be resolved (i.e. for each dependency `c sct:definitionWord x`, there exists $c' \in \mathcal{D}_{n-1}$, or $c' = c$ such that `x sct:references c'`). We create gibberish representations $T(c)$ if there is not one already, we resolve the dependencies using the gibberish representations in $\mathcal{D}_{n-1}$ to make a definition for c. All homonyms of processed concepts are also partially processed, and all the partially processed concepts are added to $\mathcal{D}_{n-1}$ to form $\mathcal{D}_n$.

If $|\mathcal{D}_{n-1}| = |\mathcal{D}_{n-2}|$, we sample a random concept c of $\mathcal{D}$ that is not partially processed, assign a gibberish representation $T(c)$ to it and add c to $\mathcal{D}_{n-1}$ to form $\mathcal{D}_n$. Note that for $i \geq 0$, $\mathcal{D}_i$ does not exclusively contain concepts in $\mathcal{D}$, but $\bar{\mathcal{D}}_i = \mathcal{D}_i \cap \mathcal{D}$ does.

This pipeline yields a set of concepts $\mathcal{D}$, where each concept $c \in \mathcal{D}$ has a gibberish representation $T(c)$ as well as a gibberish definition consistent with the internal dependencies in $\mathcal{D}$.

Example. Consider the example depicted in Fig. 2. In the first step, Sweet (adjective) and Fruit do not reference any other nodes in their definitions: they can be fully processed. In the second step, since Dessert refers to both Sweet (noun) and Sweet (adjective) and the latter was processed, it is eligible to be processed next. Moreover, since Sweet (adjective) is a homonym of Sweet (noun), it can also be processed. However, since Compote refers to both Dessert and Fruit, it may not be processed yet, since Dessert has not been processed yet. It will be processed in the following step.

3.2 Off-the-Shelf Evaluation Methodology

For each dataset $\mathcal{D}$, we perform an evaluation by comparing the performance of off-the-shelf LLMs in two different lexical semantic tasks: relation extraction and taxonomy discovery; and compare the outputs coming from two cases: on the original dataset, and its gibberish counterpart.

Relation Extraction. Given a query concept in $\mathcal{D}$, its lexical senses (i.e. written forms) and its definition, the goal of this task is to extract all relations between the concepts mentioned in the definition, including the query concept. To remain in the frame of ontology learning, we focus only on hypernymy and holonymy relationships. For instance, in Example 1, the extracted relations should be as follows: macaron is a subclass of confection, egg white is a part of macaron, icing sugar is a part of macaron, etc. Likewise, given the gibberish definition in 2 instead, we expect the same relations to be extracted, only with the concept names replaced with their gibberish counterpart. In order to retrieve a prediction, the LLM is prompted to output triples in the form: (A, r, B) where r is either `is a subclass of` or `is a part of`.

Taxonomy Discovery. Given two concepts A and B in $\mathcal{D}$, with their lexical senses and definitions, the goal of this task is to determine whether or not A is a subclass of B. Likewise, we expect that turning the lexical senses and definitions of A and B into gibberish will not change the outcome. WordNet hypernymy relations are used as a ground-truth: the predictions on the real (resp. gibberish counterpart of the) dataset are compared with the real (resp. gibberish counterpart of the) ground-truth. Indirect hypernymy relations (obtained with the transitive closure of the relation `gwn:hypernym`) are also used. Negative examples are produced by corrupting the hypernym once or twice per query (hyponym, subclass of, ?). This classification task can be evaluated with F1-score: a drop in performance should indicate that a LLM relies on the lexical senses to infer taxonomical relationships rather than textual semantic information.

Prompting. For each task/model configuration, we follow general guidelines for prompting a LLM. (1) The return is in JSON format, (2) Chain-of-Thought (CoT) [30] can be used if it improves the performance of the model, (3) One or few exemplar(s) can be used, with example(s) outside of the dataset, if it improves the performance of the model. In the **relation extraction** task, for a concept C, its written form F_C, its part-of-speech P_C, and its definition D_C, we construct a prompt $p(C)$ as shown in Listing 1.2. In the **taxonomy discovery** task, for A, B two concepts, F_A, F_B their written forms, D_A, D_B their definition, we construct a prompt $p(A, B)$ as shown in Listing 1.3. Prompt templates can be found here.

```
{FORMAT INSTRUCTIONS (Task and return format)}
{EXAMPLE(S) (zero, one or few exemplars)}

Concept: {F_C}
Part-of-speech: {P_C}
Definition: {D_C}
```

Listing 1.2. Relation extraction generic prompt $p(C)$.

```
{FORMAT INSTRUCTIONS (Task and return format)}
{EXAMPLE(S) (zero, one or few exemplars)}

Concept A: {F_A}
Definition: {D_A}

Concept B: {F_B}
Definition: {D_B}
```

Listing 1.3. Taxonomy discovery generic prompt $p(A, B)$.

3.3 Fine-Tuning Experiment

While it was previously verified that fine-tuning improves OL performance in existing domains [19], it is not clear if this statement still holds for arbitrary domains and unknown vocabularies where reasoning is required. To verify this question, after evaluating the zero/one/few-shot performance of LLMs in the gibberish domains, we propose to assess the effect of fine-tuning models on the inference performance for a specific task.

Data Split. For each dataset $\mathcal{D}$, we fine-tune a LLM for taxonomy discovery on a train split of hypernymy relations. Half of the concepts in the dataset, and their hypernymy relations, are used for training. The inverse relations are used as negatives (if A is a subclass of B, then B is not a subclass of A), alongside some randomly sampled negatives. The remaining relations are used for testing.

Prompting. We train LLMs on instructive datasets with the prefix prompt in Listing 1.4, completed using each pair of concepts in the hypernymy dataset.

```
### HUMAN:
Identify whether the statement is true or false. Answer
    with only one word: 'True' or 'False'.

CONCEPT A: {term_a} ({pos_a})
Definition: {definition_a}

CONCEPT B: {term_b} ({pos_b})
Definition: {definition_b}

```

Table 1. Dataset statistics. The 'Hypernyms' column indicates the number of retrieved hypernymy relationships within the dataset. The 'Depth' column indicates the exploration depth of the algorithm.

$\mathcal{D}$	Concepts	Hypernyms	Depth	Root Concepts
WN-sweets	244	418	5	sweet (n), sweet (a), sugar
WN-football	937	1401	5	football, team, offensive (a), defensive (a)
WN-music	1366	2497	5	musical instrument

```
Statement: '{term_a}' is a subclass of '{term_b}'.
### ASSISTANT:
```

Listing 1.4. Prefix prompt used for the fine-tuning experiment. The content between curly brackets is formatted for each pair of concepts in the dataset.

4 Experiments

In this section, we explore the off-the-shelf evaluation proposed in Subsect. 3.2, and the fine-tuning experiments described in Subsect. 3.3.

4.1 Experimental Setup

Datasets. To assess the performance variation with domain specificity, we generate three synthetic domain-specific datasets as parallel corpora from the Open English WordNet [16], using the methodology described in Sect. 3.1. They are:

- Sweets: A collection of concepts related to sweets, desserts, sweet food or sugar. In this dataset, hypernyms are frequent, and concepts are relatively well constructed from their hypernyms.
- Football: A collection of concepts related to football. This dataset, created by browsing co-topic concepts, includes less taxonomic relationships, but has its own terminology and jargon.
- Music: A collection of concepts related to musical instruments. It is the largest of the three.

Table 1 shows, for each dataset, the number of concepts, the number of hypernymy relationships, the exploration depth and the root concepts. The translator T used to generate gibberish representations of concepts is available online.[2].

Models. While this study is not comprehensive of all existing LLMs, our goal is to show a particular trend between them. In the off-the-shelf evaluation, we evaluate the following popular LLMs, with their number of parameters between parentheses: GPT-3.5 [3] (174B), GPT-4 [21] ($\geq$ 1T), Falcon-40B [1] (40B),

[2] https://github.com/htmai-880/gibberify.

LLaMa2-13B [26] (13B), and Zephyr-7B-β [27] (7B). The former two, accessed with a paid subscription, are closed-source, whereas the latter three are open-source. In the fine-tuning experiment, we consider Zephyr-7B-β [27] and Falcon-7B [1], which are both open-source. For the paid subscription models, We limit our budget to 15€ per dataset.

Specificities. We henceforth consider the three following evaluation methods:

- Ground-truth (GT)(`en`) vs `en` we compare the answers on the original English dataset against the ground-truth
- Ground-truth (GT)(`gib`) vs `gib`: we compare the answers on the gibberish dataset against the gibberish ground-truth
- `en` vs `gib`: using the answers on the original dataset as a ground-truth, we evaluate the consistency of the predictions on the gibberish dataset, regardless of their correctness.

In the relation extraction (GT(X) vs X), due to the scarcely annotated holonymy relationships in WordNet, we focus on hypernymy relationships to compute metrics. Moreover, a model prediction is processed by taking into account the inferred hypernymy relationships, using the transitive property of the relation. For instance, if a model outputs the triples (vanilla pudding, is a subclass of, custard-like pudding), and (custard-like pudding, is a subclass of, pudding), we count the triple (vanilla pudding, is a subclass of, pudding) as effectively predicted by the model. In the taxonomy discovery task, predictions that are neither "True" or "False" are ignored. Thus, macro-averaged F1-scores may not be between the macro-averaged precisions and the macro-averaged recalls.

4.2 Off-the-Shelf Evaluation

Metrics. For each model/task configuration, we compute metrics in three settings: GT(`en`) vs `en`, GT(`gib`) vs `gib`, and `en` vs `gib`. The goal is to see if the predictions with gibberish terms align with the predictions with the real terms. We compute the following metrics: precision, recall and F1-score.

Results. We first examine the results with respect the to ground-truths. It is important to mention that the English WordNet is scarcely annotated in terms of hypernymy and holonymy relationships. Consider the following example:

> *Example 3 (toffee apple).* an apple that is covered with a candy-like substance (usually caramelized sugar).

In this example, the definition obviously implies that a *toffee apple* is an *apple*, but WordNet only considers *sweet, confection* to be valid hypernyms. The incompleteness of WordNet explains why the observed performances are so low, but because our goal is a relative comparison of performances on real corpora

Table 2. Results on the relation extraction task in the GT(X) vs X setting, where X is either `en` or `gib`. Only hypernymy relations are considered.

Model	X	WN-sweets			WN-football			WN-music		
		Pre.	Rec.	F1	Pre.	Rec.	F1	Pre.	Rec.	F1
GPT-3.5	`en`	.478	.150	.228	.383	.056	.097	.397	.060	.104
	`gib`	.336	.069	.115	.371	.035	.065	.307	.029	.053
GPT-4	`en`	.583	.160	.251	–	–	–	–	–	–
	`gib`	.530	.129	.207	–	–	–	–	–	–
Falcon-40B	`en`	.573	.151	.238	.489	.067	.118	.529	.065	.116
	`gib`	.330	.080	.128	.382	.050	.088	.341	.042	.074
LLaMa2-13B	`en`	.536	.141	.223	.423	.035	.065	.434	.030	.056
	`gib`	.365	.085	.138	.341	.018	.035	.296	.014	.026
Zephyr-7B-β	`en`	.441	.158	.233	.399	.067	.115	.374	.063	.108
	`gib`	.243	.095	.137	.313	.052	.089	.261	.044	.075

and their gibberish counterpart, rather than absolute scores, it is not critical to have a high-quality ground-truth.

In both tasks, which results are reported in Table 2 and Table 3, a common trend occurs across all LLMs and in all synthetic domains: a significant performance decrease is observed when replacing real terms with gibberish. Although GPT-4 (tested on WN-sweets only because of the slowness and the costs) performs best on gibberish corpora, it suffers from the same performance drop.

While the performance on relation extraction is generally low across all LLMs with the real datasets, which we mainly attribute to the poor quality of the annotations, it is even lower with the gibberish datasets. In each case, the macro F1-score is practically halved, e.g. in WN-sweets, GPT-3.5 drops from 0.228 to 0.115, Falcon-40B drops from 0.238 to 0.128, LLaMa2-13B drops from 0.223 to 0.138, Zephyr-7B-β drops from 0.233 to 0.137. Note that the recall is low in comparison to the precision, which indicates that a LLM tends to overlook indicators that two concepts are hierarchically related. This observation aligns with the conclusion of LLMs4OL [7], according to which off-the-shelf LLMs are not sufficiently suitable for OL tasks, particularly in the case of relation extraction.

In the taxonomy discovery task, the performance of LLMs also plummets when using the gibberish dataset instead of the real one. The LLMs are relatively good at identifying whether two real concepts are hierarchically related (e.g. F1-score up to 0.940 on the WN-sweets dataset by GPT-3.5), but suffer from a large performance drop when confronted to unknown words which share the same semantic relations (e.g. the F1-score of GPT-3.5 drops from 0.940 to 0.446 when using the gibberish counterpart of WN-sweets; the same behavior is observed across all datasets and LLMs). We interpret this drop as the fact that LLMs are significantly better at leveraging semantic priors (i.e. lexical senses known from pre-training), to deduce that Concept A is a subclass of Concept B.

Table 3. Results (macro-average) on the taxonomy discovery task in the GT(X) vs X setting, where X is either `en` or `gib`.

Model	X	WN-sweets			WN-football			WN-music		
		Pre.	Rec.	F1	Pre.	Rec.	F1	Pre.	Rec.	F1
GPT-3.5	`en`	.944	.937	.940	.758	.701	.648	.829	.858	.818
	`gib`	.783	.539	.446	.640	.505	.333	.687	.537	.361
GPT-4	`en`	.949	.943	.945	–	–	–	–	–	–
	`gib`	.591	.576	.566	–	–	–	–	–	–
Falcon-40B	`en`	.775	.658	.598	.800	.648	.637	.787	.620	.613
	`gib`	.591	.575	.574	.483	.475	.478	.541	.535	.480
LLaMa2-13B	`en`	.819	.772	.750	.808	.811	.809	.785	.800	.790
	`gib`	.450	.447	.444	.533	.531	.504	.576	.556	.465
Zephyr-7B-β	`en`	.899	.897	.898	.813	.751	.759	.821	.762	.778
	`gib`	.691	.634	.621	.500	.500	.469	.530	.524	.523

Table 4. Alignment results (macro-average) on the relation extraction task in the `en` vs `gib` setting. Both hypernymy and holonymy relations are considered.

Model	WN-sweets			WN-football			WN-music		
	Pre.	Rec.	F1	Pre.	Rec.	F1	Pre.	Rec.	F1
GPT-3.5	.371	.304	.334	.263	.175	.210	.207	.138	.166
GPT-4	.504	.527	.515	–	–	–	–	–	–
Falcon-40B	.310	.303	.306	.236	.238	.237	.225	.224	.225
LLaMa2-13B	.347	.340	.344	.386	.225	.284	.374	.215	.273
Zephyr-7B-β	.214	.229	.221	.192	.180	.185	.148	.142	.145

Although the general performance drop is expected because the tested LLM would then be dealing with words it has never seen during its training, we furthermore observe that the prediction alignment is very low. In spite of analogous concepts sharing the same semantic relations with each other in the parallel corpora, the model is unable to produce analogous outputs from analogous inputs, as shown by the low F1-scores in Tables 4 and 5. This is evidence that as is, LLMs do not *reason* over semantic relationships.

Our interpretation is that the attention mechanism heavily relies on the lexical sense and the frame of a token, instead of leveraging the semantic relationships that hold between tokens. In other words, the "reasoning" abilities of LLMs for Ontology Learning are mostly limited to entities and concepts that the models have already been trained on, i.e. prior semantics. However, such a quality is critical for Ontology Learning in arbitrary domains, where hypernymy relationships must be retrieved for unknown concepts, or new concepts that share the same lexical form as some existing word (for instance, if domain-specific jargon employs existing words with different meanings).

Table 5. Alignment results (macro-average) on the taxonomy discovery task in the `en` vs `gib` setting.

Model	WN-sweets			WN-football			WN-music		
	Pre.	Rec.	F1	Pre.	Rec.	F1	Pre.	Rec.	F1
GPT-3.5	.789	.541	.465	.700	.517	.488	.738	.544	.459
GPT-4	.611	.594	.590	–	–	–	–	–	–
Falcon-40B	.541	.557	.412	.502	.495	.443	.529	.562	.352
LLaMa2-13B	.565	.570	.556	.618	.610	.586	.641	.599	.535
Zephyr-7B-β	.818	.727	.716	.557	.544	.545	.570	.572	.570

Table 6. Hypernym train-test split for the fine-tuning experiment.

$\mathcal{D}$	Train		Test	
	Positives	Negatives	Positives	Negatives
WN-sweets	189	393	229	284
WN-football	674	1043	727	567
WN-music	1367	1882	1130	851

This trend seems to hold true in both tasks, which confirms the fact that off-the-shelf LLMs are currently not suited for OL tasks on arbitrary domains.

4.3 Fine-Tuning Evaluation

Training Details. Table 6 shows the number of hypernym pairs used for the fine-tuning experiment. We use instruction tuning specifically tailored towards taxonomy discovery. In the prefix prompt documented in Listing 1.4, given two concepts A and B, the model must return "True" if A is a subclass of B and "False" otherwise. We train the model on 20 epochs, with a batch size of 4 and a learning rate of $3 \cdot 10^{-6}$. For efficient training, we quantize the model on 4 bits and use the LoRA [10] method with parameters $\alpha = 256$ and $r = 1024$.

Metrics. Similarly to the first experiment, we use Precision, Recall and F1-score to evaluate the performance of the model on the testing set.

Results. The results of the fine-tuning experiment are reported in Table 7. Two general observations can be made about the experiment. Firstly, we notice that fine-tuning drastically improves the task-specific performance of the LLM regardless the domain and corpus version. For instance, while Falcon-7B seems to be initially worse-performing than Zephyr-7B-β overall, the F1-score improves up to almost threefold (real WN-music dataset, from 0.327 to 0.874). Although not surprising for real corpora, an improvement on gibberish corpora is non-trivial: the LLMs show signs of adaptation on gibberish corpora with improved

Table 7. Taxonomy discovery results with fine-tuning in the GT(X) vs X setting, where X is either `en` or `gib`. Evaluation is performed before and after fine-tuning.

Model (X)	When	WN-sweets			WN-football			WN-music		
		Pre.	Rec.	F1	Pre.	Rec.	F1	Pre.	Rec.	F1
Falcon-7B (`en`)	Before	.564	.507	.388	.561	.504	.325	.631	.509	.327
	After	.923	.902	.907	.867	.871	.868	.874	.881	.874
Falcon-7B (`gib`)	Before	.275	.491	.352	.594	.501	.309	.314	.498	.300
	After	.725	.663	.655	.685	.687	.679	.708	.703	.683
Zephyr-7B-β (`en`)	Before	.898	.845	.853	.772	.679	.618	.783	.722	.674
	After	.905	.906	.897	.940	.939	.939	.941	.939	.940
Zephyr-7B-β (`gib`)	Before	.746	.572	.500	.740	.621	.535	.723	.589	.479
	After	.840	.816	.796	.859	.810	.817	.839	.846	.839

performance. Secondly, while the performance of a model on a gibberish corpus increases after fine-tuning, it never matches the performance of the same model fine-tuned on the real counterpart of the corpus. It is worth noting that this is a limitation of adaptation solely due to the reliance on prior semantics, since a corpus and its gibberish counterpart only differ in their input-label mapping.

Transfer Learning. In spite of the two previous observations, we can hypothesize that the improvement in performance on the gibberish corpora may indicate signs of reasoning and generalization on unseen domains, given that gibberish words are most likely not contained in the vocabulary of LLMs. To elaborate this claim, we propose another experiment: we use Zephyr-7B-β, trained for taxonomy discovery in a domain, and test it on another domain. By only using gibberish corpora, we ensure that most of the domain-specific terminology is anonymized, preventing the LLM from effectively using prior semantics. Results are reported in Fig. 3. We observe the following. Firstly, the F1-scores generally tend to increase after transfer, with the exception of the WN-music to WN-sweets case. The increase in F1-score is substantial, from 14% (WN-football to WN-sweets), up to 32% (WN-music to WN-football). This result is quite promising, as it points towards the possibility of OL on arbitrary domains with LLMs with effective pre-training. Secondly, the precision tends to drop in favor of the recall, indicating that fine-tuning makes the LLM more sensitive to syntactic clues of hypernymy relations at the cost of making them less precise. Due to the fact that both the training and the testing domains are made of gibberish words, we attribute the performance improvements of the LLM (with respect to its base version) to emerging reasoning capabilities: the fine-tuning LLM becomes more capable of abstraction and of focusing on semantic relationships between concepts, rather than the concepts themselves.

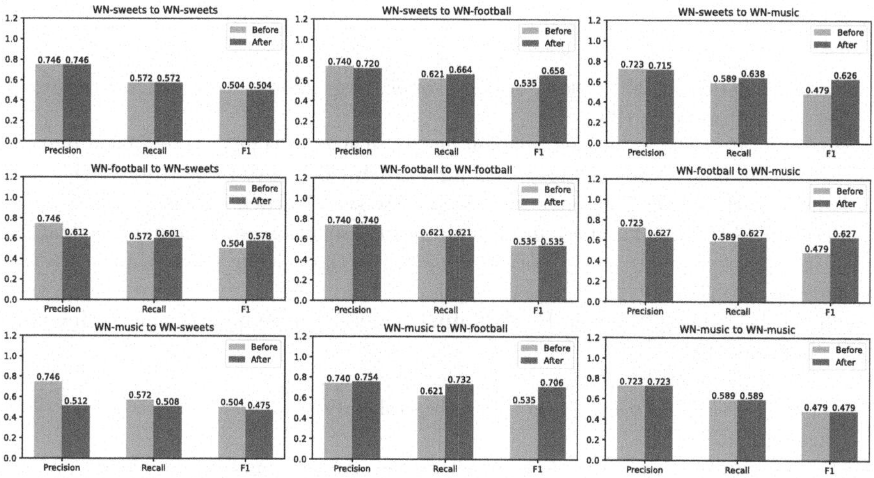

Fig. 3. Domain transfer experiment results with Zephyr-7B-β. Only gibberish corpora are selected for both training and testing.

5 Conclusion

We have explored and tested the limits of adaptability and generalizability of LLMs, and observed that LLMs do not adapt well to arbitrary domains. By creating gibberish datasets based on real data and real domains from WordNet, and using LLMs to perform ontology learning tasks on these data, it is realized that LLMs are unable to consistently retrieve the same taxonomic relationships between analogous concepts, which highlights their clear reliance on priorly learned semantics, lexical senses, and the frame of the tokens. However, we notice that after fine-tuning on gibberish data, LLMs improve at discovering hierarchies, both on the domain they were trained on and other arbitrary domains. We attribute this improvement to the emergence of reasoning with lexical semantics. Our work serves as cautionary advice for the community that LLMs do not adapt to arbitrary domains, and we hope that it can inspire future work to leverage reasoning with LLMs for Ontology Learning.

Supplemental Material Statement. Generated datasets (real and gibberish for all domains), source code for generating the synthetic datasets from the Open English WordNet, and for fine-tuning or evaluating LLMs on OL tasks are available online.[3]

Acknowledgement. The work was partially supported by EU project: enRichMyData (HORIZON-CL4-2021-DATA-01 - GA 101070284).

[3] https://github.com/boschresearch/llm-vs-gibberish-ontologies.

References

1. Almazrouei, E., et al.: Falcon-40B: an open large language model with state-of-the-art performance (2023)
2. Bodenreider, O.: The unified medical language system (umls): integrating biomedical terminology. Nucleic Acids Res. **32 Database issue**, D267–70 (2004)
3. Brown, T.B., et al.: Language models are few-shot learners (2020)
4. Caufield, J.H., et al.: Structured prompt interrogation and recursive extraction of semantics (spires): a method for populating knowledge bases using zero-shot learning (2023)
5. Cheng, D., Huang, S., Wei, F.: Adapting large language models via reading comprehension (2024)
6. GeoNames: Geonames. https://www.geonames.org/
7. Giglou, H.B., D'Souza, J., Auer, S.: Llms4ol: large language models for ontology learning (2023)
8. Gururangan, S., et al.: Don't stop pretraining: Adapt language models to domains and tasks. In: Jurafsky, D., Chai, J., Schluter, N., Tetreault, J. (eds.) Proceedings of the 58th Annual Meeting of the Association for Computational Linguistics, pp. 8342–8360. Association for Computational Linguistics (2020). https://doi.org/10.18653/v1/2020.acl-main.740
9. Hertling, S., Paulheim, H.: Olala: ontology matching with large language models. In: Proceedings of the 12th Knowledge Capture Conference 2023. K-CAP '23, New York, NY, USA, pp. 131–139. Association for Computing Machinery (2023). https://doi.org/10.1145/3587259.3627571
10. Hu, E.J., et al.: Lora: low-rank adaptation of large language models (2021)
11. Kauf, C., et al.: Event knowledge in large language models: the gap between the impossible and the unlikely (2023)
12. Li, J., Cheng, X., Zhao, W.X., Nie, J.Y., Wen, J.R.: Halueval: a large-scale hallucination evaluation benchmark for large language models (2023)
13. Li, X.L., Kuncoro, A., Hoffmann, J., de Masson d'Autume, C., Blunsom, P., Nematzadeh, A.: A systematic investigation of commonsense knowledge in large language models. In: Goldberg, Y., Kozareva, Z., Zhang, Y. (eds.) Proceedings of the 2022 Conference on Empirical Methods in Natural Language Processing, Abu Dhabi, United Arab Emirate, pp. 11838–11855. Association for Computational Linguisticss (2022). https://doi.org/10.18653/v1/2022.emnlp-main.812
14. Liu, H., Singh, P.: Conceptnet - a practical commonsense reasoning tool-kit. BT Technol. J. **22**(4), 211-226 (2004). https://doi.org/10.1023/B:BTTJ.0000047600.45421.6d
15. Mateiu, P., Groza, A.: Ontology engineering with large language models (2023)
16. McCrae, J.P., Rademaker, A., Bond, F., Rudnicka, E., Fellbaum, C.: English WordNet 2019 – an open-source WordNet for English. In: Vossen, P., Fellbaum, C. (eds.) Proceedings of the 10th Global Wordnet Conference, pp. 245–252. Global Wordnet Association, Wroclaw, Poland (2019)
17. Miller, G.A.: Wordnet: a lexical database for English. Commun. ACM **38**(11), 39–41 (1995). https://doi.org/10.1145/219717.219748
18. Min, S., et al.: Rethinking the role of demonstrations: what makes in-context learning work? (2022)
19. Moskvoretskii, V., Neminova, E., Lobanova, A., Panchenko, A., Nikishina, I.: Taxollama: wordnet-based model for solving multiple lexical sematic tasks (2024)

20. Norouzi, S.S., Mahdavinejad, M.S., Hitzler, P.: Conversational ontology alignment with chatgpt (2023)
21. OpenAI: Gpt-4 technical report (2024)
22. Petroni, F., et al.: Language models as knowledge bases? (2019)
23. Seitner, J., et al.: A large DataBase of hypernymy relations extracted from the web. In: Calzolari, N., et al. (eds.) Proceedings of the Tenth International Conference on Language Resources and Evaluation (LREC'16), Portorož, Slovenia, pp. 360–367. European Language Resources Association (ELRA) (2016)
24. Shin, S., et al.: On the effect of pretraining corpora on in-context learning by a large-scale language model. In: Carpuat, M., de Marneffe, M.C., Meza Ruiz, I.V. (eds.) Proceedings of the 2022 Conference of the North American Chapter of the Association for Computational Linguistics: Human Language Technologies, Seattle, United States, pp. 5168–5186. Association for Computational Linguistics (2022). https://doi.org/10.18653/v1/2022.naacl-main.380
25. Sun, K., Xu, Y.E., Zha, H., Liu, Y., Dong, X.L.: Head-to-tail: How knowledgeable are large language models (llm)? A.K.A. will llms replace knowledge graphs? (2023)
26. Touvron, H., et al.: Llama 2: open foundation and fine-tuned chat models (2023)
27. Tunstall, L., et al.: Zephyr: direct distillation of LM alignment (2023)
28. wan, Z., Zhang, Y., Wang, Y., Cheng, F., Kurohashi, S.: Reformulating domain adaptation of large language models as adapt-retrieve-revise (2023)
29. Wei, J., et al.: Emergent abilities of large language models (2022)
30. Wei, J., et al.: Chain-of-thought prompting elicits reasoning in large language models (2023)
31. Wei, J., et al.: Symbol tuning improves in-context learning in language models (2023)
32. Wei, J., et al.: Larger language models do in-context learning differently (2023)
33. Zhao, Z., Lee, W.S., Hsu, D.: Large language models as commonsense knowledge for large-scale task planning (2023)

Supervised Relational Learning with Selective Neighbor Entities for Few-Shot Knowledge Graph Completion

Jiewen Hou[1], Tianxing Wu[1,2(✉)], Jingting Wang[1], Shuang Wang[1,2], and Guilin Qi[1,2]

[1] Southeast University, Nanjing, China
{jiewenhou,jtwang,shuangwang,gqi}@seu.edu.cn

[2] Key Laboratory of New Generation Artificial Intelligence Technology and Its Interdisciplinary Applications, Southeast University, Ministry of Education, Nanjing, China
tianxingwu@seu.edu.cn

Abstract. Knowledge graphs have powerful reasoning capabilities, but they suffer from incompleteness and long-tail distributions of relations. Few-shot knowledge graph (KG) completion aims to address these issues by completing missing triplets for few-shot relations which only have limited existing triplets. Existing methods attempt to learn few-shot relation embeddings by utilizing the head and tail entity embeddings within the same triplets. Such entity embeddings are enhanced from their respective neighborhoods, but these methods fail to select crucial neighbor entities relevant to the relations. In this paper, to solve this problem, we propose a new Supervised Relational Learning (SuperRL) model with selective neighbor entities for few-shot KG completion. In SuperRL, we first enhance head and tail entity embeddings based on a cascaded embedding enhancement network with different neighbor entity encoders, which can select crucial neighbor entities for few-shot relations from different perspectives. We then jointly perform dual contrastive learning and metric learning to provide different supervision signals for relational learning. Extensive experiments on benchmark datasets have substantiated the superiority of SuperRL in different evaluation metrics over the state-of-the art baselines. The source code is publicly available at: https://github.com/seucoin/SuperRL.

1 Introduction

Knowledge graph (KG) consists of a set of factual triplets, where each one denoted as (h, r, t) expresses the relation r between a head entity h and a tail entity t. Large-scale knowledge graphs (KGs) [18,23,24] offer potent reasoning capabilities for various intelligent applications [5,20], but KGs are incomplete since new knowledge is always emerging over time. This inspires the exploration of KG completion, which seeks to predict the absent elements within incomplete triplets. Thus, various relational learning models [19] have been proposed to learn embeddings of entities and relations to perform KG completion. However, real-world KGs suffer from the long-tail problem, where a significant proportion of relations only have a limited number of triplets. Consequently, the performance of traditional embedding based KG completion methods

G. Demartini et al. (Eds.): ISWC 2024, LNCS 15231, pp. 144–161, 2025.
https://doi.org/10.1007/978-3-031-77844-5_8

degrades significantly when completing missing triplets for few-shot relations which only have limited existing triplets.

To address this challenge, several relational learning methods for few-shot KG completion have been proposed, including metric-based methods (e.g., GMatching [25] and FAAN [15]) and meta-learner-based methods (e.g., MetaR [2], GANA [14], and HiRe [22]). These methods focus on completing missing triplets for few-shot relations, and the core task is to predict the tail entity t for each query triplet $(h, r, ?)$ only given K reference triplets about the relation r. Metric-based methods complete missing triplets by calculating similarities with few-shot relation embeddings generated from the reference triplets, while meta-learner-based methods achieve this by transferring meta-information from the derived few-shot relation embeddings. As the embeddings of few-shot relations are initially unknown, most existing methods use the head and tail entity embeddings enhanced from their respective neighborhoods to compose entity pair embeddings, which are further utilized to generate few-shot relation embeddings. However, they overlook two types of neighbor entities crucial for representing few-shot relations, resulting in the embeddings results insufficient to high-quality few-shot KG completion.

In this study, we propose a new **Super**vised **R**elational **L**earning (**SuperRL**) model, which can select crucial neighbor entities for few-shot KG completion. We categorize such crucial neighbor entities into two groups: directly relevant entities and indirectly relevant entities. **Directly relevant entities** consist of neighbor entities from two different levels:

- **Triplet-level relevant entities** are the neighbor entities of the head entity (or the tail entity) relevant to the tail entity (or the head entity). As illustrated in Fig. 1.i, the neighbor entity `United States` is geographically relevant to the tail entity `Washington DC` and the neighbor entity `White House` holds geographical relevance to the head entity `Joe Biden`. These triplet-level relevant entities are beneficial to represent the current relation `Geo-political location` between `Joe Biden` and `Washington DC`.
- **Context-level relevant entities** are the neighbor entities of the head entity (or the tail entity) relevant to the neighbor entities of the tail entity (or the head entity). As shown in Fig. 1.ii, the neighbor entity `Southeast Asia` of the head entity `Coconut` is geographically relevant to the neighbor entity `Southeast Asian countries` of the tail entity `Malaysia`. The context-level relevant entities are important to represent the relation `Agriculture from country`.

Indirectly relevant entities are introduced based on their N-order relevance to the directly relevant entities:

- **One-order indirectly relevant entities** are the neighbor entities relevant to directly relevant entities. As shown in Fig. 1.iii, the neighbor entity `Democratic Party`, is politically relevant to the `United States` which is a directly relevant entity to the tail entity `Washington DC`. This one-order indirectly relevant entity emphasizes the political attribute of the `Geo-political location` relation, which is crucial for representing the `Geo-political location` relation.

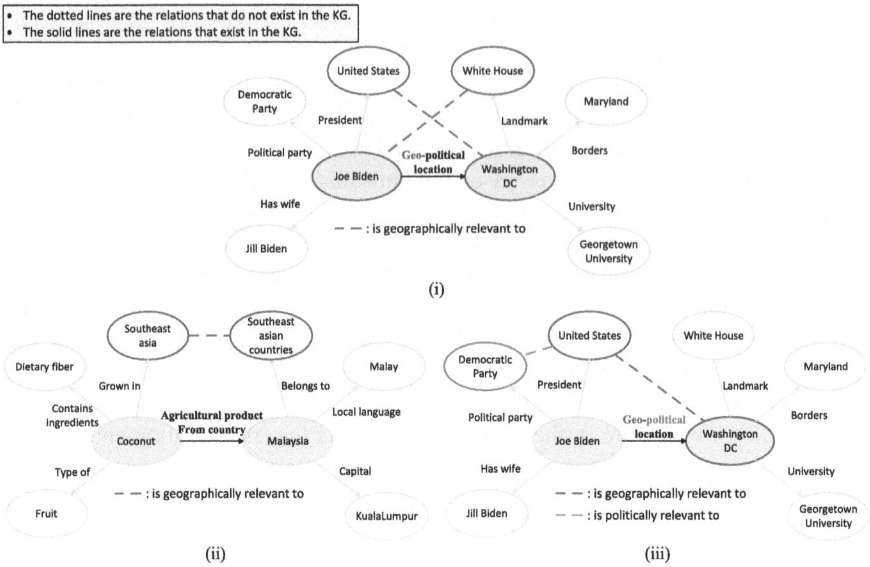

Fig. 1. An illustration of directly relevant entities and indirectly relevant entities in a KG. (i) **Triplet-level relevant entities**: the neighbor entity `United States` is geographically relevant to the tail entity `Washington DC`, and the neighbor entity `White House` is geographically relevant to the head entity `Joe Biden`. (ii) **Context-level relevant entities**: the neighbor entity `Southeast Asia` is geographically relevant to the neighbor entity `Southeast Asian countries`. (iii) **One-order indirectly relevant entities**: The neighbor entity `Democratic Party` is politically relevant to the directly relevant entity `United States`.

- ***N*-order indirectly relevant entities** are the neighbor entities relevant to $(N-1)$-order indirectly relevant entities.

In our proposed SuperRL, a cascaded embedding enhancement network is firstly established to generate entity pair embeddings enriched with the information of both directly and indirectly relevant entities for few-shot relations. To achieve this, we design two neighbor entity encoders within the network to enhance embeddings of the head and tail entities leveraging different-level directly relevant entities. Besides, such neighbor entity encoders are utilized to construct multiple enhancement layers, which are connected in a cascading manner to successively incorporate the information of indirectly relevant entities. We then apply dual contrastive learning and metric learning with entity pair embeddings to provide different supervision signals for relational learning. In dual contrastive learning, we aim to improve the consistency of entity pair embeddings enhanced by different neighbor entity encoders. In metric learning, supervision signals are introduced by calculating similarities between entity pair embeddings of the given queries and few-shot relation embeddings derived from existing triplets. Extensive experiments on two benchmark datasets demonstrate that SuperRL significantly outperforms the state-of-the-art baselines in different evaluation metrics.

In summary, this paper has the following contributions:

- We identify two types of neighbor entities (i.e., directly relevant entities and indirectly relevant entities) crucial for representing few-shot relations. They play a vital role in relational learning for few-shot KG completion.
- We propose a new supervised relational learning model (i.e., SuperRL) for few-shot KG completion. SuperRL applies a cascaded embedding enhancement network to enhance head and tail entity embeddings by encoding directly and indirectly relevant entities for few-shot relations. Dual contrastive learning and metric learning are jointly utilized to provide different supervision signals for relational learning.
- We conduct extensive experiments on two benchmark datasets for few-shot KG completion and the results show the effectiveness and superiority of SuperRL compared with baseline methods.

2 Related Work

2.1 Relational Learning for KG Completion

The key of traditional relational learning methods [19] for KG completion is to learn embeddings of entities and relations. KG embeddings preserve structural information, which can be used for KG completion. The pioneering model TransE [1] introduces the concept of using relation r as a translation for learning embeddings, expressed as $\boldsymbol{h} + \boldsymbol{r} \approx \boldsymbol{t}$ for the triplet (h, r, t). A scoring function is then employed to assess the translation quality and facilitate learning in a unified embedding space. Subsequent models, such as TransH [21] and TransR [12], incorporate relation-specific information to enhance embedding learning. ComplEx [17] learns KG embeddings in a complex space, using bilinear transformations to model relations between entities. RotatE [16] interprets the relation as a rotation between the head entity and the tail entity in a complex space. ConvE [4] and ConvKB [13] utilize convolution operators to augment entity/relation embedding learning. However, these methods require a substantial number of triplets for each relation in the training process, and their performance significantly degrades in few-shot settings where only a limited number of triplets are available for each relation. Therefore, a series of few-shot KG completion methods have been proposed to solve this problem (see Sect. 2.2 for details).

2.2 Few-Shot KG Completion

Existing few-shot KG completion methods can be categorized into two primary groups: (1) Metric-based methods: The first work in formulating few-shot KG completion is GMatching [25]. GMatching comprises a neighbor encoder that enhances entity pair embeddings from their one-hop neighbors to represent few-shot relations, and a matching processor comparing similarities between the relation representations acquired from the query and the reference set, respectively. FSRL [27] extends the setting to more shots and investigates how to integrate relation representations acquired from multiple reference triplets. FAAN [15] proposes a one-hop neighbor aggregator with dynamic attention mechanism to enhance entity pair embeddings. CIAN [11] further incorporates a cross-attention module to facilitate interactions between neighbor entities. (2) Meta-learner-based methods: MetaR [2] learns to transfer meta information of few-shot relations with the MAML training strategy [6], and generates few-shot relation embeddings by averaging the embeddings of all reference triplets. GANA [14] places increased emphasis on neighboring information and introduces a gated and attentive neighbor aggregator accordingly. HiRe [22] attempts to learn relation embeddings by jointly capturing three-level relational information.

Since few-shot KG completion lacks sufficient triplet instances, existing methods have utilized entity neighborhoods to introduce more contextual information, thereby improving the completion performance. However, the major limitation of these methods is that they neglect relevant neighbor entities crucial for learning generalizable few-shot relation embeddings, which may lower the quality of the learnt embeddings for few-shot KG completion, and we aim to solve this problem in this paper.

3 Problem Formulation

In this section, we formally define the problem of few-shot KG completion and its relevant concepts.

Definition 1 (Knowledge Graph). *A knowledge graph is a repository of factual knowledge denoted as* $\mathcal{G} = (\mathcal{E}, \mathcal{R}, \mathcal{T})$, *where* $\mathcal{E}$ *represents the set of entities,* $\mathcal{R}$ *stands for the set of relations (including high-frequency relations and few-shot relations), and* $\mathcal{T}$ *denotes the set of relational triplets defined as* $\mathcal{T} = \{(h, r, t) \in \mathcal{E} \times \mathcal{R} \times \mathcal{E}\}$.

Definition 2 (Neighbor Entity). *Given a triplet* (h, r, t) *of a few-shot relation* r*, the set of one-hop neighbor entities of the* h *and* t *is defined as* $\mathcal{N}_h$ *and* $\mathcal{N}_t$*, respectively. Each neighbor entity in* $\mathcal{N}_h$ *(or* $\mathcal{N}_t$*) is directly linked to the head entity* h *(or the tail entity* t*).*

Definition 3 (Few-Shot Knowledge Graph Completion). *Few-shot knowledge graph completion is to predict the missing tail entity for each query* $(h, r, ?)$ *of a relation* $r \in \mathcal{R}$ *only given its reference set* $\mathcal{S}_r = \{(h_i, r, t_i)|(h_i, r, t_i) \in \mathcal{G}\}$*, and* $|\mathcal{S}_r|$ *is a small number.*

For few-shot KG completion, we divide few-shot relations into three disjoint sets: $\mathcal{R}_{train}$, $\mathcal{R}_{valid}$, and $\mathcal{R}_{test}$ for training, validating, and testing, respectively. The training process is to train our model to accomplish K-shot KG completion for each few-shot relation $r \in \mathcal{R}_{train}$, where the tasks can be denoted as $\mathcal{T}_{train} = \{(\mathcal{S}_r, \mathcal{Q}_r)|r \in \mathcal{R}_{train}\}$. $\mathcal{S}_r = \{(h_i, r, t_i)\}_{i=1}^{K}$ and $\mathcal{Q}_r = \{(h_i, r, t_i)\}_{i=1}^{|\mathcal{Q}_r|}$ are the reference set and query set of r, respectively. In the process of validating and testing, our model performance is evaluated on $\mathcal{T}_{valid} = \{(\mathcal{S}_{r'}, \mathcal{Q}_{r'})|r' \in \mathcal{R}_{valid}\}$ and $\mathcal{T}_{test} = \{(\mathcal{S}_{r''}, \mathcal{Q}_{r''})|r'' \in \mathcal{R}_{test}\}$, respectively.

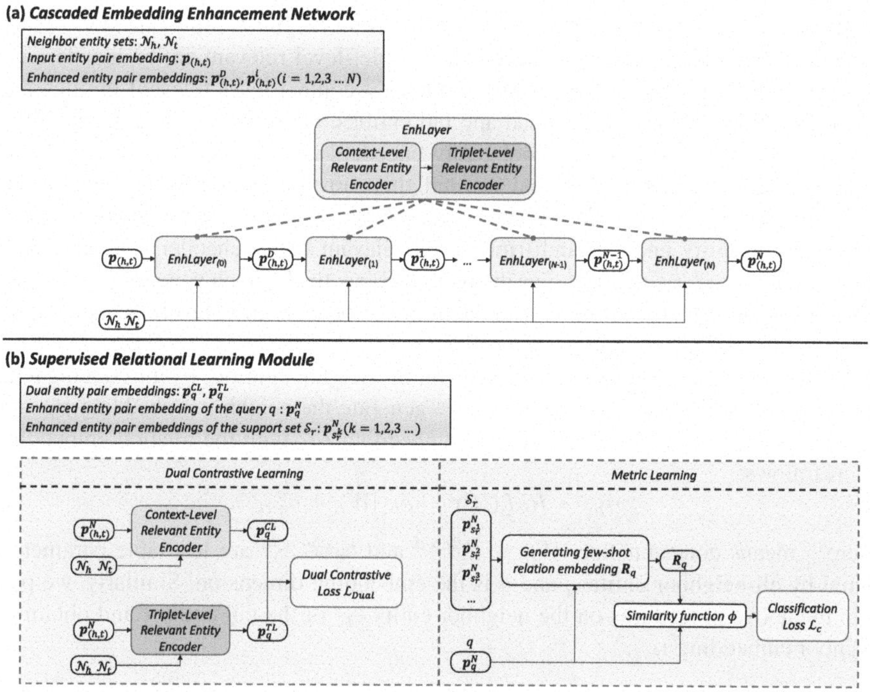

Fig. 2. The overview of SuperRL. **(a) The cascaded embedding enhancement network**, which uses neighbor entity encoders to capture the information of directly relevant entities and utilizes multiple enhancement layers to further incorporate the information of indirectly relevant entities. **(b) The supervised relational learning module**, which applies dual contrastive learning and metric learning to provide different supervision signals.

4 Methodology

In this section, we introduce SuperRL, our supervised relational learning model with selective neighbor entities for few-shot KG completion. Figure 2 provides an overview of SuperRL, which consists of two key components: (1) **Cascaded Embedding Enhancement Network**. Multiple enhancement layers consisting of different neighbor entity encoders are used for generating entity pair embeddings enriched with the information of both directly relevant entities and indirectly relevant entities for few-shot relations. (2) **Supervised Relational Learning Module**. Dual contrastive learning and metric learning provide different supervision signals with entity pair embeddings for relational learning.

4.1 Cascaded Embedding Enhancement Network

In this subsection, we introduce our designed neighbor entity encoders and the enhancement layers composed of such encoders in the proposed cascaded embedding enhancement network.

Neighbor Entity Encoders. We design two different neighbor entity encoders, which are context-level relevant entity encoder and triplet-level relevant entity encoder, and they use a cross-attention mechanism to identify context-level relevant entities and triplet-level relevant entities for head and tail entities, respectively. Specifically, given a triplet (h, r, t), the above neighbor entity encoders take the entity pair embedding $\boldsymbol{p}_{(h,t)}$ (the concatenation of $\boldsymbol{h}$ and $\boldsymbol{t}$), and the corresponding neighbor entity sets $\mathcal{N}_h = \{e_{h_i} | (h, r_{h_i}, e_{h_i}) \in \mathcal{G}\}$ and $\mathcal{N}_t = \{e_{t_j} | (t, r_{t_j}, e_{t_j}) \in \mathcal{G}\}$ as the input. Context-level relevant entity encoder and triplet-level relevant entity encoder generate entity pair embeddings $\boldsymbol{p}^{CL}_{(h,t)}$ and $\boldsymbol{p}^{TL}_{(h,t)}$ as the output, respectively. Such generated entity pair embeddings are actually enriched with the information of context-level relevant entities and triplet-level relevant entities, respectively.

We first generate neighbor embeddings for the neighbor entities by introducing relation information. Taking h as the target, we generate the neighbor embedding $\boldsymbol{n}_{h_i}$ for the neighbor entity e_{h_i} by integrating its embedding $\boldsymbol{e}_{h_i}$ with the relation embedding $\boldsymbol{r}_{h_i}$ as follows:

$$\boldsymbol{n}_{h_i} = ReLU([\boldsymbol{r}_{h_i} \| \boldsymbol{e}_{h_i}]W_n + b_n), \tag{1}$$

where $\|$ means concatenation, $W_n \in \mathbb{R}^{2d \times d}$ and $b_n \in \mathbb{R}^d$ are learnable parameters shared by all neighbor entities, and d is the embedding dimension. Similarly, we perform the above procedures on the neighbor entity e_{t_j} of the tail entity t and obtain its neighbor embedding $\boldsymbol{n}_{t_j}$.

(1) Context-Level Relevant Entity Encoder. The context-level relevant entity encoder utilizes context-level relevant entities to enhance the embeddings of the head entity h and the tail entity t. We apply a cross-attention mechanism to identify context-level relevant entities based on embedding similarities, and generate context-level neighbor representation for enhancement. Taking the head entity h as the target, the cross-attention mechanism takes $\mathcal{N}_h$ and $\mathcal{N}_t$ as the input and outputs the context-level neighbor representation $\overline{\boldsymbol{h}}_{CL}$ for h. Specifically, for each $e_{h_i} \in \mathcal{N}_h$, we transform the embedding of each $e_{t_j} \in \mathcal{N}_t$ into the query $\boldsymbol{q}^{CL}_{t_j}$, the neighbor entity embedding $\boldsymbol{e}_{h_i}$ into the key $\boldsymbol{k}^{CL}_{h_i}$, and the neighbor embedding $\boldsymbol{n}_{h_i}$ into the value $\boldsymbol{v}^{CL}_{h_i}$ with three linear transformations, $W^Q_{CL}, W^K_{CL}, W^V_{CL} \in \mathbb{R}^{d \times d}$, respectively, as follows:

$$\boldsymbol{q}^{CL}_{t_j} = \boldsymbol{e}_{t_j} W^Q_{CL}, \;\; \boldsymbol{k}^{CL}_{h_i} = \boldsymbol{e}_{h_i} W^K_{CL}, \;\; \boldsymbol{v}^{CL}_{h_i} = \boldsymbol{n}_{h_i} W^V_{CL}. \tag{2}$$

These linear transformations increase the learnable parameter space, enabling the encoder to learn optimal weights to generate few-shot relation embeddings. Then, we compute the embedding similarity $\text{Att}^{CL}_{e_{h_i}}$ of e_{h_i} with respect to $\mathcal{N}_t$ as:

$$\text{Att}^{CL}_{e_{h_i}} = \frac{\sum_{e_{t_j} \in \mathcal{N}_t} \boldsymbol{q}^{CL}_{t_j} W_{CL} \boldsymbol{k}^{CL^T}_{h_i}}{|\mathcal{N}_t|}, \tag{3}$$

where $W_{CL} \in \mathbb{R}^{d \times d}$ is a trainable weight matrix interpreting the relation between the neighbor entity e_{t_j} and the neighbor entity e_{h_i}, measuring context-level entity relevance. Afterwards, we aggregate neighbor embeddings of context-level relevant entities, generating the context-level neighbor representation $\overline{\boldsymbol{h}}_{CL}$ for h as follows:

$$\overline{\boldsymbol{h}}_{CL} = \sum_{e_{h_i} \in \mathcal{N}_h} \beta_{h_i} \boldsymbol{v}_{h_i}^{CL}, \quad \beta_{h_i} = \frac{exp(\text{Att}_{e_{h_i}}^{CL})}{\sum_{e_{h_k} \in \mathcal{N}_h} exp(\text{Att}_{e_{h_k}}^{CL})}, \tag{4}$$

where β_{h_i} denotes the attention weight of the neighbor entity e_{h_i}. A higher value of β_{h_i} indicates a stronger relevance between e_{h_i} and $\mathcal{N}_t$, thus capturing a more valuable context-level relevant entity. Correspondingly, for the tail entity t, the cross-attention mechanism takes $\mathcal{N}_t$ and $\mathcal{N}_h$ as the input, then generates the context-level neighbor representation $\overline{\boldsymbol{t}}_{CL}$ for t. Finally, we use the context-level neighbor representations $\overline{\boldsymbol{h}}_{CL}$ and $\overline{\boldsymbol{t}}_{CL}$ as well as the original input entity pair embedding $\boldsymbol{p}_{(h,t)}$ to compose the enhanced entity pair embedding $\boldsymbol{p}_{(h,t)}^{CL}$ as follows:

$$\boldsymbol{p}_{(h,t)}^{CL} = ReLU([\overline{\boldsymbol{h}}_{CL} \| \overline{\boldsymbol{t}}_{CL}] W_{E_1} + b_{E_1}) W_{E_2} + \boldsymbol{p}_{(h,t)}. \tag{5}$$

where $W_{E_1}, W_{E_2} \in \mathbb{R}^{2d \times 2d}$, $b_{E_1} \in \mathbb{R}^{2d}$ are trainable matrices.

(2) Triplet-Level Relevant Entity Encoder. The triplet-level relevant entity encoder utilizes triplet-level relevant entities to enhance the embeddings of the head entity h and tail entity t. Similarly, we apply a cross-attention mechanism to identify the triplet-level relevant entities based on embedding similarities, and generate triplet-level neighbor representation for enhancement. Taking the head entity h as the target, the cross-attention mechanism takes $\mathcal{N}_h$ and $\boldsymbol{t}$ as the input, and outputs the triplet-level neighbor representation $\overline{\boldsymbol{h}}_{TL}$ for h. Specifically, for each $e_{h_i} \in \mathcal{N}_h$, we transform the tail entity embedding $\boldsymbol{t}$ into the query $\boldsymbol{q}_t^{TL}$, the neighbor entity embedding $\boldsymbol{e}_{h_i}$ into the key $\boldsymbol{k}_{h_i}^{TL}$, and its corresponding neighbor embedding $\boldsymbol{n}_{h_i}$ into the value $\boldsymbol{v}_{h_i}^{TL}$ with three linear transformations, $W_{TL}^Q, W_{TL}^K, W_{TL}^V \in \mathbb{R}^{d \times d}$, respectively, as follows:

$$\boldsymbol{q}_t^{TL} = \boldsymbol{e}_t W_{TL}^Q, \quad \boldsymbol{k}_{h_i}^{TL} = \boldsymbol{e}_{h_i} W_{TL}^K, \quad \boldsymbol{v}_{h_i}^{TL} = \boldsymbol{n}_{h_i} W_{TL}^V. \tag{6}$$

These linear transformations increase the parameter space in the same way used in the context-level neighbor entity encoder. Then we compute the embedding similarity $\text{Att}_{e_{h_i}}^{TL}$ of e_{h_i} with respect to t as:

$$\text{Att}_{e_{h_i}}^{TL} = \boldsymbol{q}_t^{TL} W_{TL} {\boldsymbol{k}_{h_i}^{TL}}^T, \tag{7}$$

where $W_{TL} \in \mathbb{R}^{d \times d}$ is a trainable weight matrix that measures the triplet level entity relevance between e_{h_i} and t. Then we compute triplet-level neighbor representation $\overline{\boldsymbol{h}}_{TL}$ as follows:

$$\overline{\boldsymbol{h}}_{TL} = \sum_{e_{h_i} \in \mathcal{N}_h} \alpha_{h_i} \boldsymbol{v}_{h_i}^{TL}, \quad \alpha_{h_i} = \frac{exp(\text{Att}_{e_{h_i}}^{TL})}{\sum_{e_{h_j} \in \mathcal{N}_h} exp(\text{Att}_{e_{h_j}}^{TL})}, \tag{8}$$

where α_{h_i} denotes the attention weight of the neighbor entity e_{h_i}. A higher value of α_{h_i} means a stronger relevance between the i-th neighbor entity of h and the tail entity t, thus capturing a more valuable triplet-level relevant entity. Correspondingly, for the tail entity t, the cross-attention mechanism takes $\mathcal{N}_t$ and $\boldsymbol{h}$ as the input and computes the triplet-level neighbor representation $\overline{\boldsymbol{t}}_{TL}$ for t. Finally, we use the triplet-level neighbor representations $\overline{\boldsymbol{h}}_{TL}$ and $\overline{\boldsymbol{t}}_{TL}$ as well as the original input entity pair embedding $\boldsymbol{p}_{(h,t)}$ to compose the enhanced entity pair embedding $\boldsymbol{p}_{(h,t)}^{TL}$ as follows:

$$\boldsymbol{p}_{(h,t)}^{TL} = ReLU([\overline{\boldsymbol{h}}_{TL} \| \overline{\boldsymbol{t}}_{TL}]W_{E_3} + b_{E_2})W_{E_4} + \boldsymbol{p}_{(h,t)}. \tag{9}$$

where $W_{E_3}, W_{E_4} \in \mathbb{R}^{2d \times 2d}$ and $b_{E_2} \in \mathbb{R}^{2d}$ are all trainable matrices.

Enhancement Layers. The aforementioned neighbor entity encoders actually utilize directly relevant entities to enrich the embeddings of the head entity h and the tail entity t in each given triplet (h, r, t). To fully extract the information of directly relevant entities, we choose both the triplet-level and context-level relevant entity encoders to build the enhancement layer. Since indirectly relevant entities can only be introduced on the basis of directly relevant entities, we connect multiple enhancement layers in a cascading manner to further enhance $\boldsymbol{h}$ and $\boldsymbol{t}$ with the information of indirectly relevant entities, from one order to N orders successively.

The i-th enhancement layer, denoted as $EnhLayer_{(i)}$, where a context-level relevant entity encoder and a triplet-level relevant entity encoder are connected sequentially. This is the optimal connection order of the two encoders according to the experimental results, and more details are discussed in Sect. 5.4. Generally, $EnhLayer_{(0)}$ enhances $\boldsymbol{h}$ and $\boldsymbol{t}$ with the information of directly relevant entities, and it takes $\boldsymbol{p}_{(h,t)}, \mathcal{N}_h$, and $\mathcal{N}_t$ as the input. The output is the enhanced entity pair embedding $\boldsymbol{p}_{(h,t)}^{D}$. Furthermore, the output of $EnhLayer_{(0)}$ also serves as the input of $EnhLayer_{(1)}$, which takes $\boldsymbol{p}_{(h,t)}^{D}$, $\mathcal{N}_h$, and $\mathcal{N}_t$ as the input and generates the entity pair embedding $\boldsymbol{p}_{(h,t)}^{1}$ further enriched with the information of one-order indirectly relevant entities. Similarly, the input of the N-th enhancement layer includes the output of $(N-1)$-th enhancement layer $\boldsymbol{p}_{(h,t)}^{N-1}$, $\mathcal{N}_h$, and $\mathcal{N}_t$, and the output is the enhanced entity pair embedding $\boldsymbol{p}_{(h,t)}^{N}$ denoted as:

$$\boldsymbol{p}_{(h,t)}^{N} = EnhLayer_{(N)}(\boldsymbol{p}_{(h,t)}^{N-1}, \mathcal{N}_h, \mathcal{N}_t). \tag{10}$$

In summary, with an $N+1$ layers cascaded embedding enhancement network, we generate the entity pair embedding $\boldsymbol{p}_{(h,t)}^{N}$ enriched with the information of both directly relevant entities and indirectly relevant entities from one to N orders for the subsequent supervised relational learning.

4.2 Supervised Relational Learning Module

To perform supervised relational learning, we first construct the reference set $\mathcal{S}_r$ and the query set $\mathcal{Q}_r$ as follows. Given a few-shot relation $r \in \mathcal{T}_{train}$, we randomly sample K triplets to construct the K-shot reference set $\mathcal{S}_r = \{s_r^k\}_{k=1}^{K}$ where $s_r^k \equiv (h_k, r, t_k) \in \mathcal{S}_r$, and a batch of triplets to construct the query set $\mathcal{Q}_r = \{(h_i, r, t_i)\}_{i=1}^{|\mathcal{Q}_r|}$. For each triplet in $\mathcal{Q}_r$, we replace its tail entity to construct a set of negative query triplets $\mathcal{Q}_r^- = \{(h_q, r, t_q^-) \mid (h_q, r, t_q) \in \mathcal{Q}_r\}$, where $t_q^- \in \{\mathcal{C}_{h_q,r} \setminus t_q\}$. $\mathcal{C}_{h_q,r}$ is the candidate entity set generated from the KG $\mathcal{G}$. We then generate entity pair embeddings for all triplets in $\mathcal{S}_r$, $\mathcal{Q}_r$ and $\mathcal{Q}_r^-$, using the cascaded embedding enhancement network. Finally, we jointly perform dual contrastive learning and metric learning in the supervised relational learning module with these entity pair embeddings for relational learning. Dual contrastive learning is designed to maximize the consistency of entity pair embeddings enhanced with different encoders, since contrastive learning [3] can achieve high-quality embeddings in the encoding process by maximizing the consistency among positive samples, and is often used in the design of various encoders. Besides, we choose metric learning to optimize entity and relation embeddings, because it is widely used to solve the few-shot problem in machine learning, which classifies unseen instances according to their distances to few seen instances in an embedding space learned by deep learning, also achieving the state-of-the-art performance [10].

Dual Contrastive Learning. We introduce dual contrastive learning to improve the consistency of entity pair embeddings using different neighbor entity encoders. This process inherently maximizes the agreement between context-level neighbor representations and triplet-level neighbor representations for the same triplet after multi-layer enhancement. More specifically, for each query $q = (h, r, t) \in \mathcal{Q}_r$, we first enhance the output of cascaded embedding enhancement network $\boldsymbol{p}^N_{(h,t)}$, utilizing a triplet-level relevant entity encoder and a context-level relevant entity encoder, respectively. Then we obtain dual entity pair embeddings $\boldsymbol{p}^{TL}_q$ and $\boldsymbol{p}^{CL}_q$, which are enriched with triplet-level and context-level neighbor representations, respectively. Similarly, we generate dual entity pair embeddings $\boldsymbol{p}^{TL}_{q^-}$ and $\boldsymbol{p}^{CL}_{q^-}$ for each negative query q^-. Based on these, we define two contrastive loss terms for dual contrastive learning, aiming to maximize the consistency of dual entity pair embeddings for positive queries and encourage differences in dual entity pair embeddings between the positive and negative queries as:

$$\begin{aligned} \mathcal{L}_{TL} &= \frac{1}{|Q_r|} \sum_{q \in \mathcal{Q}_r} -log \frac{exp(sim(\boldsymbol{p}^{TL}_q, \boldsymbol{p}^{CL}_q)/\tau)}{\sum_i exp(sim(\boldsymbol{p}^{TL}_q, \boldsymbol{p}^{CL}_{q_i^-})/\tau)}, \\ \mathcal{L}_{CL} &= \frac{1}{|Q_r|} \sum_{q \in \mathcal{Q}_r} -log \frac{exp(sim(\boldsymbol{p}^{CL}_q, \boldsymbol{p}^{TL}_q)/\tau)}{\sum_i exp(sim(\boldsymbol{p}^{CL}_q, \boldsymbol{p}^{TL}_{q_i^-})/\tau)}, \end{aligned} \tag{11}$$

where τ denotes the temperature parameter, and the dual contrastive loss is a combination of the above two contrastive loss terms as follows:

$$\mathcal{L}_{Dual} = \mathcal{L}_{TL} + \mathcal{L}_{CL}. \tag{12}$$

Metric Learning. Inspired by [15], we adopt metric learning to complete missing triplets by calculating similarities between entity pair embeddings of the given queries and few-shot relation embeddings derived from the reference set. Specifically, given a query $q = (h, r, t) \in \mathcal{Q}_r$ and the reference set $\mathcal{S}_r = \{s_r^k\}_{k=1}^K$, we first use the cascaded embedding enhancement network to generate entity pair embeddings $\boldsymbol{p}^N_q$ (i.e., $\boldsymbol{p}^N_{(h,t)}$) and $\boldsymbol{p}^N_{s_r^k}$ for q and each $s_r^k \in \mathcal{S}_r$, respectively. We then compute the embedding similarity γ_k between $\boldsymbol{p}_q^N$ and $\boldsymbol{p}_{s_r^k}^N$ as:

$$\gamma_k = \frac{exp(\boldsymbol{p}_q^N \odot \boldsymbol{p}_{s_r^k}^N)}{\sum_{s_r^k \in \mathcal{S}_r} exp(\boldsymbol{p}_q^N \odot \boldsymbol{p}_{s_r^k}^N)}, \tag{13}$$

where $\odot$ denotes the element-wise production. The few-shot relation embedding $\boldsymbol{R}_q$ for q is generated by aggregating all $\boldsymbol{p}_{s_r^k}^N$ based on γ_k as $\boldsymbol{R}_q = \sum_{s_r^k \in \mathcal{S}_r} \gamma_k \boldsymbol{p}_{s_r^k}^N$, which emphasizes the importance of queries during relational learning. For each negative query $q^- \in \mathcal{Q}_r^-$, the generation of the few-shot relation embedding $\boldsymbol{R}_{q^-}$ is the same as above. To predict the query triplet q based on the learned few-shot relation embedding, we propose the similarity score function ϕ between $\boldsymbol{p}_q^N$ and the corresponding few-shot relation embedding $\boldsymbol{R}_q$ as $\phi(q, \mathcal{S}_r) = \boldsymbol{p}_q^N \odot \boldsymbol{R}_q$.

Here, we define a classification loss with a margin to ensure that a positive query in $\mathcal{Q}_r$ and the reference set have a higher similarity score, as well as a negative query in $\mathcal{Q}_r^-$ and the reference set should have a lower similarity score as follows:

$$\mathcal{L}_{cls} = \sum_{q \in \mathcal{Q}_r} \sum_{q^- \in \mathcal{Q}_r^-} [\gamma - \phi(q, \mathcal{S}_r) + \phi(q^-, \mathcal{S}_r)]_+, \tag{14}$$

where $[x]_+$ is the hinge loss defined as $[x]_+ = \max(0, x)$, and $\gamma > 0$ is the margin.

Training Process. We optimize SuperRL by jointly considering the classification loss and the dual contrastive loss. Our optimization $\mathcal{L}$ is defined as follows:

$$\mathcal{L} = \mathcal{L}_{cls} + \lambda \mathcal{L}_{Dual}, \tag{15}$$

where λ is a hyperparameter that controls the influence of the dual contrastive loss term. We adopt a batch sampling based meta-training procedure [27] to minimize $\mathcal{L}$ for model optimization.

5 Experiments

In this section, we present comprehensive experiments to show the performance of SuperRL and the effectiveness of its essential components.

5.1 Datasets and Evaluation Metrics

We conducted experiments on two widely used few-shot KG completion datasets, Nell-One and Wiki-One, which are constructed by [25]. For fair comparison, we followed the experimental setup of GMatching [25], where relations associated with more than 50 but less than 500 triplets are chosen as few-shot KG completion tasks. For each target relation, we used the candidate set provided by Gmatching. The statistics of both datasets are provided in Table 1. We used 51/5/11 and 133/16/34 tasks for training/validation/testing on Nell-One and Wiki-One, respectively, following the common setting in the literature. We reported MRR (mean reciprocal rank) and Hits@n (n = 1,

5) on both datasets for the evaluation of performance. MRR is the mean reciprocal rank of the correct entities, and Hits@n is the ratio of correct entities that rank in top n. We compared our proposed model against other baseline methods under 3-shot and 5-shot settings, which are the most common settings in the literature.

5.2 Baselines

We compared our model with two categories of baselines: (1) The traditional relational learning models: including TransE [1], TransH [21], DisMult [26], ComplEx [17] and ComplEx-N3 [9]. We used OpenKE [7] to reproduce the results of these models with hyperparameters reported in the original papers. The models are trained using all triplets from relations in the background knowledge graph [25] and training relations, as well as relations from all reference sets. (2) The state-of-the-art few-shot KG completion models: GMatching [25], MetaR [2], FAAN [15], CIAN [11], HiRe [22] and FSRL [27]. For HiRe and FAAN, we directly reported results obtained from the original papers. For GMatching and MetaR, we reported the results provided by [15] and [11], respectively. As FSRL [27] was initially reported in different settings, where the candidate set is much smaller, we reported the results re-implemented by [15] under the same setting with other methods. As CIAN [11] used different training data with different experimental settings, we reproduced it on the same setting as other baselines. As reported in HiRe [22], the reproduced results of GANA [14] is less competitive, we left GANA out in our comparison. All reported results are produced on the same setting and compared using the same training, validation, and test datasets.

Table 1. Statistics of the datasets.

Dataset	#Entities	#Relations	#Triples	#Tasks
Nell-One	68,545	358	181,109	67
Wiki-One	4,838,244	822	5,859,240	183

5.3 Experimental Setup

For fair comparison, we used the entity and relation embeddings pretrained by TransE [1] on both datasets, released by GMatching [25], for the initialization of SuperRL. On both datasets, we set the maximum number of neighbors as 100, and the embedding dimension is set to 100 and 50 on Nell-One and Wiki-One, respectively. We set the temperature parameter τ as 0.1, and the margin of the classification loss γ is set to 5.0. We used Adam optimizer [8] as the optimizer with an initial learning rate of $8e^{-5}$ for Nell-One and $2e^{-4}$ for Wiki-One, respectively. For all experiments except the sensitivity test, the number of enhancement layers L is set to 2 and 8 on Nell-One and Wiki-One, respectively, while the hyperparameter λ is set to 0.06 and 0.09 for 3-shot and 5-shot on both datasets. We applied mini-batch gradient descent to train our model with a batch size of 512 on both datasets. We evaluated on validation set every 10k steps and chose the best model within 300k steps based on MRR. All models are implemented by PyTorch and trained on one V100 GPU card.

5.4 Comparison with Baselines

Table 2. Comparison against state-of-the-art methods on Nell-One and Wiki-One. The best results are indicated by bold numbers, while the runner-up results are indicated by underlined numbers for each metric. The table lacks certain metric results, which are not provided in original papers.

Methods	Nell-One						Wiki-One					
	MRR		Hits@5		Hits@1		MRR		Hits@5		Hits@1	
	3-shot	5-shot	3-shot	5-shot	3-shot	5-shot	3-shot	5-shot	3-shot	5-shot	3-shot	5-shot
TransE	0.162	0.168	0.180	0.186	0.085	0.082	0.040	0.052	0.027	0.057	0.013	0.042
TransH	0.266	0.279	0.299	0.317	0.145	0.162	0.092	0.095	0.091	0.092	0.045	0.047
DisMult	0.201	0.214	0.223	0.246	0.146	0.140	0.052	0.077	0.041	0.078	0.020	0.035
ComplEx	0.228	0.239	0.252	0.253	0.165	0.176	0.064	0.070	0.053	0.063	0.029	0.030
ComplEx-N3	-	0.305	-	0.399	-	0.205	-	-	-	-	-	-
Gmatching	-	0.176	-	0.233	-	0.113	-	0.263	-	0.337	-	0.197
MetaR	0.210	0.209	0.311	0.280	0.119	0.141	0.317	0.323	0.379	0.385	0.261	0.270
FSRL	0.219	0.195	0.296	0.279	0.139	0.108	0.102	0.113	0.131	0.135	0.050	0.056
FAAN	0.247	0.279	0.309	0.364	0.183	0.200	0.298	0.341	0.368	0.395	0.228	0.281
CIAN	0.281	0.289	0.349	0.362	0.211	0.215	0.328	0.329	0.398	0.404	0.258	0.253
HiRe	-	0.306	-	0.439	-	0.207	-	0.371	-	0.419	-	0.319
SuperRL	**0.312**	**0.330**	**0.404**	**0.441**	**0.223**	**0.234**	**0.369**	**0.388**	**0.446**	**0.458**	**0.297**	**0.320**
SuperRL*	0.310	0.317	0.402	0.393	0.223	0.227	0.355	0.362	0.414	0.442	0.286	0.285

Table 2 compares SuperRL (the context-level relevant entity encoder and the triplet-level relevant entity encoder are connected sequentially in enhancement layers) and its variant SuperRL* (the triplet-level relevant entity encoder and the context-level relevant entity encoder are connected sequentially in enhancement layers) against the baselines on Nell-One and Wiki-One under 3-shot and 5-shot settings. In general, traditional KG completion methods are inferior to few-shot KG completion methods. This is because they are designed for the scenarios with sufficient training data. Overall, our SuperRL model outperforms all baseline methods under two settings on both datasets, validating its capability for few-shot KG completion, while SuperRL* is also competitive in comparisons, achieving runner-up results on most metrics. Specifically, SuperRL outperforms other methods significantly in terms of the Hits@1 metric on Nell-One, indicating that SuperRL is more inclined to rank correct triplets at the top position. This is because SuperRL introduces more precise information for few-shot KG completion by identifying directly and indirectly relevant entities. In real-world applications, Hits@1 is more crucial in KG completion, highlighting the superiority of SuperRL in practical scenarios. In addition, on the Wiki-One dataset, where the long-tail distribution of relations is more pronounced, SuperRL significantly improves Hits@5 compared with other baselines while maintaining the optimal Hits@1. This indicates that introducing directly and indirectly relevant entities can effectively tackle few-shot KG completion tasks in more challenging scenarios.

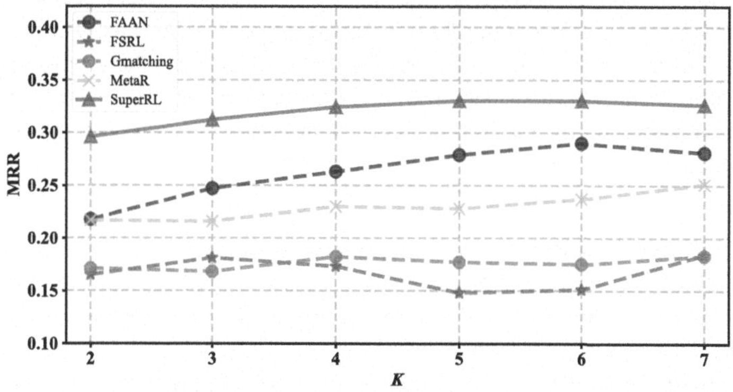

Fig. 3. Impact of few-shot size K on Nell-One.

We conducted experiments on SuperRL when varying the few-shot size K on Nell-One and Wiki-One. As other baselines lack experimental results on Wiki-One in original papers, we only present the comparison results on Nell-One in Fig. 3. Specifically, when the value of K is small, SuperRL significantly outperforms other baseline methods in terms of MRR. This is because directly and indirectly relevant entities are more qualified for few-shot KG completion when only a small number triplets are available. Furthermore, as the value of K increases, SuperRL gets relatively stable improvements compared to other baselines. This is attributed to our metric learning, which aggregates more crucial information for few-shot KG completion as the number of reference triplets increases.

5.5 Ablation Study

To validate the effectiveness of key components in SuperRL, we conducted ablation experiments on the cascaded embedding enhancement network and the supervised relational learning module on both datasets under 5-shot setting. The experimental results are shown in Table 3.

Ablation on Cascaded Embedding Enhancement Network. To verify the effectiveness of the cascaded embedding enhancement network and its different neighbor entity encoders, we removed the triplet-level relevant entity encoders, context-level relevant entity encoders, and the whole cascaded embedding enhancement network in SuperRL, respectively. After removing the context-level or triplet-level relevant entity encoders (i.e., w/o Con-Encoders or w/o Tri-Encoders), we observed a certain degree of performance decline on both datasets, revealing the effectiveness of different neighbor entity encoders. Specifically, on Wiki-One, the performance declines more significantly when removing context-level relevant entity encoders. This indicates that context-level relevant entities can effectively assist SuperRL in generating few-shot relation embeddings on Wiki-One. On Nell-One, we observed a more remarkable decline when removing triplet-level relevant entity encoders. This suggests that triplet-level relevant entities are more crucial for learning few-shot relation embeddings on Nell-One. Overall, SuperRL performs the worst compared to other variants on both datasets when removing the cascaded embedding enhancement network (w/o Enh-Network). This result highlights the significance of both directly and indirectly relevant entities, which play an essential role in relational learning for few-shot KG completion.

Ablation on Supervised Relational Learning Module. To verify the effectiveness of supervised relational learning in SuperRL, we removed dual contrastive learning (w/o $\mathcal{L}_{Dual}$) and metric learning (w/o $\mathcal{L}_{cls}$), respectively. We find that the performance of SuperRL declines significantly when removing metric learning. This demonstrates the necessity of metric learning, which generates few-shot relation embeddings from reference triplets to facilitate effective few-shot KG completion. After removing dual contrastive learning, the performance of SuperRL decreases to some extent. This verifies the role of dual contrastive learning, which can learn high-quality entity pair embeddings to further improve the performance of SuperRL.

Table 3. The ablation study on SuperRL under 5-shot link prediction. The best results are highlighted in bold, and the runner-up results are underlined for each metric.

Configuration	Nell-One			Wiki-One		
	MRR	Hits@5	Hits@1	MRR	Hits@5	Hits@1
SuperRL	**0.330**	**0.441**	**0.234**	**0.388**	**0.458**	**0.320**
SuperRL w/o Con-Encoders	0.303	0.375	<u>0.226</u>	0.338	0.438	0.248
SuperRL w/o Tri-Encoders	0.287	0.370	0.198	0.348	0.425	0.274
SuperRL w/o Enh-Network	0.125	0.141	0.069	0.180	0.226	0.111
SuperRL w/o $\mathcal{L}_{Dual}$	<u>0.306</u>	<u>0.408</u>	0.209	<u>0.367</u>	<u>0.452</u>	<u>0.288</u>
SuperRL w/o $\mathcal{L}_{cls}$	0.197	0.272	0.120	0.193	0.216	0.165

5.6 Parameter Sensitivity

We conducted sensitivity tests under 3/5-shot settings for the number of enhancement layers L and the hyperparameter λ on both datasets, which further reveals the impact

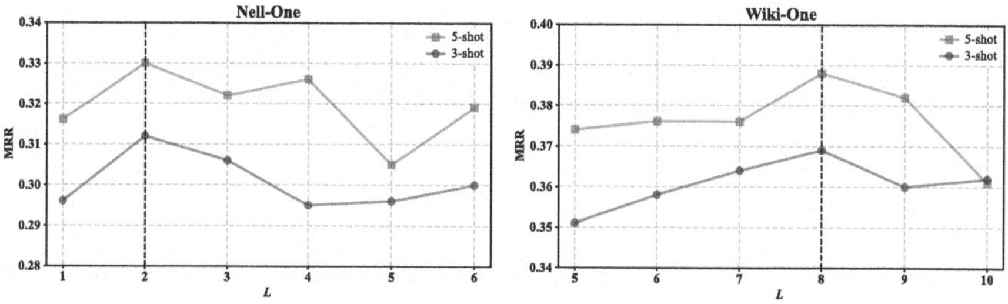

Fig. 4. Sensitivity experiments regarding the number of enhancement layers L on Nell-One and Wiki-One.

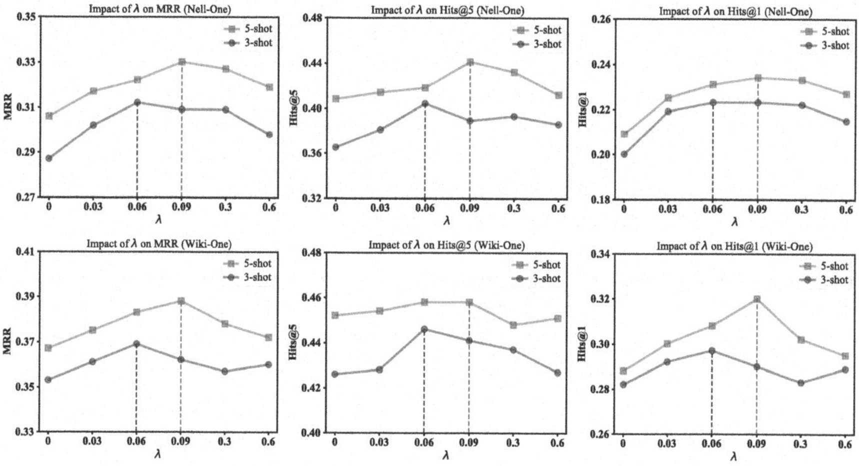

Fig. 5. Sensitivity experiments regarding the hyperparameter λ on Nell-One and Wiki-One.

of N-order indirectly relevant entities and dual contrastive learning in few-shot KG completion.

For the hyperparameter L, we performed sensitivity tests by varying L from 1 to 6 and 5 to 10 on Nell-One and Wiki-One, respectively. As shown in Fig. 4, the MRR of SuperRL reaches a peak and then declines, as the value of L increases on both datasets. The increase of MRR demonstrates the significance of indirectly relevant entities in few-shot KG completion when the order N is relatively small. However, indirectly relevant entities introduce irrelevant noise as N increases further. This reveals the duality of introducing indirectly relevant entities in few-shot KG completion. Besides, we find that the optimal L on Wiki-One is 8, which is higher than the optimal value $L = 2$ on Nell-One. One main reason is that, higher-order indirectly relevant entities may play a crucial role in few-shot KG completion on a more sparse dataset like Wiki-One.

For the hyperparameter λ, since the value of contrastive loss is significantly larger than that of the classification loss, λ should be small to ensure effective supervision from the classification loss. Thus, by varying λ in $\{0, 0.03, 0.06, 0.09, 0.3, 0.6\}$, we performed sensitivity tests on both datasets. In Fig. 5, SuperRL achieves the best results when $\lambda = 0.06$ under the 3-shot setting and $\lambda = 0.09$ under the 5-shot setting on both datasets. This highlights the significance of dual contrastive learning, which is more beneficial for few-shot KG completion as the number of reference triplets increases.

6 Conclusion

This paper explores the role of relevant neighbor entities and their impact on supervised relational learning for few-shot KG completion. We categorize these relevant neighbor entities into two main categories: directly relevant entities and indirectly relevant entities. Based on this, we propose a supervised relational learning model SuperRL leveraging these relevant neighbor entities for few-shot KG completion. SuperRL comprises a cascaded embedding enhancement network to capture the information of both directly and indirectly relevant entities, along with a supervised relational learning module that applies dual contrastive learning and metric learning to provide supervision signals. In experiments, our evaluations not only show that SuperRL significantly outperforms the state-of-the-art baselines in different evaluation metrics, but also confirms the significance of directly relevant entities and indirectly relevant entities as well as the effectiveness of our supervised relational learning model.

Acknowledgements. This work is supported by National Natural Science Foundation of China (Grant No. 62376058, 52378009, 62276063), the Fundamental Research Funds for the Central Universities (2242022R40045), ZhiShan Young Scholar Program of Southeast University, and the Big Data Computing Center of Southeast University.

References

1. Bordes, A., Usunier, N., Garcia-Durán, A., Weston, J., Yakhnenko, O.: Translating embeddings for modeling multi-relational data. In: Proceedings of NeurlIPS, pp. 2787–2795 (2013)
2. Chen, M., Zhang, W., Zhang, W., Chen, Q., Chen, H.: Meta relational learning for few-shot link prediction in knowledge graphs. In: Proceedings of EMNLP-IJCNLP, pp. 4217–4226 (2019)
3. Chen, T., Kornblith, S., Norouzi, M., Hinton, G.: A simple framework for contrastive learning of visual representations. In: Proceedings of ICML (2020)
4. Dettmers, T., Minervini, P., Stenetorp, P., Riedel, S.: Convolutional 2D knowledge graph embeddings. In: Proceedings of AAAI (2018)
5. Du, H., Le, Z., Wang, H., Chen, Y., Yu, J.: COKG-QA: multi-hop question answering over COVID-19 knowledge graphs. Data Intell. **4**(3), 471–492 (2022)
6. Finn, C., Abbeel, P., Levine, S.: Model-agnostic meta-learning for fast adaptation of deep networks. In: Proceedings of ICML, pp. 1126–1135 (2017)
7. Han, X., et al.: OpenKE: an open toolkit for knowledge embedding. In: Proceedings of EMNLP, pp. 139–144 (2018)
8. Kingma, D.P., Ba, J.: Adam: a method for stochastic optimization (2015)
9. Lacroix, T., Usunier, N., Obozinski, G.: Canonical tensor decomposition for knowledge base completion. In: Proceedings of ICML, pp. 2863–2872 (2018)
10. Li, X., Yang, X., Ma, Z., Xue, J.H.: Deep metric learning for few-shot image classification: a review of recent developments. Pattern Recogn. **138**(C) (2023)

11. Li, Y., Yu, K., Huang, X., Zhang, Y.: Learning inter-entity-interaction for few-shot knowledge graph completion. In: Proceedings of EMNLP, pp. 7691–7700 (2022)
12. Lin, Y., Liu, Z., Sun, M., Liu, Y., Zhu, X.: Learning entity and relation embeddings for knowledge graph completion. In: Proceedings of the AAAI Conference on Artificial Intelligence, vol. 29, no. 1 (2015)
13. Nguyen, D.Q., Nguyen, T.D., Nguyen, D.Q., Phung, D.: A novel embedding model for knowledge base completion based on convolutional neural network. In: Proceedings of NAACL, pp. 327–333 (2018)
14. Niu, G., et al.: Relational learning with gated and attentive neighbor aggregator for few-shot knowledge graph completion. In: Proceedings of SIGIR, pp. 213–222 (2021)
15. Sheng, J., et al.: Adaptive attentional network for few-shot knowledge graph completion. In: Proceedings of EMNLP, pp. 1681–1691 (2020)
16. Sun, Z., Deng, Z.H., Nie, J.Y., Tang, J.: RotatE: knowledge graph embedding by relational rotation in complex space. In: Proceedings of ICLR (2019)
17. Trouillon, T., Welbl, J., Riedel, S., Gaussier, E., Bouchard, G.: Complex embeddings for simple link prediction. In: Proceedings of ICML, pp. 2071–2080 (2016)
18. Vrandečić, D., Krötzsch, M.: Wikidata: a free collaborative knowledgebase. Commun. ACM **57**(10), 78–85 (2014)
19. Wang, Q., Mao, Z., Wang, B., Guo, L.: Knowledge graph embedding: a survey of approaches and applications. IEEE Trans. Knowl. Data Eng. **29**(12), 2724–2743 (2017)
20. Wang, X., Lin, T., Luo, W., Cheng, G., Qu, Y.: CKGSE: a prototype search engine for Chinese knowledge graphs. Data Intell. **4**(1), 41–65 (2022)
21. Wang, Z., Zhang, J., Feng, J., Chen, Z.: Knowledge graph embedding by translating on hyperplanes. In: Proceedings of AAAI, pp. 1112–1119 (2014)
22. Wu, H., Yin, J., Rajaratnam, B., Guo, J.: Hierarchical relational learning for few-shot knowledge graph completion. In: Proceedings of ICLR (2023)
23. Wu, T., et al.: AsdKB: a Chinese knowledge base for the early screening and diagnosis of autism spectrum disorder. In: Proceedings of ISWC, Part II, pp. 59–75 (2023)
24. Wu, T., et al.: Knowledge graph construction from multiple online encyclopedias. World Wide Web **23**, 2671–2698 (2020)
25. Xiong, W., Yu, M., Chang, S., Guo, X., Wang, W.Y.: One-shot relational learning for knowledge graphs. In: Proceedings of EMNLP, pp. 1980–1990 (2018)
26. Yang, B., Yih, W., He, X., Gao, J., Deng, L.: Embedding entities and relations for learning and inference in knowledge bases. In: Proceedings of ICLR (2015)
27. Zhang, C., Yao, H., Huang, C., Jiang, M., Li, Z., Chawla, N.V.: Few-shot knowledge graph completion. In: Proceedings of AAAI, pp. 3041–3048 (2020)

Knowledge Graphs for Enhancing Large Language Models in Entity Disambiguation

Gerard Pons(✉), Besim Bilalli, and Anna Queralt

Universitat Politècnica de Catalunya, UPC-BarcelonaTech, Barcelona, Spain
{gerard.pons.recasens,besim.bialli,anna.queralt}@upc.edu

Abstract. Recent advances in Large Language Models (LLMs) have positioned them as a prominent solution for Natural Language Processing tasks. Notably, they can approach these problems in a zero or few-shot manner, thereby eliminating the need for training or fine-tuning task-specific models. However, LLMs face some challenges, including hallucination and the presence of outdated knowledge or missing information from specific domains in the training data. These problems cannot be easily solved by retraining the models with new data as it is a time-consuming and expensive process. To mitigate these issues, Knowledge Graphs (KGs) have been proposed as a structured external source of information to enrich LLMs. With this idea, in this work we use KGs to enhance LLMs for zero-shot Entity Disambiguation (ED). For that purpose, we leverage the hierarchical representation of the entities' classes in a KG to gradually prune the candidate space as well as the entities' descriptions to enrich the input prompt with additional factual knowledge. Our evaluation on popular ED datasets shows that the proposed method outperforms non-enhanced and description-only enhanced LLMs, and has a higher degree of adaptability than task-specific models. Furthermore, we conduct an error analysis and discuss the impact of the leveraged KG's semantic expressivity on the ED performance.

Keywords: Knowledge Graphs · Entity Disambiguation · Large Language Models

1 Introduction

The association of textual mentions in a document to the entities they refer to in a Knowledge Graph (KG) is crucial for many Natural Language Processing (NLP) applications, such as question answering or information retrieval. This task is known as Entity Linking (EL), and it is a fundamental step in the transformation of unstructured text into structured knowledge. EL is usually performed as a pipeline with three different steps. The first one is Mention Detection, which detects the text spans that could possibly be linked to entities. It is followed by the Candidate Generation stage, which selects for each mention the top k entities from the KG that could refer to it, usually based

G. Demartini et al. (Eds.): ISWC 2024, LNCS 15231, pp. 162–179, 2025.
https://doi.org/10.1007/978-3-031-77844-5_9

on precomputed probability distributions from entity-mention hyperlink pairs. Finally in the Entity Disambiguation (ED) step, a final entity is selected from the previously generated set.

Usually, the ED problem is tackled by designing and training task-specific models with large amounts of data (e.g., Wikipedia dumps) [4,9]. In recent years, language models have been used for this task by making use of the mention's context in the document to disambiguate between the possible solutions [6,9, 19]. Additionally, some approaches incorporate the candidates' descriptions [23], classes [30] (e.g., the categories they are tagged with in Wikipedia) or both [4] in the model's input, by generating encodings for these text items. The addition of this knowledge allows zero-shot ED, enabling the models to classify entities that may have not been seen during training time.

Lately, new advances in Large Language Models (LLMs) such as GPT-3 [7], GPT-4 [2] or LLaMA-2 [39], have demonstrated remarkable performance in numerous NLP problems [43]. Given their large-scale and diverse training corpus, they are good candidates to perform tasks, even zero-shot ones, where general knowledge is needed for language processing, such as ED [44]. However, these LLMs still face some challenges, such as hallucination (i.e., the generation of statements that are factually incorrect) [18], and the lack of knowledge about concepts outside their training corpus. To mitigate these issues, the use of KGs to enhance LLMs has been proposed to address different problems [31]. There exist a large variety of KGs, storing information which can be encyclopedic (e.g., DBpedia [3] or YAGO [36], which extract information from Wikipedia), commonsense knowledge (e.g., ConceptNet [35], with information such as $\langle house, has, door\rangle$ or $\langle bed, usedFor, sleep\rangle$) or domain specific [1]. The explicit and structured knowledge they contain can be used to enhance the performance of LLMs, by leveraging it either during pre-training by enriching the training data [17], or during the inference stage [5,37,41]. Following the nomenclature proposed in [31], in this work we focus on KG-enhanced LLM inference, and apply it to the ED task. Our approach takes advantage of KGs to avoid retraining the LLM, and improves the effectiveness of zero-shot LLM approaches for ED.

Solving the ED problem using only LLMs would require to instruct them to choose one of the entities from the candidate set given the document containing the mention. Instead, we propose to extract the candidates' class taxonomy from a KG and use it to guide the disambiguation. For example, taking Query 1 in Fig. 1, given 'MTV awards' appearing in the context, the entity 'Justin' is more likely to be a *Musician* than a *Politician*. Thus, we can use this context to guide the LLM by eliminating invalid solutions such as 'Justin Trudeau', rather than letting the LLM directly predict the entity. Moreover, when all the remaining candidates fall directly under the same class, we retrieve the candidates' descriptions from a Knowledge Base (KB), such as Wikipedia, and append them to the disambiguation prompt (see Fig. 1, query 2). With this Retrieval Augmented Generation (RAG) [21] stage, we provide the LLM with reliable information,

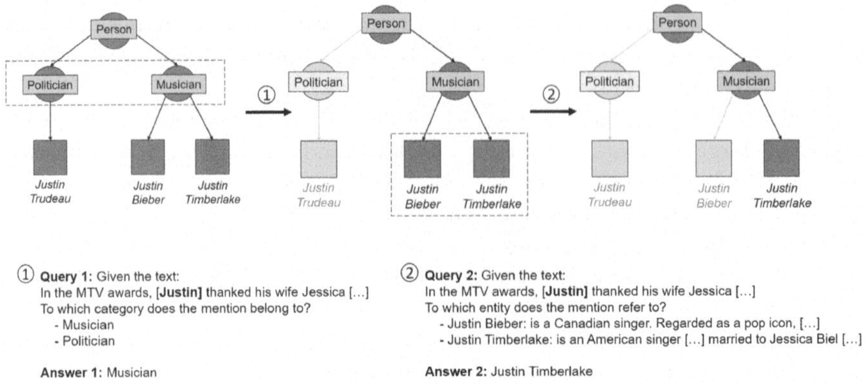

Fig. 1. Overview of the two steps of our approach.

reducing hallucination and enabling the LLM to perform predictions over new or unusual entities which may not have been present in the training corpus.

Therefore, our contributions are as follows:

- We present a method to enhance LLMs in the ED task by leveraging the candidate entity class taxonomies available in KGs. Moreover, we also augment the prompt with the entity descriptions, in order to allow the disambiguation of unseen or difficult entities.
- We evaluate the method against non-enhanced LLMs, description-only enhanced LLMs and a task-specific model by using ten ED datasets. The results show that our approach improves the disambiguation capabilities of LLMs and has a higher degree of adaptability to different domains than the task-specific model.
- We discuss how using KGs with different levels of semantic expressivity (e.g., YAGO and DBpedia) affects the proposed pruning algorithm, by studying both the ED results and the algorithm's performance.
- We study and classify the cases in which our method fails to correctly disambiguate the mention and provide insights on the possible improvements.

The remainder of the paper is structured as follows. In Sect. 2 we discuss the Related Work. In Sect. 3 we formalize the problem and present the proposed approach. In Sect. 4 we describe the different experiments, discuss the results, and conduct an error analysis. Finally, in Sect. 5 we provide our conclusions and ideas for future work.

2 Related Work

This section begins with an overview of different ED methods which leverage external information to improve their predictions. Then, the recently emerged concept of KG-enhanced LLM prompting is introduced, enumerating some of the proposed methods for tackling NLP tasks.

2.1 Knowledge-Augmented ED

Various ED approaches use model architectures that leverage the mention, its surrounding context and candidate entities to generate a solution [6,9,19]. However, some recent works incorporate additional knowledge to the model's input in order to improve the disambiguation of entities which are not present in the training dataset. This extra information is usually gathered from online sources (e.g., Wikipedia) and provided in the form of entity descriptions [23], entity types [30] or both [4]. Additionally, some works leverage the structured information contained in KGs to enhance the model's performance. In [33], information about the entity types from DBpedia and knowledge graph embeddings extracted from Wikipedia's graph structure are incorporated into the model's input. In [38], KG triples are used to train a component of the model's architecture which predicts the existence of facts between mentions in a given document. The result of this prediction is used as input for the final model, which also leverages entity types and descriptions. Finally in [27], the triples from the KG are verbalized and appended to the input sentence before being fed to the model.

These knowledge-augmented ED approaches incorporate the additional information to their model's input, which are mainly built by leveraging LLMs such as BERT [10], RoBERTa [22] or BART [20], and need to be trained or fine-tuned with large amounts of data (e.g., Wikipedia dumps with millions of entities). In contrast, in our approach we rely on the new generation of generative LLMs (e.g., GPT-3 [7], GPT-4 [2] or LLaMA-2 [39]), and solve the ED task by prompting the LLMs in a zero-shot manner without needing to train a task-specific model. This prompting approach has also been explored in [44], where the document's context and the inherent knowledge from the LLM are enriched with the entity textual descriptions, following a RAG approach [21]. RAG has been shown to be useful for incorporating new or relevant information to LLMs, and it has also been leveraged in a specific step of our proposal. However, our main focus is on the usage of KGs to obtain the class hierarchy for the candidate entities, which allows our method to solve the ED task by guiding the LLM to the correct answer (see Sect. 3.2).

2.2 KG-Enhanced LLM Prompting

LLMs can be used to solve a wide range of tasks, not just ED. However, as introduced in Sect. 1, LLMs suffer from problems such as hallucination, which can be accentuated if the information requested is outdated or not present in the training data. Retraining LLMs to incorporate this missing knowledge is expensive and time-consuming, and fine-tuning them could lead to problems such as catastrophically forgetting (i.e., the LLMs' tendency to lose previously obtained knowledge when being fine-tuned with new data) [24]. To solve these issues, KGs can be used as a source of additional structured information in different NLP tasks. In particular, information from a KG can be added to the prompt fed to the LLMs, a technique coined as KG Prompting [31], which has already been explored for Question Answering. In [41], the approach starts by identifying the entities in the question, and then the KG is queried to build subgraphs including them. After that, the LLM is prompted to comprehend and aggregate the subgraphs, and based on the consolidated result it is asked to reason over it and provide the answer. Similarly in [37], the LLM generates these subgraphs by iteratively exploring a KG to create a reasoning path over it. In each iteration, if the LLM believes that has enough information, an answer is provided. Otherwise, it is prompted to continue to traverse the graph, adding the most promising relation to the existing reasoning path each time. Finally in [5], the entities are also first extracted from the question, which are then used to retrieve the triples they participate in within the KG. Then, the triples are verbalized and appended to the prompt as context, which is fed to the LLM to obtain the answer.

In our approach, however, we solve a different task, ED, and we rely on the KG's ontology rather than on the annotated instances, guiding the disambiguation of the entities using the class hierarchy.

3 ED with KG-Enhanced LLMs

In this section we lay out the formulation of the problem to be solved and describe the two different steps of the proposed method.

3.1 Problem Formulation

Let $C = \{e_1, e_2, ...e_{|C|}\}$ be a set of k candidate entities belonging to a KG, containing a class hierarchy in which the entities are annotated, and m be a mention in a document d. The objective of ED is to assign to m the entity e it refers to, such that $e \in C$.

3.2 Method

Our proposed method for the disambiguation of the mention can be divided in two steps. First, a subgraph is generated containing the candidate entities together with their taxonomy of classes. Then, a pruning algorithm is applied to iteratively discard the candidate entities until there is only one left in the subgraph, which will be the solution (see Fig. 1). The implementation can be found in the Supplemental Material.

Subgraph Generation. Given the candidate set C for a mention m, a directed-acyclic graph (DAG) G is created from the KG, having the general class *Thing* as its 'root' (i.e., the only node without predecessors) and the candidate entities as 'leaves' (i.e., the nodes without successors). Note that G cannot be considered a tree as a node can have multiple predecessors (e.g., 'Justin Timberlake' is a linked to the class *Musician* and also to the class *Actor*).

First of all, the candidate entities are linked to the classes they belong to (see Fig. 2, step 1). Then, the classes that are not predecessors of any of the candidates

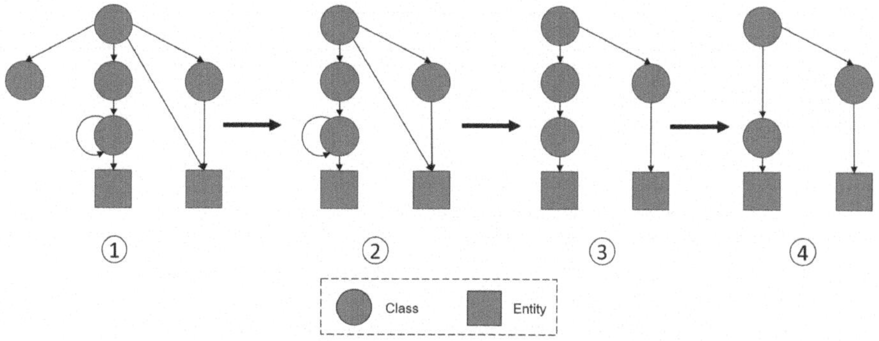

Fig. 2. Overview of the steps for the creation of the DAG.

are removed from G (see Fig. 2, step 2). Next, the relations that can be inferred by traversing G through more granular path of relations are also removed, as well as self-pointing relations (see Fig. 2, step 3). Finally, intermediate nodes which only have one direct successor and that successor is not an entity are also iteratively removed from G, linking the direct successor to the node's direct predecessors (see Fig. 2, step 4). With this last step, we aim to increase the granularity and ease the disambiguation, as the classes in the higher levels of the hierarchy tend to be more abstract (e.g., for the class *Musician*, the path from the root in DBpedia is *Thing* → *Species* → *Eukaryote* → *Person* → *Artist* → *Musician*). In some of the more complex KGs (e.g., YAGO), an entity could also be considered a class. Therefore, if there exist other entities in the candidate set that are linked to this entity, an extra preprocessing step is needed to transform the entity into a leaf, by removing the links to its direct successors while linking them to its direct predecessors.

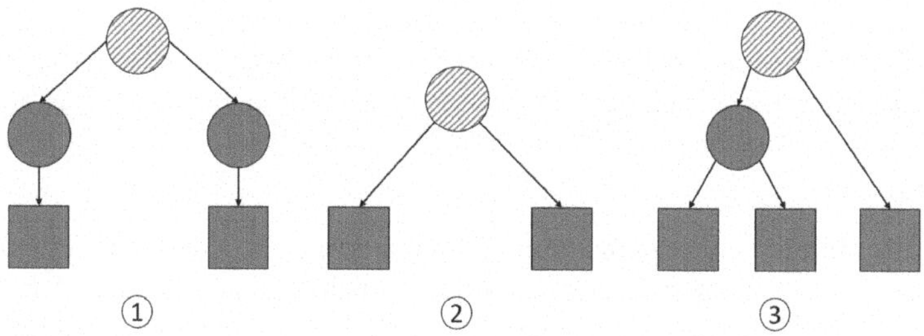

Fig. 3. Example of the three different configurations of the LCA's direct successors.

Algorithm 1: Pruning candidates

```
   Input: Subgraph G, mention m, document d and entity descriptions
   Output: Entity
1  candidates ← leaves(G);
2  while len(candidates) ≠ 1 do
3      LCA ← LCA(G, candidates);
4      directSuccessors ← directSuccessors(G, LCA);
5      if allDirSuccessorsAreClasses then
6          response ← multiChoice(directSuccessors ∪ {None}, m, d);
7          if response ≠ None then
8              G ← prune(G, directSuccessors \ {response});
9          else
10             response ← multiChoice(candidates, m, d, descriptions);
11             G ← prune(G, candidates \ {response});
12     else if allDirSuccessorsAreEntities then
13         response ← multiChoice(directSuccessors, m, d, descriptions);
14         G ← prune(G, directSuccessors \ {response});
15     else
16         D_c, D_e ← getClassesAndEntities(directSuccessors);
17         response ← multiChoice(D_c ∪ {Other}, m, d);
18         if response = Other then
19             G ← prune(G, D_c);
20         else
21             G ← prune(G, directSuccessors \ {response});
22     candidates ← leaves(G);
```

Pruning Algorithm. The pruning algorithm is outlined in Algorithm 1. Given the generated graph G and the initial candidate entities (i.e., its leaves), the algorithm starts by finding the Lowest Common Ancestor (LCA) of the candidate entities. The LCA is defined as the deepest node (i.e., the furthest from the root) which is an ancestor of all the candidates (see dashed nodes in Fig. 3). Then, the direct successors of the LCA are retrieved, which leads to three different scenarios:

1. **All the direct successors are classes (Fig. 3, case 1):** The LLM is prompted to select to which classes the mention m belongs to. All the candidate classes that are not chosen by the LLM are removed from G, along with all the nodes that have become disconnected from the root. This case corresponds to lines 5–12 in Algorithm 1.
2. **All the direct successors are entities (Fig. 3, case 2):** The LLM is prompted to directly select the entity m refers to. Here, the description of each candidate entity is retrieved from a KB and appended to the prompt. The non-selected candidates are then removed from G. This case corresponds to lines 13–15 in Algorithm 1.

3. **Direct successors are classes and entities (Fig. 3, case 3):** The direct successors are organized into classes (D_c), and entities (D_e). The LLM is then prompted to select a class from $D'_c = D_c \cup Other$, where *Other* is an additional class which encompasses D_e. If the LLM selects a class belonging to D_c, the remaining classes and the entities D_e are removed from G. If *Other* is selected, the classes from D_c are removed. Finally, the nodes which have become disconnected from the root are also removed. This case corresponds to lines 16–22 in Algorithm 1.

During the initial tests it was found that the LLM may not return a valid response when it considered that none of the presented classes matched the mention. Therefore, in *case 1* we additionally add the class *None*, which triggers a *case 2* prompt with the remaining candidates if it is selected. Finally, in order to guarantee that the LLM always has information about the entity before making a decision, the response is assessed by the LLM when a single entity is left after a *case 1* or *case 3* step. If it is negatively evaluated, a complete *case 2* prompt is triggered.

The algorithm runs until there is only one leaf (i.e., entity) left in G, which will be the final response. Therefore, in the worst-case scenario there will be k iterations.

4 Experiments

In this section we discuss the experiments performed. First, we describe the experimental settings, then we evaluate our proposal against different methods and also analyze the effect of the KG used. Finally we study the different scenarios that lead to our method failing to correctly disambiguate the mention.

4.1 Settings and Datasets

Datasets. We evaluate the approach on ten popular ED datasets, the same as in [44], which are from news and online articles (MSN [8], AQU [25], ACE04 [32], CWEB [11], R128 [34] and R500 [34]), from Wikipedia (WIKI [13], OKE15 [28] and OKE16 [29]) or from hand-crafted, brief and ambiguous sentences (KORE [15]). These datasets contain documents for which one or various mentions have been annotated with the ground truth entity they refer to. The dataset statistics are summarized in Table 1.

Candidate Sets. To allow for better comparability, we borrow the candidate sets from [44], which combine two methods to obtain sets of size 10. First, as done in previous works [4,9,19], Wikipedia hyperlink count statistics from mention-entity pairs are used to generate the candidates. If not enough candidates are found, the set is augmented by generating candidates with the BLINK model [42], which is based on dense retrieval from context and descriptions.

Table 1. Overview of ten considered datasets' statistics.

	# Docs	# Mentions	Avg. # Characters
KORE	50	144	76.4
ACE04	35	257	2285.0
OKE16	173	288	186.2
R500	357	524	164.8
OKE15	101	536	183.9
R128	113	650	818.8
MSN	20	656	3380.1
AQU	50	727	1415.9
WIKI	319	6793	1624.6
CWEB	320	11154	7575.9

Knowledge Graphs. To obtain the hierarchical representation of the classes we use YAGO [36]. It primarily leverages the information from Wikipedia's infoboxes for generating the relations between entities, and for the taxonomy it borrows the top-level representation from the schema.org ontology [12], which is further refined by carefully integrating it with the fine-grained Wikidata [40] taxonomy. Additionally, in Sect. 4.3 we study the effect of the granularity of the annotation of the classes. To this end, we use another KG with a more simple class hierarchy, DBpedia [3], which is also built on top of Wikipedia but uses a shallow and manually created ontology to define the representation of classes. Finally, to retrieve the entity descriptions we use Wikipedia as a KB, and they are truncated at 250 characters before being appended to the prompt.

Evaluation Metric. We report our results with inKB micro-F1 score (see Eq. 1). InKB means that we only consider a mention if the ground truth entity is present in the KG used. To allow comparability between KGs (i.e., YAGO and DBpedia do not have the same entities annotated), we also report the results by considering the percentage of the Gold F1 score achieved. The Gold F1 score is the maximum inKB micro-F1 score that could be obtained if the method always produced a correct answer when possible, as the candidate sets do not always contain the ground truth entity.

$$\text{micro-F1} = \frac{\text{TP}}{\text{TP} + \frac{1}{2}(\text{FP} + \text{FN})} \tag{1}$$

Additionally, given the differences in dataset sizes we report the weighted average, weighting each score by considering the number of instances of each dataset.

Large Language Models. To perform our experiments we use GPT-3.5, concretely the *gpt-3.5-turbo-1106* model from OpenAI API, setting its temperature to 0 to decrease the randomness and the creativity of the response, as we are interested in factual answers. The reason behind the selection of this LLM is in a trade-off between reasoning capabilities, operating cost and API availability.

4.2 Results

To evaluate the proposed method we compare it to a non-enhanced LLM baseline and to ChatEL [44], the only approach that to the best of our knowledge also directly prompts LLMs to solve in a zero-shot manner the ED task, without training or fine-tuning any model. Additionally, we compare it to ReFinED [4], the task-specific model, which requires extensive training, that obtained the best ED performance in the results reported in [44]:

- **Baseline:** The baseline consists in asking the LLM to directly select one of the entities within the set of candidates. Therefore, it does not have the class representation nor the entities' description. This baseline corresponds to a non-enhanced LLM approach.
- **ChatEL** [44]**:** The ED task is solved in two steps. First, the LLM is asked to describe what the mention in the document is referring to. Then, another prompt is created asking the LLM to select the candidate entity that best matches the description generated in the previous response, by also enriching the candidates with their descriptions from Wikipedia. It must be noted that in our approach an answer is always returned. However, in [44] an empty result is produced (i.e., a prediction is not performed) when the LLMs' response does not contain any candidate entity. Thus, the computation of the precision (and consequently the inKB and Gold F1-score) differs, as the number of false negatives can potentially be reduced. These observed differences in the F1-score have been mitigated by computing the achieved gold percentage, making the proposals comparable.
- **ReFinED** [4]**:** Is a ED-specific method built over the RoBERTa architecture, leveraging entity types and descriptions. It is pretrained with a Wikipedia dataset, with more than 100M mention-entity pairs, and fine-tuned on AIDA-CoNLL [16], a news related ED dataset with approximately 25.000 annotated mentions.

The results are shown in Table 2. First of all, it can be observed that the proposed approach outperforms the baseline in all of the datasets. This demonstrates that even with the vast amounts of data with which the LLMs have been trained and their reasoning capabilities, the addition of external knowledge on the prompts and the guidance during the disambiguation can be helpful to improve the performance on the ED task. One of the most frequent mistakes made by the baseline approach is to give more importance to the context than to the mention. For instance, in the sentence *'A six-game begins this Friday in Phoenix and the team hopes to get O'Neal [...]'*, the baseline links the mention to the entity 'Phoenix Suns', presumably given the basketball context. However, the mention is referring to a place, which is correctly resolved by the KG-enhanced

Table 2. Results for the inKB micro F1-score for the ED experiments with ten datasets. The ChatEL and ReFinED scores are taken from the results reported by the authors in [44]. The weighted average weights each score by taking into consideration the sizes of the datasets. The best score for each dataset is highlighted in **bold**.

		KORE	ACE04	OKE16	R500	OKE15	R128	MSN	AQU	WIKI	CWEB	Avg.	Wt. avg.
Baseline	F1-Score	68.2	89.1	59.0	77.4	64.1	68.7	82.3	62.4	69.5	65.0		
	Gold F1	76.5	95.4	82.2	85.3	82.2	83.6	94.0	96.2	89.4	89.3		
	% Gold	89.3	93.4	71.7	90.8	78.0	82.1	87.5	64.8	77.7	72.8	80.8	75.4
ReFinED [4]	F1-Score	56.7	86.4	79.4	70.8	78.1	68.0	89.1	86.1	84.1	73.8		
	Gold F1	88.0	96.9	90.3	92.1	90.3	91.1	97.0	98.1	94.4	94.3		
	% Gold	64.4	89.1	**87.9**	76.8	86.4	74.6	**91.8**	**87.7**	**89.0**	**78.2**	82.8	**82.6**
ChatEL [44]	F1-Score	78.7	89.3	75.2	82.2	75.8	78.9	88.1	76.7	79.1	70.9		
	Gold F1	88.0	96.9	90.3	92.1	90.3	91.1	97.0	98.1	94.4	94.3		
	% Gold	89.4	92.1	83.2	89.2	83.9	86.6	90.8	78.1	83.7	75.1	85.2	79.3
$Our_{DBpedia}$	F1-Score	71.3	89.4	65.9	75.4	73.5	75.0	84.2	72.0	72.5	67.7		
	Gold F1	80.1	95.7	79.8	85.6	82.2	85.9	94.1	96.3	90.4	89.4		
	% Gold	88.9	93.3	82.5	88.0	**89.3**	87.3	89.4	74.8	80.2	75.7	85.0	78.8
Our_{YAGO}	F1-Score	71.8	88.7	65.8	78.3	70.3	75.8	81.2	72.0	74.4	69.6		
	Gold F1	79.6	94.3	83.7	85.2	82.3	84.8	92.2	94.4	88.9	89.3		
	% Gold	**90.1**	**94.0**	78.6	**91.9**	85.4	**89.4**	88.0	76.2	83.6	77.9	**85.5**	81.1

approach, as in the first iteration the LLM correctly disambiguates between the classes *Organization*, *Place*, *Product* or *FictionalEntity*.

Regarding the comparison with ChatEL, it can be observed that better results are obtained by our approach in 6 out of 10 datasets, with a weighted average score of 1.8% points higher. Additionally, in the complete ChatEL evaluation GPT-4 is used, which is bigger and more powerful LLM than GPT-3.5 [2] with a cost per token more than 20 times higher.[1] Therefore, even while using a less powerful LLM, the proposed approach leads to improvements in the ED task. Additionally, the added cost of the manipulation of the graph structure (i.e., finding the LCA and pruning) is limited by the small number of candidates used in ED, which typically ranges from 5 to 30, and its execution time is two orders of magnitude lower than the LLM calls.

For the task-specific model, we can observe that it obtains a better performance in 6 of the datasets, and an average weighted score of 1.5% points higher. However, it is worth noting that it has been trained over a huge Wikipedia dataset and fine-tuned on an ED dataset about news, and for the only dataset out of these domains, KORE, our model outperforms it by more than 25% points. Therefore, the LLM methods show a greater degree of adaptability, and could compensate the decrease in performance on some datasets by not requiring the training of specific models.

[1] https://openai.com/pricing.

4.3 KG Expressivity Impact

In this section we evaluate how the differences in the semantic expressivity of the taxonomy of classes in the KG affects our approach. Concretely, we explore if reducing the granularity of the taxonomy affects its disambiguation capabilities. To this end, we use YAGO and DBpedia KGs, whose statistics are summarized in Table 3. It can be observed that YAGO has more than a thousand times as many classes as DBpedia, and nearly doubles the average depth of the path from an entity to the root. Therefore, YAGO has a more granular class representation and also annotates more semantic interpretations of the entities. For instance, as it is exemplified in Fig. 4, in the annotation of Barcelona in YAGO a distinction is made between its representation as a *Place* and as a *Organization*, whereas in DBpedia Barcelona is only considered as a *Place*. Additionally, we can also observe the difference in the number of classes and its granularity. For example, DBpedia stops at the city level, while YAGO classifies the municipalities also within their country and region.

To evaluate the two KGs under study, we repeat the same experimental settings as in Sect. 4.1 for DBpedia, keeping in mind that the inKB entities do not completely overlap on both KGs, thus affecting the Gold F1-score. The results can be seen in Table 2, where in 7 out of 10 datasets the more granular class representation, YAGO, has a better performance, and the weighted average score is 2.4% points higher. This reinforces the hypothesis that having a more semantically rich class taxonomy can help in the disambiguation task. We can observe that YAGO does not outperform DBpedia primarily in the OKE datasets, which

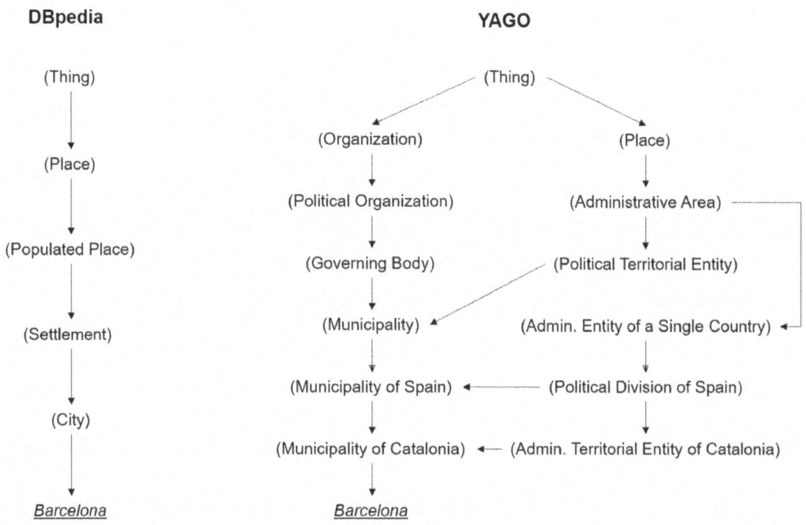

Fig. 4. Class representation of the entity Barcelona in DBpedia (left) and YAGO (right) KGs.

contain a large number of mentions referring to generic occupations (e.g., Governor, Judge, Engineer, etc.). For instance, in the second iteration of the method for the sentence *'As governor, Reagan raised taxes [...]'*, the disambiguation is between the entity 'Governor' which is the ground truth answer, and the class *Head of Government*, which has other entities as successors (e.g., 'Governor of California'). This causes a *case 3* (see Sect. 3.2) disambiguation between *Head of Government* and *Other*, which leads to the LLM selecting the former as it properly fits the context.

Table 3. Metric comparisons from YAGO and DBpedia KGs [14].

	DBpedia	YAGO
# Instances	5,044,223	6,349,359
# Classes	760	819,292
Avg. tree depth	3.51	6.61
Avg. branching factor	4.53	8.48

Regarding the number of iterations both KGs exhibit a similar behavior, having a mean value close to 2.2 (see Table 4). Therefore, even though YAGO has a deeper taxonomy, it is compensated by its superiority in semantic expressivity and mitigated by the elimination of intermediary nodes in the preprocessing step (see Sect. 3.2). Hence, given that the execution time of the graph manipulation is two orders of magnitude lower than the LLM calls, using deeper graphs does not significantly affect the performance.

Table 4. Percentage of disambiguated entities in which the pruning algorithm reached a final single entity within the specified number of iterations.

	Iterations						Avg. Iterations
	1	2	3	4	5	6	
YAGO	26.24%	37.36%	26.60%	8.30%	1.32%	0.15%	2.21
DBpedia	23.57%	43.00%	26.68%	6.12%	0.42%	0.01%	2.18

4.4 Error Analysis

We thoroughly examined and categorized the scenarios that led to our method producing an incorrect disambiguation, as understanding them is crucial for assessing the capabilities and limitations of LLMs in this task.

Ground Truth Errors. These errors consider the inaccuracies in the annotation of the datasets. For instance, in the sentence *'[...] it is required excellent English communication skills [...]'*, the mention English is annotated as 'England' instead of 'English Language'.

KG Errors. These errors encompass the problems derived from the annotation of the entities' classes in the KGs. For example, in the sentence *'Mars, Galaxy and Bounty are chocolate [...]'* the ground truth answer 'Bounty (chocolate bar)' is wrongly annotated in DBpedia as an *Architectural Structure*, causing the pruning algorithm to fail. Additionally, the annotations could also suffer from inconsistencies. For instance, the 'Supreme Court of Florida' falls under the *Organization* class, while the 'Supreme Court of California' is considered a *Building*.

Ambiguous Errors. Some datasets contain sentences with high degree of ambiguity. For instance, in the sentence *'Justin, Stefani and Kate are among the most popular people both on MTV and Twitter'*, the disambiguation between 'Justin Timberlake' and 'Justin Bieber' is not clear as both are popular celebrities in those platforms and have collaborated with the other mentioned artists. Moreover, there are some ground truth labels that could be argued to be incorrect. For example, in the sentence *'accepted the post of principal and only teacher at a primary school in rural Blaauwbosch, Newcastle.'*, principal is annotated in the ground truth as 'Principal (Academia)', yet for primary schools in the UK a more appropriate term would be 'head teacher', which is also found in the candidate set.

LLM Errors. Finally, some errors are produced by the LLM's response. These are usually originated by the LLM missing information from the context and incorrectly resolving the entity or by wrongly interpreting the mention and assigning it to an erroneous class.

In Table 5, all the errors from the two smaller datasets (i.e., KORE and ACE2004) have been classified according to the presented types of error. This study has not been extended to all the datasets as it is unfeasible due to their sizes. Regarding the ground truth error, it corresponds to the sentence *'Onassis married Kennedy on October 20, 1968'*, where the mention Onassis is annotated as 'Jacqueline Kennedy Onassis' instead of 'Aristotle Onassis'. For the KG errors, 2 are originated from a missing class annotation and 1 from a wrong labeling of an entity. Also, 3 errors for the ambiguous sentences are originated by the context not being sufficient to disambiguate the mention and in 2 of them the LLM's response could arguably be considered also correct (e.g., in the sentence *'The Isle of Wight festival in 1970 was the biggest at its time'*, the mention could be both referring to the musical festival and to the concrete festival's edition). Finally, 5 of the LLM errors are caused by missed context (e.g., in the short sentence *'Tiger lost the US Open'*, the mention Tiger, likely referring to Tiger

Woods, helps to disambiguate between 'US Open (tennis)' and 'US Open (golf)' but it is missed by the LLM) and 7 by a wrong interpretation of the class (e.g., in the sentence *'[...] ran adjacent to an advertisement for a golf tournament on Fox Sports sponsored by Sun Microsystems.'* the mention is interpreted as a TV program rather than a TV channel).

These last LLM errors could potentially be solved by using LLMs with more powerful reasoning capabilities. To explore this idea, a small experiment with GPT-4 and Mistral Large [26] has been run, where the models are able to correctly disambiguate 8 and 7 of these 12 errors, respectively.

Table 5. Error types for the ACE2004 and KORE datasets, using YAGO as the KG.

Error Type	# Errors
LLM error	12
Ambiguous error	5
KG error	3
Ground truth error	1

5 Conclusions

In this work we present a novel method to enhance LLMs with KGs to solve the ED task. For this purpose, we leverage the entities' class taxonomy annotated in a KG to gradually prune the candidates' search space. Additionally, when the disambiguation is at the entity level we add the entities' descriptions to the prompt. This proposal allows solving the ED task without training task-specific models or fine-tuning them on domain-specific or new data, which is a time-consuming and expensive process. In the experiments we show that the proposed method outperforms both non-enhanced and description-enhanced LLM approaches, and that it has a higher degree of adaptability to different domains than task-specific methods, which rely on the data they have been trained with. Additionally, we observe how using more semantically expressive KGs improves the ED results without degrading the pruning algorithm's performance. Finally, we analyze the different disambiguation errors and classify them according to their type, drawing conclusions about them. Specifically, and as a future line of work, the usage of more powerful LLMs could be studied, which could help in the disambiguation of difficult mentions.

Supplemental Material Statement: Datasets and scripts containing the prompts and the algorithms can be found in the attached repository.[2]

[2] https://github.com/gerardponsrecasens/KGLLMs4ED.

Acknowledgements. This work is supported by the Horizon Europe Programme under GA.101093164 (ExtremeXP) and the Spanish Ministerio de Ciencia e Innovación under project PID2020-117191RB-I00/ AEI/10.13039/501100011033 (DOGO4ML). Anna Queralt is a Serra Húnter Fellow.

Disclosure of Interests. The authors have no competing interests to declare that are relevant to the content of this article.

References

1. Abu-Salih, B.: Domain-specific knowledge graphs: a survey. J. Netw. Comput. Appl. **185**, 103076 (2021)
2. Achiam, J., et al.: GPT-4 technical report. arXiv preprint arXiv:2303.08774 (2023)
3. Auer, S., Bizer, C., Kobilarov, G., Lehmann, J., Cyganiak, R., Ives, Z.: DBpedia: a nucleus for a web of open data. In: Aberer, K., et al. (eds.) ASWC/ISWC -2007. LNCS, vol. 4825, pp. 722–735. Springer, Heidelberg (2007). https://doi.org/10.1007/978-3-540-76298-0_52
4. Ayoola, T., Tyagi, S., Fisher, J., Christodoulopoulos, C., Pierleoni, A.: ReFinED: an efficient zero-shot-capable approach to end-to-end entity linking. In: NAACL (2022)
5. Baek, J., Aji, A.F., Saffari, A.: Knowledge-augmented language model prompting for zero-shot knowledge graph question answering. In: Proceedings of the First Workshop on Matching From Unstructured and Structured Data (MATCHING 2023) (2023). https://api.semanticscholar.org/CorpusID:260063238
6. Barba, E., Procopio, L., Navigli, R.: ExtEnD: extractive entity disambiguation. In: Proceedings of the 60th Annual Meeting of the Association for Computational Linguistics (Volume 1: Long Papers), pp. 2478–2488 (2022)
7. Brown, T., et al.: Language models are few-shot learners. In: Advances in Neural Information Processing Systems, vol. 33, pp. 1877–1901 (2020)
8. Cucerzan, S.: Large-scale named entity disambiguation based on Wikipedia data. In: Proceedings of the 2007 Joint Conference on Empirical Methods in Natural Language Processing and Computational Natural Language Learning (EMNLP-CoNLL), pp. 708–716 (2007)
9. De Cao, N., Izacard, G., Riedel, S., Petroni, F.: Autoregressive entity retrieval. In: 9th International Conference on Learning Representations, ICLR 2021, Virtual Event, Austria, 3–7 May 2021. OpenReview.net (2021). https://openreview.net/forum?id=5k8F6UU39V
10. Devlin, J., Chang, M.W., Lee, K., Toutanova, K.: BERT: pre-training of deep bidirectional transformers for language understanding. arXiv preprint arXiv:1810.04805 (2018)
11. Gabrilovich, E., Ringgaard, M., Subramanya, A.: FACC1: freebase annotation of clueweb corpora, version 1 (release date 2013-06-26, format version 1, correction level 0) (2013)
12. Guha, R.V., Brickley, D., Macbeth, S.: Schema.org: evolution of structured data on the web. Commun. ACM **59**(2), 44–51 (2016)
13. Guo, Z., Barbosa, D.: Robust named entity disambiguation with random walks. Semantic Web **9**(4), 459–479 (2018)
14. Heist, N., Hertling, S., Ringler, D., Paulheim, H.: Knowledge graphs on the web-an overview. Knowl. Graphs eXplainable Artif. Intell., 3–22 (2020)

15. Hoffart, J., Seufert, S., Nguyen, D.B., Theobald, M., Weikum, G.: KORE: keyphrase overlap relatedness for entity disambiguation. In: Proceedings of the 21st ACM International Conference on Information and Knowledge Management, pp. 545–554 (2012)
16. Hoffart, J., et al.: Robust disambiguation of named entities in text. In: Proceedings of the 2011 Conference on Empirical Methods in Natural Language Processing, pp. 782–792 (2011)
17. Hu, L., Liu, Z., Zhao, Z., Hou, L., Nie, L., Li, J.: A survey of knowledge enhanced pre-trained language models. IEEE Trans. Knowl. Data Eng. (2023)
18. Ji, Z., et al.: Survey of hallucination in natural language generation. ACM Comput. Surv. **55**(12), 1–38 (2023)
19. Le, P., Titov, I.: Improving entity linking by modeling latent relations between mentions. In: Proceedings of the 56th Annual Meeting of the Association for Computational Linguistics, pp. 1595–1604. Association for Computational Linguistics, Melbourne, Australia, July 2018. https://doi.org/10.18653/v1/P18-1148
20. Lewis, M., et al.: BART: denoising sequence-to-sequence pre-training for natural language generation, translation, and comprehension. In: Proceedings of the 58th Annual Meeting of the Association for Computational Linguistics, pp. 7871–7880. Association for Computational Linguistics, Online, July 2020. https://doi.org/10.18653/v1/2020.acl-main.703
21. Lewis, P., et al.: Retrieval-augmented generation for knowledge-intensive NLP tasks. In: Advances in Neural Information Processing Systems, vol. 33, pp. 9459–9474 (2020)
22. Liu, Y., et al.: RoBERTa: a robustly optimized BERT pretraining approach. arXiv preprint arXiv:1907.11692 (2019)
23. Logeswaran, L., Chang, M.W., Lee, K., Toutanova, K., Devlin, J., Lee, H.: Zero-shot entity linking by reading entity descriptions. In: Proceedings of the 57th Annual Meeting of the Association for Computational Linguistics (2019)
24. Luo, Y., Yang, Z., Meng, F., Li, Y., Zhou, J., Zhang, Y.: An empirical study of catastrophic forgetting in large language models during continual fine-tuning. CoRR abs/2308.08747 (2023). https://doi.org/10.48550/ARXIV.2308.08747
25. Milne, D., Witten, I.H.: Learning to link with Wikipedia. In: Proceedings of the 17th ACM Conference on Information and Knowledge Management, pp. 509–518 (2008)
26. Mistral AI: Mistral Large (2024). https://mistral.ai/news/mistral-large/
27. Mulang', I.O., Singh, K., Prabhu, C., Nadgeri, A., Hoffart, J., Lehmann, J.: Evaluating the impact of knowledge graph context on entity disambiguation models. In: Proceedings of the 29th ACM International Conference on Information & Knowledge Management, pp. 2157–2160 (2020)
28. Nuzzolese, A.G., Gentile, A.L., Presutti, V., Gangemi, A., Garigliotti, D., Navigli, R.: Open knowledge extraction challenge. In: Gandon, F., Cabrio, E., Stankovic, M., Zimmermann, A. (eds.) SemWebEval 2015. CCIS, vol. 548, pp. 3–15. Springer, Cham (2015). https://doi.org/10.1007/978-3-319-25518-7_1
29. Nuzzolese, A.G., Gentile, A.L., Presutti, V., Gangemi, A., Meusel, R., Paulheim, H.: The second open knowledge extraction challenge. In: Sack, H., Dietze, S., Tordai, A., Lange, C. (eds.) SemWebEval 2016. CCIS, vol. 641, pp. 3–16. Springer, Cham (2016). https://doi.org/10.1007/978-3-319-46565-4_1
30. Onoe, Y., Durrett, G.: Fine-grained entity typing for domain independent entity linking. In: Proceedings of the AAAI Conference on Artificial Intelligence, vol. 34, pp. 8576–8583 (2020)

31. Pan, S., Luo, L., Wang, Y., Chen, C., Wang, J., Wu, X.: Unifying large language models and knowledge graphs: a roadmap. IEEE Trans. Knowl. Data Eng. (2024)
32. Ratinov, L., Roth, D., Downey, D., Anderson, M.: Local and global algorithms for disambiguation to Wikipedia. In: Proceedings of the 49th Annual Meeting of the Association for Computational Linguistics: Human Language Technologies, pp. 1375–1384 (2011)
33. Ristoski, P., Lin, Z., Zhou, Q.: KG-ZESHEL: knowledge graph-enhanced zero-shot entity linking. In: Proceedings of the 11th Knowledge Capture Conference, pp. 49–56 (2021)
34. Röder, M., Usbeck, R., Hellmann, S., Gerber, D., Both, A.: N^3-a collection of datasets for named entity recognition and disambiguation in the NLP interchange format. In: LREC, pp. 3529–3533 (2014)
35. Speer, R., Chin, J., Havasi, C.: ConceptNet 5.5: an open multilingual graph of general knowledge. In: Proceedings of the AAAI Conference on Artificial Intelligence, vol. 31 (2017)
36. Suchanek, F.M., Kasneci, G., Weikum, G.: YAGO: a core of semantic knowledge. In: Proceedings of the 16th International Conference on World Wide Web, pp. 697–706 (2007)
37. Sun, J., et al.: Think-on-graph: deep and responsible reasoning of large language model with knowledge graph (2023)
38. Ayoola, T., Fisher, J., Pierleoni, A.: Improving entity disambiguation by reasoning over a knowledge base. In: NAACL (2022)
39. Touvron, H., et al.: Llama 2: open foundation and fine-tuned chat models. arXiv preprint arXiv:2307.09288 (2023)
40. Vrandečić, D., Krötzsch, M.: Wikidata: a free collaborative knowledgebase. Commun. ACM **57**(10), 78–85 (2014)
41. Wen, Y., Wang, Z., Sun, J.: MindMap: knowledge graph prompting sparks graph of thoughts in large language models. In: Proceedings of the 62nd Annual Meeting of the Association for Computational Linguistics (2024)
42. Wu, L., Petroni, F., Josifoski, M., Riedel, S., Zettlemoyer, L.: Scalable zero-shot entity linking with dense entity retrieval. In: Proceedings of the 2020 Conference on Empirical Methods in Natural Language Processing (EMNLP), pp. 6397–6407. Association for Computational Linguistics, Online, November 2020. https://doi.org/10.18653/v1/2020.emnlp-main.519
43. Yang, J., et al.: Harnessing the power of LLMs in practice: a survey on ChatGPT and beyond. ACM Trans. Knowl. Discovery Data (2023)
44. Ding, Y., Zeng, Q., Weninger, T.: ChatEL: entity linking with chatbots. In: COLING-LREC (2024)

Unaligned Federated Knowledge Graph Embedding

Deyu Chen[1], Hong Zhu[1], Jinguang Gu[2], Rusi Chen[3], and Meiyi Xie[1(✉)]

[1] School of Computer Science and Technology, Huazhong University of Science and Technology, Wuhan 430074, China
{deyuchen,zhuhong,xiemeiyi}@hust.edu.cn

[2] Department of Computer Science and Technology, Wuhan University of Science and Technology, Wuhan 430065, China
simon@wust.edu.cn

[3] State Grid Hubei Electric Power Research Institute, Wuhan, China

Abstract. Recently, knowledge graph embedding (KGE) methods under the federated learning paradigm have received much attention. Its privacy-preserving decentralized training method effectively utilizes the knowledge graphs held by different clients. Existing federated KGE frameworks collaboratively train the global model by aggregating aligned entity embeddings among clients. However, in real-world scenarios, the lack of aligned entities and the high heterogeneity among knowledge graphs constrain their potential. To address these issues, we propose a federated KGE framework that does not depend on any aligned set but uses structure information. The framework introduces a set of basis edges to model the general structure information. Then, we use two separate modules on clients to encode structure and feature representations, respectively. Finally, clients only upload structure parameters for aggregation on the server. The framework uses a new unaligned federated KGE paradigm to tackle the heterogeneity of multi-source knowledge graphs. Experimental results on benchmark datasets show that UniFE achieves superior results even compared to federated KGE frameworks using the aligned set.

Keywords: Knowledge graph embedding · Federated learning · Heterogeneous data

1 Introduction

Knowledge graphs (KGs) are widely used data structures that model facts as (h, r, t) representing head entity h connected to tail entity t through relation r. Many large-scale knowledge graphs have been proposed and used on many downstream tasks [16,17,22]. Since knowledge graphs are usually incomplete, the knowledge graph completion (KGC) task is proposed, which predicts missing links based on the observed triplets to discover new facts. A popular solution [2,

G. Demartini et al. (Eds.): ISWC 2024, LNCS 15231, pp. 180–198, 2025.
https://doi.org/10.1007/978-3-031-77844-5_10

20] is to embed the observed triplets in a low-dimensional space to find potential connections of entities, known as knowledge graph embedding (KGE).

The application of KGs relies on the availability of large-scale data. However, organizations tend to maintain their private knowledge graphs, and laws also restrict data sharing across organizations, such as the GDPR[1]. So the KGs objectively become data silos due to commercial or privacy agreements [13].

Federated learning (FL) is a learning paradigm proposed recently, which allows clients to learn a global model jointly without data sharing directly [15]. In order to better utilize multi-source KGs with privacy-preserving, some works [4,5,30] proposed and explored the federated knowledge graph completion (FKGC) task which doing KGC task in the federated setting. The task is set to have overlapping entities among clients without overlapping relations. The server aggregates the parameter of aligned entities among clients to train a centralized global model. The paradigm improved the performance of the KGC task while maintaining privacy preservation. It also alleviated large graphs' computing resource consumption and data maintenance costs through server aggregation.

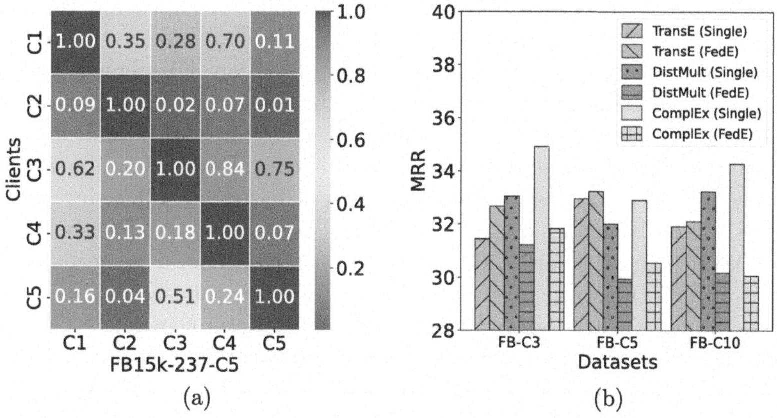

Fig. 1. (a) An example of inter-client aligned entity proportion on FB15k-237-C5. The proportion is calculated by dividing the number of aligned entities between two clients and the entities' number of client owning more entities. (b) The MRR performance of *Single* setting and FedE using different KGE methods.

In real-world scenarios, the combination of KGE and FL has more challenges. First, entity alignment is a costly work and a significant research problem. Figure 1(a) shows the aligned entity investigation for the federated KGE benchmark dataset. The result represents the aligned entity set between two clients as a percentage of the client with the larger entity set.[2] The investigation

[1] https://gdpr-info.eu.

[2] The specific calculation for each cell: $\frac{|\mathcal{E}_x \cap \mathcal{E}_y|}{max(|\mathcal{E}_x|,|\mathcal{E}_y|)}$, where $\mathcal{E}_x$ and $\mathcal{E}_y$ are the entity sets owned by the corresponding clients.

demonstrates that aligned entities are often fewer or even unavailable in the heterogeneous federated setting. Second, simple aggregation of highly heterogeneous clients often leads to adverse results. The performance comparison between local training (*Single* setting) and average aggregation method FedE [4] in heterogeneous environments shown in Fig. 1(b), and the results show that an increase in heterogeneity often corresponds to a decrease in performance that is even worse than local training. Entities may also have different features in distinct contexts, so it is necessary to adopt better approaches than direct aggregation. Finally, the holders of KGs may be concerned about uploading their complete entity list to the server for reasons. The less information transmitted to the server brings a lower contribution cost and the more willing the clients are to participate [1].

These issues lead us to explore federated knowledge graph embedding learning without any aligned set. We introduce the structure perspective, which aims at the general structure representation for heterogeneous knowledge graphs. Structure information is a crucial feature in graph-related tasks. Existing works propose parameter aggregation among different graphs through decoupled learning [8,14,21] and generative approaches [29], which have been effective on tasks such as federated graph classification but not considered the multi-relational data. Inductive KGE models provide the feasibility of capturing the general patterns over knowledge graphs using meta-learning [3,6].

To address the above challenges, we proposed an **Un**al**i**gned **F**ederated Knowledge Graph **E**mbedding framework, UniFE for short, which does not depend on any aligned set for federated KGE. Our framework follows the common setting of FL with a server and a set of clients. Due to no aligned set, we intuitively use a set of desensitized basis edges based on adjacency structure of entities as the bridge among clients. Then, we construct the Basis Structure Graph (BSG) using the basis edges to represent the general patterns on KGs. Finally, we learn the structure representation of entities based on the BSG. To tackle the adverse effect on aggregation of highly heterogeneous KGs, we use separate modules on clients: the structure representation module and the feature representation module, inspired by the decoupled learning [8,14,21]. The server aggregates only the parameters related to structure learning. Moreover, in order to validate the effectiveness, we evaluate our proposed framework in unaligned setting for FKGC benchmark datasets. The results demonstrate that our framework outperforms existing FKGC baselines, even if they use the aligned set.

In summary, main contributions of our work are as follows:

- We consider a more realistic scenario for the FKGC task without any aligned set among clients. For the new task, we provide the structure perspective for learning KGE models in heterogeneous federated setting.
- We propose a heterogeneous federated KGE framework, UniFE. The framework encodes the general structure patterns among clients, uses decoupling learning the feature representations and structure representations of entities, and supports plugging in different existing KGE methods.

- We conduct extensive experiments on the FKGC benchmark datasets without aligned set. Experimental results show that our framework is effective in the unaligned setting.

2 Related Work

2.1 Knowledge Graph Embedding

In recent years, many KGE models have been proposed. They aim to map entities and relations into low-dimensional spaces to find unobserved facts. TransE [2] is a representative approach based on a translation mechanism that keeps the entities and relations in space with the constraint that $h + r \approx t$. DistMult [28] uses tensor decomposition, which only handles symmetric relations due to the use of diagonal matrices. ComplEx [24] introduces complex embeddings to solve the problem of modeling asymmetric relations. RotatE [20] models the relations as the rotation from the source entity to the target entity in the complex space, and it can infer the composition pattern. ConvE [7] introduces a multi-layer convolutional network model that effectively models common scenarios about the nodes with high indegree.

2.2 GNN for Multi-relational Data

Graph neural networks [12], which aggregate the neighbor embeddings and generate representations of nodes, do not consider the problem in multi-relational data scenarios. R-GCN [18] extends to relation-specific aggregation of node neighbors, enabling an encoder for relational data. SACN [19] combined the benefit of GCN and ConvE using learnable weights for more accurate embeddings of graph nodes. CompGCN [25] jointly embeds nodes and relations to improve effectiveness. It also solves the over-parameterization problem of previous methods and can be easily generalized to them.

2.3 Federated Learning over Knowledge Graphs

Federated learning uses data decentralized across different clients to train a global model under privacy-preserving. It alleviates the lack of data and computing resources on the clients, which is a promising approach to training large, effective models. FedAvg [15] first proposed a paradigm for FL, proving common initialization and average aggregation of parameters to be effective.

FedE [4] first defines the FKGC task and proposes a federated KGE framework based on FedAvg. Its main idea is to optimize the global model using average aggregation of aligned entity embeddings. FedEC [5] introduces embedding-contrastive learning to tackle the problem of data heterogeneity. It extends FedE to alleviate the adverse effects of heterogeneity by maximizing the agreement between the global embeddings and locally updated embeddings. FedLU [30] maintains local and global models on each client. It uses mutual distillation from two models and only aggregates global models to avoid drift between local optimization and global convergence due to high heterogeneity. However, this line of work relies on the paradigm proposed by FedE, aggregating only through aligned entities among clients.

DP-FLames [10] proposes three inference attacks under above paradigm to quantify the privacy risks of federated KGE. Then, it proposes a differential private federated KGE with private selection and an adaptive privacy budget allocation policy to mitigate the privacy threat. Since our setting does not have explicitly aligned entities, it avoids the three attacks.

Additionally, existing works [8,21] studied FL over graphs for tasks such as graph classification, but the features of multi-relational data have yet to be considered. Other works [3,6] focus on inductive KGE and knowledge extrapolation in the federated setting, which differs from our goal.

3 Preliminaries

A knowledge graph is defined as $\mathcal{G} = (\mathcal{E}, \mathcal{R}, \mathcal{T})$, where $\mathcal{E}$ denotes a set of entities, $\mathcal{R}$ denotes a set of relations, and $\mathcal{T}$ denotes a set of triplets. Large-scale knowledge graphs are usually incomplete, and the KGC task is to predict missing links based on existing triplets. A popular solution is the KGE models, which embed entities and relations to low-dimensional vector spaces to predict the triplets formed as $(h, r, ?)$ or $(?, r, t)$ to be a true fact or not.

The FKGC task typically has two roles: a centralized server S and a set of clients with local knowledge graphs $\{\mathcal{G}_i\}_{i=1}^{C}$ of number C. The task aims to enhance the local clients' performance of the KGC task by aggregating the embeddings of overlapped entities among clients.

FedE [4] first proposed a federated knowledge graph embedding framework. The server performs a global initialization $\mathbf{E}_1^g$ for entities during initialization. In communication round r, it utilizes the global embedding $\mathbf{E}_r^g$ aggregated from the previous round $r-1$. The global embedding is conducted with a permutation $\mathbf{P}^c\mathbf{E}_r^g$ to each client $c \in C$. Once a local training of l epochs is completed, the local embedding $\mathbf{E}^c$ is obtained. After all clients have completed their training, the weights uploaded by the clients are aggregated as follows:

$$\mathbf{E}_{r+1}^g = (\mathbb{1} \oslash \sum_{c=1}^{C} \mathbf{v}^c) \otimes \sum_{c=1}^{C} \mathbf{P}^{c\top} \mathbf{E}_{r+1}^c, \tag{1}$$

where $\mathbb{1}$ represents all-one vector, $\mathbf{v}^c$ represents existence vector of client c, $\oslash$ and $\otimes$ represents element-wise division and multiply respectively. The framework repeats this process to minimize the average local training objective.

Notably, we assume that the clients' knowledge graphs do not have overlapping entities or relations, which presents a significant challenge compared to prior works [4,5], as there is no aligned set as a bridge among clients. We denote the task as unaligned FKGC, which is formalized as follows:

Given a centralized server S and a set of clients with local knowledge graphs $\{\mathcal{G}_i\}_{i=1}^{C}$ of number C, $\bigcap_{i=1}^{C} \mathcal{G}_i = \varnothing$. The unaligned FKGC aims to establish a set of general basis representations $\mathcal{B} = \{b_1, b_2, ..., b_n\}$ among different KGs and aggregate the locally learned parameters of basis representations on the server, which enhances the effectiveness of KGC for the clients.

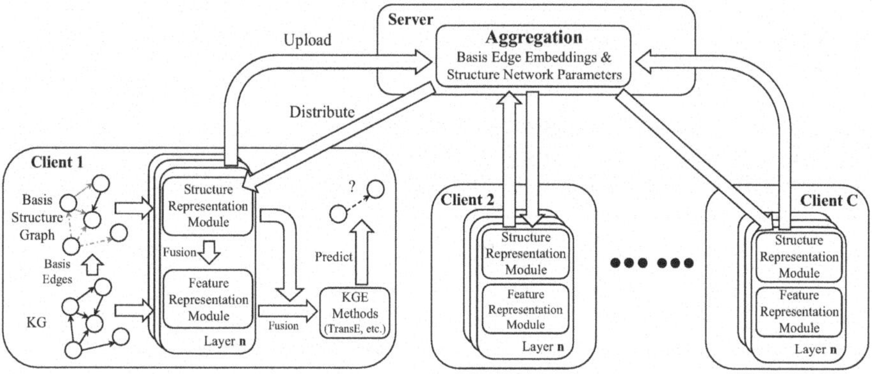

Fig. 2. The overview of UniFE. The framework uses the server-client FL architecture. Each client contains a structure representation module and a feature representation module. It protects client privacy better by only aggregating the structure parameters, which avoids the transfer of aligned entity embeddings.

4 Methodology

To solve the above issues, we proposed an **Un**al**i**gned **F**ederated Knowledge Graph **E**mbedding framework, UniFE. We focus on improving the KGC task in the heterogeneous federated environment without any aligned set. In order to address the absence of aligned entities among clients, an intuitive idea is to find a set of general structure representations over clients' KGs called basis edges. Our proposed framework constructs the Basis Structure Graphs to guide structure learning through the basis edges. For the data heterogeneity among clients, we use two separate modules to learn the feature and structure representations of entities on clients. The framework applies the fusion operation at each layer to enhance the encoding expression [21]. Finally, we only upload structure parameters to the server for aggregation, which avoids the adverse effect of global aggregation on local entity feature embeddings. The overview of our proposed framework is shown in Fig. 2.

In this section, we first introduce the modeling of general structure representations on KGs in Sect. 4.1. Next, we describe the local training procedure mainly using two separate modules in Sect. 4.2. Finally, we describe the global aggregation procedure in Sect. 4.3. The overall algorithm for the proposed framework is described in Algorithm 1.

Algorithm 1: UniFE Framework

Require: number of clients C, selected faction of clients F, number of local epoch E and batch size m, learning rate η.

Server: Initialize basis embeddings $\mathbf{B}$ and structure encoder parameters w^s;
Clients: Each client initialize feature embeddings $\mathbf{H}^f$ and feature parameters w_c^f, then traverse to get relation-specific degree set $\mathcal{D}_c$ and generate BSGs;
for round $t = 0, 1, ...$ **do**
  $C_{sub} \leftarrow \lfloor F \times C \rfloor$;
  Server distributes $\mathbf{B}$ and w^s to each client;
  for each client $c \in C_t$ **in parallel do**
    $\mathbf{B}_t^c, w_t^c \leftarrow LocalTraining(c, \mathbf{B}_t^c, w_t^{s_c})$;
  end
  $\mathbf{B}_{t+1} \leftarrow \{\mathbf{b}_{t+1} \leftarrow \sum_{c=1}^{C} \frac{N_c(b)}{N(b)} \mathbf{b}_t^c\}$;
  $w_{t+1}^s = \sum_{c=1}^{C} \frac{|\mathcal{D}_c|}{|\mathcal{D}|} w_{t_c}^s$;
end
// Ignore clients' locally held and updated parameters for clarity.
Function $LocalTraining(c, \mathbf{B}, w^s)$:
  for each local epoch e from 1 to E **do**
    $\mathcal{T}_m \leftarrow$ (split triplets $\mathcal{T}_c$ into batches of size m);
    for batch $n \in \mathcal{T}_N$ **do**
      Update two modules by Eq. 3 to 7 and compute loss L by Eq. 8;
      $\mathbf{B} \leftarrow \mathbf{B} - \eta \nabla L$;
      $w^s \leftarrow w^s - \eta \nabla L$;
    end
  end
  return $\mathbf{B}, w^s$;
end

4.1 Basis Structure Modeling

Our framework considers KGE models in a highly heterogeneous federated setting without any aligned set. The existing FKGE paradigm requires maintaining a dictionary of entity mappings corresponding to each client on the server, which does not satisfy our task. Therefore, it is necessary to create a set of basis edges that can represent general structure patterns across different KGs.

Some works [3,9] explore modeling transferable information on KGs, which show that relative positions and interactions between relations are effective transferable features. Inspired by them, we design a way to model a node-level basis structure.

We first generate the BSGs from the structure of the KGs. The BSG is used to model the adjacent structure information of entities in corresponding KG, where entities are used as nodes and a specific adjacent structure pattern corresponds to an edge, called a basis edge. Figure 3(a) shows a typical example of transferable structure information. We can observe that nodes at corresponding

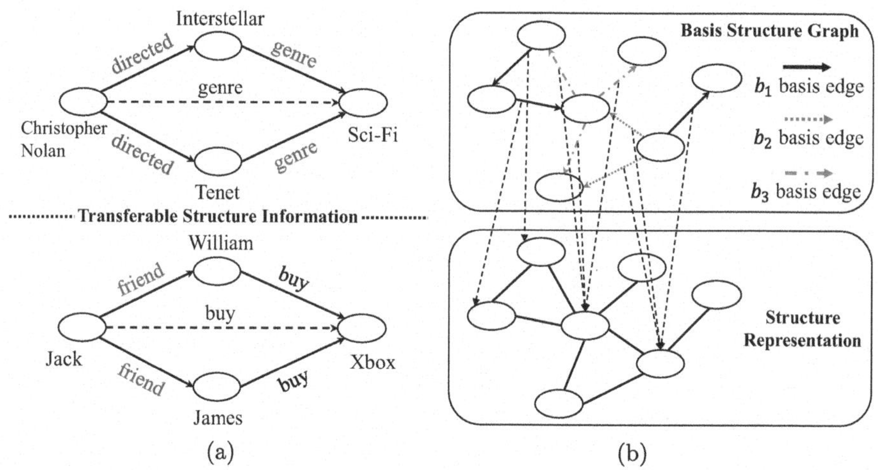

Fig. 3. (a) An example of transferable structure information about relative positions and interactions between different relations. (b) The process of generating structure representations over BSG. Relation-specific adjacent patterns correspond to different basis edges, and the aggregation of the basis edges obtains the structure representation.

positions in two KGs have the same degree composition. The degree is often applied as typical domain-invariant information in many graph-related tasks [21,26]. For multi-relational data, we consider entity connections under relations as slices. One slice represents structure within this relational domain. In UniFE, we intuitively consider the different relation-specific degrees as different patterns.

Specifically, we create a set of basis edges based on relation-specific degree sets. For a client's KG, $\mathcal{G}_c = (\mathcal{E}_c, \mathcal{R}_c, \mathcal{T}_c)$, where $\mathcal{E}_c$, $\mathcal{R}_c$, and $\mathcal{T}_c$ represent the set of entities, relations, and triplets on the client c, respectively. The set $\mathcal{D}_c$ of relation-specific degrees is generated by traversing the entities $e \in \mathcal{E}_c$, which compute the degree of each e with r as the outgoing edge, i.e., to compute the tail entities' number of distinct $(e_i, r_j, ?)$ in $\mathcal{T}_c$. The relation-specific degree set obtained:

$$\mathcal{D} = \{(e_1, r_1) : d_{11}), (e_1, r_2) : d_{12}, \ldots, (e_m, r_n) : d_{mn}\}, \tag{2}$$

where (e_i, r_j) represents the tuple composed of different entities and relations, and d_{ij} represents the number of tail entities under the tuple.

We use basis edges $\mathcal{B} = \{b_1, b_2, \ldots, b_k\}$ based on the relation-specific degree set to replace the edges in the original KG, i.e., the tuple $(e_i, r_i) = d$ in the relation-specific degree set, the corresponding edge is set to b_d basis edge. Traversing entities and corresponding relations generates BSG for the client's KGs, which denotes the structure patterns' composition of the entities, as shown in Fig. 3(b).

4.2 Local Training Procedure

Entity Structure Representation Module. The entity structure representation module learns structure representations of entities on the BSG. For the basis edges set $\mathcal{B}$, the module receives the embeddings of the basis edges $\mathbf{B} = \{\mathbf{b}_1, \mathbf{b}_2, \ldots, \mathbf{b}_k\}$ from the server. Then, it generates the input structure embedding $\mathbf{h}^s \in \mathbf{H}^s$ by the aggregation of the outgoing basis edges of entities as follows:

$$\mathbf{h}_e^s = \frac{1}{|O(e)|} \sum_{b_d \in O(e)} d^{-1} \mathbf{b}_d, \tag{3}$$

where $O(e)$ represents outgoing basis edges collection of entity e on the BSG, and $\mathbf{h}_e^s$ represents the structure embedding of entity e. The structure representation aggregates the adjacent relation-specific structure patterns of the entities. For each basis pattern to have the same importance, we multiply the basis edge embeddings by the reciprocal of its degree.

The structure representation module only focuses on the general structure information among clients. Since entities and relations have no alignment part with each other among clients, there is no need to model the attributes of edges. During the structure representations training process, specific relations are hidden. Based on the structure embeddings, a graph convolutional network (GCN) [12] is used. This network is initialized with parameters from the server distribution. The updating process of the structure representation at each layer is as follows:

$$\mathbf{H}^{s_{l+1}} = f(\hat{A}\mathbf{H}^{s_l}\mathbf{W}^l), \tag{4}$$

where $\hat{A} = \tilde{D}^{-\frac{1}{2}}(A + I)\tilde{D}^{-\frac{1}{2}}$ is the normalized adjacency matrix with added self-loop, and $\tilde{D}$ defined as $\tilde{D}_{ii} = \sum_j (A + I)_{ij}$, $\mathbf{H}^{s_l}$ represents the entity hidden state of the l-th layer, which is the structure embeddings at the 0-th layer, i.e., $\mathbf{H}^{s_0} = \mathbf{H}^s$, and $\mathbf{W}^l$ is the transformation matrix of the l-th layer.

Entity Feature Representation Module. The entity feature representation module uses a multi-relational graph neural network encoder to learn features on the original KG. We use the fusion operation before feature encoding and output, which concatenates the feature and structure embeddings to enhance the encoding expression. Specifically, in order to benefit from the structure information, the entity feature representations and the structure representations are fused through the linear layer before each convolution layer and output layer, as in the following equation:

$$\mathbf{h}_e = \mathbf{W}_{fusion}[\mathbf{h}_e^f; \mathbf{h}_e^s] + b_{fusion}, \tag{5}$$

where $\mathbf{h}_e$ is the entity representation after fusing the feature representation $\mathbf{h}_e^f \in \mathbf{H}^f$ and structure representation $\mathbf{h}_e^s$ of entity e, $\mathbf{W}_{fusion}$ and b_{fusion} are the transformation matrix and bias, and $[\cdot;\cdot]$ is the vector concatenate operation.

Then, the fused representation is used as the entity representation input into the CompGCN [25] layer to get the feature representation of entities and relations, and the entity representation is updated as follows:

$$\mathbf{h}_e^{l+1} = f\left(\sum_{(e',r)\in N(e)} \mathbf{W}_{\lambda(r)}^l \phi(\mathbf{h}_{e'}^l, \mathbf{h}_r^l)\right), \tag{6}$$

where $N(e)$ is the set of outgoing neighbors of entity e, $f(\cdot)$ is the activation function, $\mathbf{W}_{\lambda(r)}^l$ is the relation-type specific parameter in layer l, i.e., using different transformation matrix for original relations, inverse relations, and the self-loop, respectively, $\phi(\cdot,\cdot)$ is composition operator, such as vector subtraction, multiplication, circular-correlation.

The relation representations are updated by the transformation matrix at each layer as follows:

$$\mathbf{h}_r^{l+1} = \mathbf{W}_{rel}^l \mathbf{h}_r^l, \tag{7}$$

where $\mathbf{W}_{rel}^l$ is the relation transformation matrix of layer l.

Training Objective To train the proposed model, we optimize binary cross-entropy loss with label smoothing [7] for the observed triplets on each client as follows:

$$L = \frac{1}{n} \sum_{(h,r,t)\in T} (y \cdot log\sigma(S(h,r,t)) + (1-y) \cdot log\sigma(1 - S(h,r,t))) \tag{8}$$

where y is the label vector, σ is the activation function, $S(\cdot)$ is the score function.

4.3 Global Update Procedure

In the global aggregation stage, each client uploads only the parameters of the structure network and the basis embeddings to the server at communication round t, as follows:

$$\mathbf{b}_{t+1} = \sum_{c=1}^{C} \frac{N_c(b)}{N(b)} \mathbf{b}_t^c, \tag{9}$$

$$w_{t+1}^s = \sum_{c=1}^{C} \frac{|\mathcal{D}_c|}{|\mathcal{D}|} w_{t_c}^s, \tag{10}$$

where $\mathbf{b}$ and w^s represent basis embeddings and structure network parameters after aggregation, respectively, and $N_c(b)$ and $N(b)$ represent the number of the basis embeddings participating in the aggregation on the current client and all selected clients, $|\mathcal{D}|$ represents the entity-relation composition number of all selected clients.

This aggregation is privacy-preserving because structure networks and basis embeddings are insensitive. Moreover, the basis embeddings indirectly improve the whole framework. They generate entity structure representation, which enhances the feature representation module through the fusion operation. The basis embeddings also improve relation embeddings through entity-relation composition in layers of the feature representation module.

5 Experiments

In this section, we evaluate the following questions through experiments: 1) Does the performance of the proposed framework have enough potential for applications? 2) Is each module of the proposed framework effective? 3) Does the proposed framework have an advantage in convergence speed when it does not need to consider different contexts of entities? 4) Are there any stricter private settings?

5.1 Experimental Settings

Datasets. In order to evaluate the effectiveness of our proposed framework, we used FB15k-237-C3, -C5, and -C10 for heterogeneous FKGC task [30] and NELL-995-Fed3 [4]. The first three datasets are generated from FB15k-237 [23] by a clustering-based partition algorithm, which enables it to conform more to the realistic data distribution. The NELL-995-Fed3 is to randomly assign the relations of NELL-995 [27] to three clients and distribute triplets to clients based on the relations. This dataset is not divided for evaluating heterogeneity but can be used to evaluate the general applicability of our framework. It must be emphasized that in our proposed framework, the entity embeddings of each client are initialized independently, i.e., entities with identical names of different clients can be regarded as distinct instances, and they are invisible to each other, conforming with our setting. The data statistics are shown in Table 1.

Table 1. The statistics of datasets. It shows the average number of entities, relations, and triplets for different numbers of clients.

Dataset	Clients	Entities	Relations	Triplets
FB15k-237-C3	3	6262.7	79.0	103372.0
FB15k-237-C5	5	5119.0	47.4	62023.2
FB15k-237-C10	10	2176.9	23.7	31011.6
NELL-995-Fed3	3	33453.7	66.7	51404.3

Baselines. We compare our proposed framework in the unaligned setting with three existing federated knowledge graph embedding frameworks using the aligned entity set. FedE [4] first proposed the federate KGE framework, FedEC [5] first introduces contrastive learning to solve the heterogeneity of KGs, and FedLU [30] is the state-of-art federated KGE framework currently, which addresses data heterogeneity by maintaining different local and global models and transferring knowledge through mutual knowledge distillation. We use predictions of local models as results of FedLU.

The scoring of triplets uses several typical score functions TransE [2], DistMult [28], and ComplEx [24] for the baselines. Note that our framework used the composition of entities and relations, which is unsuitable to be applied to score functions with the unequal dimensions of the entity and relation embeddings such as RotatE [20]. Additionally, we implemented a convolution-based method ConvE [7] for UniFE. Since negative sampling is not used, we only set the comparison with the *Single* setting.

Evaluation Metrics. Following common evaluation metrics, we use the clients' average Hits at N (Hits@N) and Mean Reciprocal Rank (MRR) to evaluate the link prediction performance. The results use the rank in the *filtered* setting [2], which filters out the triplets that appear in the training, validation, or test set during the evaluation.

Implementation Details. We use Adam optimizer [11] with a learning rate 0.001. For the baselines, we refer to the implementation provided by Zhu et al. [30] and follow the main parameters provided. We use the higher results of the previously reported experiments and our reproduction for some existing experiments. The embedding dimension of entity and relation is 256. For fair comparisons, UniFE set the dimension of entity and relation embeddings to 128 because we have two modules. The number of basis edges is set to 50. The batch size is set to 1024. The experiments for *Single* setting evaluate the average MRR on the validation set every 10 epochs and use the early stop with patience of 3. For the federated setting, we use 3 local training epochs, evaluate the average MRR on the validation set every 5 communication rounds, and use the early stop with patience of 3.

5.2 Main Results

The main results of link prediction on FB15k-237-C3, -C5, -C10, and NELL-995-Fed3 are shown in Table 2 about MRR and Hits@1, which are the metrics that have significant influences on the downstream applications.

Based on these results, our proposed framework performs better than the *Single* setting. Specifically, on FB15k-237-C3, for TransE, DistMult, ComplEx, and ConvE, our approach achieves a relative improvement of 8.02%, 12.95%, 9.22%, and 4.57% in MRR, respectively. On the FB15k-237-C5, -C10, and NELL-995-Fed3, the relative improvement in MRR ranges from 1.91% to 14.50%. This improvement proves that our framework can benefit from KGs for different clients while preserving privacy.

Compared to FedE, our approach achieves an average relative improvement in MRR of 14.47%, 16.11%, 16.35%, and 18.27% on FB15k-237-C3, -C5, -C10, and NELL-995-Fed3, respectively. FedE uses average aggregation for aligned entity embeddings between clients. We can observe that FedE performs worse than *Single* setting in some cases, e.g., the ComplEx on FB15k-237-C3. This indicated that the same entity has different representations in different contexts. The average aggregation of highly heterogeneous KGs has an adverse effect in this situation. Our results relative to FedE and *Single* setting show that our approach can handle data heterogeneity better.

Table 2. Main results of link prediction on FB15k-237-C3, -C5, -C10, and NELL-995-Fed3. **Bold** numbers denote the best results with the same KGE methods in different settings.

KGE	Setting	FB15k-237-C3		FB15k-237-C5		FB15k-237-C10		NELL-995-Fed3	
		MRR	Hits@1	MRR	Hits@1	MRR	Hits@1	MRR	Hits@1
TransE	Single	31.44	19.48	32.94	20.47	31.99	19.58	23.53	10.67
	FedE	32.66	20.25	33.23	20.66	32.10	19.86	19.92	7.98
	FedEC	33.15	20.78	33.58	21.13	32.75	20.40	20.35	8.28
	FedLU	33.83	21.53	34.36	21.94	33.47	21.13	23.64	11.32
	UniFE	**33.96**	**23.14**	**35.02**	**23.81**	**33.67**	**22.56**	**24.82**	**14.56**
DistMult	Single	33.04	22.17	32.00	21.85	33.23	22.90	26.37	18.72
	FedE	31.21	21.04	29.94	19.95	30.17	20.43	23.79	17.14
	FedEC	32.85	20.92	29.25	18.13	31.28	20.37	25.85	18.46
	FedLU	34.93	23.18	33.65	22.46	34.83	24.40	26.67	19.23
	UniFE	**37.32**	**26.77**	**36.64**	**26.09**	**36.67**	**26.24**	**28.32**	**19.50**
ComplEx	Single	34.92	24.05	32.89	23.13	34.28	23.58	28.73	21.07
	FedE	31.82	21.41	30.54	19,88	30.06	19.80	26.34	18.96
	FedEC	34.58	22.44	31.30	19.63	32.53	20.59	28.89	20.68
	FedLU	37.10	25.38	35.66	24.05	36.33	25.14	29.04	**21.16**
	UniFE	**38.14**	**27.86**	**36.82**	**26.63**	**36.86**	**26.53**	**29.28**	20.93
ConvE	Single	36.94	26.55	35.39	25.18	35.03	24.91	29.62	19.98
	UniFE	**38.63**	**27.72**	**38.31**	**27.51**	**37.58**	**26.67**	**32.43**	**23.29**

Compared to FedEC and FedLU, our approach improves the average MRR across all settings by 11.65% and 3.62%, respectively. FedEC uses embedding-contrastive learning to tackle data heterogeneity, while FedLU maintains two models, local and global, and uses mutual distillation to tackle data heterogeneity. The restrictions of the above two approaches lie in the coverage of aligned entities among clients. The above results demonstrate that our approach outperforms results in the highly heterogeneous federated environment by mining and aggregating general structure information.

Furthermore, the absolute accuracy of our proposed framework is only for showing its potential, as the required conditions are different from existing methods. For question 1), we propose a learning paradigm for the FKGC task that has better privacy preservation and more general applicability without weakening performance in highly heterogeneous environments.

5.3 Ablation Study

In order to demonstrate the necessity and effectiveness of our proposed modules, we designed experiments by initializing them differently or removing modules. Specifically, we propose some variants:

- **w/o struct. 128/256:** The variant does not use the structure representation module. It initializes entity embeddings independently. For fair comparison and to observe the effect of embedding dimensions on the entity feature module, we used 128 and 256 dimensions. The former is used to evaluate the actual effect of single modules, and the latter doubles the parameters to compare the UniFE having two modules.
- **w/o struct. agg.:** The variant uses the structure representation module without any aggregation. It co-initializes basis embeddings and structure network parameters but initializes others independently.
- **w/ ent. init.:** The variant uses the structure representation module with basis embeddings and structure network parameters aggregation. It co-initializes basis embeddings and structure network parameters. Additionally, it co-initializes the entity feature embeddings.
- **w/ ent. agg.:** The variant uses the structure representation module with basis embeddings and structure network parameters aggregation. It co-initializes basis embeddings and structure network parameters. Additionally, it co-initializes the entity feature embeddings and uses entity feature aggregation with reference to FedE.

Table 3. Ablation study with different initialization and modules for UniFE. **Bold** numbers denote the best results and underline numbers denote the second best results in different variants.

Setting	FB15k-237-C3		FB15k-237-C5		FB15k-237-C10		NELL-995-Fed3	
	MRR	Hits@1	MRR	Hits@1	MRR	Hits@1	MRR	Hits@1
w/o struct. 128	34.78	24.15	32.79	22.08	32.23	21.90	29.70	20.95
w/o struct. 256	38.35	**27.96**	36.26	25.79	34.52	24.18	30.95	21.57
w/o struct. agg.	37.78	26.88	37.89	26.96	36.17	25.54	30.69	21.11
w/ ent. init.	<u>38.48</u>	27.62	**38.42**	**27.72**	<u>37.19</u>	<u>26.18</u>	32.36	22.86
w/ ent. agg.	37.81	26.90	37.79	27.11	36.91	25.98	**32.76**	<u>22.99</u>
UniFE	**38.63**	<u>27.72</u>	<u>38.31</u>	<u>27.51</u>	**37.58**	**26.67**	<u>32.43</u>	**23.29**

Table 3 shows the ablation study for the different variant models. From the results, we obtain the following observations:

1. Compared to *w/o struct. 128*, UniFE has an average relative 13.42% improvement of MRR. When compared to *w/o struct. 256*, UniFE has an average relative 5.01% improvement of MRR. Note that from the absolute amount of parameters, *w/o struct. 256* doubles the parameters of the feature representation module, which is more than the structure representation module with basis edges' number of 50. Moreover, this variant cannot aggregate parameters without aligned entity embeddings. The results demonstrate the parameter efficiency and potential of UniFE.

2. Compared to *w/o struct. agg.*, UniFE has an average relative 3.23% improvement of MRR. The results demonstrate the effectiveness of structure parameter aggregation.
3. The variant of *w/ ent. init.* obtained comparable results to UniFE. It concluded that different initializations of entity embeddings do not significantly influence. Our framework does not use co-initialization of entity embeddings, which is privacy-preserving without affecting performance.
4. Compared to *w/ ent. agg.* on FB15k-237-C3, -C5, -C10, *w/ ent. init.* and UniFE have average relative 1.40% and 1.79% improvements of MRR, respectively. The results show that the average aggregation of entity embeddings in highly heterogeneous environments has an adverse impact while bringing the risk to clients' privacy.
5. On NELL-995-Fed3, *w/ ent. agg.* have average relative 1.24% and 1.02% improvements of MRR compared with *w/ ent. init.* and UniFE. The results demonstrate that the average aggregation of entities has certain effects in the general setting that is not highly heterogeneous. Our framework's structure aggregation and entity aggregation do not conflict if realistic conditions are available.

For question 2), the results of the ablation study show that each module of our proposed framework is effective.

5.4 Further Analysis

Convergence Speed. Figure 4(a) illustrates the MRR results on the validation set of FB15k-237-C5 when TransE is used for UniFE and baselines. From the results, our proposed framework has a comparable convergence speed with FedLU, and our convergence speed exceeds FedE and FedEC. The trend of convergence on other datasets is roughly the same. For question 3), the results demonstrate the favorable learning efficiency of our framework with less use of client information.

Stricter Privacy Setting. The client's willingness to engage in FL is related to the information transferred to the server. Specifically, less information transmitted to the server brings a lower contribution cost, and clients are more willing to participate [1]. So, we conducted experiments to analyze the impact of the number of basis edges on our framework. Figure 4(b) shows the model's MRR results when using different numbers of basis edges. The results show that the MRR tends to increase and then decrease in the range of the basis edges' number from 10 to 100. The number of basis edges needs a suitable value to model the general structure information among different KGs.

Based on these results, we consider whether minimizing the number of parameters exchanged further is possible. We design a variant with a stricter privacy setting for exploring question 4). The variant is based on a plain intuition that lower relation-specific degrees represent more specific structure patterns, while higher relation-specific degrees represent more broad structure patterns. So we

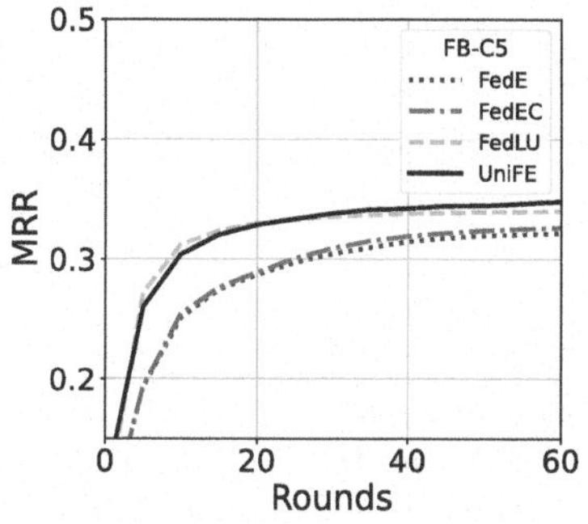

(a)

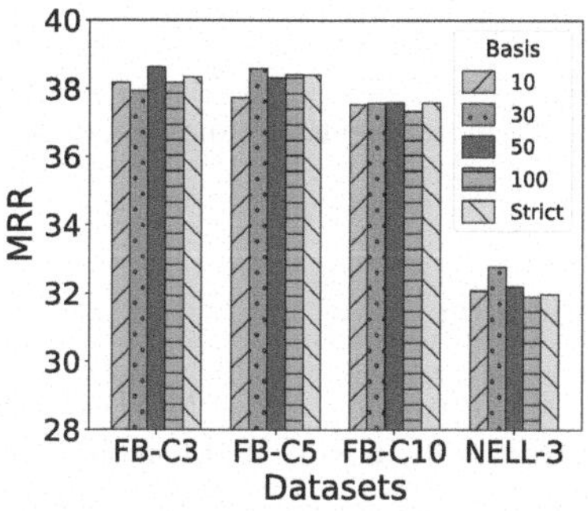

(b)

Fig. 4. (a) The MRR results with communication rounds on validation set of FB15k-237-C5. (b) The average MRR results of link prediction with different number of basis edges.

use the original number of relation-specific degrees when it is less than 20, whereas greater than 20, every ten items use the same basis edge, i.e., 20 to 29, 30 to 39, 40 to 49, and 50+ use different four basis edges.

From the results, compared to the default basis edges' number of 50, *Strict* setting further reduces the number of parameters and brings almost no performance loss. It is also a promising work on how to design basis edges for scenarios with higher privacy requirements.

6 Conclusion and Future Work

In this paper, we consider a more realistic scenario of the FKGC task, the heterogeneous federated environment without any aligned set. For the new setting, we propose UniFE, an unaligned federated knowledge graph embedding framework. The framework uses the pre-defined basis edges modeling the general structure information and two separate modules to learn the structure representations and feature representations in clients' local training. The clients only upload the structure parameters to the server for aggregation. This new learning paradigm does not depend on any aligned set and tackles the heterogeneity of multi-source KGs. We conducted extensive experiments on benchmark datasets, and the results demonstrate the effectiveness of our framework. In the future, we plan to explore more modeling approaches for general structure information over KGs and try to apply them to more tasks in the federated setting, such as the inductive KGC task.

Supplemental Material Statement: Source code for baselines and datasets FB15k-237-C3, -C5, -C10 are available at https://github.com/nju-websoft/FedLU. The dataset NELL-995-Fed3 is available at https://github.com/zjukg/FedE. Source code for UniFE is available at https://github.com/deyu-chen/UniFE.

Acknowledgements. The work was supported by the State Grid Corporation Science and Technology Project: Application research of a new generation of artificial intelligence in the security analysis and decision-making of future power grid (5100-202099522A-0-0-00).

References

1. Bi, X., Gupta, A., Yang, M.: Understanding partnership formation and repeated contributions in federated learning: an analytical investigation. Manag. Sci. (2023)
2. Bordes, A., Usunier, N., García-Durán, A., Weston, J., Yakhnenko, O.: Translating embeddings for modeling multi-relational data. In: Advances in Neural Information Processing Systems 26: 27th Annual Conference on Neural Information Processing Systems 2013, pp. 2787–2795 (2013)
3. Chen, M., et al.: Meta-learning based knowledge extrapolation for knowledge graphs in the federated setting. In: Proceedings of the Thirty-First International Joint Conference on Artificial Intelligence. IJCAI 2022, pp. 1966–1972 (2022)
4. Chen, M., Zhang, W., Yuan, Z., Jia, Y., Chen, H.: Fede: embedding knowledge graphs in federated setting. In: IJCKG'21: The 10th International Joint Conference on Knowledge Graphs, pp. 80–88 (2021)
5. Chen, M., Zhang, W., Yuan, Z., Jia, Y., Chen, H.: Federated knowledge graph completion via embedding-contrastive learning. Knowl. Based Syst. **252**, 109459 (2022)
6. Chen, M., et al.: Meta-knowledge transfer for inductive knowledge graph embedding. In: SIGIR '22: The 45th International ACM SIGIR Conference on Research and Development in Information Retrieval, pp. 927–937 (2022)
7. Dettmers, T., Minervini, P., Stenetorp, P., Riedel, S.: Convolutional 2D knowledge graph embeddings. In: Proceedings of the Thirty-Second AAAI Conference on Artificial Intelligence, (AAAI-18), the 30th innovative Applications of Artificial Intelligence (IAAI-18), and the 8th AAAI Symposium on Educational Advances in Artificial Intelligence (EAAI-18), pp. 1811–1818 (2018)
8. Dwivedi, V.P., Luu, A.T., Laurent, T., Bengio, Y., Bresson, X.: Graph neural networks with learnable structural and positional representations. In: The Tenth International Conference on Learning Representations. ICLR 2022 (2022)
9. Galkin, M., Yuan, X., Mostafa, H., Tang, J., Zhu, Z.: Towards foundation models for knowledge graph reasoning. In: The Twelfth International Conference on Learning Representations. ICLR 2024 (2024)
10. Hu, Y., et al.: Quantifying and defending against privacy threats on federated knowledge graph embedding. In: Proceedings of the ACM Web Conference 2023. WWW 2023, Austin, TX, USA, 30 April 2023–4 May 2023, pp. 2306–2317 (2023)
11. Kingma, D.P., Ba, J.: Adam: a method for stochastic optimization. In: 3rd International Conference on Learning Representations. ICLR 2015 (2015)
12. Kipf, T.N., Welling, M.: Semi-supervised classification with graph convolutional networks. In: 5th International Conference on Learning Representations (2017)
13. Li, Q., Diao, Y., Chen, Q., He, B.: Federated learning on non-IID data silos: an experimental study. In: 38th IEEE International Conference on Data Engineering. ICDE 2022. pp. 965–978 (2022)

14. Liu, Y., Zheng, Y., Zhang, D., Lee, V.C.S., Pan, S.: Beyond smoothing: unsupervised graph representation learning with edge heterophily discriminating. In: Thirty-Seventh AAAI Conference on Artificial Intelligence. AAAI 2023, Thirty-Fifth Conference on Innovative Applications of Artificial Intelligence. IAAI 2023, Thirteenth Symposium on Educational Advances in Artificial Intelligence. EAAI 2023, pp. 4516–4524 (2023)
15. McMahan, B., Moore, E., Ramage, D., Hampson, S., Arcas, B.A.: Communication-efficient learning of deep networks from decentralized data. In: Proceedings of the 20th International Conference on Artificial Intelligence and Statistics. AISTATS 2017, vol. 54, pp. 1273–1282 (2017)
16. Ren, H., et al.: LEGO: latent execution-guided reasoning for multi-hop question answering on knowledge graphs. In: Proceedings of the 38th International Conference on Machine Learning. ICML 2021, vol. 139, pp. 8959–8970 (2021)
17. Ruiz, C., Ren, H., Huang, K., Leskovec, J.: High dimensional, tabular deep learning with an auxiliary knowledge graph. In: Advances in Neural Information Processing Systems 36: Annual Conference on Neural Information Processing Systems 2023. NeurIPS 2023 (2023)
18. Schlichtkrull, M., Kipf, T.N., Bloem, P., van den Berg, R., Titov, I., Welling, M.: Modeling relational data with graph convolutional networks. In: Gangemi, A., et al. (eds.) ESWC 2018. LNCS, vol. 10843, pp. 593–607. Springer, Cham (2018). https://doi.org/10.1007/978-3-319-93417-4_38
19. Shang, C., Tang, Y., Huang, J., Bi, J., He, X., Zhou, B.: End-to-end structure-aware convolutional networks for knowledge base completion. In: The Thirty-Third AAAI Conference on Artificial Intelligence. AAAI 2019, The Thirty-First Innovative Applications of Artificial Intelligence Conference. IAAI 2019, The Ninth AAAI Symposium on Educational Advances in Artificial Intelligence. EAAI 2019, pp. 3060–3067 (2019)
20. Sun, Z., Deng, Z., Nie, J., Tang, J.: Rotate: knowledge graph embedding by relational rotation in complex space. In: 7th International Conference on Learning Representations. ICLR 2019 (2019)
21. Tan, Y., Liu, Y., Long, G., Jiang, J., Lu, Q., Zhang, C.: Federated learning on non-IID graphs via structural knowledge sharing. In: Thirty-Seventh AAAI Conference on Artificial Intelligence. AAAI 2023, Thirty-Fifth Conference on Innovative Applications of Artificial Intelligence. IAAI 2023, Thirteenth Symposium on Educational Advances in Artificial Intelligence. EAAI 2023, pp. 9953–9961 (2023)
22. Tang, Z., Pei, S., Peng, X., Zhuang, F., Zhang, X., Hoehndorf, R.: Neural multi-hop logical query answering with concept-level answers. In: 22nd International Semantic Web Conference, ISWC 2023, vol. 14265, pp. 522–540 (2023)
23. Toutanova, K., Chen, D.: Observed versus latent features for knowledge base and text inference. In: Proceedings of the 3rd Workshop on Continuous Vector Space Models and Their Compositionality. CVSC 2015, pp. 57–66 (2015)
24. Trouillon, T., Welbl, J., Riedel, S., Gaussier, É., Bouchard, G.: Complex embeddings for simple link prediction. In: Proceedings of the 33nd International Conference on Machine Learning. ICML 2016, vol. 48, pp. 2071–2080 (2016)
25. Vashishth, S., Sanyal, S., Nitin, V., Talukdar, P.P.: Composition-based multi-relational graph convolutional networks. In: 8th International Conference on Learning Representations. ICLR 2020 (2020)
26. Wu, J., He, J., Xu, J.: Demo-net: degree-specific graph neural networks for node and graph classification. In: Proceedings of the 25th ACM SIGKDD International Conference on Knowledge Discovery and Data Mining, pp. 406–415 (2019)

27. Xiong, W., Hoang, T., Wang, W.Y.: Deeppath: a reinforcement learning method for knowledge graph reasoning. In: Proceedings of the 2017 Conference on Empirical Methods in Natural Language Processing. EMNLP 2017, pp. 564–573 (2017)
28. Yang, B., Yih, W., He, X., Gao, J., Deng, L.: Embedding entities and relations for learning and inference in knowledge bases. In: 3rd International Conference on Learning Representations. ICLR 2015 (2015)
29. Zhang, K., Yang, C., Li, X., Sun, L., Yiu, S.: Subgraph federated learning with missing neighbor generation. In: Advances in Neural Information Processing Systems 34: Annual Conference on Neural Information Processing Systems 2021. NeurIPS 2021, pp. 6671–6682 (2021)
30. Zhu, X., Li, G., Hu, W.: Heterogeneous federated knowledge graph embedding learning and unlearning. In: Proceedings of the ACM Web Conference 2023. WWW 2023, pp. 2444–2454 (2023)

Finetuning Generative Large Language Models with Discrimination Instructions for Knowledge Graph Completion

Yang Liu[1], Xiaobin Tian[1], Zequn Sun[1(✉)], and Wei Hu[1,2]

[1] State Key Laboratory for Novel Software Technology, Nanjing University, Nanjing 210023, China
yliu20.nju@gmail.com, xbtian.nju@gmail.com, {sunzq,whu}@nju.edu.cn
[2] National Institute of Healthcare Data Science, Nanjing University, Nanjing 210093, China

Abstract. Traditional knowledge graph (KG) completion models learn embeddings to predict missing facts. Recent works attempt to complete KGs in a text-generation manner with large language models (LLMs). However, they need to ground the output of LLMs to KG entities, which inevitably brings errors. In this paper, we present a finetuning framework, DIFT, aiming to unleash the KG completion ability of LLMs and avoid grounding errors. Given an incomplete fact, DIFT employs a lightweight model to obtain candidate entities and finetunes an LLM with discrimination instructions to select the correct one from the given candidates. To improve performance while reducing instruction data, DIFT uses a truncated sampling method to select useful facts for finetuning and injects KG embeddings into the LLM. Extensive experiments on benchmark datasets demonstrate the effectiveness of our proposed framework.

Keywords: Knowledge graph completion · Large language model · Instruction tuning

1 Introduction

Knowledge graphs (KGs) store real-world facts in multi-relational structures, where nodes represent entities and edges are labeled with relations to describe facts in the form of triplets like (`head entity`, `relation`, `tail entity`). KGs often face the incompleteness problem [12], which adversely affects the performance of downstream knowledge-intensive applications such as question answering [11,24] and recommender systems [13]. KG completion models are designed to resolve the incompleteness issue by inferring the missing facts based on the facts already in KGs. Conventional KG completion models are based on KG embeddings. Given an incomplete fact where either the head or tail entity is missing and requires prediction, *embedding-based models* first compute the plausibility for candidate entities using an embedding function of entities and relations and then rank them to obtain predictions. Entity and relation embeddings

G. Demartini et al. (Eds.): ISWC 2024, LNCS 15231, pp. 199–217, 2025.
https://doi.org/10.1007/978-3-031-77844-5_11

can be learned based on either graph structures [1,3,35,39] or text attributes [17,20,29,30,36].

In recent years, motivated by the impressive performance of generative pre-trained language models (PLMs) such as T5 [22] and BART [16], some models convert KG completion to a sequence-to-sequence generation task [4,23,33]. Given an incomplete fact, *generation-based models* first construct a natural language query with text attributes of the given entity and relation, and then ask a generative PLM to generate an answer directly. Finally, they ground the answer to the entities in the KG, which, however, inevitably brings errors.

More recently, some work attempts to conduct KG completion using large language models (LLMs), such as ChatGPT and LLaMA [27]. Given an incomplete fact, KICGPT [31] first constructs query prompts with demonstration facts and the top-m candidate entities predicted by a pre-trained KG completion model. Then, it engages in a multi-round online interaction with ChatGPT using these query prompts. Finally, it rearranges these candidates according to the response of ChatGPT. This method may not make full use of the reasoning ability of LLMs because the LLMs (e.g., ChatGPT) may not fit the KG well. Besides, the multi-round interaction costs too much. In contrast, KG-LLM [37] converts KG completion queries to natural language questions and finetunes LLMs (e.g., LLaMA-7B) to generate answers. It then uses a heuristic method to ground the output of LLMs to KG entities: if the output text contains an entity name, then this entity is selected as the answer. The errors in such a grounding process cause KG-LLM to lag behind the state-of-the-art KG completion models. Besides, generation-based models obtain multiple output texts and rank them by the generation probabilities, which is time-consuming and unsuitable for LLMs.

To address the above issues and fully exploit the reasoning ability of LLMs, we propose DIFT that finetunes LLMs with discrimination instructions for KG completion. To avoid the grounding errors in generation-based models, DIFT constructs discrimination instructions that require LLMs to select an entity from the given candidates as the answer. Specifically, it first employs a lightweight embedding-based model to provide the top-m candidate entities for each incomplete fact, and adds the names of these entities to the prompts as candidate answers to the KG completion query. Then, it finetunes an LLM with parameter-efficient finetuning methods like LoRA [14] to select one entity name from the prompt as the output. In this way, the LLM gets enhanced by finetuning and can always generate entities in the KG instead of unconstrained generation.

However, training the LLM with parameter-efficient finetuning methods is still costly. To further reduce the computation cost of finetuning, we design a truncated sampling method that can select useful samples from the KG for instruction construction. Let us assume that we get an example for finetuning with the query $q = (h, r, ?)$ and the answer entity t. We use the pre-trained embedding-based model to compute the score of the fact (h, r, t) and the rank of t. Then, the truncated sampling method decides whether to discard the example based on the score of the fact and the rank of the answer entity. To unleash the graph reasoning ability of the LLM on KGs, we inject the embedded knowledge of queries and candidate entities into the LLM to further enhance it.

In summary, our main contributions are threefold:

- We propose a new KG completion framework, namely DIFT, which leverages discrimination instructions to finetune generative LLMs. DIFT does not require grounding the output of LLMs to entities in KGs.
- We propose a truncated sampling method to select useful KG samples for instruction construction to improve finetuning efficiency. We also inject KG embeddings into LLMs to improve finetuning effectiveness.
- Experiments show that DIFT advances the state-of-the-art KG completion results, with 0.364 Hits@1 on FB15K-237 and 0.616 on WN18RR.

The remaining sections of this paper are structured as follows. In Sect. 2, we delve into the existing research on knowledge graph completion. Section 3 provides a detailed exposition of our proposed framework. We then present our experimental results and analyses in Sect. 4. Finally, in Sect. 5, we conclude this paper and outline potential avenues for future research.

2 Related Work

Related studies can be divided into embedding- and generation-based models.

2.1 Embedding-Based KG Completion

Embedding-based KG completion methods compute prediction probability with entity and relation embeddings learned from either structural or textual features. We divide existing embedding-based models into two categories: structure-based models and PLM-based models.

Structure-Based Models. These models learn embeddings using structural features such as edges (i.e., triplets), paths or neighborhood subgraphs. Therefore, they can be categorized into three groups. The first group comprises triplet-based embedding models to preserve the local relational structures of KGs. They interpret relations as geometric transformations [3,25] or utilize semantic matching methods for scoring triplets [1,19]. The second group contains path-based models [6,34], which predominantly learn probabilistic logical rules from relation paths to facilitate reasoning and infer missing entities. The models in the third group use various deep neural networks to encode the subgraph structures of KGs. CompGCN [28] captures the semantics of multi-relational graphs of KGs based on the graph convolutional networks (GCN) framework. Instead, HittER [5] uses Transformer to aggregate relational neighbor information. Recently, NBFNet [39] employs a flexible and general framework to learn the representation of entity pairs, demonstrating strong performance among structure-based models.

PLM-Based Models. PLM-based models employ PLMs (e.g., BERT [10]) to encode the text attributes of entities and relations in facts, and compute prediction probabilities using the output embeddings. KG-BERT [36] is the first PLM-based KG completion model, which verifies that PLMs are capable of capturing the factual knowledge in KGs. It turns a fact into a natural language sentence by concatenating entity and relation names, and then predicts whether this sentence is correct or not. Following KG-BERT, some subsequent works make improvements in different aspects. StAR [29] divides each fact into two asymmetric parts and encodes them separately with a Siamese-style encoder. SimKGC [30] introduces three types of negatives for efficient contrastive learning. CoLE [17] promotes structure-based models and PLM-based models mutually through a co-distillation learning framework. These works are all embedding-based models. They obtain query embeddings and entity embeddings with encoder-only PLMs like BERT.

2.2 Generation-Based KG Completion

Different from embedding-based models that need to learn entity, relation or fact embeddings, generation-based models convert KG completion as a text generation task. These models first translate a KG completion query into a natural language question and then ask a generative language model (e.g., T5 [22] and BART [16]) to give an answer. Finally, they ground answers to entities in KGs using some matching methods. To compare with traditional KG completion models that rank entities based on their scores, generation-based models generate multiple entities with beam search or sampling and rank them by the generation probabilities. GenKGC [33] converts KG completion to sequence-to-sequence generation task to achieve fast inference speed. KGT5 [23] designs a unified framework for KG completion and question answering, but discards the pre-trained weights and trains T5 from scratch. KG-S2S [4] proposes to employ a generative language model to solve different forms of KG completion tasks including static KG completion, temporal KG completion, and few-shot KG completion [15]. Although these works provide some insight into how to conduct KG completion with LLMs, simply replacing PLMs with current LLMs is infeasible as finetuning LLMs on KGs is time-consuming and takes many computational resources.

With the emergence of LLMs, several works attempt to adapt LLMs for KG completion. KG-LLM [37] performs instruction tuning on KG completion tasks with relatively smaller LLMs (e.g., LLaMA-7B, ChatGLM-6B) and surpasses ChatGPT and GPT-4, but it still lags behind state-of-the-art KG completion models. KICGPT [31] employs an embedding-based model as the retriever to generate an ordered candidate entity list and designs an in-context learning strategy to prompt ChatGPT to re-rank the entities with a multi-round interaction. KICGPT is the most similar work to our proposed method DIFT, because we also employ an embedding-based model to obtain candidate entities and provide them to LLMs. However, accessing closed-source LLMs like ChatGPT is costly as the inference cost grows linearly with the number of missing facts. In contrast, we propose an effective and efficient method to finetune open-source LLMs.

3 The DIFT Framework

In this section, we describe the proposed DIFT framework for KG completion.

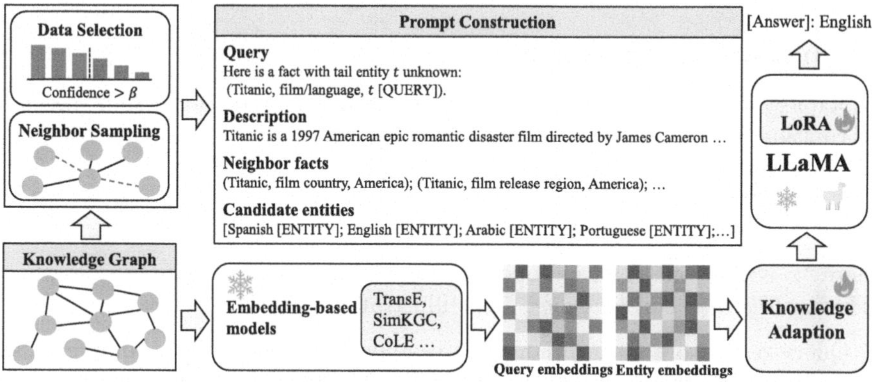

Fig. 1. Illustration of the proposed DIFT framework.

3.1 Notations

We start by introducing the definitions and notations used in this paper.

Knowledge Graph. A KG is denoted as $\mathcal{G} = (\mathcal{E}, \mathcal{R}, \mathcal{T})$. $\mathcal{E}$ is the set of entities, and $\mathcal{R}$ is the set of relations. $\mathcal{T} = \{(h, r, t) | h, t \in \mathcal{E}, r \in \mathcal{R}\}$ is the set of facts. We denote a fact as (h, r, t), in which h is the head entity, t is the tail entity, and r is the relation between h and t. Furthermore, the available text attributes of $\mathcal{G}$ encompass entity names, relation names, and entity descriptions.

Knowledge Graph Completion. KG completion (a.k.a. link prediction) aims to predict the missing entity given an incomplete fact. To be more specific, given an incomplete fact $(h, r, ?)$ or $(?, r, t)$, the purpose of KG completion is to find the missing entity t or h from the entity set $\mathcal{E}$.

3.2 Framework Overview

Figure 1 shows the overall framework of the proposed DIFT. In general, DIFT finetunes an LLM $\mathcal{M}$ on a given KG $\mathcal{G}$ with the help of an embedding-based model $\mathcal{M}_E$ which has been trained on $\mathcal{G}$ in advance. To elaborate, take a tail prediction query $q = (h, r, ?)$ as an example, we feed q into $\mathcal{M}_E$ to get the top-m predicted entities $\mathcal{C} = [e_1, e_2, \dots, e_m]$ where m is a predefined hyperparameter.

Subsequently, we construct a discrimination instruction $\mathcal{P}(q)$ based on the query q and the candidate entities $\mathcal{C}$. Finally, $\mathcal{P}(q)$ is fed into $\mathcal{M}$ to select the most plausible entity. In this way, we ensure that $\mathcal{M}$ always predicts an entity in $\mathcal{E}$ as the answer, avoiding grounding the unconstrained output texts from $\mathcal{M}$ to entities. For efficient finetuning, we employ $\mathcal{M}_E$ to score the instruction samples and only keep samples with high confidence. Additionally, to enhance the graph reasoning ability of $\mathcal{M}$, we design a knowledge adaption module to inject the embeddings of q and candidate entities in $\mathcal{C}$ obtained from $\mathcal{M}_E$ into $\mathcal{M}$.

3.3 Instruction Construction

For a query $q = (h, r, ?)$, we construct the prompt $\mathcal{P}$ by integrating four pieces of information: Query $\mathcal{Q}$, Description $\mathcal{D}$, Neighbor facts $\mathcal{N}$ and Candidate entities $\mathcal{C}$, which can be represented as:

$$\mathcal{P}(q) = [\mathcal{Q}; \mathcal{D}; \mathcal{N}; \mathcal{C}], \tag{1}$$

where ";" is the concatenation operation between texts. We give an example of querying (*Titanic*, *film language*, ?), as illustrated in Fig. 1.

Query refers to a natural language sentence containing the incomplete fact $(h, r, ?)$. Instead of designing a complex natural language question to prompt off-the-shelf LLMs, we simply concatenate the entity and relation names in the form of a triplet and indicate which entity is missing. During the finetuning process, the LLM $\mathcal{M}$ will be trained to fit our prompt format.

Description is the descriptive text of h, which contains abundant information about the entity. This additional information helps the LLM $\mathcal{M}$ get a better understand of the entity h. For instance, we depict *Titanic* in Fig. 1 as *a 1997 American epic romantic disaster film directed by James Cameron.*

Neighbor Facts are obtained by sampling facts related to the entity h. As there may be numerous facts associated with h, we devise a straightforward yet effective sampling mechanism, namely relation co-occurrence (*RC*) sampling. It is rooted in relation co-occurrence, and streamlines the number of facts while ensuring the inclusion of relevant information. The intuition behind RC sampling lies in the observation that the relations frequently co-occurring with r are considered to be crucial to complete $(h, r, ?)$. For example, the relations *film language* and *film country* in Fig. 1 often co-occur, because the language of a film is closely related to the country where it is released. Therefore, we can infer that the language of *Titanic* is highly likely to be English from the fact that it is an American film. Drawing on the above observation, we sort the neighboring relations of h based on their frequency of co-occurrences with r and subsequently select facts containing these relations until a preset threshold γ is reached.

Candidate Entities are the names of top-m entities ranked by the KG embedding model $\mathcal{M}_E$. We retain the order of candidate entities since the order reflects the confidence of each entity from $\mathcal{M}_E$. We instruct the LLM $\mathcal{M}$ to select an entity from the given candidates, thereby avoiding the grounding errors.

3.4 Truncated Sampling

We design a sampling method to select representative samples to reduce instruction data. The main idea is to opt for high-confidence samples indicated by $\mathcal{M}_E$, thereby empowering $\mathcal{M}$ to acquire intrinsic semantic knowledge of $\mathcal{M}_E$ efficiently. By finetuning $\mathcal{M}$ on these selected instruction samples, we effectively mitigate the computational burden associated with training.

We take the sample fact (h, r, t) with query $(h, r, ?)$ and answer entity t as an example. We denote the sample fact as s. Specifically, we assess the confidence of s from both global and local perspectives. The global confidence $Conf_{\text{global}}(s)$ is computed as $\frac{1}{R(h,r,t)}$, where $R(h, r, t)$ is the ranking of t for the query $(h, r, ?)$. We name it as the global confidence because it measures the ranking of t among all candidates in the KG.

Considering that the global confidence ignores the differences between two queries whose answer entities are in the same rank, inspired by [32], we present the local confidence to measure the score of a fact itself. The local confidence $Conf_{\text{local}}(s)$ is computed as $f(h, r, t)$, i.e., the score of s obtained from $\mathcal{M}_E$. It is worth noting that $Conf_{\text{local}}(s)$ is assigned as 0 if t is not ranked within the top-m. Finally, the confidence of s is determined by the weighted sum of global and local confidence, expressed as follows:

$$Conf(s) = Conf_{\text{global}}(s) + \alpha \times Conf_{\text{local}}(s), \tag{2}$$

where α serves as a hyperparameter to balance the global and local confidence. Subsequently, we introduce a threshold β and keep the samples with confidence greater than β as the final instruction data.

3.5 Instruction Tuning with Knowledge Adaption

Given the prompt $\mathcal{P}(q)$, we finetune the LLM $\mathcal{M}$ to generate the entity name of t. The loss of instruction tuning is a re-construction loss:

$$\mathcal{L}_{\mathcal{M}} = -\sum_{i=1}^{N} \log p(y_i \,|\, y_{<i}, \mathcal{P}(q)), \tag{3}$$

where N denotes the number of tokens in the entity name of t, y_i $(i = 1, 2, \ldots, N)$ represents the i-th token, and $p(y_i \,|\, y_{<i}, \mathcal{P}(q))$ signifies the probability of generating y_i with $\mathcal{M}$ given the prompt $\mathcal{P}(q)$ and tokens that have been generated.

The facts provided in $\mathcal{P}(q)$ are presented in the text format, losing the global structure information of KGs. Therefore, we propose to inject the embeddings learned from KG structure into $\mathcal{M}$ to further improve its graph reasoning ability. We align the embeddings from $\mathcal{M}_E$ with the semantic space of $\mathcal{M}$, to get the knowledge representations:

$$\hat{\mathbf{e}} = \mathbf{W}_2(\text{SwiGLU}(\mathbf{W}_1 \cdot \mathbf{e} + \mathbf{b}_1)) + \mathbf{b}_2, \tag{4}$$

where $\hat{\mathbf{e}}$ denotes the knowledge representation obtained based on the embeddings $\mathbf{e}$. $\mathbf{W}_1 \in \mathbb{R}^{d_1 \times d_0}$, $\mathbf{b}_1 \in \mathbb{R}^{d_1}$, $\mathbf{W}_2 \in \mathbb{R}^{d_2 \times d_1}$, and $\mathbf{b}_2 \in \mathbb{R}^{d_2}$ are trainable weights.

Table 1. The statistics of datasets.

Datasets	#Entities	#Relations	#Training	#Validation	#Testing
FB15K-237	14,541	237	272,115	17,535	20,466
WN18RR	40,943	11	86,835	3,034	3,134

d_0 is the embedding dimension of $\mathcal{M}_E$, d_2 is the hidden size of $\mathcal{M}$, and d_1 is a hyperparameter. SwiGLU is a common activation function used in LLaMA [27].

Considering that $\mathcal{M}_E$ scores a fact based on the embeddings of the query q and the candidate entity t, we inject the knowledge representations of q and all candidate entities in $\mathcal{C}$ into $\mathcal{M}$. We add two special placeholders "[QUERY]" and "[ENTITY]" to indicate that there will be a knowledge representation from $\mathcal{M}_E$, as shown in Fig. 1. Specifically, we place a "[QUERY]" after the missing entity in $\mathcal{Q}$ and an "[ENTITY]" after each entity name in $\mathcal{C}$.

4 Experiments

4.1 Experiment Setup

Datasets. In the experiments, we use two benchmark datasets, FB15K-237 [26] and WN18RR [8], to evaluate our proposed framework. FB15K-237 consists of real-world named entities and their relations, constructed based on Freebase [2]. On the other hand, WN18RR contains English phrases and the semantic relations between them, constructed based on WordNet [18]. Notably, these two datasets are updated from their previous versions (i.e., FB15K and WN18 [3]) respectively, they both removed some inverse edges to prevent data leakage. For a detailed overview, the statistics of these two datasets are shown in Table 1.

Evaluation Protocol. For each test fact, we conduct both head entity prediction and tail entity prediction by masking the corresponding entities, respectively. The conventional metrics are ranking evaluation metrics, i.e., Hits@k ($k = 1, 3, 10$) and mean reciprocal rank (MRR). Hits@k is the percentage of queries whose correct entities are ranked within the top-k, and MRR measures the average reciprocal ranks of correct entities. In our framework, the finetuned LLM selects an entity as the answer from the ranking list of candidates. To assess its performance and make the results comparable to existing work, we move the selected entity to the top of the ranking list, and other candidates remain unchanged. We then use Hits@k and MRR to assess the reranked candidate list. We report the averaged results of head and tail entity prediction under the filtered ranking setting [3].

Implementation Details. We run our experiments on two Intel Xeon Gold CPUs, an NVIDIA RTX A6000 GPU, and Ubuntu 18.04 LTS. Text attributes are taken from KG-BERT [36]. We select three representative embedding-based models to experiment with DIFT, namely, TransE, SimKGC, and CoLE. Each embedding-based model is pre-trained on the training set. We obtain the top 20 predicted entities for each query in the validation set and test set. We also obtain the embeddings of all queries and entities for knowledge adaption.

As for the instruction tuning, we select LLaMA-2-7B[1] as the LLM. We employ LoRA [14] for parameter-efficient finetuning. The hyperparameters of LoRA are set to $r = 64$, alpha = 16, and dropout = 0.1. We introduce LoRA for all query and value projection matrices in the self-attention module of Transformer. To further speed up the finetuning process, we quantize the LLM by QLoRA [9], which quantizes the LLM parameters to 4 bits by introducing Double Quantization with 4-bit NormalFloat data type. Inspired by KICGPT [31], we partition the validation set into two parts according to 9:1. The first part is used to finetune the LLM to follow the instructions, and the second part is used for hyperparameter selection. Note that we do not use the training data of each benchmark to construct instructions. Since the embedding-based model has learned the training data, it would rank the correct entity at the first in the candidate list for most training facts. If we use these candidate lists to construct instructions, the LLM would learn a tricky solution to pick the first candidate as an answer, which is not the goal of our finetuning.

4.2 Baselines

Embedding-Based Models. We choose eight *structure-based models* as baselines. Three triplet-based models are selected, including TransE [3], RotatE [25], and TuckER [1]. We also choose two path-based models. Neural-LP [34] is the first model that learns logic rules from relation paths and NCLR [6] is the state-of-the-art path-based model. The remaining models are all graph-based. CompGCN [28] employs GCNs to encode the multi-relational graph structure of the KG, while HittER [5] leverages the Transformer architecture. NBFNet [39] currently performs best among the structure-based models. We also select five *PLM-based models* as the competitors, namely KG-BERT [36], StAR [29], MEM-KGC [7], SimKGC [30], and CoLE [17]. Note that, SimKGC stands the state-of-the-art link prediction model on WN18RR, which benefits from efficient contrastive learning. CoLE promotes PLMs and structure-based models mutually to achieve the best performance on FB15K-237 among PLM-based models. To ensure a fair comparison, we present results derived solely from N-BERT, the PLM-based KG embedding module within CoLE, rather than the entire CoLE framework.

Generation-Based Models. We select three generation-based KG completion models, all of which are either based on BART or T5, namely, GenKGC [33], KGT5 [23], and KG-S2S [4]. Further, we select two recent models based on LLMs as baselines. $\text{ChatGPT}_{\text{one-shot}}$ is a baseline proposed by AutoKG [38], and KICGPT evaluates it on the whole test sets of FB15K-237 and WN18RR for comparison. KICGPT is the most competitive KG completion model, which employs

[1] https://huggingface.co/meta-llama/Llama-2-7b-chat-hf.

Table 2. Link prediction Results. We mark the best scores in terms of each metric in **bold** and the second-best scores are underlined. We reproduce the results of TransE, SimKGC and CoLE using their source code and hyperparameters. The results of Neural-LP are obtained from [21]. The results of GenKGC, KGT5 and KG-S2S are obtained from [4]. The results of other baselines are taken from their respective original papers.

Models	FB15K-237				WN18RR			
	MRR	Hits@1	Hits@3	Hits@10	MRR	Hits@1	Hits@3	Hits@10
Embedding-based								
TransE	0.312	0.212	0.354	0.510	0.225	0.016	0.403	0.521
RotatE	0.338	0.241	0.375	0.533	0.476	0.428	0.492	0.571
TuckER	0.358	0.266	0.394	0.544	0.470	0.443	0.482	0.526
Neural-LP	0.237	0.173	0.259	0.361	0.381	0.368	0.386	0.408
NCRL	0.300	0.209	-	0.473	0.670	0.563	-	**0.850**
CompGCN	0.355	0.264	0.390	0.535	0.479	0.443	0.494	0.546
HittER	0.373	0.279	0.409	0.558	0.503	0.462	0.516	0.584
NBFNet	0.415	0.321	0.454	**0.599**	0.551	0.497	0.573	0.666
KG-BERT	-	-	-	0.420	0.216	0.041	0.302	0.524
StAR	0.365	0.266	0.404	0.562	0.551	0.459	0.594	0.732
MEM-KGC	0.346	0.253	0.381	0.531	0.557	0.475	0.604	0.704
SimKGC	0.338	0.252	0.364	0.511	0.671	0.595	0.719	0.802
CoLE	0.389	0.294	0.429	0.572	0.593	0.538	0.616	0.701
Generation-based								
GenKGC	-	0.192	0.355	0.439	-	0.287	0.403	0.535
KGT5	0.276	0.210	-	0.414	0.508	0.487	-	0.544
KG-S2S	0.336	0.257	0.373	0.498	0.574	0.531	0.595	0.661
$\text{ChatGPT}_{\text{one-shot}}$	-	0.267	-	-	-	0.212	-	-
KICGPT	0.412	0.327	0.448	0.581	0.564	0.478	0.612	0.677
LLaMA + TransE	0.232	0.080	0.321	0.502	0.202	0.037	0.360	0.516
LLaMA + SimKGC	0.236	0.074	0.335	0.503	0.391	0.065	0.695	0.798
LLaMA + CoLE	0.238	0.033	0.387	0.561	0.374	0.117	0.602	0.697
DIFT + TransE	0.389	0.322	0.408	0.525	0.491	0.462	0.496	0.560
DIFT + SimKGC	0.402	0.338	0.418	0.528	**0.686**	**0.616**	**0.730**	0.806
DIFT + CoLE	**0.439**	**0.364**	**0.468**	0.586	0.617	0.569	0.638	0.708

RotatE to provide the top-m predicted entities for each query and re-ranks these candidates with ChatGPT through multi-round interactions. We also report

Table 3. Results of ablation study

Models	FB15K-237				WN18RR			
	MRR	Hits@1	Hits@3	Hits@10	MRR	Hits@1	Hits@3	Hits@10
DIFT	**0.439**	**0.364**	0.468	0.586	**0.617**	**0.569**	**0.638**	0.708
w/o truncated sampling	0.423	0.338	0.459	0.587	0.600	0.537	**0.638**	**0.712**
w/o RC sampling	0.434	0.354	0.468	**0.588**	0.614	0.564	0.636	0.708
w/o description	0.436	0.358	0.467	0.586	0.603	0.548	0.630	0.705
w/o neighbors	0.438	0.360	**0.469**	**0.588**	0.610	0.558	0.637	0.708
w/o knowledge adaption	0.437	0.358	0.468	0.587	0.612	0.560	0.637	0.708

the performance of DIFT without finetuning, denoted by LLaMA+TransE, LLaMA+SimKGC, and LLaMA+CoLE, respectively.

4.3 Main Results

We report the link prediction results on FB15K-237 and WN18RR in Table 2. Generally speaking, our proposed framework DIFT achieves the best performance in most metrics on two datasets. Compared with the selected embedding-based models TransE, SimKGC, and CoLE, DIFT improves the performance of these models on both datasets, significantly in terms of Hits@1. Without finetuning, the performance of DIFT drops dramatically, which demonstrates that it is necessary to finetune the LLM for KG completion task.

Compared with the LLM-based model $\text{ChatGPT}_{\text{one-shot}}$, DIFT consistently outperforms it in terms of Hits@1, regardless of the integration with any of the embedding-based models. This indicates that prompting ChatGPT with in-context learning is less effective than finetuning a smaller LLM with the help of existing embedding-based models for link prediction. Compared with the most competitive baseline model KICGPT which also provides the LLM with candidate entities, the relative improvement brought by DIFT is less. However, KICGPT needs multi-round interactions with ChatGPT, which has 175B parameters. In contrast, DIFT finetunes a small LLaMA with only 7B parameters.

Comparing different metrics, we find that the performance improvement is more significant on Hits@1 while less significant on Hits@10. In DIFT, we ask the LLM to select the plausible entity from the given candidate list. Given that the correct entity is more likely to be ranked in the top 10 entities rather than outside the top 10, the LLM is more likely to select an entity in the top 10 as the answer. Thus, the improvement is more obvious on Hits@1 rather than Hits@10.

We also find that the performance improvement on FB15K-237 is more significant than that on WN18RR. This discrepancy can be attributed to the stark disparity in density between the two datasets: FB15K-237 is considerably denser than WN18RR, implying a richer reservoir of knowledge. More knowledge leads to better improvement since the knowledge is provided for the LLM to comprehend in the form of prompts and embeddings.

4.4 Ablation Study

For the ablation study, we select CoLE as the embedding-based model to provide candidate entities since DIFT with CoLE performs best overall on both datasets. We evaluate the effectiveness of two kinds of sampling mechanisms, i.e., *truncated sampling* and *RC sampling*, as well as three kinds of support information, i.e., *description*, *neighbors*, and embeddings used in *knowledge adaption*.

From the results presented in Table 3, it is evident that all components contribute a lot to DIFT. Among all these components, truncated sampling has the most substantial impact on performance. The Hits@1 score experiences a degradation of at least 5.6% in the absence of truncated sampling. This shows that this mechanism can effectively select useful instruction data for the LLM to learn intrinsic semantic knowledge of the embedding-based model.

We can also observe that the impact of description, neighbors, and RC sampling differs significantly between the two datasets. Without description, the Hits@1 will drop more on WN18RR. This is attributed to WN18RR being a sparse KG with less structural information compared with FB15K-237. Therefore, it needs additional description to enrich entity information, aiding in the differentiation between similar entities. In addition, neighbor information is also more important for WN18RR. This is because many correct entities will directly appear in the neighbor facts of WN18RR, facilitating the LLM in making accurate predictions. Instead, the improvement of Hits@1 is more significant on FB15K-237 than WN18RR for RC sampling. We posit that this is attributed to FB15K-237 being highly dense, with each entity having numerous neighbor facts. Many of these facts are irrelevant to the query, leading to interference. Hence, RC sampling can minimize irrelevant facts and enhance effectiveness.

As for knowledge adaption, we observe consistent performance improvements across the two datasets, indicating good generality and robustness.

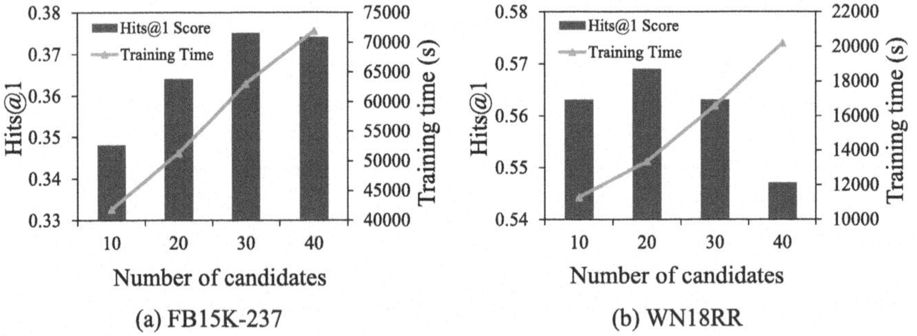

Fig. 2. Hits@1 results and training time of DIFT on FB15K-237 and WN18RR along with the numbers of candidate entities.

4.5 Further Analyses

Effect of the Number of Candidates. In Sect. 4.3, we set the number of candidate entities m provided by the embedding-based model to 20. Here we investigate the effect of m on the performance and the training time of DIFT. The results are shown in Fig. 2. First, for the training time, we find that it grows linearly when we increase m. It is intuitive since increasing m leads to longer prompts. Second, as for the performance of DIFT, we find that the performance is best when m is set to 30 on FB15K-237, and there is a slight drop when m is set to 40. The same observation can be found on WN18RR if we continue to increase m after 20. This indicates that blindly increasing the number of candidate entities cannot improve performance. Third, we find that the performance is best when m is set to 30 on FB15K-237 and 20 on WN18RR. That is to say, to achieve the best performance, DIFT needs more candidate entities on FB15K-237 than WN18RR. We think that this discrepancy arises from the generally inferior performance of models on FB15K-237 compared to WN18RR. Consequently, to ensure the presence of answer entities within the prompts, a larger m is advisable on FB15K-237 than on WN18RR.

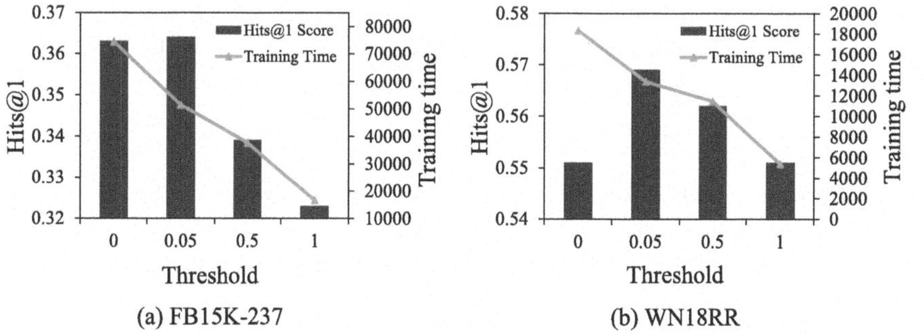

Fig. 3. Hits@1 results and training time of DIFT on FB15K-237 and WN18RR along with the threshold for truncated sampling.

Effect of Truncated Sampling Thresholds. In Sect. 3.4, we use a threshold β to control the quantity of instruction data. To investigate the impact of β on the performance and the training time of DIFT, we conduct an experiment by setting different values for β. In particular, we change β from 0.05 in the main experiments to 0, 0.5, and 1.0 respectively. The results are shown in Fig. 3. We have the following observations. First, with β increasing, the quantity of instruction data decreases, and therefore the training time also decreases accordingly. Second, the performance drops when we set β to 0 on both datasets, which indicates that increasing the quantity of instruction data does not necessarily improve the performance, and its quality also affects the performance. Third, if we strictly ensure that the quality of the instruction data is high enough, i.e., we set β to 0.5 or 1.0, the performance of DIFT also drops. We think there are mainly two reasons: (1) When β is set to 0.5 or 1.0, the limited instruction data is not enough to finetune the LLM sufficiently. (2) Instruction data with high confidence usually places the answer entity among the first few in the candidate list. Therefore, finetuning the LLM with this data will cause the LLM to always choose the top-ranked entities, regardless of whether they are correct.

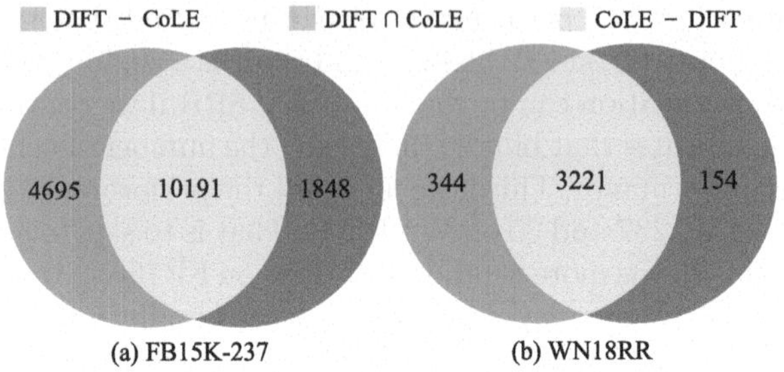

Fig. 4. Correct predictions of DIFT and CoLE on FB15K-237 and WN18RR. The light blue area represents the accurate triplets predicted by DIFT, excluding those that can also be predicted by CoLE. The dark green area illustrates the overlapping triplets predicted accurately by DIFT and CoLE. The light green area represents the accurate triplets predicted by CoLE, excluding those that can also be predicted by DIFT. (Color figure online)

Comparison of DIFT and Basic Embedding Models. We further investigate the predictions of DIFT in comparison with those of the selected embedding-based model. For this analysis, we continue to employ CoLE as the embedding-based model to analyze the results. We draw Venn diagrams to highlight both their shared and individual correct predictions, as illustrated in Fig. 4. It is obvious that in addition to the shared correct predictions, DIFT can also get some correct predictions by itself. Conversely, we observe instances where CoLE makes correct inferences that DIFT fails to replicate. Based on the divergence between the correct predictions of DIFT and CoLE, we can conclude that the LLM does not repeat the predicted entities by CoLE blindly, instead, it can reason the missing facts based on its knowledge obtained in the pre-training stage.

Comparison of Different Versions of the LLM. In the main experiment, we employ LLaMA-2-7B-Chat as the LLM for DIFT. In order to investigate the influence of different versions of the LLM on the performance of DIFT, we experiment with the foundation version, denoted as LLaMA-2-7B-Foundation. The results are shown in Table 4. DIFT with LLaMA-2-7B-Foundation performs slightly better than that with LLaMA-2-7B-Chat on FB15K-237, but the observation is the opposite on WN18RR. Generally speaking, DIFT achieves a similar performance no matter which version of the LLM are employed. It demonstrates the robustness and generalization of DIFT for different LLM versions.

Table 4. Link prediction Results of different versions of LLaMA-2-7B.

Models	FB15K-237				WN18RR			
	MRR	Hits@1	Hits@3	Hits@10	MRR	Hits@1	Hits@3	Hits@10
LLaMA-2-7B-Chat								
DIFT + TransE	0.389	0.322	0.408	0.525	0.491	0.462	0.496	0.560
DIFT + SimKGC	0.402	0.338	0.418	0.528	0.686	0.616	0.730	0.806
DIFT + CoLE	0.439	0.364	0.468	0.586	0.617	0.569	0.638	0.708
LLaMA-2-7B-Foundation								
DIFT + TransE	0.393	0.328	0.409	0.525	0.481	0.450	0.486	0.552
DIFT + SimKGC	0.405	0.341	0.420	0.530	0.682	0.608	0.731	0.806
DIFT + CoLE	0.439	0.363	0.468	0.587	0.619	0.571	0.641	0.710

Table 5. Influence of the order of candidates

Ordered finetuning	Ordered inference	FB15K-237				WN18RR			
		MRR	Hits@1	Hits@3	Hits@10	MRR	Hits@1	Hits@3	Hits@10
✓	✓	0.439	0.364	0.468	0.586	0.686	0.616	0.730	0.806
✓	✗	0.328	0.168	0.441	0.584	0.484	0.233	0.712	0.806
✗	✓	0.423	0.333	0.466	0.589	0.627	0.500	0.731	0.809
✗	✗	0.417	0.324	0.464	0.591	0.625	0.493	0.736	0.808

4.6 The Finetuning Learns What?

In this section, we investigate what the LLM learns during our finetuning process. DIFT employs a lightweight embedding-based model to provide candidate entities for both finetuning and inference. A natural question arises: Does the LLM learn the preference of the embedding-based model predictions or the knowledge in the KG? To answer this question, we design the following experiment to evaluate the effect of the candidate order in both the finetuning and inference stages.

Effect of the Order of Candidates. DIFT takes the top-m predicted entities from the embedding-based model as the candidates for the LLM. We retain the order of candidates because we assume that the order reflects the knowledge learned by the embedding-based model. Here, to investigate the influence of the order of candidates, we shuffle the candidates in the finetuning or inference stages to ask the LLM to select an entity from the shuffled candidate list. Remember that the shuffled candidate list is only used for entity selection, we move the selected entity to the top of the ranking list from the embedding-based model for evaluation. Results are shown in Table 5, and we have the following observations.

On FB15K-237, we employ CoLE as the embedding-based model. We can find that the performance drops dramatically if we finetune the LLM with ordered candidates but shuffle the candidates during inference. We think the reason is that ordered candidates instruct the LLM to select within the top few entities as they are more plausible. Therefore, the LLM still focus on the top few candidates during inference, even though the candidates are shuffled. When we finetune the LLM with shuffled candidates, we find that the performance changes slightly whether the candidates are shuffled or not during inference. The reason is that the LLM has no idea about the preference that the top few candidates are more plausible, so it can not benefit from the order of candidates.

On WN18RR, we use SimKGC as the embedding-based model and similar observations can be found. However, we find that the performance of DIFT is even worse than SimKGC when we finetune the LLM with shuffled candidates. This demonstrates that the LLM can not outperform SimKGC solely based on its inherent knowledge without prediction preferences.

Based on the above analyses, it appears that our DIFT not only captures prediction preferences but also primarily acquires knowledge from the KG.

Case Study. To explore how DIFT improves performance compared with the selected embedding-based models, we conduct a case study on DIFT (integrating CoLE), TransE, SimKGC, and CoLE. Table 6 presents the Hits@1 results of the four models on three queries from FB15K-237, in which the entities marked with horizontal lines at the bottom are the answers. In the first two cases, DIFT consistently performs accurately while the other models all predict wrong entities.

- In Case 1, the contextual description of the head entity, "*It tells the story of an aspiring actress named Betty Elms, newly arrived in Los Angeles ...*", offers ample support to determine the answer "Los Angeles", and our DIFT generates the correct entity name, indicating that DIFT has improved contextual inference capability compared with the embedding-based models.
- In Case 2, neither the description nor the neighbor information provides clues to *Shonda Rhimes*' gender. It is difficult for embedding-based models to infer the correct entity based on such incomplete knowledge. Instead, DIFT has open knowledge and powerful commonsense reasoning ability, allowing it to overcome this limitation and predict the correct answers. This case shows the complementarity of embedding-based models and LLMs in our framework.
- In Case 3, despite DIFT inferring an "incorrect" entity "*The Last King of Scotland*", it is crucial to highlight that the underlying issue is associated with the dataset, not DIFT itself. This is because the language of "*The Last King of Scotland*" is also English, but FB15K-237 lacks this specific knowledge. This case demonstrates that DIFT is capable of leveraging open knowledge in LLMs, surpassing the constraints of closed knowledge in KGs.

Table 6. Case study on three queries from FB15K-237. Correct answers are underlined.

	Case 1	Case 2	Case 3
Head entity	Mulholland Drive	Shonda Rhimes	?
Relation	*featured film locations*	*gender*	*film language*
Tail entity	?	?	English language
DIFT	Los Angeles	Female	The Last King of Scotland
TransE	Paris	Male	Pan's Labyrinth
SimKGC	Berkeley	Male	The Illusionist
CoLE	New York City	Male	The Illusionist

5 Conclusion and Future Work

In this paper, we propose a novel KG completion framework DIFT. It finetunes generative LLMs with discrimination instructions using LoRA, which does not involve grounding the output of LLMs to entities in KGs. To further reduce the computation cost and make DIFT more efficient, we propose a truncated sampling method to select facts with high confidence for finetuning. KG embeddings are also added into the LLMs to improve the finetuning effectiveness. Experiments show that DIFT achieves state-of-the-art results on KG completion. In future work, we plan to support other KG tasks such as KGQA and entity alignment.

Supplemental Material Statement: Source code and datasets are available on GitHub: https://github.com/nju-websoft/DIFT.

Acknowledgments. This work was funded by National Natural Science Foundation of China (No. 62272219), Postdoctoral Fellowship Program of CPSF (No. GZC20240685), and CCF-Tencent Rhino-Bird Open Research Fund.

References

1. Balazevic, I., Allen, C., Hospedales, T.M.: TuckER: tensor factorization for knowledge graph completion. In: EMNLP-IJCNLP, pp. 5185–5194 (2019)
2. Bollacker, K.D., Evans, C., Paritosh, P.K., Sturge, T., Taylor, J.: Freebase: a collaboratively created graph database for structuring human knowledge. In: SIGMOD, pp. 1247–1250 (2008)
3. Bordes, A., Usunier, N., García-Durán, A., Weston, J., Yakhnenko, O.: Translating embeddings for modeling multi-relational data. In: NIPS, pp. 2787–2795 (2013)
4. Chen, C., Wang, Y., Li, B., Lam, K.: Knowledge is flat: a Seq2Seq generative framework for various knowledge graph completion. In: COLING, pp. 4005–4017 (2022)

5. Chen, S., Liu, X., Gao, J., Jiao, J., Zhang, R., Ji, Y.: HittER: hierarchical transformers for knowledge graph embeddings. In: EMNLP, pp. 10395–10407 (2021)
6. Cheng, K., Ahmed, N.K., Sun, Y.: Neural compositional rule learning for knowledge graph reasoning. In: ICLR (2023)
7. Choi, B., Jang, D., Ko, Y.: MEM-KGC: masked entity model for knowledge graph completion with pre-trained language model. IEEE Access **9**, 132025–132032 (2021)
8. Dettmers, T., Minervini, P., Stenetorp, P., Riedel, S.: Convolutional 2D knowledge graph embeddings. In: AAAI, pp. 1811–1818 (2018)
9. Dettmers, T., Pagnoni, A., Holtzman, A., Zettlemoyer, L.: QLoRA: efficient finetuning of quantized LLMs. arXiv:2305.14314 (2023)
10. Devlin, J., Chang, M., Lee, K., Toutanova, K.: BERT: pre-training of deep bidirectional transformers for language understanding. In: NAACL, pp. 4171–4186 (2019)
11. Du, H., Le, Z., Wang, H., Chen, Y., Yu, J.: COKG-QA: multi-hop question answering over COVID-19 knowledge graphs. Data Intell. **4**, 471–492 (2022)
12. Galárraga, L., Razniewski, S., Amarilli, A., Suchanek, F.M.: Predicting completeness in knowledge bases. In: WSDM, pp. 375–383 (2017)
13. Guo, Q., et al.: A survey on knowledge graph-based recommender systems. IEEE Trans. Knowl. Data Eng. **34**, 3549–3568 (2022)
14. Hu, E.J., et al.: LoRA: low-rank adaptation of large language models. In: ICLR (2022)
15. Ji, S., Pan, S., Cambria, E., Marttinen, P., Yu, P.S.: A survey on knowledge graphs: representation, acquisition, and applications. IEEE Trans. Neural Netw. Learn. Syst. **33**, 494–514 (2022)
16. Lewis, M., et al.: BART: denoising sequence-to-sequence pre-training for natural language generation, translation, and comprehension. In: ACL, pp. 7871–7880 (2020)
17. Liu, Y., Sun, Z., Li, G., Hu, W.: I know what you do not know: knowledge graph embedding via co-distillation learning. In: CIKM, pp. 1329–1338 (2022)
18. Miller, G.A.: WordNet: a lexical database for English. Commun. ACM **38**, 39–41 (1995)
19. Nayyeri, M., et al.: Dihedron algebraic embeddings for spatio-temporal knowledge graph completion. In: ESWC (2022)
20. Omeliyanenko, J., Zehe, A., Hotho, A., Schlör, D.: CapsKG: enabling continual knowledge integration in language models for automatic knowledge graph completion. In: ISWC (2023)
21. Qu, M., Chen, J., Xhonneux, L.A.C., Bengio, Y., Tang, J.: RNNLogic: learning logic rules for reasoning on knowledge graphs. In: ICLR (2021)
22. Raffel, C., et al.: Exploring the limits of transfer learning with a unified text-to-text transformer. J. Mach. Learn. Res. **21**, 1–67 (2020)
23. Saxena, A., Kochsiek, A., Gemulla, R.: Sequence-to-sequence knowledge graph completion and question answering. In: ACL, pp. 2814–2828 (2022)
24. Saxena, A., Tripathi, A., Talukdar, P.P.: Improving multi-hop question answering over knowledge graphs using knowledge base embeddings. In: ACL, pp. 4498–4507 (2020)
25. Sun, Z., Deng, Z., Nie, J., Tang, J.: RotatE: knowledge graph embedding by relational rotation in complex space. In: ICLR (2019)
26. Toutanova, K., Chen, D., Pantel, P., Poon, H., Choudhury, P., Gamon, M.: Representing text for joint embedding of text and knowledge bases. In: EMNLP, pp. 1499–1509 (2015)
27. Touvron, H., et al.: LLaMA: open and efficient foundation language models. arXiv:2302.13971 (2023)

28. Vashishth, S., Sanyal, S., Nitin, V., Talukdar, P.P.: Composition-based multi-relational graph convolutional networks. In: ICLR (2020)
29. Wang, B., Shen, T., Long, G., Zhou, T., Wang, Y., Chang, Y.: Structure-augmented text representation learning for efficient knowledge graph completion. In: WWW, pp. 1737–1748 (2021)
30. Wang, L., Zhao, W., Wei, Z., Liu, J.: SimKGC: simple contrastive knowledge graph completion with pre-trained language models. In: ACL, pp. 4281–4294 (2022)
31. Wei, Y., Huang, Q., Zhang, Y., Kwok, J.T.: KICGPT: large language model with knowledge in context for knowledge graph completion. In: EMNLP-Findings, pp. 8667–8683 (2023)
32. Xie, R., Liu, Z., Lin, F., Lin, L.: Does William Shakespeare really write Hamlet? Knowledge representation learning with confidence. In: AAAI, pp. 4954–4961 (2018)
33. Xie, X., et al.: From discrimination to generation: knowledge graph completion with generative transformer. In: WWW, pp. 162–165 (2022)
34. Yang, F., Yang, Z., Cohen, W.W.: Differentiable learning of logical rules for knowledge base reasoning. In: NeurPS (2017)
35. Yang, Y., Ye, Z., Zhao, H., Meng, L.: A novel link prediction framework based on gravitational field. Data Sci. Eng. **8**, 47–60 (2023)
36. Yao, L., Mao, C., Luo, Y.: KG-BERT: BERT for knowledge graph completion. arXiv:1909.03193 (2019)
37. Yao, L., Peng, J., Mao, C., Luo, Y.: Exploring large language models for knowledge graph completion. arXiv:2308.13916 (2023)
38. Zhu, Y., et al.: LLMs for knowledge graph construction and reasoning: recent capabilities and future opportunities. arXiv:2305.13168 (2023)
39. Zhu, Z., Zhang, Z., Xhonneux, L.A.C., Tang, J.: Neural Bellman-Ford networks: a general graph neural network framework for link prediction. In: NeurIPS, pp. 29476–29490 (2021)

BLINK: Blank Node Matching Using Embeddings

Alexander Becker(✉), Mohamed Ahmed Sherif, and Axel-Cyrille Ngonga Ngomo

DICE Group, Department of Computer Science, Paderborn University, Paderborn, Germany
beckeral@campus.upb.de, {mohamed.sherif,axel.ngonga}@upb.de
https://dice-research.org/

Abstract. Knowledge graphs (KGs) differ significantly over multiple different versions of the same data source. They also often contain blank nodes that do not have a constant identifier over all versions. Linking such blank nodes from different versions is a challenging task. Previous works propose different approaches to create signatures for all blank nodes based on named nodes in their neighborhood to match blank nodes with similar signatures. However, these works struggle to find a good mapping when the difference between the KGs' versions grows too large. In this work, we propose BLINK, an embedding-based approach for blank node linking. BLINK merges two KGs' versions and embeds the merged graph into a latent vector space based on translational embeddings and subsequently matches the closest pairs of blank nodes from different graphs. We evaluate our approach using real-world datasets against state-of-the-art approaches by computing the blank node matching for isomorphic graphs and graphs that contain triple changes (i.e., added or removed triples). The results indicate that BLINK achieves perfect accuracy for isomorphic graphs. For graph versions that contain changes, such as having up to 20% of triples removed in one version, BLINK still produces a mapping with an *Optimal Mapping Deviation Ratio* of under 1%. These results show that BLINK leads to a better linking of KGs over different versions and similar graphs adhering to the linked data guidelines.

Keywords: Knowledge graphs · Data Integration · Linked Data · Blank Nodes · Blank Node Matching

1 Introduction

Knowledge graphs (KGs) evolve over time where the updated KG versions normally include added, corrected, and deleted triples. While relational databases often create transaction logs describing changes to previous versions [11], RDF KGs are often distributed as a set of triples without any transaction history. Approaches such as [1] create versioning strategies composing single triple

G. Demartini et al. (Eds.): ISWC 2024, LNCS 15231, pp. 218–236, 2025.
https://doi.org/10.1007/978-3-031-77844-5_12

changes to hierarchies. Handling blank nodes is challenging because the identifiers of blank nodes from different graphs do not share global identifiers. Moreover, RDF tools and libraries normally do not keep the same blank node identifiers after processing [9]. This causes the need to rename them or completely delete and re-add parts of the graph that are only connected by one or multiple blank nodes [1].

According to the linked data guidelines [3], KGs should be linked to each other to add context to data and create opportunities to gain insights by combining different data sources. For KGs with multiple versions, links must be created between the different versions to not lose connectivity to other graphs or add unnecessary redundancy [33] when publishing new versions. Creating links is not a big challenge for entities that are named by a URI but is a nontrivial problem for blank nodes that can have different local names over different versions.

Addressing this problem is important as blank nodes are widely popular in semantic web standards [21]. For instance, blank nodes are used as a way to model lists as defined in the RDF 1.1 standard [27] and recommended by SKOS [16]. Furthermore, blank nodes are used to model simple existential statements. For example, if it is certain that a professor offers a course in the next semester but it is not yet determined how the course is named, a blank node may be used to signal that there is going to be a course, but no other information is available yet. Blank nodes are also used in ontology languages. For example, in the OWL2 standard [22], restrictions are modeled using blank nodes:

```
_:x a owl:Restriction.
_:x owl:onProperty author.
_:x owl:allValuesFrom Researcher.
```

Blank nodes are also used in a variety of other contexts that require matching them, as discussed in [19], and are widely used in different KGs with more than 66% of all domains of the BTC-2012 dataset [12] using at least some blank nodes [15].

In this paper, we present BLINK, an approach for blank node linking that computes a mapping between the blank nodes of two graphs by first merging the two graphs into one merged graph and computing entity embedding vectors for the blank nodes in the merged graph. We then split the blank nodes of the merged graphs into two sets based on what graph they originated from and create a mapping between the two sets based on the distances between the latent vector embeddings of the blank nodes.

This paper is structured as follows: Sect. 2 contains the necessary definitions to formally define the problem of graph matching and error measures used to evaluate the quality of mappings. In Sect. 3, we give an overview of related work tackling the same problems we solve in this work. We then present our approach in Sect. 4. Section 5 contains experiments where we compare our approach to other algorithms on real-world KGs and synthetic ones. Finally, we conclude our findings and explain how this work can be extended in the future in Sect. 6.

2 Preliminaries

Definition 1 (Knowledge Graph). *A Knowledge Graph (KG) $G(\mathcal{R}, \mathcal{B}, \mathcal{P}, \mathcal{L})$ is a set of triples $(s, p, o) \in (\mathcal{R} \cup \mathcal{B}) \times \mathcal{P} \times (\mathcal{R} \cup \mathcal{L} \cup \mathcal{B})$, where $\mathcal{R}$ is the set of all resources, $\mathcal{B}$ is the set of all blank nodes, $\mathcal{P}$ is the set of all predicates, and $\mathcal{L}$ the set of all literals.*

Definition 2 (Blank Radius). *The blank radius of a blank node is the minimum number of triples we need to traverse to find a non-blank node. For example, if a blank node is directly connected to a non-blank node, the blank radius is 1. If the blank node is only connected to other blank nodes, but at least one of them is connected to a non-blank node, the blank radius is 2. The blank radius of a graph is the maximum blank radius of all blank nodes in the graph.*

Definition 3 (Blank node component (BComponent)). *Each blank node is part of exactly one BComponent which is defined as the maximal subgraph that contains the blank node and consists only of triples containing blank nodes as subject and object (as defined in [18]).*

Definition 4 (Graph Mapping). *A mapping between two graphs $G(\mathcal{R}, \mathcal{B}, \mathcal{P}, \mathcal{L})$, and $G'(\mathcal{R}', \mathcal{B}', \mathcal{P}', \mathcal{L}')$ is a function M that maps all resources, literals, predicates, and blank nodes from G to G'. Formally $M : (\mathcal{R} \times \mathcal{B} \times \mathcal{P} \times \mathcal{L}) \rightarrow (\mathcal{R}' \times \mathcal{B}' \times \mathcal{P}' \times \mathcal{L}')$.*

Mapping named resources, predicates, and literals is a straightforward task as only the URI or literal is to be matched. On the other hand, matching blank nodes is a non-trivial task as blank nodes do not always have a unique injective property and two blank nodes may have the same connections to other nodes making it impossible to differentiate them.

Definition 5 (Isomorphism). *Two graphs G, and G' are isomorphic, iff there exists a bijective mapping function M between them, so that $(s, p, o) \in G \iff (M(s), M(p), M(o)) \in G'$.*

Definition 6 (Graph Delta). *The difference between two graphs G, G', denoted $\Delta(G, G')$, is defined as the number of triples that need to be added or removed to make the graphs isomorphic. $\Delta(G, G')$ is computed as the number of triples that need to be added to G and G' so that G and G' are isomorphic. Formally, $\Delta(G, G') = |\{(s, p, o) \in G \wedge (s, p, o) \notin G'\}| + |\{(s, p, o) \in G' \wedge (s, p, o) \notin G\}|$.*

While the previous definition defines the number of different triples between two graphs, which cannot be 0 for different graphs, as blank nodes are only named locally and differ between different documents [31], we define a similar function Δ_M to measure the quality of a mapping function M. Δ_M measures the graph delta between two graphs after a mapping M is applied to one of them that renames blank nodes.

Definition 7 (Mapping Delta). $\Delta_M(G, G') = |\{(s,p,o) \in G \wedge (M(s), M(p), (o)) \notin G'\}| + |\{(M(s)^{-1}, M(p)^{-1}, M(o)^{-1}) \in G' \wedge (s,p,o) \notin G\}|$.

To evaluate the mapping functions and measure their quality relatively to the optimal mapping function achieving the lowest possible value of Δ_M in cases where the graphs are not isomorphic, we define *the Optimal Mapping Deviation Ratio (OMDR)* as follows:

Definition 8 (Optimal Mapping Deviation Ratio (OMDR)). *Let G and G′ be two non-isomorphic graphs:* $OMDR_M(G, G') = \dfrac{\Delta_M(G, G')}{\Delta_{optimal}(G, G')}$.

As we require that the graphs are non-isomorphic, the function is well-defined. If the mapping given to the function is optimal, i.e., needs the same number of triple additions and deletions to make the graphs isomorphic as the optimal mapping, the OMDR is 1. In the case where the mapping M leads to a value of Δ_M twice as high as that of the optimal mapping, the OMDR will be 2. Mapping algorithms therefore try to minimize their Δ_M to have an OMDR as close to 1 as possible. Two different non-optimal mappings can be compared by using the ratio of their respective OMDRs.

The two main problems we solve with our approach are the *isomorphism task* and the *differential task*, as defined in [18]. For solving the *isomorphism task*, two isomorphic graphs are given as input, such that there exists a mapping leading to $\Delta_M = 0$. The RDF triples are not given in the same order to prevent blank node matching algorithms from using the order of the two graphs as a criterion for matching the graphs. The isomorphism task does not aim to find out whether two graphs are isomorphic efficiently, as studied in [10], but we aim here to find a mapping for cases where the isomorphism of two graphs is already known.

The main goal of the *differential task* is to map two different graphs or two different versions of the same graph to each other while minimizing the Δ between the two graphs, where $\Delta \neq 0$. We want to minimize the Δ_M, i.e., the amount of required triple additions and deletions, to make the graphs as isomorphic as possible.

3 Related Work

The blank node matching problem can be interpreted as an assignment problem that can be optimized using the *Hungarian* algorithm [23]. The approach proposed in [30] is able to find the optimal solution in a case when there is no triple containing blank nodes as both subject and object, but cannot correctly handle graphs with multiple connected blank nodes. Other algorithms to match blank nodes focus on computing a signature value for each blank node based on the triples they are part of and then map the blank nodes with closest signatures to each other [4]. *Tzitzikas et al.* [30] propose the SIGN algorithm that computes the signature based on the `rdf:type` value for the blank node, the predicate and subject of incoming triples, and the predicate and object of outgoing triples. *Lantzaki et al.* [18] extend the SIGN approach with the R-SIGN algorithm that includes the order of neighboring blank nodes into the signature. As the R-SIGN approach works with a variable radius it is able to match blank nodes far away from any non-blank nodes. *Oraskari and Törmä* [26] also build upon the SIGN algorithm by iteratively recomputing the signatures to include nodes further away in the signature computation if the current signature is not unique. Hogan [13,14] creates canonical labels for blank nodes based on a coloring of blank nodes assigned by hashing the neighborhood of them to decide if two graphs are isomorphic. *Lee et al.* [20] use the *MapReduce* process to match blank nodes if they have a high similarity score based on a high amount of similar triples with a configurable threshold.

While our approach focuses on matching blank nodes between different graphs, there are also methods for linking named entities across different graphs. *Trivedi et al.* [28] propose LinkNBed where they learn representations of entities and relations across multiple graphs and also take duplicates into account by utilizing the embedding, the neighborhood and attributes of an entity. *Buneman* and *Staworko* try to solve the graph alignment problem using bisimulation [6] using different alignment methods like similarity alignment and overlap alignment.

Another related research area to our work is that of *Knowledge graph embedding (KGE)* algorithms that can be used to create latent space vector representations of nodes. In recent years, dozens of such KGE techniques have been developed, we list here only a few of them. RESCAL [25] computes a three-way factorization of an adjacency tensor representing the input KG. The adjacency tensor is then decomposed into a product of a core tensor and embedding matrices. HolE [24] uses circular correlation as its compositional operator. ComplEx [29] is a *KGE* model using latent factorization, in which complex valued embeddings are utilized for handling a large variety of binary relations including symmetric and anti-symmetric relations. On the other hand, TransE [5] is an energy-based KGE model, in which a relation r between two entities h and t corresponds to a translation of their embeddings. More details on knowledge graph embedding approaches and applications can be found in [7,32]. These and other embedding models can be used for computing the embedding vectors for our approach.

4 Approach

BLINK takes two graphs G and G' as input and creates a mapping M from G to G' minimizing $\Delta_M(G, G')$. The key idea of BLINK is to compute an embedding for the union of both graphs G^+ and match the blank nodes that are close in the latent embedding vector space. We divide our approach into three parts: First, we propose a method to match G and G' into a single graph G^+ in Sect. 4.1. In Sect. 4.2, we then give an overview of the embedding model we use. Finally in Sect. 4.3, we present our algorithm BLINK to compute a mapping from the embedding vectors of G^+.

4.1 Preprocessing/Graph Merging

We start our approach by merging the two input KGs into one with the following procedure. We insert every triples that does not involve blank nodes from both G and G' into G^+. To be able to distinguish from which graph a blank node originated, we extend the local name of each blank node in its originating graph to create a globally unique name. The global name consists of a symbol ◀ that is not contained in any URI in the graphs, then a 0 if the blank node originates from G or a 1 if the blank node originates from G', another ▶ to terminate the global identifier part and concatenate the locally unique name the blank node had in the graph it originates from. We then add the triples with the renamed blank nodes to G^+. Note that BLINK does not rely on keeping the local name the same but is only kept for easier evaluation. Instead, the local names could also be mapped to random strings without impacting the performance of BLINK. We only need to distinguish from which graph the node came from and to distinguish the blank node from other blank nodes coming from the same graph.

The merged model G^+ now contains all the necessary information for the embedding algorithm. An example of this algorithm is shown in Fig. 1. Figures 1a and 1b contain the two graphs G and G' respectively while Fig. 1c contains the merged graph. Note that because of the nature of the construction of G^+, there are no direct connections from any blank node of G to any blank node of G'. By merging all triples containing only named resources, we share knowledge between the two graphs enabling the embedding process to take more training data into account for computing the latent space vectors of named resources and thereby making them more stable against being pushed away by connections to blank nodes from different graphs.

4.2 Embedding

Our approach utilizes a translation-based embedding model based on TransE [5]. TransE aims to make the sum of the head entity embedding and relation embedding equal to the tail entity embedding as shown in Eq. 1, with γ being a margin parameter, σ being the sigmoid function, and $\mathrm{emb}(x)$ returning the embedding vector of x. We use the default $\gamma = 4$ for our approach as implemented within the DICE embeddings framework [8]. Our matching is based on the fact that similar nodes have similar latent space embedding vectors. To not lose any information, we also include literals in the embedding process.

$$\hat{y}_i(\text{head}, \text{rel}, \text{tail}) = \sigma(\gamma - \|\mathrm{emb}(\text{head}) + \mathrm{emb}(\text{rel}) - \mathrm{emb}(\text{tail})\|_2) \qquad (1)$$

The main challenge to overcome is the fact that we do not have any connections between any blank node from G to any blank node from G'. Going with our example in Fig. 1c, there is no connection from `◀0▶b1` to `◀1▶b2` and no connection from `◀1▶b1` to `◀0▶b2` even though `_:b1` from G and `_:b1` from G' as well as `_:b2` from G and `_:b2` from G' are semantically equivalent. This would lead the embedding process to push the latent space vectors of `◀0▶b2` and

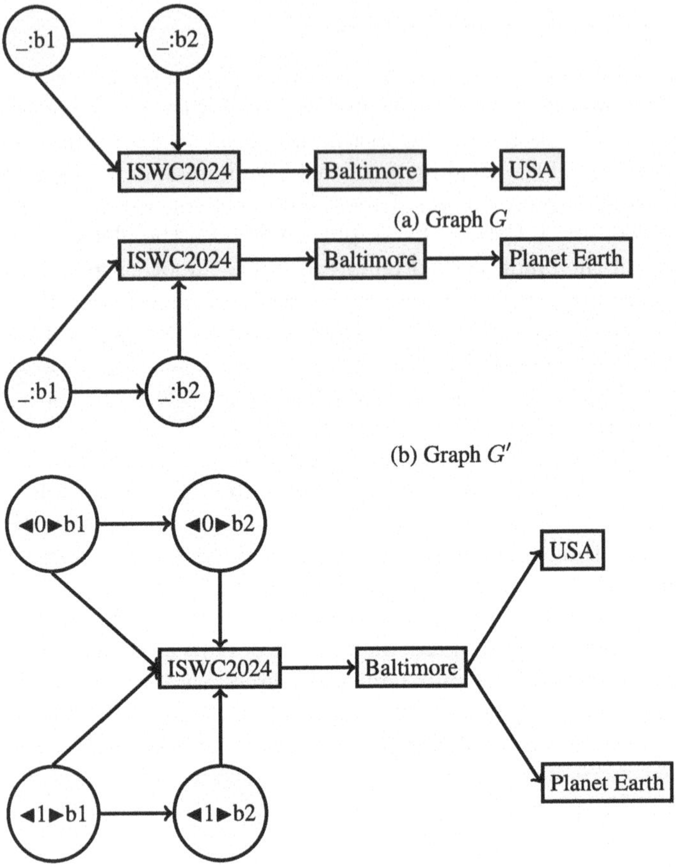

(a) Graph G

(b) Graph G'

(c) Merged graph G^+

Fig. 1. An example of how our preprocessing would merge two graphs into one.

`◀1▶b2` away from each other as there is a connection from `◀0▶b1` to `◀0▶b2` but not from `◀0▶b1` to `◀1▶b2`.

Therefore we have to adapt the training process and change the way the target value is decided.

Normally, the neural network should handle each input triple x_i= (head, rel, tail) in such a way that $\hat{y}_i$=1 if the triple exists in the graph and $\hat{y}_i$=0 if the triple does not exist in the graph. But this would not be the case with our previously defined challenge. Therefore, we have changed the target function as shown in Eq. 2.

$$y_i(\text{head, rel, tail}) = \begin{cases} 1 & :(\text{head, rel, tail}) \in G^+ \\ 0.5 & :\text{head and tail are both blank nodes} \wedge \text{ head } \in G \wedge \text{ tail } \in G' \\ 0.5 & :\text{head and tail are both blank nodes} \wedge \text{ head } \in G' \wedge \text{ tail } \in G \\ 0 & :\text{otherwise} \end{cases} \quad (2)$$

We then adapt the binary cross entropy (BCE) loss function to ignore the triples with y_i=0.5 in the loss function computation by multiplying the result of the BCE loss function with a term to ignore said triples as shown in Eq. 3. These two changes result in the model ignoring any triple that contains blank nodes originating from two different graphs preventing the embedding vectors of similar blank nodes from being pushed away from each other.

$$L(y_i, \hat{y}_i) = -\sum_{i=1}^{N} (y_i \log(\hat{y}_i) + (1 - y_i)\log(1 - \hat{y}_i)) \cdot ((y_i - 0.5)^2 \cdot 4) \tag{3}$$

4.3 Matching

Let B be the set of all blank nodes in G and B' be the set of all blank nodes in G'. We then compute the pairwise *Euclidean distance* between the embedding vectors of all blank nodes within B and all embedding vectors of all blank nodes within B' into the distance matrix D with $D_{i,j}$ being the Euclidean distance between the embedding vectors of B_i and B'_j. Let $M=\emptyset$ be the resulting mapping of the algorithm. Then our matching algorithm proceeds to match the closest blank nodes until there are no unmatched blank nodes left in B or B' as shown in Algorithm 1. By using this algorithm we get a one-to-one mapping for all blank nodes mapping the most similar blank nodes to each other if $|B|=|B'|$. If the number of blank nodes is not the same in both graphs then this algorithm computes the most probable $\min(|B|, |B'|)$ matches and leaves the remaining nodes without a matched blank nodes from the other graph. By removing already matched blank nodes from the yet-to-be-matched nodes and the distance matrix, we ensure that we do not run into problems if multiple blank nodes have the

Algorithm 1. MatchBlankNodes(B, B', D)

Input: The set of blank nodes of both graphs B and B' and a matrix D containing the pairwise euclidean distances of all embedding vectors of the nodes of B to the nodes of B'
Output: A mapping M between the blank nodes
while $B \neq \emptyset \wedge B' \neq \emptyset$ **do**
  $(i, j) \leftarrow \arg\min_{(i,j)} D_{i,j}$
  $M \leftarrow M \cup (B_i, B'_j)$
  $B \leftarrow B - \{B_i\}$
  $B' \leftarrow B' - \{B'_j\}$
  $D'_{k,l} \leftarrow D_{k,l} \quad \forall \quad (k,l) \quad 1 \leq k < i \wedge 1 \leq l < j$
  $D'_{k,l} \leftarrow D_{k+1,l} \quad \forall \quad (k,l) \quad i < k \leq |B| \wedge 1 \leq l < j$
  $D'_{k,l} \leftarrow D_{k,l+1} \quad \forall \quad (k,l) \quad 1 \leq k < i \wedge j < l \leq |B'|$
  $D'_{k,l} \leftarrow D_{k+1,l+1} \quad \forall \quad (k,l) \quad i < k \leq |B| \wedge j < l \leq |B'|$
  $D \leftarrow D'$
end while
return M

same connections to other nodes and therefore very similar embedding vectors. Otherwise, it would be possible for multiple blank nodes of one graph to match with a single blank node from the other graph which would leave some blank nodes of the other graph without a matching blank node.

5 Evaluation and Results

To evaluate our approach, we conducted experiments using real-world KGs. We compare the results of our approach with multiple different numbers of training epochs to current state-of-the-art algorithms described in Sect. 3.

Research Questions. We aim to answer the following research questions:

Q_1. Does the accuracy of BLINK increase with a larger number of training epochs?
Q_2. How does a *higher number of BComponents* affect BLINK for the isomorphism task?
Q_3. Is BLINK able to match blank nodes correctly for *larger BComponents* coming from isomorphic graphs?
Q_4. How is the accuracy impacted by adding triples that contain existing blank nodes as subjects and random strings as predicates and objects?
Q_5. Are the approaches robust concerning added triples with blank nodes as subjects and random known relations and entities from the graph as predicates and objects?
Q_6. What effect does *splitting up BComponents* have on the accuracy of the approaches?

Setup. We present the results for BLINK using $\{16, 32, 64, 128, 256\}$ training epochs dubbed BLINK $_{[\#epochs]}$. The embedding and matching of our approach use the DICE embeddings library[1] [8]. We use an embedding dimension of 32 and a batch size of 1024 for our experiments. To make the results reproducible, we use 1 as a seed for random number computation wherever applicable. As a baseline or matching quality, we use the signature algorithm [30] extended by [18], dubbed SIGN, and the radius-based signature algorithms [18] with $\{2, 3, 1000\}$ as parameters for the radius dubbed R-SIGN $_{[radius]}$. We also report the result for not mapping any blank nodes as NO MAPPING and the best achieveable Δ_M dubbed OPTIMAL MAPPING.

Datasets. The first and second datasets we use for our experiment are subsets of LINKEDGEODATA [2]. In particular, we use the last 30000 lines of the *MilitaryThingNode* and *CraftNode* subset of LINKEDGEODATA because of the high number of triples containing blank nodes. Statistics regarding the datasets are listed in Table 1. As a third dataset, we use a synthetic dataset dubbed Syn_l with l being the number of layers generated by us representing one big BComponent created by starting with a single blank node and subsequently adding a layer

[1] Version 0.0.5 https://pypi.org/project/dicee/0.0.5/.

of $4^{\text{layer index}}$ blank nodes around it and therefore increasing the blank radius of the graph by one. All blank nodes, except for the first one, have 4 random connections to blank nodes of the previous layer. The outermost layer consists of 4^{l+1} named resources again randomly connected with 4 links to blank nodes of the previous layer.

Table 1. Dataset statistics for the used datasets showing in order: number of triples, number of blank nodes, number of blank nodes only connected to other blank nodes, number of triples containing at least one blank node, number of triples containing two blank nodes, the blank radius, and the number of BComponents of the graph. The *CraftNode* dataset consists of only 29980 triples because there are 20 duplicate triples in the last 30000 lines of the dataset.

Dataset	|Triples|	|BNodes|	|BBNodes|	|BTriples|	|BBTriples|	BRadius	|BC|
Military	30000	2827	1452	30000	2749	2	78
CraftNode	29980	4739	2815	29980	3846	2	893
Syn$_l$	$\sum_{i=1}^{l} 4 \cdot 4^i$	$\sum_{i=1}^{l} 4^{i-1}$	$\sum_{i=1}^{l} 4^{i-2}$	$\sum_{i=1}^{l} 4 \cdot 4^i$	$\sum_{i=1}^{l} 4 \cdot 4^{i-1}$	l	1

5.1 Isomorphism Mapping

As input for the *isomorphism task*, we created two copies of the same dataset, where we changed the order of one of them to prevent the algorithms from making decisions based on the order of triples. As both dataset instances contain the exact same triples, the optimal solution for matching the blank nodes results in Δ_M=0.

Q1: Accuracy over Different Numbers of Training Epochs. The results for the *MilitaryThingNode* dataset are shown in Fig. 2. As expected, the Δ_M is 60000 if no blank nodes are matched because every triple in the dataset contains at least one blank node. Therefore, no triple from one graph is equal to any triple in the other graph and all triples from one graph have to be removed and all triples from the other graph have to be added to make both graphs equal. The SIGN algorithm can reduce the Δ_M to 2980 while the R-SIGN algorithm obtains an optimal result for all radii. This result is expected, as the R-SIGN algorithm is proven to produce the optimal result for the *isomorphism task* in case the radius parameter is at least as big as the blank radius of the graph [18]. The mapping of BLINK achieves a Δ_M of 2882, 782, and 44 for 16, 32, and 64 training epochs, respectively. Starting at 128 training epochs, BLINK produces a perfect mapping. This answers our first research question, Q_1, indicating that our embedding process indeed puts similar blank nodes closer to each other in the embedding space the more epochs we train. Accordingly, the quality of the mapping produced by BLINK increases with an increasing number of training epochs.

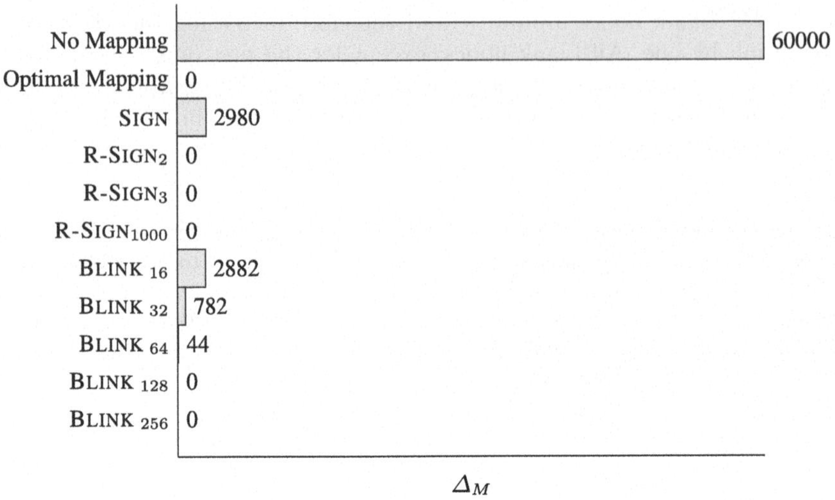

Fig. 2. Δ_M for the isomorphism task using the *MilitaryThingNode* dataset for the blank node matching algorithms from Sect. 5.

Q2: Higher Number of BComponents. The mapping Δ for the *CraftNode* dataset is shown in Fig. 3. The SIGN algorithm can match the graphs up to a Δ_M of 7174 while the R-SIGN algorithms can find a perfect mapping as the blank radius of this radius is only 2. BLINK achieves a Δ_M of 9496 and 4658 for 16 and 32 epochs respectively. Starting at 64 epochs, BLINK produces an optimal mapping, which again confirms our answer for Q_1. The number of blank nodes that are only connected to other blank nodes and especially the number of BComponents in this dataset are larger than in the *MilitaryThingNode* dataset which shows that BLINK is also able to handle datasets with less known URIs and more possibilities for incorrect matches. This answers our research question Q_2.

Q3: Large BComponents. To answer our research question Q_3, we conducted an experiment with the Syn_l dataset with l=$\{1, 2, 3, 4, 5, 6, 7\}$ to find out how well BLINK can handle different BComponent sizes. The results are presented as a heatmap in Fig. 4. After only 16 training epochs, BLINK can find a perfect matching for the synthetic datasets up to a radius of 5. For a radius of 6, BLINK requires more training epochs as there is a small Δ_M for 16 epochs but it can produce a perfect result after 32 epochs. The task gets harder when the blank radius is 7, but even then BLINK can compute an optimal mapping after 64 epochs. This answers our research question Q_3. Interestingly, even the signature and radius-based signature algorithms with a radius smaller than the blank radius achieve perfect accuracy. This happens because the extended version of the signature algorithm [18] creates deterministic counters for adjacent blank nodes enhancing the performance massively for isomorphic graphs in comparison to the default SIGN algorithm [30].

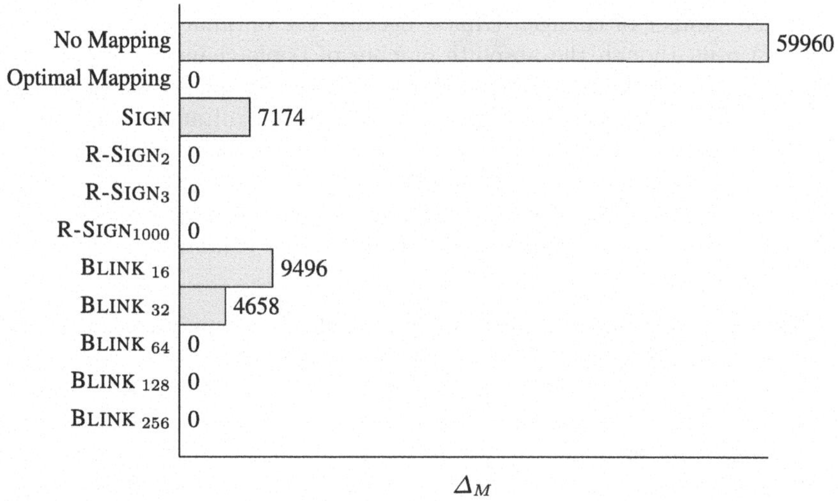

Fig. 3. Δ_M for the isomorphism task using the *CraftNode* dataset for the blank node matching algorithms from Sect. 5.

5.2 Differential Mapping

For the *differential task*, we focus on how well the approaches perform when changing the dataset. We simulate different versions of a dataset by adding and removing triples from one graph instance. In this case, the optimal mapping solution would have a Δ_M equal to the number of added and removed triples. We evaluate the results of this set of experiments using the *Optimal Mapping Deviation Ratio* (OMDR) as defined in Definition 8. As the OMDR depends on the Δ_M of the optimal mapping as its denominator, the OMDR can increase

	Syn_1	Syn_2	Syn_3	Syn_4	Syn_5	Syn_6	Syn_7
Optimal Mapping	0	0	0	0	0	0	0
No Mapping	32	160	672	2720	10912	43680	174752
SIGN	0	0	0	0	0	0	0
R-SIGN$_2$	0	0	0	0	0	0	0
R-SIGN$_3$	0	0	0	0	0	0	0
R-SIGN$_{1000}$	0	0	0	0	0	0	0
BLINK 16	0	0	0	0	0	84	28954
BLINK 32	0	0	0	0	0	0	758
BLINK 64	0	0	0	0	0	0	0
BLINK 128	0	0	0	0	0	0	0
BLINK 256	0	0	0	0	0	0	0

Fig. 4. Δ_M for the isomorphism task using synthetic datasets.

for a higher number of changed triples, because the optimal mapping also has a higher Δ even though the absolute number of triple changes increases. The optimal Δ for this task is determined by the number of triples added or removed from the dataset instance we change. Interestingly, 1% of added triples would result in an optimal Δ of 300, while 10% would result in Δ=3000. Therefore, the reported numbers in Figs. 5, 6, and 7 are not to be compared over different columns because the OMDR base is different in each column. A higher OMDR in column c_1 is not worse than the OMDR in another column c_2 if the optimal Δ is smaller in column c_1.

Q4: Adding Triples with New Objects. For the first experiment of this task, we use the *MilitaryThingNode* dataset and add new triples with existing subject URIs, random predicate URIs, and random object URIs to one instance of the dataset. We want to evaluate how the algorithms can deal with new additions to the dataset and at what percentage of new triples the performance starts to drop. We therefore conduct this experiment with $\{2, 4, 6, 8, 10, 20, 50\}\%$ of added triples. Figure 5 shows the results of the experiment. Even for 2% of added triples, no signature-based algorithm produces a mapping with less than 10 times more needed changes to make the graphs isomorphic in comparison to the optimal mapping. BLINK, however, is able to compute a perfect result after 128 training epochs, mapping no blank node incorrectly to its equivalent blank node in the other graph. Even for only 16 training epochs, BLINK only has an optimal mapping deviation of almost half of the signature algorithms. These results show that BLINK can quickly produce results outperforming the state of the art and slowly converge to the smallest Δ_M achievable for the given dataset.

	2%	4%	6%	8%	10%	20%	50%
Optimal Mapping	1.000	1.000	1.000	1.000	1.000	1.000	1.000
No Mapping	101.000	51.000	34.333	26.000	21.000	11.000	5.000
SIGN	14.333	11.848	10.720	9.514	9.457	7.128	4.129
R-SIGN$_2$	10.743	10.515	10.048	9.178	9.241	7.084	4.120
R-SIGN$_3$	10.743	10.515	10.048	9.178	9.241	7.084	4.120
R-SIGN$_{1000}$	10.743	10.515	10.048	9.178	9.241	7.084	4.120
BLINK $_{16}$	5.780	3.413	2.620	2.228	1.993	1.494	1.321
BLINK $_{32}$	2.870	2.253	1.941	1.811	1.709	1.441	1.195
BLINK $_{64}$	1.067	1.065	1.068	1.068	1.041	1.055	1.143
BLINK $_{128}$	1.000	1.000	1.000	1.082	1.001	1.002	1.019
BLINK $_{256}$	1.000	1.000	1.000	1.020	1.000	1.000	1.002

Fig. 5. Optimal Mapping Deviation Ratios for the differential task with random triples added to the *MilitaryThingNode* dataset. The different columns show the Δ for different percentages of added triples.

Q5: Adding Triples with Existing Objects. For the second experiment of the *differential task*, we aim to answer research question Q_5. We start with the *MilitaryThingNode* dataset, but instead of adding triples with random predicates and objects, we add triples with already existing predicates and objects. We want to find out if BLINK is also able to compute good mappings between the two graphs if not only new entities are added and linked to existing entities but existing entities are linked to other already existing entities. This is important because in real-world applications new links between existing entities can be added to complete a knowledge graph as in link prediction [34] or through manual completion of the knowledge graph. We conduct the experiment with $\{1, 2, 4, 6, 8, 10, 20\}$ % of added triples. The results of this experiment are shown in Fig. 6. For a small amount of 1% added triples, all algorithms are able to generate mapping for some blank node. However, the SIGN algorithm still only achieves an OMDR of 19.26. The radius-based sign algorithms all achieve the same result again as the radius of the dataset remains 2. They achieve an OMDR of 11.193. BLINK produces a more accurate mapping at just 16 epochs of training with an Optimal Mapping Deviation Ratio of 11.907, i.e., almost twice as accurate as the R-SIGN algorithms. With a growing number of epochs, BLINK can produce a result that is even more accurate with an OMDR of 3.72. For a higher number of added triples (10%), all algorithms are closer to the number of changes required with the optimal mapping. Not mapping any blank nodes results in an OMDR of 21 which is surpassed by the SIGN algorithm with a deviation ratio of 9.858. The R-SIGN algorithms only marginally beat the SIGN algorithm in accuracy with a deviation ratio of 9.749. BLINK, however, is still able to produce a nearly accurate mapping with a deviation ratio of 1.977 for 16 epochs and 1.286 for 256 training epochs. This result indicates that BLINK can correctly match blank nodes even if the dataset gets altered by adding more links between the existing resources in the dataset. BLINK is more robust against changes than the SIGN and R-SIGN algorithms for different amounts of added triples and outperforms their mapping for all numbers of training epochs we tested. Furthermore, training of BLINK would lead to an even smaller Δ_M computed by BLINK allowing the user to choose how much time should be invested into finding a high-quality mapping by increasing or lowering the number of training epochs. This answers our research question Q_5.

Q6: Removing Triples. For the third experiment of the *differential task* task, we removed a different number of triples from the dataset. To prevent completely removing blank nodes, we made sure that each blank node is still contained in at least one triple. We conducted the experiment with $\{1, 2, 4, 6, 8, 10, 20\}$ % of removed triples to determine how many triples are necessary for BLINK and the other algorithms to work and at what percentage of triple removal the performance starts to drop. Because of the triple removal, some of the BComponents get split up which poses an extra challenge for the signature-based algorithms. The amount of BComponents is shown in Table 2.

The results of this experiment are shown in Fig. 7. Like the last experiment, our results show that BLINK outperforms all signature-based algorithms. The

	1%	2%	4%	6%	8%	10%	20%
Optimal Mapping	1.000	1.000	1.000	1.000	1.000	1.000	1.000
No Mapping	201.000	101.000	51.000	34.352	26.000	21.000	11.002
SIGN	19.260	13.827	14.432	11.805	9.707	9.858	7.025
R-SIGN$_2$	11.193	10.543	13.392	11.367	9.463	9.749	6.999
R-SIGN$_3$	11.193	10.543	13.392	11.367	9.463	9.749	6.999
R-SIGN$_{1000}$	11.193	10.543	13.392	11.367	9.463	9.749	6.999
BLINK$_{16}$	11.907	5.730	3.380	2.596	2.213	1.977	1.487
BLINK$_{32}$	6.787	2.817	2.210	1.953	1.778	1.637	1.403
BLINK$_{64}$	3.613	1.390	1.442	1.447	1.422	1.406	1.318
BLINK$_{128}$	3.807	1.250	1.295	1.331	1.346	1.329	1.292
BLINK$_{256}$	3.720	1.163	1.220	1.251	1.310	1.286	1.278

Fig. 6. Optimal Mapping Deviation Ratios for the differential task with triples containing known predicates and objects added to the *MilitaryThingNode* dataset. The different columns show the deviation for different percentages of added triples.

Table 2. The number of BComponents for the dataset versions with different percentages of triples removed.

Removed Triples	0%	1%	2%	4%	6%	8%	10%	20%
BComponents	78	99	107	133	156	197	215	354

OMDR of BLINK is less than half of the OMDR of all other algorithms for all tested percentages of removed triples. Even when removing 20% of triples from the graph, BLINK computes a mapping with only a 0.3% higher Δ_M than the optimal mapping. Meanwhile, the signature algorithms only achieve a 627.6% higher Δ_M than the optimal possible mapping. The OMDR for BLINK stays almost constant for a different number of removed triples (and therefore split up BComponents) with OMDRs between 1.000 and 1.008 for 256 training epochs. This answers our last research question Q_6. Our results indicate that BLINK is robust against splitting up BComponents as well as overall missing triples in the graph.

	1%	2%	4%	6%	8%	10%	20%
Optimal Mapping	1.000	1.000	1.000	1.000	1.000	1.000	1.000
No Mapping	199.000	99.000	49.000	32.333	24.000	19.000	9.000
SIGN	31.913	22.043	16.250	13.323	11.868	10.077	6.285
R-SIGN$_2$	23.920	18.833	15.232	12.917	11.675	9.970	6.276
R-SIGN$_3$	23.920	18.833	15.232	12.917	11.675	9.970	6.276
R-SIGN$_{1000}$	23.920	18.833	15.232	12.917	11.675	9.970	6.276
BLINK $_{16}$	10.493	5.760	3.412	2.597	2.192	1.956	1.494
BLINK $_{32}$	3.653	2.367	1.670	1.481	1.337	1.261	1.175
BLINK $_{64}$	1.107	1.107	1.032	1.024	1.019	1.008	1.012
BLINK $_{128}$	1.000	1.000	1.000	1.006	1.004	1.000	1.003
BLINK $_{256}$	1.000	1.000	1.008	1.000	1.000	1.003	1.003

Fig. 7. Optimal Mapping Deviation Ratios for the differential task with random triples removed from the *MilitaryThingNode* dataset. The different columns show the deviation for different percentages of removed triples.

6 Conclusion and Future Work

In this paper, we propose BLINK, an approach for matching blank nodes that works by merging two graphs, embedding the merged graph into a latent vector space, and subsequently matching the blank nodes that are closest to each other in the embedding space. The experiments regarding the *isomorphism task* show that BLINK's accuracy is up to par with current state-of-the-art algorithms, as it also finds the optimal mapping solution after a sufficient number of epochs. For the *differential task*, our finding is that BLINK significantly outperforms other algorithms and in most cases computes a solution that is very close to the optimal mapping.

Further studies need to be carried out to assess the impact of using different embedding models and loss functions on the accuracy of the mapping. It is also worth investigating whether removing a part of the triples based on a low gain of information, similar to the process described in [17], results in a better runtime/accuracy tradeoff than using all triples for the embedding vector computation. It might also be beneficial to combine BLINK with signature-based approaches to reduce the time it takes to compute a matching. For example, blank nodes that have BComponent matches with the other graph can be computed quickly by using R-SIGN [18]. BLINK could then be used to match blank nodes that do not have an equivalent BComponent in the other graph.

Supplemental Material Statement: Source code for merging graphs and signature-based algorithms as well as the delta computation and the source code for the embedding process, training files, datasets, blank node mappings, created models, and a CSV of computed embedding vectors for each entity are available from our Github[2].

Acknowledgements. This work has been supported by the Ministry of Culture and Science of North Rhine-Westphalia (MKW NRW) within the project SAIL under the grant no NW21-059D. This work has been supported within the project "WHALE" (LFN 1-04) funded under the Lamarr Fellow Network programme by the Ministry of Culture and Science of North Rhine-Westphalia (MKW NRW). This project has received funding from the European Union's Horizon Europe research and innovation programme under grant agreement No 101070305.

References

1. Auer, S., Herre, H.: A versioning and evolution framework for RDF knowledge bases. In: Virbitskaite, I., Voronkov, A. (eds.) PSI 2006. LNCS, vol. 4378, pp. 55–69. Springer, Heidelberg (2007). https://doi.org/10.1007/978-3-540-70881-0_8
2. Auer, S., Lehmann, J., Hellmann, S.: LinkedGeoData: adding a spatial dimension to the web of data. In: Bernstein, A., et al. (eds.) ISWC 2009. LNCS, vol. 5823, pp. 731–746. Springer, Heidelberg (2009). https://doi.org/10.1007/978-3-642-04930-9_46
3. Berners-Lee, T.: Linked-data design issues. W3C design issue document (2009). https://www.w3.org/DesignIssues/LinkedData.html
4. Berners-Lee, T., Connolly, D.: Delta: an ontology for the distribution of differences between RDF graphs. World Wide Web **4**(3), 4–3 (2004). http://wwww3.org/DesignIssues/Diff
5. Bordes, A., Usunier, N., Garcia-Duran, A., Weston, J., Yakhnenko, O.: Translating embeddings for modeling multi-relational data. In: Burges, C., Bottou, L., Welling, M., Ghahramani, Z., Weinberger, K. (eds.) Advances in Neural Information Processing Systems, vol. 26. Curran Associates, Inc. (2013). https://proceedings.neurips.cc/paper_files/paper/2013/file/1cecc7a77928ca8133fa24680a88d2f9-Paper.pdf
6. Buneman, P., Staworko, S.: RDF graph alignment with bisimulation. Proc. VLDB Endow. **9**(12), 1149–1160 (2016). https://doi.org/10.14778/2994509.2994531
7. Cao, J., Fang, J., Meng, Z., Liang, S.: Knowledge graph embedding: a survey from the perspective of representation spaces. ACM Comput. Surv. **56**(6) (2024). https://doi.org/10.1145/3643806
8. Demir, C., Ngomo, A.C.N.: Hardware-agnostic computation for large-scale knowledge graph embeddings. Softw. Impacts (2022)
9. Fiorelli, M., Pazienza, M.T., Stellato, A., Turbati, A.: Version control and change validation for RDF datasets. In: Garoufallou, E., Virkus, S., Siatri, R., Koutsomiha, D. (eds.) MTSR 2017. CCIS, vol. 755, pp. 3–14. Springer, Cham (2017). https://doi.org/10.1007/978-3-319-70863-8_1
10. Grohe, M., Schweitzer, P.: The graph isomorphism problem. Commun. ACM **63**(11), 128–134 (2020)
11. Haerder, T., Reuter, A.: Principles of transaction-oriented database recovery. ACM Comput. Surv. (CSUR) **15**(4), 287–317 (1983)

[2] https://github.com/becker-al/BLINK.

12. Harth, A.: Billion triples challenge data set (2012). http://km.aifb.kit.edu/projects/btc-2012/
13. Hogan, A.: Skolemising blank nodes while preserving isomorphism. In: Proceedings of the 24th International Conference on World Wide Web, pp. 430–440 (2015)
14. Hogan, A.: Canonical forms for isomorphic and equivalent RDF graphs: algorithms for leaning and labelling blank nodes. ACM Trans. Web **11**(4) (2017). https://doi.org/10.1145/3068333
15. Hogan, A., Arenas, M., Mallea, A., Polleres, A.: Everything you always wanted to know about blank nodes. J. Web Semant. **27-28**, 42–69 (2014). https://doi.org/10.1016/j.websem.2014.06.004, https://www.sciencedirect.com/science/article/pii/S1570826814000481, Semantic Web Challenge 2013
16. Isaac, A., Summers, E.: SKOS simple knowledge organization system primer. W3C note, W3C (2009). https://www.w3.org/TR/2009/NOTE-skos-primer-20090818/
17. Karegowda, A.G., Manjunath, A., Jayaram, M.: Comparative study of attribute selection using gain ratio and correlation based feature selection. Int. J. Inf. Technol. Knowl. Manag. **2**(2), 271–277 (2010)
18. Lantzaki, C., Papadakos, P., Analyti, A., Tzitzikas, Y.: Radius-aware approximate blank node matching using signatures. Knowl. Inf. Syst. **50** (2017). https://doi.org/10.1007/s10115-016-0945-9
19. Lantzaki, C., Tzitzikas, Y.: Tasks that require, or can benefit from, matching blank nodes. CoRR abs/1410.8536 (2014). http://arxiv.org/abs/1410.8536
20. Lee, T., Im, D.H., Won, J.: Similarity-based change detection for RDF in MapReduce. Procedia Comput. Sci. **91**, 789–797 (2016)
21. Mallea, A., Arenas, M., Hogan, A., Polleres, A.: On blank nodes. In: Aroyo, L., et al. (eds.) ISWC 2011. LNCS, vol. 7031, pp. 421–437. Springer, Heidelberg (2011). https://doi.org/10.1007/978-3-642-25073-6_27
22. Motik, B., Patel-Schneider, P.: OWL 2 web ontology language mapping to RDF graphs (second edition). W3C recommendation, W3C (2012). https://www.w3.org/TR/2012/REC-owl2-mapping-to-rdf-20121211/
23. Munkres, J.: Algorithms for the assignment and transportation problems. J. Soc. Ind. Appl. Math. **5**(1), 32–38 (1957). https://doi.org/10.1137/0105003
24. Nickel, M., Rosasco, L., Poggio, T.: Holographic embeddings of knowledge graphs. In: Proceedings of the Thirtieth AAAI Conference on Artificial Intelligence. AAAI'16, pp. 1955–1961 (2016)
25. Nickel, M., Tresp, V., Kriegel, H.: A three-way model for collective learning on multi-relational data. In: Getoor, L., Scheffer, T. (eds.) Proceedings of the 28th International Conference on Machine Learning. ICML 2011, Bellevue, Washington, USA, 28 June–2 July 2011, pp. 809–816. Omnipress (2011). https://icml.cc/2011/papers/438_icmlpaper.pdf
26. Oraskari, J., Törmä, S.: RDF-based signature algorithms for computing differences of IFC models. Autom. Construct. **57** (2015). https://doi.org/10.1016/j.autcon.2015.05.008
27. Patel-Schneider, P., Hayes, P.: RDF 1.1 semantics. W3C recommendation, W3C (2014). https://www.w3.org/TR/2014/REC-rdf11-mt-20140225/
28. Trivedi, R., Sisman, B., Dong, X.L., Faloutsos, C., Ma, J., Zha, H.: LinkNBed: multi-graph representation learning with entity linkage. In: Gurevych, I., Miyao, Y. (eds.) Proceedings of the 56th Annual Meeting of the Association for Computational Linguistics (Volume 1: Long Papers), pp. 252–262. Association for Computational Linguistics, Melbourne, Australia (2018). https://doi.org/10.18653/v1/P18-1024, https://aclanthology.org/P18-1024

29. Trouillon, T., Welbl, J., Riedel, S., Gaussier, É., Bouchard, G.: Complex embeddings for simple link prediction. In: International Conference on Machine Learning, pp. 2071–2080. PMLR (2016)
30. Tzitzikas, Y., Lantzaki, C., Zeginis, D.: Blank node matching and RDF/S comparison functions. In: Cudré-Mauroux, P., et al. (eds.) ISWC 2012. LNCS, vol. 7649, pp. 591–607. Springer, Heidelberg (2012). https://doi.org/10.1007/978-3-642-35176-1_37
31. Völkel, M., Enguix, C.F., Kruk, S.R., Zhdanova, A.V., Stevens, R., Sure-Vetter, Y.: Semversion - versioning RDF and ontologies. Technical report. Universität Karlsruhe (TH) (2005)
32. Wang, Q., Mao, Z., Wang, B., Guo, L.: Knowledge graph embedding: a survey of approaches and applications. IEEE Trans. Knowl. Data Eng. **29**(12), 2724–2743 (2017)
33. Yang, L., Huang, L., Lu, H., Xu, F.: Removal mechanism of redundant blank nodes in linked data. In: 2018 13th IEEE Conference on Industrial Electronics and Applications (ICIEA), pp. 1118–1121 (2018). https://doi.org/10.1109/ICIEA.2018.8397878
34. Zamini, M., Reza, H., Rabiei, M.: A review of knowledge graph completion. Information **13**(8), 396 (2022)

Distilling Event Sequence Knowledge From Large Language Models

Somin Wadhwa[1,2(✉)], Oktie Hassanzadeh[1], Debarun Bhattacharjya[1], Ken Barker[1], and Jian Ni[1]

[1] IBM Research, Yorktown Heights, NY, USA
{hassanzadeh,debarunb,kjbarker}@us.ibm.com
[2] Northeastern University, Boston, USA
wadhwa.s@northeastern.edu

Abstract. Event sequence models have been found to be highly effective in the analysis and prediction of events. Building such models requires availability of abundant high-quality event sequence data. In certain applications, however, clean structured event sequences are not available, and automated sequence extraction results in data that is too noisy and incomplete. In this work, we explore the use of Large Language Models (LLMs) to generate event sequences that can effectively be used for probabilistic event model construction. This can be viewed as a mechanism of distilling event sequence knowledge from LLMs. Our approach relies on a Knowledge Graph (KG) of event concepts with partial causal relations to guide the generative language model for causal event sequence generation. We show that our approach can generate high-quality event sequences, filling a knowledge gap in the input KG. Furthermore, we explore how the generated sequences can be leveraged to discover useful and more complex structured knowledge from pattern mining and probabilistic event models. We release our sequence generation code and evaluation framework, as well as corpus of event sequence data.

Keywords: Knowledge Graphs · Large Language Models · Knowledge Distillation

1 Introduction

Building probabilistic models from event sequence data has numerous practical applications across different domains when plentiful high-quality event data is available. For example, in Finance, event models can be used to predict stock market trends and make informed investment decisions. In Healthcare, event models can help identify patterns and correlations in patient data to improve diagnoses and treatment plans. In the field of Cybersecurity, these models can

Supplementary Information The online version contains supplementary material available at https://doi.org/10.1007/978-3-031-77844-5_13.

G. Demartini et al. (Eds.): ISWC 2024, LNCS 15231, pp. 237–255, 2025.
https://doi.org/10.1007/978-3-031-77844-5_13

be used to detect and prevent potential cyber attacks by analyzing the sequence of events leading up to a breach. A common characteristic of the data in these domains is that sequences are clearly associated with an entity (e.g., a company, a person, or a device). There are however other domains where such a clean association between events and entities may not be possible. One such application is news event analysis [8,13,18,30]. While various news sources record and describe newsworthy events, it is often not possible to automatically put together coherent sequences of events, because each event may involve multiple topics and actors, and many correlated and unrelated events may be occurring simultaneously or in close proximity

Prior work has addressed this challenge by devising automated mechanisms for extracting narratives [29,33], topic detection and tracking [2], and timeline summarization [16]. While these different categories of solutions have been successful in a range of applications, the outcome is inherently noisy and not in the form of structured event sequences useful for the construction of event models. Prior work has shown little success in automatically turning narratives into structured sequences. In this paper, we explore a novel mechanism for creating structured event sequences in such domains, using generative language models.

Large Language Models [7,31,38] have recently become the dominant paradigm in a range of natural language processing (NLP) tasks [11] and often beat traditional approaches on a number of challenging tasks, including complex arithmetic reasoning [22] and open-domain question answering [23]. In this paper, our goal is to examine the capability of LLMs to generate structured event sequences useful for event analysis. Our aim is to use LLMs directly for generation of event sequences, as opposed to improving prior extraction methods that would rely on high-quality and comprehensive sources describing detailed event sequences for a wide variety of events. Our hypothesis is that LLMs trained on large corpora have already gathered the required knowledge of plausible event sequences and therefore can be suitably guided to produce diverse and high-quality event sequences. To effectively distill this knowledge, we use event-related concepts in Wikidata [36], a comprehensive general-domain knowledge graph, to guide the sequence generation. This can be viewed as a novel mechanism for knowledge-guided text generation [42] and symbolic knowledge distillation [39]. We then use these generated sequences for pattern mining and learning probabilistic event models, as a way of further structuring the underlying knowledge. Figure 1 shows our overall framework along with examples from our experiments of patterns mined from an LLM-generated event sequence collection, as a well as a simple model learned from the collection.

In summary, we make the following contributions:

1. We devise a new iterative in-context prompting strategy for generating high-quality event sequences using LLMs. To the best of our knowledge, we are the first to use LLMs to generate structured event sequences for the purpose of analyzing various event models.

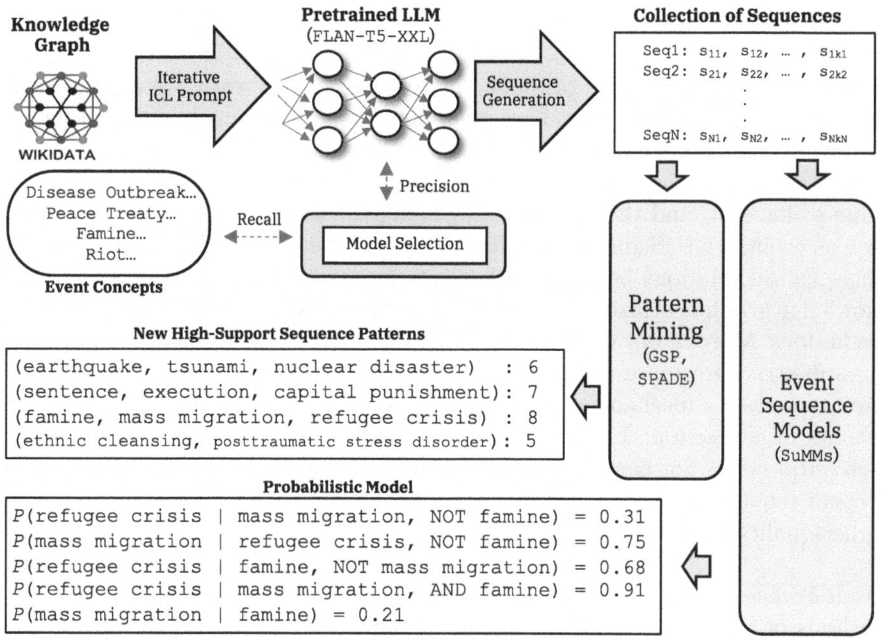

Fig. 1. An overview of our framework for distilling event sequence knowledge from LLMs, along with examples portraying potential use cases. We show that by **(1)** starting with a sparse knowledge graph such as Wikidata, we can generate targeted event sequences. Owing to the inherent sparsity in the underlying KG, we can **(2)** use LLMs to carry out a portion of the evaluation (i.e. precision) to select an optimal model. On this new generated sequence dataset, we then **(3)** apply classical pattern-mining algorithms (e.g., GSP) to identify potentially interesting `has_cause` and `has_effect` event sequence chains, and **(4)** learn summary Markov models (SuMMs) to identify potential influencing events for particular event types of interest; these are both illustrations of extracting complex structured knowledge from the generated sequences.

2. We compile high-quality event sequences using our generation mechanism, based on a curated set of high-level event concepts (classes) from Wikidata that represent newsworthy events.
3. We develop an evaluation framework and conduct experiments to show the value of LLM-powered event sequence generation on replicating and augmenting knowledge in structured representations such as knowledge graphs.
4. We further demonstrate the practical usefulness of our approach by leveraging downstream pattern mining and probabilistic event models.

Our code and generated sequence data are included in the supplementary material available at https://doi.org/10.5281/zenodo.13308920.

2 Related Work

News Event Analysis. The primary applications of our work are around news event analysis and forecasting. Liang [45] presents a taxonomy of different flavors of event prediction in the literature. Our target event prediction applications fall under the "Semantic Prediction" category, with time and location details not being of interest, and the primary goal being the prediction of "event profiles" such as event types. Seminal work in this area is the work of Radinsky et al. [30] where causal relations between past events are extracted from text and then a knowledge graph is utilized to generalize the extracted relations in order to make predictions. More recent work has explored the use of graph sequence mining over a graph structure representation of events extracted from text [8], with graph mining used as a mechanism of extracting useful relations from large and noisy outputs of extraction. The application of building event sequence models over such outputs has not been explored. Our paper explores an alternative approach of event sequence generation that is capable of generating longer and potentially higher-quality sequences.

Event Sequence Extraction from Text. There is a wealth of literature on different methods of extracting sequences from textual corpora. Norambuena et al. [29] present a comprehensive survey of automated methods of narrative extraction. Narratives contain several elements including events, participants (actors/protagonists), time, and space. The task of event detection itself is a highly challenging task and the topic of extensive research [9,24,41], which has its root in the Topic Detection and Tracking (TDT) task [33]. This line of work started out as a DARPA-sponsored initiative with the same name [3]. Another closely related task is news timeline summarization [16]. While pattern mining algorithms have been applied to the output of such extractions, e.g. for creation of "domain templates" [14], we are not aware of any attempts to use the extractions to construct event models for analysis or prediction. This is mainly due to the fact that the output of such methods often result in very short and noisy sequences, not suitable for the majority of event sequence models.

Sequential Pattern Mining and Event Sequence Models. Sequential pattern mining and related approaches have been the subject of extensive research [15,26–28]. These algorithms take in a set of sequences (or "sequential records") with a set of unique events (or "items") and often a "minimum support" threshold, and return as output a ranked set of all frequent sequences in a given sequence collection (or database) meeting the minimum support threshold. There is also a long line of work on statistical and probabilistic models for analysis of different kinds of event sequences. Our focus in this paper is on multivariate event sequences, i.e., sequences of various event types without timestamps. Markov models for sequences [5,32] and long short-term memory (LSTM) [20] models are examples of prediction models. We leverage a more recent family of models – Summary Markov models [6] – for some of the experiments in this paper that involve analyzing generated event sequences.

3 Knowledge-Guided Event Sequence Generation

Through utilizing LLMs, we model event prediction as a *conditional generation task* under zero and iterative few-shot settings. Our targets are linearized sequences of event concepts. We begin by prompting a large language model (with in-context exemplars) with an event trigger y_1 to generate the next concept from a defined set of labels, and repeat this process until we get a sequence of desired length. Formally, given an event trigger $\mathcal{T}$, we model the probability of generating linearized string y of length T containing N unique event concepts that follow $\mathcal{T}$ in sequence:

$$p_{\text{LM}}(y|\mathcal{T}) = \prod_{t=2}^{T} p(y_t|\mathcal{T}, y_{<t-1}) \quad (1)$$

This is the standard conditional language modeling objective. We try multiple prompting techniques and qualitatively observe optimal results with an *iterative* in-context few-shot prompting strategy (Fig. 2). Specifically, we start with a set of six randomly selected examples of the form – "What usually follows event X?". This approach follows the incremental prompting procedure from [25]. Based on the model output (Y) from a pre-specified vocabulary, we append this same example to the original prompt *in conjunction* (i.e. "What usually follows event X and Y?") with ICL examples of the same form. As shown in Fig. 2, our iterative technique serves dual purposes: (i) it leverages in-context learning; and (ii) eliminates the need for implementing complex resolvers to post-process model outputs. We repeat this process until a sequence of a desired minimum length m is achieved (in our experiments, $m = 3$) or we've exhausted a maximum number of tries ($k = 10$ in our experiments) to generate an in-domain event type.

Identifying Event Concepts. With incremental prompting we curate a new dataset of high-level event concepts (classes) from Wikidata that represent newsworthy events. To do so, we query Wikidata for event concepts that have links to Wikinews articles and are instances of classes that are a subclass of the `occurrence` class, i.e., indicating they are newsworthy event classes. We gathered 50 top-level classes for these event concepts, each having multiple labels (e.g. `conflict` → `conflict (psychological), dispute, disagreement, etc.`). This yielded a total of 202 unique event labels for the 50 top-level classes. Most of these event concepts have *some* causal relations (i.e. `has_cause` or `has_effect`). We use these relation pairs as in-context exemplars to create our prompts. We then generate event sequences through iterative in-context prompting (Fig. 2). Full length prompts used in all our experiments are provided in the Appendix.

To generate new event sequences in a zero-shot setting, we start with an event trigger (e.g. a concept like `workplace accident`), create a prompt with instructions describing desired relationships and a few in-context exemplars (ICL prompt), and constrained the model output to the original 50 event concept labels to generate the next event in the sequence (full text of the prompt is provided in the supplementary material). We append the model output to another

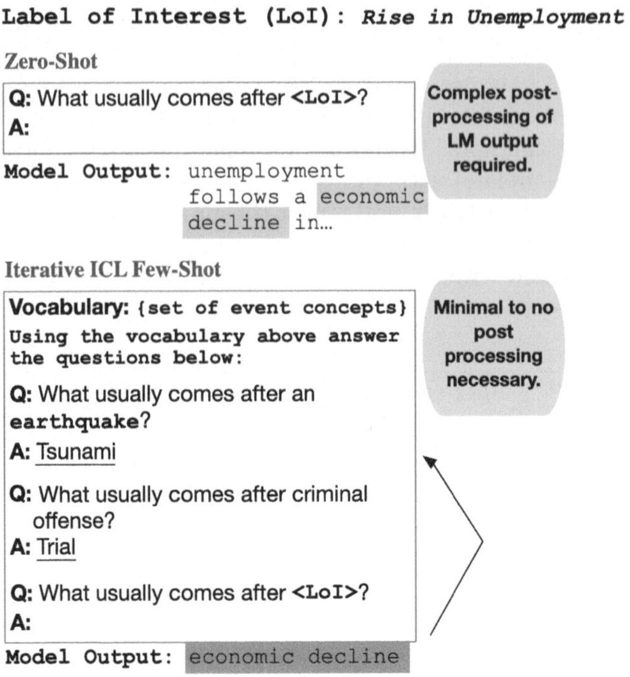

Fig. 2. Illustration of our approach to elicit event sequence knowledge given a *label of interest*. Use of instructional in-context exemplars substantially reduces the need for post-processing LLM output in addition to constraining the output label space.

ICL prompt with *conjunctive* event examples (i.e. questions of the form "What happens after X, Y, and Z"). We repeat this process until we reach a pre-defined maximum sequence length (in this case, 10) or until the model fails to generate an in-vocabulary response in k maximum attempts (in this case, $k = 3$). In this process, we test the following two ablations –

Number of Exemplars. We varied the number of in-context exemplars between 1–12. This is in addition to the zero-shot experiments described in the main paper. We evaluated recall (i.e. proportion of references captured by the resulting output sequences) for all generated outputs in an automated way through matching lexical alignment with Wikidata references. We observed none to marginal improvements by varying the number of exemplars beyond 3 in the initial trigger prompt, and beyond 5 in the second iterative prompt.

Selection of Specific Exemplars. Selecting in-context examples is an incredibly noisy process [44]. We started with a static set of randomly selected examples, however owing to Wikidata's inherent label imbalance (political and economic events dominate newsworthy concepts), this led to erratic results, i.e. high recall on similar concepts but not otherwise.

We then tested a dynamic selection method where every instance of the prompt would contain examples similar to `target_label`. To achieve this, we used BERT embeddings [12] to retrieve (using cosine distance) examples from the reference set. This approach however led to a lower macro-recall and, upon manual inspection of outputs, we observed a high degree of redundancy, i.e. generated outputs were copied from the ICL exemplars.

To solve for these issues, we reverted to the static prompt examples but manually selected a mix of event topics to be included in the prompt. Our current selection of the prompt yields higher macro-recall than both of the aforementioned techniques tested. While we believe there may be better techniques to select ideal candidates for ICL exemplars [1,4] and understand how their compositionality affects specific outputs, we consider such an analysis to be beyond the scope of our work.

We repeat this sequence generation procedure on all 202 event concepts, generating 2,276 event sequences with an average length of 5.7 labels per sequence.

4 Assessing the Quality of LLM-Generated Event Sequences

Open-ended text generation in a task like event sequencing, with extremely sparse reference data, poses unique challenges to the evaluation of model outputs [37]. The traditional scheme to evaluate discrete model outputs has been to calculate precision and recall for the generated outputs against a predefined reference test set. However, under open-world settings and particularly when a sparse KG like Wikidata is used as reference data, a missing causal relation between two event classes in a sequence may very well be a valid relation. Therefore, it is not possible to automatically derive an accurate measure of precision and recall purely using Wikidata as reference data. We take a multi-pronged evaluation approach to assess the quality and usefulness of the generated event sequences across multiple tasks. This section presents our approach in evaluating the quality of generated event sequences, along with the results of this evaluation. An evaluation of the usefulness of the generated event sequences is presented in Sect. 5.

4.1 Human Evaluation of Cause-Effect Prediction Accuracy of LLMs

To quantify how well model outputs correlate with human assessments, we first conduct a small-scale human evaluation on a different, independent event-commonsense reasoning dataset: ATOMIC [21]. ATOMIC consists of event-centered pairs of instances of the form `IsAfter` (`Y` comes after `X`) and `Causes` (`X` causes `Y`). We use these instances as input prompts to the model and then ask human annotators to evaluate model outputs. Specifically, we show human annotators anonymized model outputs and true references and elicit their preferences given a trigger event.

To generate outputs, we follow the same strategy as above for a set of 200 randomly selected event-centered input instances (100 each of the type 'X `Causes` Y' and 'Y `IsAfter` X')[1]. We then present the model output and the true reference from ATOMIC to three human annotators. For example, a typical instance presented to human evaluators was of the form:

```
Input Instance: PersonX drops out of high school
Response 1: PersonX gets a job
Response 2: PersonX turns PersonX's life around
Type: IsAfter
```

One of the *responses* above is the LLM output, while the other is the true reference. The human evaluators are then asked to answer the following questions–

- Are both responses *functionally* similar?
- Which response do you prefer?
- Which response, if any, is completely irrelevant?

We find that in an overwhelming majority of the cases, the models generate output that is semantically equivalent to the reference (even though there is no direct lexical alignment), or output that the humans prefer over the true reference. Based on the responses from human evaluators[2], we observe that humans found 65.82% of response pairs *functionally* equivalent. That is, even though not lexically aligned, they meant the same thing. In 27.64% of the instances the humans preferred the model-generated event instance over the true reference. In only 6.55% of instances did the humans prefer the true reference over the model-generated output.[3] These results reinforce our underlying assertion that LLMs are capable of event-centered reasoning, and therefore could produce high-quality event sequence collections.

4.2 Evaluation of Recall

Despite the sparsity of causal relations in Wikidata, one can still reasonably estimate recall through pairwise comparisons of generated event classes to the existing causal relations in Wikidata. We build a reference set of causal relations in Wikidata by curating a list of all the pairs of event concepts that have any of the several causal relations[4] in Wikidata in any direction, including `has_cause (P828)`, `has_immediate_cause (P1478)`, `has_contributing_factor (P1479)`, and `has_effect(P1542)`. Our results show that this is an effective mechanism of comparing recall across methods, as larger models that are expected to have better accuracy yield higher recall scores.

[1] Complete details about ATOMIC are available in Table 1 in [21].

[2] We observe strong inter-rater agreement with a Fleiss kappa, $\kappa = 0.81$; conflicting response labels were aggregated through majority vote.

[3] Additional details on these experiments are available in the supplementary material (Appendix).

[4] www.wikidata.org/wiki/Wikidata:List_of_properties/causality.

4.3 Evaluation of Precision

To overcome sparsity in reference data, prior work has generally relied on human evaluations [10] for estimating precision, which entails looking at pairs of events and asking annotators whether or not the events in question have a causal relationship. Such a process for potentially thousands of event pairs (like in our case) can be very cost prohibitive. Furthermore, recent research [19,46,47] indicates that pre-trained language models themselves might outperform lay human annotators such as those found on Amazon Mechanical Turk. For instance, [19] demonstrated that labeling data under a few-shot chain-of-thought prompt ("explain-then-annotate" setting) surpasses crowdworker annotations on relevance assessments. Following these results, we use LLMs for evaluating precision and for selecting the most optimal model. We propose evaluating precision for model selection as a binary classification task. Given two events e_1, e_2, an *evaluator* model must evaluate whether e_1 reasonably leads to e_2 under a `has_cause` or `has_effect` relationship. To do this, we start with a large instruction-tuned model (in our case, Flan-T5-XXL (11B) [11]) and adopt instructional in-context few shot prompting to classify whether or not e_1 reasonably leads to e_2, and for the model to provide a justification for its results. While we hypothesize that such an approach may yield noisy results, a small manual assessment as well as our results comparing different models with different evaluator models indicate that this approach yields reliable results for comparing different models, and a reasonable estimate of the overall precision of the model. Note that the evaluator performs only a simple binary classification task that has a very high accuracy even in smaller models.

4.4 Settings

We performed all our model inference related experiments on two NVIDIA V100 GPUs. We used the Huggingface library v4.26.1 [40] and publicly available model checkpoints.[5]. Classical pattern mining algorithms (GSP, SPADE) were implemented in Python through the use of `spmf`[6] library v1.4. For event sequence generation, we use in-context learning under zero shot settings for all LLMs, with `top-k` sampling ($k = 50$, in conjunction with `top-p`, where $p = 0.95$). To identify influencing events from Summary Markov Models (SuMMs), we use implementations from [6] and split the dataset (generated from LLMs) into train/dev/test sets (70%/15%/15%) to generate results reported in Table 2. BSuMMs and OSuMMs were learned with hyperparameters of $\alpha = 0.1$, $\gamma = 0.5$ and a look-back (κ) window of 4.

4.5 Results

Table 1 summarizes our results from these experiments. While prior work as proven the concept of LLM-as-a-judge [47] when much larger LLMs like GPT-4 are used, here we use less resource-intensive LLMs not for evaluation of the

[5] https://huggingface.co/docs/transformers/model_doc/flan-t5
[6] pypi.org/project/spmf/.

absolute quality of the generated sequences, but for comparison of the relative performance of models

Since we use our models for dual purposes – for generating *and* evaluating event sequences, owing to this inherent conflict we find it prudent to independently assess these evaluator models. To ensure robustness of our results, we use multiple evaluator models and find no significant difference between evaluated precision across different models used as evaluators with the largest model performing marginally better as a precision evaluator.

Table 1. Evaluation of LLM-generated sequences. For the purpose of evaluating recall (R), we count event pairs `(e₁, e₂)` if such a pair exists in Wikidata. For evaluating precision (P), we treat correctness of all generated event pairs `(e₁, e₂)` as a standard classification task. Best-performing model scores are in bold.

	Precision Evaluator Model (P)			R	F-1
	Flan-T5-Large	*Flan-T5-XL*	*Flan-T5-XXL*		
Flan-T5-Large (783M) [11]	0.73	0.72	0.72	0.47	0.57
Flan-T5-XL (3B)	0.75	0.75	0.78	0.49	0.60
Open-Research LLaMA (3B) [35]	0.70	0.69	0.72	0.45	0.55
Flan-T5-XXL (11B)	**0.79**	**0.79**	**0.81**	**0.54**	**0.65**

4.6 Discussion

We observed in our analysis that some event triggers did not produce any sequences. Out of the 202 unique input event triggers in our data, 8 event triggers yielded sequences of length 1, i.e., no sequences. This means that the underlying model could not select a relevant event concept from the provided vocabulary that might follow the given trigger.

5 Knowledge Distillation Through Event Sequence Analysis

Given a high-quality collection of event sequences generated by utilizing LLMs, we use pattern mining to discover high-support sequence patterns not directly derivable from the knowledge graph, and learn probabilistic models to discover complex event sequence rules.

5.1 Mining New Patterns

In order to derive new, unseen relationships (`has_cause` or `has_effect`) between the extracted event classes, we use the generated event sequence collection followed by classical frequent itemset mining algorithms like GSP [34] and SPADE

[43] to derive new high support patterns. This aspect of the overall workflow is illustrated in the middle section of Fig. 1, where high-support patterns are mined from event sequences.

The classical pattern mining algorithms we use to mine for new event patterns are both Apriori-based approaches. Under both methods, given two sequences of the same event concept class

$$\alpha =< a_1, a_2, .., a_n > \text{ and } \beta =< b_1, b_2, .., b_n > \tag{2}$$

α is a subsequence of β denoted as $\alpha \subseteq \beta$ iff there exists a set of values $1 \leq j_1 < j_2 < ... < j_n \leq m$ such that $a_1 \subseteq b_{j1}, a_2 \subseteq b_{j2}, ..., a_n \subseteq b_{jn},$; then β is a supersequence of α. Given multiple such sequences and a support threshold, the task here is to find a set of frequent event subsequences. GSP is depicted in Algorithm 1). SPADE uses a"vertical database format", which stores sequences as lists of itemsets associated with their IDs (referred to as "id-lists"), which allows faster support counting. The algorithm organizes the search space into equivalence classes, and avoids multiple scans of the sequences.

Algorithm 1. Generalized Sequential Pattern (GSP) Mining Algorithm

Input: Database of sequences D, minimum support threshold min_sup
Output: Set of all sequential patterns SP
$SP \leftarrow \emptyset$
$C_1 \leftarrow$ set of all individual items in D that meet min_sup
$L_1 \leftarrow$ filter candidates in C_1 by min_sup
$k \leftarrow 2$
while $L_{k-1} \neq \emptyset$ **do**
  $C_k \leftarrow$ generate_candidates(L_{k-1})
  for each sequence $s \in D$ **do**
    for each candidate $c \in C_k$ **do**
      if c is contained in s **then**
        increment support count of c
      end if
    end for
  end for
  $L_k \leftarrow$ filter candidates in C_k by min_sup
  $SP \leftarrow SP \cup L_k$
  $k \leftarrow k + 1$
end while
return SP

Examples of Mined Patterns. Following are example outputs from application of GSP on LLM outputs.

Mined Pattern Example 1.

`Pattern: Civil Disorder` *(Q686984)* → `Democratization` *(Q1064441)* → `Energy Crises` *(Q8413663)* `Support: 5`
The pattern above occurs with a support value of 5 i.e. at least supported by 5 super-sequences. Empirically, we can find support for such a pattern in history.[7]. In 1994, the country of South Africa democratized post civil disorder. This led to an increased energy demand over the following decade, eventually culminating in a full blown energy crises starting 2003.

Mined Pattern Example 2.

`Pattern: Famine` *(Q168247)* → `Refugee Crises` *(Q20898283)* → `Post Traumatic Stress Disorder` *(Q202387)*
`Support: 5`
The pattern above again occurs with a support value of 5 i.e. at least supported by 5 super-sequences. Similar to the previous example, evidence supporting such an event tranisiton can be found in real life.[8]. During the Great Irish Famine people were forced to relocate and flee Ireland causing a refugee crises. A great number of these individuals suffered from mental health crises (e.g. PTSD) due to the events directly associated with the famine.

5.2 Identifying Influencing Sets Through Summary Markov Models

Learning about potential *influencing events* that lead to a given event type in a large set of event sequences is an important aspect of analyzing multivariate event sequences, i.e. events *without time stamps*, like the ones generated by our models. Classic k_{th} order Markov chains capture these dynamics by modeling the probability of observing a particular event type given the preceding k events in-sequence. The recent family of summary Markov models (SuMMs) [6] generalize other well known Markov models for event sequences by leveraging a function that summarizes historical event occurrences, and identifying the subset of event types that affect the probability of occurrence of event types of interest; this forms the influencing set.

We use the LLM-generated sequences to learn two types of SuMMs: binary SuMMs (BSuMMs) and ordinal SuMMs (OSuMMs). In BSuMMs, it is only the presence or absence of an event in the relevant history that has an effect on the occurrence of other events, while in OSuMMs the order of the events is also taken into account. We refer the reader to Sects. 3.3 and 3.4 in [6] for complete formal definitions and methods for learning SuMMs over event sequence collections. Briefly, given a subset of event labels of interest $\mathbf{X} \in \mathcal{L}$ and a set of parameters $\Theta_X = \{\theta_{x|h}\}$, where $\theta_{x|h}$ is the probability of a given event label $x \in \mathbf{X}$ occurring at any position in the sequence given the historical event

[7] https://en.wikipedia.org/wiki/South_African_energy_crisis
[8] https://en.wikipedia.org/wiki/Great_Famine_(Ireland)

occurrences h, *influencing* and *non-influencing* event sets can be formally defined as label sets $\mathbf{U} = \mathcal{L} \setminus \mathbf{U}$ are influencing sets for event labels $\mathbf{X}$ such that they minimally determine the probability of observing any particular label of interest x_i for a given position i in the sequence.

Evaluation: SuMMs Vs LSTMs. Following the evaluation strategy implemented in [6], we focus on individual labels of interest and conduct an evaluation around probabilistic prediction. Consequently, we select negative log loss as the evaluation metric. Table 2 summarizes our results on the test set for both BSuMMs and OSuMMs, along with a simple LSTM baseline. We observe that models trained on event sequences generated from larger models (e.g. Flan-T5-XXL) fare better than the ones generated from their smaller counterparts (e.g. Flan-T5-Large). We treat this observation as a proxy for generated event sequence quality. That is, better quality sequences lead to better predictive models.

Table 2. Negative log likelihood (*lower magnitude is better*) averaged over interest labels from LLM-generated (Flan-T5-XXL) event sequences. Lookback window (k) for LSTM was fixed to 5. Best-performing data generator model scores are in bold.

(↓) Data Generator Model	BSuMMs	OSuMMs	LSTM
Flan-T5-Large (783M) [11]	-63.49	-84.29	-109.28
Flan-T5-XL (3B)	-63.20	-92.65	-121.23
Open-Research LLaMA (3B) [35]	-110.57	-101.29	-190.68
Flan-T5-XXL (11B)	**-57.99**	**-78.64**	**-108.89**

Qualitative Assessment. Fig. 1 shows examples of learned influencing sets using BSuMMs for `refugee crisis` and `mass migration` events. Two events `mass migration` and `famine` are identified as influencing events for `refugee crisis`. The model indicates that the occurrence of both `mass migration` and `famine` together has a 0.91 probability of resulting in `refugee crisis` as a part of a sequence of events. On the other hand the occurrence of `mass migration` in the absence of `famine` has a 0.31 probability of resulting in `refugee crisis`. BSuMMs and OSuMMs deploy a greedy score-based forward and backward search strategy to efficiently discover the minimal influencing sets. Overall, the discovery of influencing sets from LLM-generated data provides a mechanism of distilling complex symbolic knowledge from the output of LLMs.

We provide two more examples below of influencing sets derived from the application of SuMMs. For each example, we show evidence supporting the accuracy of the extracted knowledge. Overall, these results show the high quality and usefulness of the distilled event sequence knowledge.

Influencing Set Example 1. The following example identifies "Hate Crimes" as a predecessor to the occurrence of "Civil Disorder" related events.

```
X: Civil Disorder (Q686984)
Parent: Hate Crime (Q459409)
```

- $P(\texttt{Civil Disorder}|\texttt{NO Hate Crime}) = 0.12$
- $P(\texttt{Civil Disorder}|\texttt{Hate Crime}) = 0.55$

In the example above, we see that the likelihood of a civil disorder is greatly influenced by the occurrence of a hate crime.

Influencing Set Example 2. The following example identifies "Disease Outbreaks" and "Lockdowns" as precursors to the institution of "Travel Restrictions".

`X:Travel Restriction` *(Q87745167)*
`Parents: Disease Outbreak` *(Q3241045)*, `Lockdown` *(Q6665312)*

- $P(\texttt{TR}|\texttt{NO Outbreak, NO Lockdown}) = 0.0.0001$
- $P(\texttt{TR}|\texttt{Lockdown, NO Outbreak}) = 0.0.29$
- $P(\texttt{TR}|\texttt{NO Lockdown, Outbreak}) = 0.26$

Quite intuitively, we see here the likelihood of Travel Restrictions directly correlate with the institution of Disease Outbreaks and Lockdowns (since the latter have been lately associated with the former).

Error Analysis. We observed that in some cases, the identified influencing sets for some event concepts were not correct or, at times, illogical. Qualitatively, we observe that this occurs with rare event types that do not appear often either in the underlying knowledge graph, or in the LLM-generated set of event sequences. Consequently, SuMMs fail to identify logical influencing sets. For example, for the event type `United States Presidential Impeachment`, BSuMM model identified `unequal treaty` as the influencing event.

6 Conclusions and Future Work

In this paper, we presented methods of distilling event sequence knowledge from large language models. We first presented an approach of generating high-quality event sequences through knowledge-guided generation using LLMs. We then conducted a three-pronged quantitative and qualitative evaluation of our results. First, we evaluated LLM-generated event sequences in absolute terms through manual evaluation and automated evaluation using standard accuracy metrics. Second, we looked at some qualitative examples of *newly* identified high support sequences not already present in our base knowledge graph i.e. Wikidata. Finally, we gauge how probabilistic models like SuMMs fare when trained on LLM-generated data. We found that through our carefully-designed elicitation procedure, LLMs are capable of producing high-quality event sequences that can be used for the downstream tasks of pattern mining and the construction of probabilistic event models such as SuMMs.

This work demonstrates the utility of large language models for extracting event-related information and helps researchers better navigate the complex interaction between event-related entities. While we have demonstrated some use-cases for the resulting dataset of event sequences – mining logical rules/-patterns and extracting influencing event types – the resulting datasets in this work and those from other domains could themselves be a useful resource for researchers, as one may leverage them suitably to inform or justify decision-making. We make our code and datasets publicly available for future research. Here, we outline a number of directions for future work:

- In this paper, we used Wikidata as our base source of knowledge. The event concepts found on Wikidata often appear in the pre-training datasets of large language models. We did not consider more complex, domain-specific datasets of non-timestamped events (e.g. Healthcare, Finance). Applying LLMs to generate domain-specific events may require considerable amounts of data to fine-tune these models, and collecting such supervision to train these models at scale may be prohibitively expensive.
- A key element of our evaluation strategy (precision) involves the use of the same language models that were used to generate the sequences being evaluated in the first place. Through qualitative examples and past research on using LLMs as annotators, we observe that such a strategy yields a noisy but useful signal for evaluating model performance. However, an ideal and accurate evaluation of model outputs should involve the use of human annotators and a validation of the use of larger LLMs as a part of LLMs-as-a-judge [47] evaluation strategy. Furthermore, our use of smaller models was justified in part due to the simplicity of the precision evaluation task, which can be posed as a binary classification task. It will be interesting to evaluate the correctness of post-hoc explanations generated by models for their corresponding output during precision evaluation, as such explanations are key to the usefulness of the distilled knowledge, particularly in critical decision support applications.
- In the context of our domain of interest in this paper (news event analysis), an exciting avenue for future research is to study the effect of utilizing structured knowledge distilled from LLMs in a pipeline for future event prediction, and a comparison with the performance of human forecasters. Recent work [17] claims that LLMs, without symbolic knowledge elicitation, come close and in some cases surpass the ability of a "crowd aggregate of competitive forecasters" in making accurate forecasts in the form of answering forecast questions on online platforms such as the Good Judgment Open ((https://www.gjopen.com)). Two research questions arise: 1) Could a neurosymbolic approach utilizing distilled symbolic knowledge complement or outperform a purely LLM-based solution? 2) Would distilled high-quality structured knowledge provide better explainability and therefore be a more reliable tool as a part of a human-AI collaboration mechanism for event forecasting?

Supplemental Material Statement: Our supplementary material is available at https://doi.org/10.5281/zenodo.13308920 and includes code and prompts used for event sequence generation and benchmarking, as well as the base KG and sample output files. `README.md` has all the details. `Appendix.pdf` contains our prompts and human evaluation details.

References

1. Agrawal, S., Zhou, C., Lewis, M., Zettlemoyer, L., Ghazvininejad, M.: In-context examples selection for machine translation. In: Findings of the Association for Computational Linguistics: ACL 2023, pp. 8857–8873. Association for Computational Linguistics, Toronto, Canada (2023). https://doi.org/10.18653/v1/2023.findings-acl.564
2. Allan, J.: New York, 1st edn. Springer (2012). https://doi.org/10.1007/978-1-4615-0933-2
3. Allan, J., Carbonell, J.G., Doddington, G., Yamron, J., Yang, Y.: Topic detection and tracking pilot study final report. In: Proceedings of the DARPA Broadcast News Transcription and Understanding Workshop, February, 1998 (1998). https://doi.org/10.1184/R1/6626252.v1
4. An, S., et al.: How do in-context examples affect compositional generalization? In: Proceedings of the 61st Annual Meeting of the Association for Computational Linguistics, Volume 1, Long Papers, pp. 11027–11052. Association for Computational Linguistics, Toronto, Canada (2023). https://doi.org/10.18653/v1/2023.acl-long.618
5. Begleiter, R., El-Yaniv, R., Yona, G.: On prediction using variable order Markov models. J. Artif. Intell. Res. **22**, 385–421 (2004). https://doi.org/10.1613/jair.1491
6. Bhattacharjya, D., Sihag, S., Hassanzadeh, O., Bialik, L.: Summary Markov models for event sequences. In: Raedt, L.D. (ed.) Proceedings of the Thirty-First International Joint Conference on Artificial Intelligence, IJCAI-22, pp. 4836–4842. International Joint Conferences on Artificial Intelligence Organization (2022). https://doi.org/10.24963/ijcai.2022/670
7. Brown, T., et al.: Language models are few-shot learners. In: Larochelle, H., Ranzato, M., Hadsell, R., Balcan, M., Lin, H. (eds.) Advances in Neural Information Processing Systems, vol. 33, pp. 1877–1901. Curran Associates, Inc. (2020). https://proceedings.neurips.cc/paper_files/paper/2020/file/1457c0d6bfcb4967418bfb8ac142f64a-Paper.pdf
8. Cekinel, R.F., Karagoz, P.: Event prediction from news text using subgraph embedding and graph sequence mining. World Wide Web **25**, 2403–2428 (2022). https://doi.org/10.1007/s11280-021-01002-1
9. Chen, M., et al.: Event-centric natural language processing. In: ACL (2021)
10. Chiang, C.H., Lee, H.y.: Can large language models be an alternative to human evaluations? In: Proceedings of the 61st Annual Meeting of the Association for Computational Linguistics, Volume 1, Long Papers, pp. 15607–15631. Association for Computational Linguistics, Toronto, Canada (2023).https://doi.org/10.18653/v1/2023.acl-long.870
11. Chung, H.W., et al.: Scaling instruction-finetuned language models (2022)
12. Devlin, J., Chang, M.W., Lee, K., Toutanova, K.: BERT: pre-training of deep bidirectional transformers for language understanding. In: Proceedings of the 2019 Conference of the North American Chapter of the Association for Computational Linguistics: Human Language Technologies, Volume 1, Long and Short Papers, pp. 4171–4186. Association for Computational Linguistics, Minneapolis, Minnesota (2019). https://doi.org/10.18653/v1/N19-1423
13. Du, X., et al.: RESIN-11: schema-guided event prediction for 11 newsworthy scenarios. In: Proceedings of the 2022 Conference of the North American Chapter of the Association for Computational Linguistics: Human Language Technologies: System Demonstrations, pp. 54–63. Association for Computational Linguistics, Seattle, Washington (2022). https://doi.org/10.18653/v1/2022.naacl-demo.7

14. Filatova, E., Hatzivassiloglou, V., McKeown, K.: Automatic creation of domain templates. In: Proceedings of the COLING/ACL 2006 Main Conference Poster Sessions, pp. 207–214. Association for Computational Linguistics, Sydney, Australia (2006). https://aclanthology.org/P06-2027
15. Fournier-Viger, P., Lin, J.C.W., Kiran, R.U., Koh, Y.S.: A survey of sequential pattern mining. Data Sci. Pattern Recogn. **1**(1), 54–77 (2017)
16. Gholipour Ghalandari, D., Ifrim, G.: Examining the state-of-the-art in news timeline summarization. In: Proceedings of the 58th Annual Meeting of the Association for Computational Linguistics, pp. 1322–1334. Association for Computational Linguistics (2020). https://doi.org/10.18653/v1/2020.acl-main.122
17. Halawi, D., Zhang, F., Yueh-Han, C., Steinhardt, J.: Approaching human-level forecasting with language models (2024)
18. Hassanzadeh, O., et al.: Knowledge-based news event analysis and forecasting toolkit. In: Proceedings of the Thirty-First International Joint Conference on Artificial Intelligence, IJCAI 2022, Vienna, Austria, 23-29 July 2022, pp. 5904–5907 (2022). https://doi.org/10.24963/ijcai.2022/850
19. He, X., et al.: AnnoLLM: making large language models to be better crowdsourced annotators (2023)
20. Hochreiter, S., Schmidhuber, J.: Long short-term memory. Neural Comput. **9**(8), 1735–1780 (1997). https://doi.org/10.1162/neco.1997.9.8.1735
21. Hwang, J.D., et al.: COMET-ATOMIC 2020: on symbolic and neural commonsense knowledge graphs. In: AAAI (2021)
22. Imani, S., Du, L., Shrivastava, H.: MathPrompter: mathematical reasoning using large language models. In: Proceedings of the 61st Annual Meeting of the Association for Computational Linguistics, Volume 5: Industry Track, pp. 37–42. Association for Computational Linguistics, Toronto, Canada (2023). https://doi.org/10.18653/v1/2023.acl-industry.4
23. Kamalloo, E., Dziri, N., Clarke, C., Rafiei, D.: Evaluating open-domain question answering in the era of large language models. In: Proceedings of the 61st Annual Meeting of the Association for Computational Linguistics, Volume 1: Long Papers, pp. 5591–5606. Association for Computational Linguistics, Toronto, Canada (2023). https://doi.org/10.18653/v1/2023.acl-long.307
24. Li, M., et al.: Connecting the dots: event graph schema induction with path language modeling. In: Proceedings of the 2020 Conference on Empirical Methods in Natural Language Processing (EMNLP), pp. 684–695. Association for Computational Linguistics (2020). https://doi.org/10.18653/v1/2020.emnlp-main.50
25. Li, S., Zhao, R., Li, M., Ji, H., Callison-Burch, C., Han, J.: Open-domain hierarchical event schema induction by incremental prompting and verification. In: Proceedings of the 61st Annual Meeting of the Association for Computational Linguistics, Volume 1, Long Papers, pp. 5677–5697. Association for Computational Linguistics, Toronto, Canada (2023). https://doi.org/10.18653/v1/2023.acl-long.312
26. Mabroukeh, N.R., Ezeife, C.I.: A taxonomy of sequential pattern mining algorithms. ACM Comput. Surv. **43**(1) (2010). https://doi.org/10.1145/1824795.1824798
27. Mannila, H., Toivonen, H., Verkamo, A.I.: Discovery of frequent episodes in event sequences. Data Min. Knowl. Disc. **1**, 259–289 (1997)
28. Mooney, C.H., Roddick, J.F.: Sequential pattern mining – approaches and algorithms. ACM Comput. Surv. **45**(2) (2013). https://doi.org/10.1145/2431211.2431218

29. Norambuena, B.K., Mitra, T., North, C.: A survey on event-based news narrative extraction. ACM Comput. Surv. **55**(14s) (2023). https://doi.org/10.1145/3584741
30. Radinsky, K., Davidovich, S., Markovitch, S.: Learning causality for news events prediction. In: Proceedings of the 21st World Wide Web Conference 2012, WWW 2012, Lyon, France, April 16-20, 2012, pp. 909–918. ACM (2012). https://doi.org/10.1145/2187836.2187958
31. Raffel, C., et al.: Exploring the limits of transfer learning with a unified text-to-text transformer. J. Mach. Learn. Res. **21**(1) (2020)
32. Raftery, A.: A model for high-order Markov chains. J. Roy. Stat. Soc. B **47**(3), 528–539 (1985)
33. Santana, B.S., Campos, R., Amorim, E., Jorge, A., Silvano, P., Nunes, S.: A survey on narrative extraction from textual data. Artif. Intell. Rev. **56**(8), 8393–8435 (2023). https://doi.org/10.1007/s10462-022-10338-7
34. Srikant, R., Agrawal, R.: Mining sequential patterns: generalizations and performance improvements. In: Apers, P., Bouzeghoub, M., Gardarin, G. (eds.) EDBT 1996. LNCS, vol. 1057, pp. 1–17. Springer, Heidelberg (1996). https://doi.org/10.1007/BFb0014140
35. Touvron, H., et al.: LLaMA: open and efficient foundation language models. arXiv preprint arXiv:2302.13971 (2023)
36. Vrandečić, D., Krötzsch, M.: Wikidata: a free collaborative knowledgebase. Commun. ACM **57**(10), 78–85 (2014). https://doi.org/10.1145/2629489
37. Wadhwa, S., Amir, S., Wallace, B.: Revisiting relation extraction in the era of large language models. In: Proceedings of the 61st Annual Meeting of the Association for Computational Linguistics, Volume 1: Long Papers, pp. 15566–15589. Association for Computational Linguistics, Toronto, Canada (2023). https://doi.org/10.18653/v1/2023.acl-long.868
38. Wei, J., et al.: Finetuned language models are zero-shot learners. In: International Conference on Learning Representations (2022). https://openreview.net/forum?id=gEZrGCozdqR
39. West, P., et al.: Symbolic knowledge distillation: from general language models to commonsense models. In: Proceedings of the 2022 Conference of the North American Chapter of the Association for Computational Linguistics: Human Language Technologies, pp. 4602–4625. Association for Computational Linguistics, Seattle, United States (2022). https://doi.org/10.18653/v1/2022.naacl-main.341
40. Wolf, T., et al.: Transformers: state-of-the-art natural language processing. In: Proceedings of the 2020 Conference on Empirical Methods in Natural Language Processing: System Demonstrations, pp. 38–45. Association for Computational Linguistics (2020). https://doi.org/10.18653/v1/2020.emnlp-demos.6
41. Xiang, W., Wang, B.: A survey of event extraction from text. IEEE Access **7**, 173111–173137 (2019). https://doi.org/10.1109/ACCESS.2019.2956831
42. Yu, W., et al.: A survey of knowledge-enhanced text generation. ACM Comput. Surv. **54**(11s) (2022). https://doi.org/10.1145/3512467
43. Zaki, M.J.: SPADE: an efficient algorithm for mining frequent sequences. Mach. Learn. **42**, 31–60 (2004). https://api.semanticscholar.org/CorpusID:5387869
44. Zhang, Y., Feng, S., Tan, C.: Active example selection for in-context learning. In: Proceedings of the 2022 Conference on Empirical Methods in Natural Language Processing, pp. 9134–9148. Association for Computational Linguistics, Abu Dhabi, United Arab Emirates (2022). https://doi.org/10.18653/v1/2022.emnlp-main.622
45. Zhao, L.: Event prediction in the big data era: a systematic survey. ACM Comput. Surv. **54**(5) (2021). https://doi.org/10.1145/3450287

46. Zhao, M., et al.: LMTurk: few-shot learners as crowdsourcing workers in a language-model-as-a-service framework. In: Findings of the Association for Computational Linguistics: NAACL 2022, pp. 675–692. Association for Computational Linguistics, Seattle, United States (2022). https://doi.org/10.18653/v1/2022.findings-naacl.51
47. Zheng, L., et al.: Judging LLM-as-a-judge with MT-bench and chatbot arena (2023)

□

Correction to: Multi-view Transformer-Based Network for Prerequisite Learning in Concept Graphs

Zhichun Wang, Yifeng Shao, Boci Peng, Bangqi Li, Yun Li, Qianren Wang, and Nijun Li

Correction to:
Chapter 4 in: G. Demartini et al. (Eds.): *The Semantic Web – ISWC 2024*, LNCS 15231, https://doi.org/10.1007/978-3-031-77844-5_4

In the originally published version of the chapter 4 the author names was erroneously reflected as "Bangui Li" instead of "Bangqi Li". The author name has been updated.

The updated version of this chapter can be found at
https://doi.org/10.1007/978-3-031-77844-5_4

G. Demartini et al. (Eds.): ISWC 2024, LNCS 15231, p. C1, 2026.
https://doi.org/10.1007/978-3-031-77844-5_14

Author Index

G. Demartini et al. (Eds.): ISWC 2024, LNCS 15231, pp. 257–259, 2025.
https://doi.org/10.1007/978-3-031-77844-5

The manufacturer's authorised representative in the EU is Springer Nature Customer Service Centre GmbH, Europaplatz 3, 69115 Heidelberg, Germany. If you have any concerns regarding our products, please contact ProductSafety@springernature.com

Printed and bound by CPI Group (UK) Ltd, Croydon, CR0 4YY
01/10/2026
02225908-0007